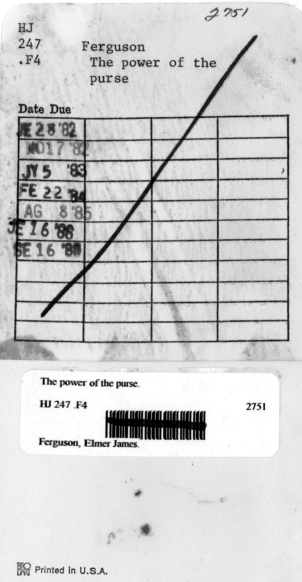

THE POWER OF THE PURSE

A History of American Public Finance, 1776-1790

The Institute of Early American History and Culture is sponsored jointly by the College of William and Mary and Colonial Williamsburg, Incorporated. Publication of this book has been assisted by a grant from the Lilly Endowment, Inc.

A HISTORY OF
AMERICAN PUBLIC FINANCE, 1776-1790

THE POWER OF THE PURSE

By

E. James Ferguson

PUBLISHED FOR THE
Institute of Early American History and Culture
AT WILLIAMSBURG, VIRGINIA

By The University of North Carolina Press · Chapel Hill

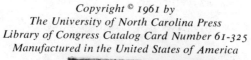

To
Louise

Preface

THIS book is essentially history rather than economics. It grew out of general reading in contemporary sources. Public finance entered into every discussion of political or constitutional issues, but the significance of what I read was often obscure to me. When books on financial history were not enlightening, I was led to explore the subject in an effort to comprehend.

The work was begun under the direction of Professor Merrill Jensen of the University of Wisconsin, who has given me his valuable criticism and encouragement at every stage of the research and writing. I have gained much from intellectual communion with my colleague, Whitney Bates, who is an expert on Revolutionary finance and possibly the one person who will read these pages without feeling at any point that the meaning is obscure. In that critical hiatus likely to occur between research and scholarly publication, this book owes much to past and present members of the council and staff of the Institute of Early American History and Culture, particularly Lester J. Cappon, who had confidence in its ultimate merit. James Morton Smith and Frederick Hetzel greatly improved the manuscript in editing it for publication. The Institute twice granted financial aid for research.

Librarians have been unfailingly cooperative. I wish particularly to thank the directors and staffs of the Manuscript Division of the Library of Congress, the Fiscal Records Section of the National Archives, the Division of Public Records of the Pennsylvania Historical and Museum Commission, the Massachusetts Historical Society, the American Philosophical Society, the Pennsylvania Historical Society, the Maryland Hall of Records, the New York Public Library, the New York Historical Society, the American Antiquarian Society, and the William L. Clements Library. A grant from the University of Maryland supplied funds for typing the manuscript.

CONTENTS

Preface   vii

List of Tables   xi

Introduction   xiii

PART I
THE REVOLUTION

1. Currency Finance   3
2. Square Dollars   25
3. Return to the States   48
4. Mass Expropriation   57
5. Business, Government, and Congressional Investigation   70

PART II
NATIONALIST ASCENDANCY, 1781-1783

6. Counterrevolution in Finance   109
7. Reign of the Financier   125
8. The Aristocracy Suppressed   146

PART III
POSTWAR ERA

9. Settlement of Individual Accounts   179
10. Settlement of State Accounts   203
11. The Economics of Disunion   220
12. Speculation in the Public Debt   251

PART IV
NATIONAL PUBLIC FINANCE

13. Funding: The People and the Creditors   289
14. Assumption: The Compromise of 1790   306
15. The Threads Tied   326

Bibliographical Essay   344

Index   349

List of Tables

Treasury Disbursements and Allocations Through 1781   28
Emissions of Continental Currency, 1775-81   30
Depreciation of Old Continental Currency, 1777-81   32
Old Money Requisitions to 1780   34
State Credits to 1780   34
Loan Office Returns, 1777-81   38
Foreign Aids to 1780   40
Federal Income to 1780   43
Indent Account, 1785-89   227
Receipts and Expenditures, Nov. 1, 1784 to 1789,
    Excluding Indents   236-237
Federal Debt in Massachusetts: Concentration   273
Federal Debt in Massachusetts: Transfer   275
Federal Debt in Maryland: Concentration   276
Federal Debt in Maryland: Transfer   277
Public Debt in Pennsylvania: Concentration   278
Public Debt in Pennsylvania: Transfer   279
Federal Debt in Rhode Island: Concentration   280
Federal Debt in Rhode Island: Transfer   282
Subscriptions at the Treasury: Concentration   283

Introduction

"The situation of our public debts and the very great embarrassments which attended all our concerns on that account, were the principal causes, of that revolution which has given us the Constitution."

—Letter on Hamilton's funding
Proposals dated New York,
Feb. 3, 1790.[1]

O UR conception of Revolutionary finance was until recently based on the writings of nineteenth-century scholars who were engaged in the defense of sound money against silverites and inflationists. Because the keystone of public finance in early America was fiat money, they enlarged upon its failures as an object lesson for their own generation. Delving into the colonial past, they exposed the currency depreciation that occurred in New England and the Carolinas; for them this sufficed as a general description of colonial public finance.[2] Carrying the narrative forward into the American Revolution, they portrayed the dramatic fall of Continental currency in a setting of general disorder and military weakness. In their view, the same obsession with paper money was the primary source of

---

1. *Md. Jour. and Baltimore Advertiser,* Feb. 12, 1790.
2. The case against paper money as drawn by nineteenth-century historians rested heavily on the data and opinions supplied by William Douglass, *A Discourse Concerning the Currencies of the British Plantations in America* (Boston, 1740), which was a partisan document. The best nineteenth-century work on the colonies is Andrew M. Davis, *Currency and Banking in the Province of the Massachusetts-Bay,* American Economic Assn., *Publications,* 3rd ser., 1 (1900), no. 4.

national difficulties in the "critical period" of the Confederation.[3] The denouement was the rise of the Federalists and Alexander Hamilton, who rescued the country from its errors.

Events of the twentieth century have undermined the position these writers sought to defend. Now that fiat money and managed economies are the rule, a more favorable view of colonial finance is possible—one that takes cognizance of its successful operation in many colonies and its contribution to the economic growth of the country.[4] Seen in the context of later wars and revolutions and not as a lesson in political economy, the financial expedients to which the United States resorted during the Revolution appear reasonable if not inevitable. The alteration in viewpoint is essential to a knowledge of the early history of the nation. The political issues of the day, which turned largely on the question of public finance, lack meaning if the typical modes of finance pursued from colonial times are regarded only as inept blunders and not as a viable system adapted to America's agrarian circumstances.

Public finance was a more controversial subject in the eighteenth century than it is now. The way a government collects and spends money always confers differential benefits upon individuals—a fact well understood by eighteenth-century Americans, who fully appreciated the function of economic interest in politics. But they reserved for economic factors a higher role in shaping the general institutions of society. The power of the purse was to them the

3. Charles J. Bullock, *The Finance of the United States from 1775 to 1789, with Especial Reference to the Budget* (Madison, 1895), University of Wisconsin, *Bulletin, Economics, Political Science and History Series*, I, no. 2; William Graham Sumner, *The Financier and the Finances of the American Revolution* (New York, 1891). Both of these books, especially Sumner's biography of Morris, were major scholarly productions. Less meritorious although a pioneer work, was Albert S. Bolles, *Financial History of the United States from 1774 to 1789* (New York, 1879). The treatment of the period in Davis R. Dewey, *Financial History of the United States* (N. Y., 1903), was circumspect, avoiding gross errors of fact or judgment, but handicapped by his reliance on secondary accounts.

4. See Curtis P. Nettels, *The Money Supply of the American Colonies Before 1720* (Madison, 1934), University of Wisconsin, *Studies in the Social Sciences and History*, XX. Most influential in shaping a new viewpoint are two articles by the economist, Richard A. Lester, "Currency Issues to Overcome Depressions in Pennsylvania, 1723 and 1729," *Jour. of Pol. Economy*, 46 (1938), 324-75, and "Currency Issues to Overcome Depressions in Delaware, New Jersey, New York and Maryland, 1715-1737," *ibid.*, 47 (1939), 182-217. He recapitulates the material in *Monetary Experiments, Early American and Recent Scandinavian* (Princeton, 1939). See Curtis Nettels' review of this book in *Eng. Hist. Rev.*, 56 (1941), 333.

determinant of sovereignty, and upon its location and extent depended the power of government, the existence of civil rights, and the integrity of representative institutions. Their basic premise was that popular control of taxation ensured the rights of the citizen; but power over taxation was also an instrument with which to enlarge the sphere of private liberty against the authority of the state. Conscious of pursuing the traditions of Parliament in its struggle against the Crown, the Americans as colonists manipulated their control of taxation to wrest authority from British governors. After independence, they tried to safeguard the sovereignty of their new states under the Articles of Confederation by denying Congress the right to tax.

The war for independence, however, gave birth to Congressional functions requiring money expenditures and, most important, created a large domestic and foreign debt. How the debt was to be paid—whether by the states or by Congress—became the pivotal issue in the relations between the states and the nascent central government. Until 1787 the movement to strengthen the Union was almost wholly directed towards settling the debt upon Congress and giving Congress the right to collect taxes. With the adoption of the Constitution and the enactment of the Hamiltonian funding program in 1790, the movement was consummated: Congress acquired both debts and taxes.

Disputes over public finance also expressed divergent social philosophies. The broadest cleavage in American society was that which ranged mercantile capitalists and their allies against agrarians both great and small. In colonial times the provinces had devised methods of public finance suited to their predominantly agrarian circumstances—methods which included fiat money, agricultural credit, and certain cheap and painless ways of discharging public debts. The alternative, which was embraced by the mercantile capitalists surging to the fore with the Revolution, consisted of "sound money" backed by specie, funded debts, government banks, and sanctity of contract. Apart from the question of whether Congress or the states should collect taxes and assume mastery of debts, there was a further question as to the methods by which finance should be conducted and debts paid. Any action had a differential effect upon social groups, not only in its immediate economic consequences, but in its compatibility with their ways of life.

Much of the history of Revolutionary America proceeds inexorably from questions of government finance, taxation, and debt payment, which, however abstruse, are essential to understanding. The present work deals with these questions, and in this sense it is designed to be a fully elaborated financial history. But it is also an essay in historical interpretation. Its higher goal is to trace the political and constitutional progress of the nation in terms of the issues of public finance.

THE POWER OF THE PURSE

A History of American Public Finance, 1776-1790

PART I

THE REVOLUTION

*"In this city of Kanbalu is the mint of the grand khan,
who may truly be said to possess the secret of the al-
chemists, as he has the art of producing money . . . He
causes the bark to be stripped from . . . mulberry-trees . . .
This . . . is made into paper, resembling (in substance) that
which is manufactured from cotton, but quite black. When
ready for use, he has it cut into pieces of money of different sizes, nearly square, but somewhat longer than they
are wide . . . The coinage of this paper money is authenti-
cated with as much form and ceremony as if it were actually
of pure gold or silver; for to each note a number of officers,
specially appointed, not only subscribe their names, but
affix their signets also . . . the act of counterfeiting it is
punished as a capital offence. When thus coined in large
quantities, this paper currency is circulated in every part
of the grand khan's dominions; nor dares any person at
the peril of his life, refuse to accept it in payment. All of
his subjects receive it without hesitation, because, wherever
their business may call them, they can dispose of it again in
the purchase of merchandise they may have occasion for;
such as pearls, jewels, gold, or silver. With it, in short,
every article may be procured."*

—*Travels of Marco Polo,*
Book 2, no. 10.

I

Currency Finance

"It is in the memory of every gentleman, that, before the beginning of the Revolution, every State issued paper money; it answered the exigencies of Government in a considerable degree."

—Samuel Livermore in the
House of Representatives,
Feb. 9, 1790.

Few modern nations have a currency which is convertible upon demand into gold or silver, and the spectacle of a depreciating currency is so common that although it may elicit disapproval, it hardly incurs moral censure unless carried to an extreme. Over the generations, in fact, most nations have devaluated their currencies and partially or wholly repudiated their debts. From a twentieth-century viewpoint, the activities of the American governments during the Revolution fall into a recognizable pattern.

The pattern was less familiar in the eighteenth century, when currency mining was a relatively unadvanced art. Analogies to later epics of depreciation symbolized by the fall of the mark, the lire, the franc, or more appropriately, the assignat, the yen, and the Confederate dollar are really less relevant to a consideration of the motives and policies of our Revolutionary forebears than an examination of colonial precedents. During the Revolution, Americans were merely pursuing a legitimate tradition with no thought of unorthodoxy or innovation. In colonial times their governments had habitually employed fiat money; indeed the whole system of public finance was based on it.

The use of fiat money was a solution to the problem created by a shortage of coin and the absence of banking institutions. The colonies mined no precious metals themselves, and the coin brought in by commerce flowed outward in purchase of British commodities. An undeveloped country, America could not produce enough to buy the goods needed for its economic development; more was always imported than American cargoes of tobacco, wheat, furs, and naval stores could procure; hence an unfavorable balance of trade existed with Britain. The gap was bridged by advances of credit from British merchants, but the flow of hard money was toward Britain rather than America. What coin existed in the colonies came mainly from trade with the Spanish and French West Indies. Its circulation was largely confined to merchants, and its stay was likely to be of short duration— it was a commodity for export rather than a medium of exchange. There were no banks or credit institutions to enlarge the money supply by employing the available specie to back a paper medium.[1]

The colonies tried various ways of coping with the problem. Barter was common in rural areas, and staple products such as tobacco, wheat, and even deerskins, were by law declared a medium of exchange. Much business was accomplished without cash payments. Storekeepers usually gave a year's credit to farmers, accepting their crops in payment. Merchants dealt with one another on account, settling balances only at long intervals. Early in the eighteenth century, the colonies tried to attract foreign coin by giving it an artificial value, fixing such rates that hard money with a silver or gold content equivalent to £100 British sterling had a legal value of £133 to £178 in different provinces.[2] The results were dubious. As the colonies grew in wealth and population, the money supply became increasingly inadequate to the requirements of the economy. The

1. This chapter is adapted from the author's article, "Currency Finance: An Interpretation of Colonial Monetary Practices," *Wm. and Mary Qtly.*, 3rd ser., 10 (1953), 153-80. It has an extensive bibliography.

2. The colonies used pounds and shillings as a standard of value. When provincial governments began overvaluing coin, the Board of Trade prepared a royal proclamation, issued in 1704, which established a double standard for colonial pounds and British sterling; at the so-called proclamation rate, £100 sterling was worth £133 in colonial proclamation money. However, many of the colonies raised the legal value of coin even higher; when they issued paper currency, they transferred these different values to their bills. Nettels, *Money Supply*, 162-81, 229-49.

inhabitants felt the need of a medium of exchange which, unlike coin, would not "make unto itself wings and fly away."[3]

The solution was fiat money. It was issued for general economic purposes through "land banks"—the primary mode of social welfare activity in which colonial governments engaged. The legislature printed "bills of credit" which were lent out at low interest, usually 5 percent. The loan was secured by mortgages taken on the borrower's property. An individual could get only a limited sum, and after an initial period of grace, when he was liable only for the annual interest, he had to repay the principal over a period of years. As he spent the proceeds of the loan in buying land, making improvements, or paying debts, the bills entered into general circulation. As he and other borrowers repaid the government, the bills were canceled and retired. Then they were reissued, or successive banks were established to keep up a continuous flow of loans. The colonies thus used their wealth in land as the basis of credit, creating a medium of exchange out of "*solid* or *real* property . . . melted down and made to circulate in paper money or bills of credit."[4]

In the eighteenth century, land banks became the panacea for economic depression. When trade worsened, specie went out of circulation and the dearth of a circulating medium was keenly felt. The injection of money and credit into the economy was, from all appearances, so often beneficial as to confirm the idea that paper money was the cure for depression. A modern economist finds the tactics of colonial government analogous to those of the New Deal and in some ancestral relationship to present-day Keynesian doctrine.[5] Except in New England, few contemporaries doubted that land banks stimulated the economic growth of the country. In the middle colonies, where they were most successful, the loans served as a substitute for taxes. Interest received by the government was sufficient

3. The phrase occurs in a circular sent out to the states by Congress during the Revolution. Worthington C. Ford, ed., *Journal of the Continental Congress, 1774-1789* (Wash., 1904-37), XV, 1057. Hereafter cited *Journals.*

4. The quotation is from an Address of the Maryland House of Delegates to their Constituents (1787), Broadsides, Portfolio 28, no. 24, Rare Books Division, Lib. Cong. The best modern work on colonial finance over the span it covers is an unpublished doctoral dissertation, Leslie Van Horn Brock, The Currency of the American Colonies, 1700-1764 (Univ. of Mich., 1941).

5. Lester, *Monetary Experiments;* a less enthusiastic treatment is Theodore Thayer, "The Land-Bank System in the American Colonies," *Jour. of Econ. Hist.,* 13 (1953), 145-59.

to pay most of the ordinary cost of administration. Pennsylvania managed a land bank almost continuously after 1723 without mishap. For more than twenty-five years before the French and Indian War, the interest received by the government supported expenses without the necessity of direct taxes. Relative freedom from taxation probably contributed to Pennsylvania's remarkable growth.[6]

The other middle colonies were also fortunate in their experiments. New Jersey enacted three separate loans up to 1735, and the interest enabled the government to suspend direct taxation for sixteen years prior to 1751. Delaware issued land bank notes from 1723 to 1746, with apparent benefit to the province.[7] New York extended its land bank of 1737 until the last installment of the principal was due for repayment in 1768, when all classes demanded its renewal, and in 1771 the bank was reinstituted by virtue of a special act of Parliament. Governor Tryon's report in 1774 showed that the interest from loans comprised about half the provincial revenue—an amount which nearly matched expenses in time of peace. In Maryland the first land bank was established in 1733. Its notes fell considerably below par, but later rose to nominal value. In 1769 a new bank was begun, and it functioned without incident until the Revolution.[8]

6. Isaac Sharpless, *Two Centuries of Pennsylvania History* (Phila., 1900), 115-16, 119, 134-36; Albert S. Bolles, *Pennsylvania, Province and State* (Phila., 1899), I, 243-51, 262-65, 396-98; Lester, "Currency Issues in Pennsylvania," *Jour. of Pol. Economy*, 46 (1938), 357, 369; Brock, Currency of the Colonies, 74-84; Thomas Pownall, *The Administration of the Colonies*, 4th edn. (London, 1768), 220-21; Carl Van Doren, ed., *Letters and Papers of Benjamin Franklin and Richard Jackson, 1753-1785* (Phila., 1947), 81. No general property tax was enacted after 1717 until the outbreak of the French and Indian War. See James T. Mitchell and Henry Flanders, eds., *The Statutes at Large of Pennsylvania, 1782-1801* (Harrisburg, 1896-1911), III, 128, 138, 408-17, V, 201-12, 352-61.

7. Richard P. McCormick, *Experiment in Independence, New Jersey in the Critical Period, 1781-1789* (New Brunswick, 1950), 190-91; Brock, Currency of the Colonies, 93-99, 391-409; Henry Phillips, *Historical Sketches of the Paper Currency of the American Colonies, Prior to the adoption of the Federal Constitution* (Roxbury, Mass., 1865-66), 67-76; Lester, "Currency Issues in Delaware, New Jersey, New York and Maryland," *Jour. of Pol. Economy*, 47 (1939), 183-99. Donald L. Kemmerer, *Path to Freedom, the Struggle for Self Government in Colonial New Jersey, 1703-1776* (Princeton, 1940) does not subscribe to the popular passion for paper money but leaves no doubt that New Jersey's experiments were successful.

8. *The Colonial Laws of New York from the Year 1664 to the Revolution* (Albany, 1894), II, 1015-40, IV, 708-10; Edmund B. O'Callaghan, ed., *Documents Relative to the Colonial History of the State of New York* (Albany, 1853-87), VIII, 452-54; Kathryn L. Behrens, *Paper Money in Maryland* (Baltimore, 1923),

Land banks were less successful in New England and the south. Virginia never adopted one, but in North and South Carolina land bank loans figured in the early depreciation of paper money. Similarly, the land banks of the New England colonies, particularly Rhode Island, contributed to the decline of currency in that area and brought on the first statutory regulation of paper money by Parliament.

Land bank emissions eased the revenue problems of colonial governments in some degree because taxes were more easily collected when citizens had access to money. But the difficulties of war finance drove the colonies to another use of paper money. It is this system of "currency finance" that is most important as the background of governmental practice during the Revolution.

The ordinary expenses of colonial governments were small. Officials drew fees rather than salaries, and the few public services were usually handled by local government. Such provinces as Pennsylvania and New York spent no more than £5,000 a year apart from war expenses.[9] Taxation was adjusted to these limited needs. Imposts and excise taxes afforded a maintaining fund, while direct levies on polls and property raised what other funds were needed. But revenues could not be freely expanded. Heavy duties on imports drove off trade or caused smuggling, and direct taxes, if levied in specie, struck the citizens with undisguised force and often took a long time to collect.

It was difficult or impossible for governments to borrow from their own citizens. The wealth of the country did not exist in liquid form. Private capital was tied up in lands or commodities, and no

Johns Hopkins Univ., *Studies in Historical and Political Science*, XLI, no. 1, 9-58; Clarence P. Gould, *Money and Transportation in Maryland, 1720-1765* (Baltimore, 1915), Johns Hopkins Univ., *Studies in Historical and Political Science,* XXXIII, no. 1, 87-105, 111; *Laws of Maryland made since M,DCC,LXIII . . .* (Annapolis, 1787), Nov. sess., 1769, ch. XIV.

9. See A State of the Annual Expense of the several Establishments of the British Colonies in North America . . . , Public Record Office (London), C. O., 323/19, f. 13 (Lib. Cong. photostats). Massachusetts had the highest costs, about £18,000 in 1760. South Carolina's peace-time expenditures the same year were £8,000. The other colonies spent less than £5,000. Bolles, *Pennsylvania*, I, 376, reports a statement of William Penn in 1775 that Pennsylvania's ordinary expenditures were £3,000. As late as 1774, £5,000 was the cost of government in New York, exclusive of expenses originating in war. O'Callaghan, ed., *N.Y. Col. Docs.*, VIII, 453-54.

banks or business corporations had yet been formed.[10] When war or other emergencies required large outlays, colonial governments discovered no alternative to paper money. Massachusetts first employed it in 1696, and eventually all the colonies took it up. Currency finance became the ordinary recourse in war, and it was adapted to the regular operation of government in time of peace. Although practice varied in details, the colonies developed something like a uniform system conducted on the basis of known principles. Massachusetts, the single exception, went on a sound money basis in the 1750's. Elsewhere the methods can be described in general terms.

To meet war expenditures or financial emergencies, colonial legislatures printed money as needed and put it into the hands of the officials who bought supplies or paid the troops. The act which authorized the emission nearly always assigned specific taxes to its redemption. If import duties produced about £5,000 a year, the income for four years ahead might be allocated to redeem £20,000 in bills of credit. If a further emission of money was necessary, the legislature might pledge the impost for a further term or commit the general property tax. Taxes for years ahead were appropriated to the withdrawal of money emitted in a single year.[11]

This system was merely a way of anticipating tax revenues and had somewhat the character of a forced loan; yet there was little objection on grounds of principle, and the procedure answered nicely to the general situation. Its primary virtue was its avoidance of any transactions in specie. There was no need to find hard money either to pay present expenses or future debts. Wholly by its own action, in default of moneylenders, the government obtained a credit by pledging the assets it could command.

The money issued by the government was not convertible into gold or silver, and its value was not sustained by the promise of interest, although sometimes interest was paid. It was usually, but not

10. Robert Morris wrote in 1781: "To expect loans within the United States presupposes an Ability to lend, which does not exist in any considerable number of the inhabitants. The personal property, not immediately engaged either in commerce or the improvement of lands, was never very considerable." Francis Wharton, ed., *The Revolutionary Diplomatic Correspondence of the United States* (Wash., 1889), IV, 532-33.

11. For an enlightening discussion of the theory of currency finance, see "Thoughts on Banks and Paper Money," *Daily Advertiser* (N.Y.), Feb. 2, 1786. Joseph Dorfman, *The Economic Mind in American Civilization* (N.Y., 1946), I, 141-78, samples formal theorizing.

always, legal tender in private transactions. Regardless of any stipulation on the face of the notes, the basic security was the fund assigned to their withdrawal. Taxes and other incomes of the government had to be sufficient to create a general use for the bills and thus ensure their negotiability. Since the money was created and upheld solely by political acts, confidence in the government was essential to its value. The holder had to be confident that withdrawals would be continuous and that future governments would have both the will and the ability to collect taxes. When this confidence existed, the money passed readily in day-to-day transactions without undergoing much scrutiny. But colonial legislators had some grasp of the quantity theory of money and understood that the amount must not exceed too far the requirements of trade at existing price levels, or depreciation would occur regardless of guarantees.

Under conditions prevailing in colonial America, currency finance facilitated the retirement of public debts, and the ease with which the debt could be retired was in rough proportion to its size. If it was large, paper money was plentiful and widely distributed; the government could withdraw a large fraction of the outstanding currency every year by levying heavy taxes payable in the certificates of indebtedness themselves. As withdrawals shortened the supply of currency to the point where collections were difficult, the debt ceased to be a problem, and the remaining currency could be left in circulation to serve the needs of trade. It was gratifying to the colonists that fiscal operations did not at any point involve specie, which had to be drawn from overseas. Common opinion distinguished between debts which had to be paid in specie and those which could be extinguished by the withdrawal of a paper medium. Specie debts were regarded as privileged, onerous, hard to discharge; paper money or certificate debts were the ordinary thing, comfortably suited to the country's abilities. The means of payment lay at hand, and the people were taxed in a medium that was accessible to them.[12]

12. A circular issued by Congress in 1779 distinguished between the ease of paying public debts by withdrawals of a paper medium and the hardship imposed upon the taxpayer by having to redeem them in specie, contrasting the happy circumstances of the United States with the difficulties Britain would face when the debts of war were paid. American debt could be canceled by withdrawals of paper money which was in the country and within reach of the people, whereas Britain "must provide for the discharge of her immense debt by taxes to be paid

Begun in war, currency finance was adapted to the ordinary functions of government in time of peace.   It should be noted that other
means than currency were used to anticipate future income.   Colonial
governments, and to a much greater extent the state governments
of the Revolution, issued various kinds of warrants and certificates
which, though often given an extensive circulation, did not serve
as a medium of exchange to the same degree as paper money.   With
certain exceptions, however, all these notes were issued and redeemed
on the same terms as currency.   A basic pattern therefore emerges:
the governments met expenses by issuing a paper medium, whether
currency or certificates, directly to individuals; they redeemed this
paper, not by giving specie to those who held it, but by accepting
it for taxes or other payments.   This was the system of currency
finance.

It prevailed in all the colonies except Massachusetts, where the
government after 1751 met expenses by floating loans among its citizens, issuing short-term, interest-bearing "treasury notes."[13]   The
significant difference between these notes and the bills used elsewhere (which sometimes bore interest and were called treasury notes)
lay in the fact that the interest and principal were actually paid in
hard money.   Issued in relatively large denominations, Massachusetts' notes were an investment security rather than a medium of exchange.   During the French and Indian War, the province departed
from the strict rectitude of her fiscal procedures so far as to pay her
soldiers in certificates which were redeemable only in the taxes;
otherwise she maintained her system until the Revolution.

Massachusetts was alone in having a specie-backed paper and a
government credit based on voluntary loans.   Her ability to sustain
a rigorous system is partly explained by the fact that her trade
brought in an extraordinary amount of coin which enabled the people to pay taxes in specie.   It cannot be denied, however, that the
inhabitants were imbued with a pecuniary zeal not found in other
colonies·   Fiscal administration was always more exacting in Mas-

in specie, in gold or silver perhaps now buried in the mines of Mexico or
Peru, or still concealed in the brooks and rivulets of Africa or Indostan." *Journals,* XV, 1057.

13. The following account is derived from Davis, *Currency and Banking in
Massachusetts,* and a contemporary analysis in a letter from Governor Bernard to
the Board of Trade, Aug. 1, 1764, PRO, C. O., 323/19, f. 33-35.

sachusetts. The annual budget was the highest in the colonies. The towns were more efficient units than the county governments of the middle and southern provinces.

Even in Massachusetts financial decorum was a late achievement: the colony had once been notorious for currency depreciation. First to resort to paper money, Massachusetts had combined land bank and direct emissions to increase the volume of circulating paper. If her economy had been isolated, it might have absorbed her own bills without much difficulty, but a deluge of paper money poured in from adjacent Rhode Island. This little colony sported with land banks, issuing enormous sums on loan to preferred individuals, who were known to make a business of re-lending the money at higher rates of interest—sometimes to natives of Massachusetts.

In New England's unitary economy, it was impossible to stop the entry of Rhode Island bills, whose bulk laid over and depressed the currency of Massachusetts. An additional strain resulted from large emissions during Massachusetts' rather extensive participation in the Anglo-French wars of the period. As a result, her money depreciated steadily, then more rapidly, until 1751, when conservative and mercantile elements managed to carry through a small revolution. The hard money paid by Britain as compensation for the colony's expenditures in King George's War was used to redeem outstanding bills, which were called in and exchanged for specie at an average rate of 7½ to 1. The transition to a sound money system was difficult, requiring several years; but Massachusetts was aided by another large British payment, and her system stood the test of the French and Indian War. She continued to back treasury notes with specie until the Revolution.

Outside New England, the only provinces which did not keep their paper money in a fair degree of order were the Carolinas. Depreciation was severe in these colonies. Although much of the devaluation occurred early in the eighteenth century, when the land was thinly populated and undeveloped, it is clear that the legislature of North Carolina took no pains to support its first emissions. The bills steadily depreciated, and in 1748 they were called in to be exchanged at a rate of 7½ to 1. The new money fluctuated thereafter around a point considerably below its nominal value, but it was rising near the end of the colonial period due to the British government's close control over the legislature.[14]

South Carolina's circumstances were considerably different. Currency depreciation was confined to the period before 1731 when the infant colony was under a heavy financial strain from war. Finding the situation favorable to their interests, debtor elements tried to maintain the downward trend, but were overcome after a bitter struggle. The currency was stabilized in 1731 at the rate of 7 to 1 of sterling, which remained unchanged until the Revolution. During its maturity, the province had a stable currency and a record of successful management.[15]

The vicissitudes of New England and the Carolinas drew the attention of later historians, who scarcely discussed other colonies except to quote exchange rates to show that here too paper money depreciated. If currency passed below its legal value in exchange for specie or in the purchase of sterling bills of exchange, they inferred that it was unsound, that too much had been issued, or that people lacked confidence in it. While this was certainly true in Rhode Island, Massachusetts, and the Carolinas, the moderate discount that occurred in other colonies had no such implication. It was largely the result of conditions of international trade.[16]

14. The most coherent account of North Carolina's tangled finances is in Brock, *Currency of the Colonies*, 106-13, 428-46, Table XXII. North Carolina's paper money suffered, among other things, from the fact that commodities were employed as a tender in all transactions and in the public mind were the "money of the province"; Mattie Erma Parker, *Money Problems of Early Tar Heels* (Raleigh, 1942), 7-8. Like Virginia and Maryland, North Carolina also established public tobacco warehouses whose receipts for deposits constituted another medium of exchange.

15. About £106,500 in legal tender bills circulated permanently without any provision for redemption. The government met annual expenses by issuing "public orders" and "tax certificates" which, although not legal tender, provided a supplemental currency, which passed at par with legal tender bills. William Roy Smith, *South Carolina as a Royal Province, 1719-1776* (N.Y., 1903), 228-79; Robert L. Meriwether, *The Expansion of South Carolina, 1729-1765* (Kingsport, Tenn., 1940), 8-9; Brock, *Currency of the Colonies*, 115-27; Alexander Hewatt, *An Historical Account of the Rise and Progress of the Colonies of South Carolina and Georgia* (London, 1779), II, 58.

16. The term *specie,* as used here, means hard money as opposed to paper money. It was also used to denote the standard of value which colonies placed on their money—which varied according to the amount of silver the money legally represented. Exchange rates are discussed in Anne Bezanson, Robert D. Gray, and Miriam Hussey, *Prices in Colonial Pennsylvania* (Phila., 1935), 314-36. A contemporary analysis may be found in the valuable public letters of Robert Carter Nicholas, provincial treasurer of Virginia, "Paper Money in Colonial Vir-

Payments between Britain and the colonies were normally accomplished in bills of exchange. American merchants who shipped cargoes to Britain received drafts upon British mercantile houses which they either used themselves or sold in colonial ports. If total shipments from America did not earn enough sterling bills of exchange to pay for imports and to service debts, such bills became scarce in America and their value rose in terms of currency. Since specie could be employed in international payments, it too increased in value relative to currency. Circumstances beyond the control of colonial governments affected the rate of exchange, regardless of how scrupulously they managed their paper money or how good its credit was at home.

In the middle colonies, the discount on paper money was never great enough to impair its credit or utility. Historians agree that Pennsylvania "maintained the system without fear of repudiation and to the manifest benefit of the province." During the half century before the Revolution, the domestic price level in Pennsylvania was more uniform than in any succeeding period of equal length.[17] The emissions of New Jersey and Delaware were regarded as stable and said to have passed usually at par with those of Pennsylvania. New York's currency was highly esteemed, and the colony's ability to keep its bills at par was a "subject for special commendation."[18]

Maryland's first emission depreciated, though well-secured, apparently because tobacco remained the primary medium of exchange. By 1764, however, province bills were reported "locked up in the Chests of the Wealthy" for the sake of the interest falling due on

ginia," *Wm. and Mary Qtly.,* 1st ser., 20 (1911-12), 254-56. See also Jerman Baker to Duncan Rose, Feb. 15, 1764, *ibid.,* 12 (1903-4), 241.

17. See Adam Smith's famous observation in *Wealth of Nations,* Modern Library edn. (N.Y., 1937), 311; Lester, "Currency Issues in Pennsylvania," *Jour. of Pol. Economy,* 46 (1938), 373; and the concluding chapter in Bezanson and others, *Prices in Colonial Pennsylvania.*

18. McCormick, *Experiment in Independence,* 190-91, 233-34; Brock, *Currency of the Colonies,* 66-74, 93-99, 336-53, 391-409; Lester, "Currency Issues in Delaware, New Jersey, New York and Maryland," *Jour. of Pol. Economy,* 47 (1939), 185-86, 192, 199, 207, 216; Phillips, *Historical Sketches of Paper Currency,* I, 67-76; Richard S. Rodney, *Colonial Finances in Delaware* (Wilmington, 1928), 23; Carl Lotus Becker, *History of Political Parties in the Province of New York, 1760-1776* (Madison, 1909), Univ. of Wisconsin, *Bulletin, History Series,* II, no. 1, 66-67. Clarence W. Loke, The Currency Question in the Province of New York, 1764-1771 (unpublished master's thesis, Univ. of Wisconsin, 1941), Appendix D, surveys newspaper price quotations for tea, pork, wheat, sugar, and molasses, finding them stable from 1760 to 1775.

them. In spite of large emissions after that date, her bills held their value. "As a colony," writes a modern scholar, "Maryland had solved the problem of a paper currency."[19]

Virginia managed until 1755 without paper money, relying upon tobacco notes as a local medium of exchange. After the French and Indian War forced her to resort to currency emissions, her bills held their value until 1760. Then a sharp break in tobacco prices marked the onset of a long and severe depression. During the next several years, planters could hardly market their crops, and prices remained very low. The absence of planter balances ordinarily arising from tobacco sales in Britain caused a shortage of specie and bills of exchange within the colony. Planters who were under pressure to pay British creditors had to bid high for bills of exchange, and they accepted discounts on Virginia currency ranging up to 50 and 60 percent. Although there was not enough specie to provide a medium of exchange, the legislature proceeded with plans to retire wartime emissions, and the treasurer of the province, John Robinson, probably rendered a public service when he restored some £100,000 to circulation by secret loans to hard-pressed planters. By the end of the decade, however, Virginia's currency was restored, and it was reported that British merchants who had formerly complained of her paper money were among its warmest advocates.[20]

Constancy of value was not in many minds the sole test of a currency. Another criterion is suggested by Thomas Pownall's remark that in spite of depreciation in New England, "it was never yet objected that it [depreciation] injured them in trade." Thomas Hancock, one of the greatest merchants in America, was not convinced that paper money was an unmitigated evil. Of the legislation which placed Massachusetts on a sound money basis, he complained:

19. Jerman Baker to Duncan Rose, Feb. 15, 1764, *Wm. and Mary Qtly.*, 1st ser., 12 (1903-4), 240; Behrens, *Paper Money in Maryland*, 9-58; Gould, *Money and Transportation in Maryland*, 87-105.

20. Although there is no good modern account of Virginia's financial history, David John Mays, *Edmund Pendleton, 1721-1803* (Cambridge, 1952), presents a vivid story of the depression years, told as an incident of the long-term decline of tobacco planting. Mays has a full account of the Robinson affair. Two contemporary sources are "Paper Money in Colonial Virginia," *Wm. and Mary Qtly.*, 1st ser., 20 (1911-12), 254-56, and letters to the Assembly's agent in London, "Proceedings of the Virginia Committee of Correspondence, 1759-67," *Va. Mag. of Hist. and Biog.*, 10 (1902-3), 337-56; 11 (1903-4), 1-25, 131-43, 345-57; 12 (1904-5), 1-14, 225-40, 353-64. See also Brock, *Currency of the Colonies*, 467-97; George Louis Beer, *British Colonial Policy, 1754-1765* (N.Y., 1907), 179-88.

"This d——d Act has turn'd all Trade out of doors and it's impossible to get debts in, either in Dollars or Province Bills."[21] It is possible that a steady and continuing inflation was not wholly injurious to an expanding country whose people seldom had fixed incomes or a large accumulation of liquid capital.

Even if stability is taken as the sole rule in judging the success of colonial currency, the record is not black. The depreciation in New England was mainly Rhode Island's fault, and elsewhere North Carolina was the chief offender. The colonies, of course, did not have complete freedom to act. Each felt in varying degree the restraint of British authority. Nevertheless, the predominant fact was not the failure of paper money but its success and good credit—in the colonies from New York to Maryland, in Virginia, and in South Carolina during its later development.

Older historical studies tend to exaggerate the debtor-creditor conflict over paper money in colonial times. It is evident that when currency was reasonably well handled, such conflicts did not become serious. The details of any currency emission were a public question; the existence of the practice itself was not. Ideally, men of property would have preferred coin or a currency convertible upon demand into precious metals, but most of them shared the popular belief that there was no alternative to the existing system. They were not afraid of it as long as the government was under aristocratic control. When Parliament passed the Restraining Act of 1764 forbidding the enactment of legal tender laws, protests were entered by New York, Pennsylvania, Maryland, Virginia, and South Carolina—colonies which were scarcely in the grip of leveling elements. As the legal tender status of paper money was the crux of any conflict between debtors and creditors, these protests against the Restraining Act of 1764 would have been inconceivable if propertied men had felt they had anything to fear. "Contrary to the traditions that historians have perpetuated," writes a modern student of economic thought, "a critical analysis of the contemporary literature indicates that the proponents as well as the critics were not poor debtors or agrarians, but for the most part officials, ministers, merchants, and men of substance and learning in general."[22]

21. Pownall, *Administration of the Colonies*, 220, 221; William T. Baxter, *The House of Hancock* (Cambridge, 1945), 112.
22. Dorfman, *Economic Mind*, I, 142.

Pennsylvania's currency was held in universal esteem and regarded as a principal factor in the colony's growth and prosperity. In his widely read work on colonial affairs, Thomas Pownall wrote that there "never was a wiser or a better measure, never one better calculated to serve the uses of an encreasing country . . . never a measure more steadily pursued, nor more faithfully executed for forty years together."[23] Merchants and traders of Philadelphia formally opposed the Restraining Act of 1764, and the colonial agent, Benjamin Franklin, fought the enactment of the law and tried his best to get it repealed. In arguing his case before the British ministry and members of Parliament, Franklin cited restrictions upon paper money as one of the main reasons for the alienation of the American provinces from the mother country.[24]

New York merchants were also incensed by the Restraining Act. The Assembly appointed a committee of New York county members whose duties included corresponding with other provinces and the colonial agent to secure the act's repeal. Governor Moore espoused the cause and repeatedly urged the Board of Trade to sanction an emission on the terms desired by the province. The Assembly refused aid to British troops unless the Crown approved a currency bill, and, according to Carl Becker, opposition to the Townshend Acts was partly rooted in this grievance. Popular unrest was eventually stilled not only by the repeal of the Townshend duties, but also by a special act of Parliament which allowed the colony to issue paper money.[25]

Public opinion in Maryland seems to have been nearly unanimous in favor of paper money. Among the beneficiaries of the currency system were many of the most prominent men, who got loans from

23. Pownall, *Administration of the Colonies*, 185.
24. Merchant petition in Samuel Hazard, *The Register of Pennsylvania* (Phila., 1828-35), II, 222-23; [John Dickinson], "The Late Regulations Respecting the British Colonies on the Continent of America, Considered . . . ," *The Political Writings of John Dickinson* (Wilmington, 1801), I, 54-58. Franklin's lobby against the act of 1764 is discussed in Lewis James Carey, *Franklin's Economic Views* (N.Y., 1928), 1-24.
25. Becker, *Political Parties in New York*, 26-27, 69-80, 88; John H. Hickcox, *A History of the Bills of Credit or Paper Money Issued by New York from 1709 to 1789* (Albany, 1866), 43-46; Arthur M. Schlesinger, *Colonial Merchants and the American Revolution, 1763-1776* (N.Y., 1918), 55-56; *Journals of . . . the General Assembly of the Colony of New York, 1743-1765* (N.Y., 1766), II, 779, 799; O'Callaghan, ed., *N.Y. Col. Docs.*, VII, 820-21, 878, 884-85, VIII, 1, 72, 169-70, 189, 206.

the government. The list included a "surprising number" of merchants. After the Parliamentary restrictions were enacted in 1764, all classes concurred in the need for further emissions, and Maryland's agents in London were directed to lobby for the repeal of the act.[26]

The notorious depreciation of North Carolina's currency does not seem to have been a major factor in her sectional antagonisms. Both houses of a legislature presumably dominated by the "court house ring" petitioned the Crown in 1768 to approve paper money legislation. At a time when the Regulator Movement had begun to split the colony into warring factions, Governor Tryon added his pleas to those of the legislature. His letter to the Board of Trade repeated familiar arguments which, coming from less responsible sources, have often been dismissed as the pretense of debtors trying to evade their obligations. He said that much distress arose from the lack of a larger circulating medium.[27]

In South Carolina, the early struggle between debtors and creditors was never quite forgotten, but in time the memory grew so dim that the contemporary historian David Ramsay, a native of the colony, could write: "From New-York to Georgia there had never been in matters relating to money, an instance of a breach of public faith." On the basis of his personal recollection, he claimed that the use of paper money "had been similar from the first settlement of the colonies, and under proper restriction had been found highly advantageous." Another historian of the province, Alexander Hewatt, was an extreme foe of paper money at the time he acknowledged its value to a "growing colony" like South Carolina if kept within bounds.[28]

Virginia's treasurer, Robert Carter Nicholas, expressed the views of a conservative planter. In a public defense of the government's conduct, he declared that the outbreak of the French and Indian

26. Gould, *Money and Transportation in Maryland*, 105, 109; Behrens, *Paper Money in Maryland*, 45, 47-48.
27. William L. Saunders, ed., *The Colonial Records of North Carolina* (Raleigh, 1886-90), VII, 679-82, VIII, 11-12.
28. David Ramsay, *The History of the American Revolution* (Dublin, 1793), 432, 437; Hewatt, *Historical Account of South Carolina and Georgia*, I, 155-56, 205-06, II, 54-58. A modern historian remarks that the Crown had so long protected Charleston merchants against inflation they had become "oblivious of danger." Smith, *South Carolina as a Royal Province*, 279.

War had made paper money unavoidable. Nicholas understood the dangers of a paper medium and was conversant with the arguments against it, including the pamphlet of William Douglass, its ardent foe in New England; but he felt that the evils it sometimes produced did not arise from paper money as such: "They have been chiefly, if not totally owing either to these Bills of Credit not being established upon proper Funds or to a Superabundance of them or to some Mismanagement." Granting a risk was involved, Nicholas believed that many colonies had derived great benefit from paper money and he thought it had been helpful to Virginia.

Nicholas's view was akin to that of a conservative New York merchant, John Watts, who was highly critical of the Restraining Act of 1764. Like many others, he thought the act would put a virtual end to paper money in the colonies. "The use of paper money is abolished as an evil," he complained, "when, properly treated, it is the only medium we have left of commerce and the only expedient in an exigency. Every man of estate here abominates the abuse of paper money, because the consequences fall upon himself, but there is just the same difference in the use and abuse of it as there is in food itself."[29]

After the Revolution, many people remembered the successful use of paper money in former times. In 1786 a correspondent to a New York newspaper recalled: "Before the commencement of the late war, when public faith was still in possession of vestal chastity, divers of the states, then provinces, had large sums in circulation at full value, depending on funds calculated to redeem only five to ten per centum per annum of the amount issued; consequently it must be from ten to twenty years before the whole would be redeemed; and yet, tho' the money drew no interest . . . it circulated freely and at its full nominal value on a perfect equality with specie."[30] Noting that Continental currency held its value during the first year or two of the Revolution without any security behind it, David Ramsay explained in his *History of the American Revolution:* "This was in some degree owing to a previous confidence, which had been

29. "Paper Money in Colonial Virginia," *Wm. and Mary Qtly.,* 1st ser., 20 (1911-12), 232-33, 244-47, 251, 254. Watts is quoted in Leonard Woods Labaree, *Conservatism in Early American History* (N.Y., 1948), 51.

30. "Thoughts on Banks and Paper Money," *Daily Advertiser* (N.Y.), Feb. 2, 1786.

begotten by honesty and fidelity, in discharging the engagements of government."[31]

The Revolution destroyed that confidence, at least among propertied men, for they believed that paper money could never be a reliable instrument in an era when, as they said, the policy of government was dictated by the multitude. Most people, however, never lost their affection for it. "From the earliest settlement of America," declared a petition addressed to the Pennsylvania legislature in 1785, "most of our improvements have been aided by the medium of paper currency . . . and your petitioners are persuaded that . . . public faith might be restored, and the ancient system revived, to the great ease of the inhabitants and emolument of the community." Such an appeal invoked common knowledge.[32]

As the Revolution itself revealed, the use of paper money was subject to limitations, particularly as a mode of war finance. A system in which the public debt can be increased only by enlarging the currency supply must lead under the stress of prolonged war to a serious depreciation. The greatest test in colonial times was the French and Indian war, and the colonies made a considerable financial effort: New York emitted £535,000; Pennsylvania, whose currency normally stood at £80,000, issued £540,000; Virginia authorized £440,000.[33] According to estimates of the Board of Trade, the North American provinces spent £2,500,000 sterling beyond their ordinary costs of government, of which about £800,000 represented expenditures of Massachusetts, the sound money colony. The remaining £1,700,000 consisted almost entirely of currency or certificates issued upon no other security than taxes.[34]

Despite the volume of paper, little or no depreciation seems to have occurred in most provinces. A booming war economy absorbed a greater amount of currency, and the colonies benefited from British expenditures in America. The most vital aid, however, was a large British subsidy which the colonies received as compensation

31. Ramsey, *History of the Revolution,* 437.
32. *Penn. Packet,* Mar. 4, 1785.
33. Brock, Currency of the Colonies, Tables XV, XVIII, XXVIII; An Account of the Tender and Amount of the Bills of credit . . . in . . . Pennsylvania since . . . 1749, PRO, C. O., 323/19, f. 85; "Proceedings of the Virginia Committee of Correspondence," *Va. Mag. of Hist. and Biog.,* 11 (1903-4), 355-57.
34. A State of the Debts incurred by the British Colonies in North America for the extraordinary Expences of the last War . . . , PRO, C. O., 323/19, f. 19.

for expenditures in behalf of the empire. Beginning in 1756 and made available in sterling bills of exchange from year to year, the entire subsidy came to over £1,150,000 sterling, nearly half the expenditures of the colonies.

The war had scarcely ended when the colonies began to retire their debts. Virginia's currency was down to £206,000 by 1767, and although two small postwar emissions restored some money to circulation, only £54,391 was afloat in 1773. Pennsylvania, no longer tax free, made regular withdrawals until the Revolution, and in New York an acute shortage of currency existed by 1768. A speaker in the House of Commons observed in 1766 that the colonies had already retired £1,755,000, and that most of the remaining debt of £760,000 could be written off within two years, a fact which justified the British decision to tax the colonies. How much this happy situation was the result of British subsidies is hard to know. Unquestionably the grants were of crucial importance to their chief recipients, Massachusetts and Connecticut; without them, these provinces and perhaps others might have gone through a cycle of currency depreciation and repudiation. As it was, the colonies emerged from the war with a conviction that their methods worked. Currency finance had stood the test.[35]

British policy with respect to colonial currency is a neglected subject. From the one considerable treatment available, it appears that the British government usually acknowledged the necessity of colonial emissions and acquiesced in them.[36] Before 1740, the Board of Trade was "reluctantly sympathetic and essentially reasonable" in sanctioning both land bank loans and direct emissions. However, it always opposed making currency a legal tender in private transactions, even though it approved laws for this purpose. Generally speaking, the Board tried to regulate colonial issues by ensuring that the amounts were reasonable, that funds for redemption were

---

35. Serious depreciation was apparently confined to New Hampshire and North Carolina. See PRO, C. O., 323/19, f. 29; Brock, Currency of the Colonies, 437, 476-77. British subsidies are discussed in Beer, *British Colonial Policy*, 52-57; and Lawrence H. Gipson, "Connecticut Taxation and Parliamentary Aid Preceding the Revolutionary War," *Amer. Hist. Rev.*, 36 (1931), 731. See also "Paper Money in Colonial Virginia," *Wm. and Mary Qtly.*, 1st ser., 20 (1911-12), 228, 234; *Jour. of N.Y. Assembly, 1743-1765*, II, 799; O'Callaghan, ed., *N.Y. Col. Docs.*, VII, 820-21, 843-45; T. C. Hansard, Publisher, *Parliamentary History of England* (London, 1806-20), XVI, 204; PRO, C.O., 323/19, f. 19.

36. Brock, Currency of the Colonies, 168-243, 476-508, 520-27, 558-63.

adequate, and that emissions were withdrawn within a limited period of time. Control was exerted largely through instructions to governors, who were ordered to refuse assent to laws which did not have a clause suspending their operation until Crown approval had been received.[37]

Supervision was not effective and lapsed almost completely during periods of war. As currency emissions were the only way the provinces could furnish aid, governors were allowed to approve acts without a suspending clause if the Board's other stipulations were satisfied. The colonies took advantage of their bargaining position to procure assent to laws which did not comply with the Board's requirements. Neither governors nor the Crown could afford to scrutinize too closely the modes by which assistance was given.

War still hindered the enforcement of policy, but British control tightened after 1740. Rhode Island's emissions were a flagrant abuse, hard to ignore, and the Board appears to have been more susceptible to complaints of British merchants claiming injury from legal tender laws. Mercantile and creditor interests in Britain eventually carried their appeals to Parliament, with the result that the standing instructions of the Board of Trade were given statutory effect.[38]

The currency act of 1751 applied only to New England. It did not abolish the paper money system in that area, as is sometimes supposed, but merely established rules for continuing it. After bills in present circulation were retired, no more paper money was to be legal tender in private transactions. The provinces were allowed to continue emitting bills from year to year to pay governmental expenses, provided they committed taxes sufficient to redeem them within two years—a provision flexible enough to accommodate a moderate expansion of the currency. In event of war or other emergency, all curbs would be relaxed as to amounts which could be issued, provided taxes were voted capable of redeeming the bills within five years. The act of 1751 left the colonies outside New England undis-

37. Example of the Board's instructions may be found in Leonard W. Labaree, ed., *Royal Instructions to British Governors, 1670-1776* (N.Y., 1935), I, 218-38; O'Callaghan, ed., *N.Y. Col. Docs.*, VI, 949, VII, 463-64.

38. Oliver M. Dickerson, *American Colonial Government* (Cleveland, 1912), 314-19.

turbed; within that area its major effect was to prohibit legal tender laws and to rule out land banks.[39]

The Restraining Act of 1764 was passed at the end of the French and Indian War, when the colonies had large sums outstanding. As first drafted, it would have applied the curbs imposed on New England to all the colonies, but in its final form it merely prohibited legal tender laws and required that existing legal tender currencies be sunk at their expiration dates. Many colonies protested, in the belief that the legal tender feature was an essential prop to their money.[40] Experience was to show, however, that the restriction did not materially impair the workings of the currency system.

As the quarrel between Britain and the colonies progressed, it appears that British policy regarding paper money was subordinated to the larger purpose of securing a permanent civil list.[41] Attempts were made to trade approval of colonial emissions for the grant of a fixed revenue to the Crown. Even so, the colonies made headway against British restraints, though they could not again make their money legal tender. New York was allowed to renew its land bank in 1771, and after a long struggle, New Jersey got consent for the establishment of a land bank in 1774. Pennsylvania continued to emit currency and in 1773 renewed its land bank. Maryland issued £173,000 to pay war debts and over half a million dollars to finance improvements and establish a land bank. Virginia's council annulled two land bank acts passed by the lower house, but the province emitted £40,000 for other purposes. Held under close rein by the British governor, North Carolina issued treasury notes and debenture bills, while South Carolina emitted "public orders" and "tax certificates" which were, in effect, a paper currency. Finally, in 1773 Parliament explicitly legalized colonial monetary practices as they were being carried on under the restrictive acts of 1751 and 1764.[42]

39. 24 Geo. II, C. 53, Danby Pickering, ed., *The Statutes at Large from Magna Charta to the End of the Eleventh Parliament of Great Britain, Anno 1761* (London, 1762-1807), XX, 306-9.

40. For the statute, see 4 Geo. III, C. 34, *ibid.*, XXVI, 103-5; for the colonial protest, see Van Doren, ed., *Letters of Franklin and Jackson*, 116, 139, 169.

41. Brock, Currency of the Colonies, 409-11; Phillips, *Historical Sketches of Paper Currency*, 69-71; Dickerson, *American Colonial Government*, 316.

42. 10 Geo. III, C. 35, Pickering, ed., *Statutes at Large*, 306; *Col. Laws of N.Y.*, V, 149-70; *Acts . . . of the Province of New Jersey . . .* (Burlington, 1776), 419-41 (act of March 11, 1774); Mitchell and Flanders, eds., *Statutes of Pennsylvania*, VII, 100-7, 204-11, VIII, 15-22, 204-20, 264-83, 284-300, 417-23, 447-55;

Had the Revolution not occurred, Britain might have reached a general solution of colonial monetary problems. As early as 1754, Richard Jackson and Benjamin Franklin exchanged plans to form one or more land banks based on capital loaned from the Bank of England or subscribed by private investors. It was expected that land bank notes would provide a circulating medium for all the North American colonies. Later, when the Stamp Act was under discussion, Franklin and Thomas Pownall broached a similar scheme as an alternative method of gaining revenue from the colonies. They envisaged a continental land bank with a branch office in each province, centrally managed in Britain. The bank was to issue legal tender notes on loan at 5 percent interest, the principal to be repaid over a period of ten years. The notes were to circulate throughout the American colonies. Franklin and Pownall worked on this scheme for three or four years.[43]

By 1767 the petitions of the colonies against the restrictive act of 1764 had convinced a majority of the Privy Council that its repeal was advisable. The Council was willing to allow the colonies to establish loan offices which would emit legal tender notes valid for all transactions except payment of sterling debts. A bill for this purpose was written, and the groundwork was prepared for its introduction into the House of Commons. Franklin, Jackson, and Pownall hoped to realize their plan for establishing an intercolonial land bank, backed by British capital. However, the whole subject became entangled in the current effort to raise a revenue in America. The colonial agents learned that the Commons would probably insist that the income arising from any loan offices in America be subject to the appropriation of the Crown. Since they could not risk this outcome, they gave up the project. Commenting that he had hoped to make better use of his plan for a continental land bank,

---

Laws of Maryland . . . , Nov. sess., 1766, ch. XXVI; Nov. sess., 1769, ch. XIV; Nov. sess., 1773, ch. XXVI; "Paper Money in Colonial Virginia," *Wm. and Mary Qtly.*, 1st ser., 20 (1911-12), 236-37, 262; Phillips, *Historical Sketches of Paper Currency*, I, 206-8; Parker, *Money Problems of Early Tar Heels*, 13; Smith, *South Carolina as a Royal Province*, 275-79; Brock, Currency of the Colonies, Tables XXIV, XXVI, XXVII. For the act of 1773, see 13 Geo. III, C. 57, Pickering, ed., *Statutes at Large*, 113-14.

43. Van Doren, ed., *Letters of Franklin and Jackson*, 41-54; Carey, *Franklin's Economic Views*, 19-24; Verner Crane, "Benjamin Franklin and the Stamp Act," Colonial Society of Massachusetts, *Transactions*, 32 (1937), 57-59; Pownall, *Administration of the Colonies*, 186-87, 230-53; Dickinson, *Political Writings*, I, 58.

Pownall published the details of it in the 1768 edition of his *Administration of the Colonies*.[44] Any further effort to solve colonial monetary problems under British auspices was forestalled by the Revolution.

Upon reviewing the evidence, it appears that the impression of colonial public finance conveyed by later scholars gives a misleading background for a financial history of the Revolution. The efforts of the American provinces to create a medium of exchange, provide agricultural credit, and equip government with the means of incurring and discharging responsibilities, hardly constitute a "dark and disgraceful" picture, nor, on the whole, a record of failure. Most colonies handled their currency with discretion and were successful in realizing the purposes associated with its use. Except for Massachusetts, where depreciation had given it a bad name, paper money was the "ancient system" which by the time of the Revolution had existed as long as most people could remember. Mindful of its dangers, men of property still accounted it a useful and necessary device. Perhaps their sense of security was in some degree based upon false premises—British restraints may have accounted for the conservative management of paper money in certain colonies. Governors and their appointive councils certainly repulsed many a drive for paper money legislation. But if the British connection afforded them a sheltered environment, the propertied and aristocratic classes of American society were in most provinces unaware of it. The legislatures which they dominated continued to emit paper money as a regular procedure. In time of war, all the colonies but one were unreservedly committed to currency finance as the only way of meeting the situation. Emissions might then be overlarge, as the Revolution was to prove, but the common need precluded any nice regard for the effect upon contracts.

44. See Van Doren, ed., *Letters of Franklin and Jackson*, 196-97; Franklin to Joseph Galloway, June 13, 1767, Albert H. Smyth, ed., *The Writings of Benjamin Franklin* (N.Y., 1905-7), V, 25-28; Osgood Hanbury and Capel Hanbury to Charles Hammond, George Steuart, and John Brice, May 6, 21, 1767, Black Books, V, 19, 20, Md. Hall of Records, Annapolis; Letters of Charles Garth, provinical agent, *passim*, Historical Commission of South Carolina, microfilm collection of the Ill. Hist. Survey, Univ. of Illinois; *Jour. of N. Y. Assembly, 1743-1765*, II, 779, 799; "Proceedings of the Virginia Committee of Correspondence, 1759-1767," *Va. Mag. of Hist. and Biog.*, 10 (1902-3), 337-56, 11 (1903-4), 1-25, 131-43, 345-57, 12 (1904-5), 1-14, 225-40, 353-64; Misc. Papers Relating to America, British Museum, Add. Mss., 22680, no. 9, Lib. Cong. photostats; Theodore Thayer, "Land-Bank System in the Colonies, *Jour. of Econ. Hist.*, 13 (1953), 158-59.

Square Dollars

*"He made our Wives and Daughters fine
And pleas'd most everybody
He bought the Rich their costly Wine
The Poor their Flip and Toddy . . ."*

—"Mournful Lamentation on the
Death of Paper Money, 1781"[1]

A REVOLUTION, a war, the dissolution of government, the creating of it anew, cruelty, rapine, and devastation in the midst of our very bowels. These, sir," wrote Robert Morris, "are circumstances by no means favorable to finance."[2] A resolute critic of the paper emissions and economic controls upon which Congress relied to prosecute the war, Morris was not ordinarily given to extenuating the failures of Congressional policy. In this case he wrote for the benefit of the French ministry, hoping to put a better face on the government's financial difficulties. His comment shows only his awareness of a fact which he and other conservative reformers of the period often found convenient to ignore: the pattern of events which led to the depreciation of paper money and the impoverishment of the central government was fixed by circumstances which Congress had no power to control.

Open war developed in the summer of 1775 when the regular colonial governments were being superseded by revolutionary assemblies. The force of events required an army and the extension

1. *Magazine of History*, Extra Numbers, no. 21 (1922), 200.
2. Morris to Franklin, Nov. 27, 1781, Wharton, ed., *Diplomatic Correspondence*, V, 15.

of aid to patriot resistance groups in the provinces. Congress had to assume the functions of a central government. The issuance of paper money was the only way to finance the war—in any case, the habit of resorting to currency emissions was so ingrained in the colonists that nothing else was seriously considered. Since any scheme to support widespread military operations with thirteen provincial currencies would have posed insuperable difficulties, Congress adopted a Continental currency. In June 1775 it issued two million dollars and another million in July; before the end of the year the total was six million.[3]

Care was taken to support the value of this money. Following the beaten path of colonial procedure, Congress pledged the faith of the thirteen colonies to its redemption. Each colony was made responsible for the withdrawal of a certain share or quota of the total emission. Three million was to be redeemed between 1779 and 1782 and the remaining three million between 1782 and 1786. Continental bills bore no interest and were printed in small denominations; it was clear that they were intended to be a medium of exchange rather than treasury notes of the sort employed by Massachusetts. Although Congress requested the states to receive them for taxes, it did not ask that they be made legal tender.[4]

The war soon consumed these emissions, creating the need for others, and by the time independence was declared, Congress was issuing its twentieth million. Before the end of 1776 the total was $25,000,000, all of which remained in circulation. It was near the limit of what the economy could absorb without depreciation, according to contemporary estimates, and since the states were also printing money, it is not surprising that Continental currency began to fall in value. The initial decline was slowed, possibly because cash payments had become universal, replacing the credit transactions normal in colonial times, and thus creating a need for a greater volume of money.[5] In addition, real price advances and an expanding war economy absorbed a larger circulating medium—the discount

3. Congress acted upon the recommendation of the New York Provincial Congress. Peter Force, ed., *American Archives* (Wash., 1837-53), 4th ser., II, 845, 1016, 1281.

4. *Journals*, II, 103, 105, 221, III, 390, 457.

5. See Henry Laurens's observation, Edmund G. Burnett, ed., *Letters of the Members of the Continental Congress* (Wash., 1921-36), II, 488.

on Continental money was still slight in the fall of 1776. But it required no particular foresight to predict the consequences if the war should last a long time. Richard Henry Lee had prudently agreed with some of his tenants to substitute payments in kind for payments in cash, and the great merchant Robert Morris was already prophesying that force must one day be used to compel the acceptance of paper money.[6]

Currency finance required some sort of balance between emissions and withdrawals, but Congress had little power to control either. War expenditures could not be kept within bounds, nor could Congress effect withdrawals of paper money. Continental money fell to destruction in the widening gap between income and expenditure. Congress continued to print money until its value was almost gone, convinced that the only alternative was to abandon the war, happy in the end that "any quantity of brown paper" would serve the purpose.[7]

The expense of the war far exceeded anything in colonial experience. As the conflict broadened, it stimulated a business boom and caused a real price inflation, which was in turn spurred by government and private buying.[8] A seller's market prevailed throughout the war; domestic products and services rose in price, and scarce foreign articles were extravagantly dear. Since Congress seldom, if ever, had funds equal to its immediate obligations, it could not afford the economies of advance planning. Forced to construct the apparatus of government amidst the havoc and crisis of war, it was further handicapped by a realization that public opinion would tolerate little centralization of power. Until the end of the fighting, supply and procurement remained a hurried improvisation in the face of emergency.

6. Lee to Patrick Henry, May 26, 1777, and Lee to George Wythe, Oct. 19, 1777, James C. Ballagh, ed., *The Letters of Richard Henry Lee* (N.Y., 1911, 1914), I, 297, 334-37; Robert Morris to Silas Deane, Dec. 21, 1776, Force, *American Archives*, 5th ser., III, 1334.

7. Henry Laurens to the President of South Carolina, Dec. 1, 1777, Burnett, ed., *Letters,* II, 578.

8. Prices fluctuated greatly from time to time and place to place, making scattered contemporary observations as to real price advances during the war unreliable. Anne Bezanson, *Prices and Inflation During the American Revolution* (Phila., 1951), is the most thorough study. Prices were erratic, but the advance ranged from 50 percent to 100 percent over prewar prices. See pp. 61, 88, 323.

The universal disorder virtually exempted public officers from effective supervision, and costs were increased—no one knows how much—by inefficiency, waste, and corruption. Almost all federal procurement officers were merchants, and it was an uncontradicted belief, occasionally proved, that they speculated with public money, embezzled funds and supplies, used public wagons and ships to transport their own goods, and deliberately bid up prices in order to increase their commissions on purchases. A further drain on federal resources arose from excessive personnel employed in noncombatant service with the army. A host of soldiers and hired civilians were kept at tasks requiring only a fraction of their time.

The real expense of the war was therefore enormous. A member of Congress lamented: "The Avarice of our people and the extravagant prices of all commodities, joined with imperfect management of our Affairs, would expend the mines of Chili and Peru."[9] Estimates vary, but through 1781 the annual cost to Congress was perhaps $20,000,000 specie. The following table gives some idea of the magnitude of domestic expenditures, without allowing for foreign expenditures or the growth of a floating debt.[10]

TREASURY DISBURSEMENTS AND ALLOCATIONS THROUGH 1781
OLD CONTINENTAL CURRENCY

		Specie Value[11] (arbitrary valuation)
1775-1776	$ 20,064,666	$20,064,666
1777	26,426,333	24,986,646
1778	66,965,269	24,289,438
1779	149,703,856	10,794,620
	$263,160,124	$80,135,370

9. John Henry, Jr., to the Governor of Maryland, Feb. 14, 1778, Burnett, ed., *Letters*, III, 85.

10. This table, which is exceptionally complete, is from the Statement of the Receipts and Expenditures of Public Monies during the Administration of the Finances by Robert Morris, published Feb. 16, 1791, on order of a House committee appointed Mar. 19, 1790, on Robert Morris's memorial. Hereafter cited Receipts and Expenditures (1791). Compare Jonathan Elliot, "The Funding System of the United States and Great Britain . . . ," *House Document No. 15*, 28th Cong., 1st sess., 1843-44, II, 10. Samuel Osgood, who was well informed, estimated federal expenditures through 1783 at $150,000,000 specie. Osgood to William Gordon, Jan. 19, 1786, Samuel Osgood Papers, N. Y. Hist. Soc.

11. The specie values given here are far too high because they are based on

1780	$82,908,320		$2,500,000
	891,236	(new emission)	500,000
			$3,000,000
1781	$11,408,095		$ 285,202
	1,179,249	(new emission)	589,624
	320,049	specie	320,049
	747,590	(expended by financier)	747,590
			$1,942,465

Members of Congress understood the management of currency finance, and, knowing how heavily the war effort depended upon maintaining the value of the currency, they were greatly concerned about its depreciation. In a vain effort to husband its resources, Congress authorized new issues of money only in small amounts; through most of 1777 emissions were in driblets of one and two millions. It made no difference. The demands were so pressing that money had to be printed every month, then every fortnight. Congress stuffed the maw of the Revolution with paper money.[12] By the spring of 1778, emissions were five and ten millions at a time, and expenditures were about a million a week.[13]

The states could levy taxes; theoretically, they should have been withdrawing currency, preserving its value by reducing the amount

the Continental scale of depreciation, which overvalued paper money. The scale of depreciation adopted by Congress stated the value of paper money in terms of specie from week to week from the date in 1777 when its depreciation was presumed to have begun.

12. See John Henry, Jr., to the Governor of Maryland, Feb. 14, 1778, Burnett, ed., *Letters*, III, 85.

13. Historians of Revolutionary finance are not certain as to the amount of old Continental currency issued, but the above schedule is probably correct. A statement prepared by Joseph Nourse in 1785, which must be accepted as authoritative, gives a figure of $200,000,000. The emissions he cites have been checked in the *Journals*. Besides these, Congress issued $16,500,000 in 1777 and $25,000,000 in 1778. These emissions were voided after Congress had spent the money. They were exchangeable for other bills, but a table for 1779 in the *Journals* shows that only $15,300,000 was exchanged, leaving $26,000,000 outstanding. After this date, further exchanges could scarcely have been carried out because Congress had stopped emissions and had no money. The remainder of the voided bills— all but $7,784,000—was probably exchanged for loan certificates. State of Accounts of the Several States with the United States, Force Purchase, Item no. 6, U. S. Finance, Div. of Mss., Lib. Cong.; *Journals*, XV, Appendix.

in circulation. But, as Franklin observed, they had not in the early years of the war, "the Consistency for collecting heavy taxes."[14] The state governments were embryonic and sometimes wracked by internal commotion. Their legality was not firmly established, and they were more disposed to court a popular following than levy rigorous taxes which would suggest an onerous comparison with the enemy. Having so recently opposed taxation by Parliament, the American people were sensitive on the subject.[15]

EMISSIONS OF CONTINENTAL CURRENCY

1775	$ 6,000,000
1776	19,000,000
1777	13,000,000
1778	63,400,000
1779	124,800,000
	$226,200,000
new emission currency, 1780 and 1781	$ 1,592,222[16]

State revenue systems also suffered from the incidents of war. Normal incomes from import and export duties were cut off, and it was scarcely possible to lay taxes on polls or property when men were leaving their occupations to join the army. British military operations added to the disorder. Hence, the states laid no taxes of any significance in 1775 and 1776. As Gouverneur Morris declared, it would have been "madness."[17]

By the time state governments were firmly seated and politically able to collect taxes, all paper money—Continental as well as state

14. "Of the Paper Money of the United States (1784)," Smyth, ed., *Writings of Franklin*, IX, 231-32.

15. When Congress first emitted paper money, Governor Colden of New York wrote the Earl of Dartmouth, June 7, 1775: "The Congress are well aware that an attempt to raise money by immediate assessment upon the people would give a disgust that might ruin all their measures. . . ." O'Callaghan, ed., *N. Y. Col. Docs.*, VIII, 579.

16. *American State Papers, Finance*, 3rd ser., Documents, Legislative and Executive of the United States . . . selected and edited by Walter Lowrie and Matthew St. Clair Clarke (Wash., 1832), I, 58, and citations listed in footnote 13.

17. *Journals*, XII, 1048-52. Morris's statement was prepared for French consumption; it was unlike him. On the absence of state taxation, see Ralph V. Harlow, "Some Aspects of Revolutionary Finance," *Amer. Hist. Rev.*, 35 (1929-30), 62.

currency—had gone into a decline, bringing on a series of consequences from which escape was difficult. Before taxes could be
collected, the income expected from them was eroded by depreciation. The state governments functioned only by issuing larger
quantities of paper money, from which they realized less and less
income. Unable to avoid spending every dollar they could lay hands
on, they put Continental money back into circulation as fast as it
came into their treasuries. The withdrawals necessary to sustain its
value were not made.

People laid the depreciation of currency to one cause or another
as factional motive suggested. It was possible to blame a multitude
of conditions that increased the expense of war: inefficiency, waste,
and corruption in federal administration, or the avarice of profiteers.
One could denounce the state governments for truckling to popular
favor and failing to collect taxes, or one might say that the Union
was at fault in denying Congress the power to tax. All these crit-
icisms pointed up a facet of the situation, but members of Congress, who had to act within the limits of what was politically feasible and practically attainable, could find no solutions.

Depreciation first began in the summer or fall of 1776, in consequence not only of the volume of emissions, but also the military
crisis. As Washington retreated and the British menaced Philadelphia, the faith of the thirteen states pledged to the redemption
of Continental money may have seemed a most doubtful guarantee.
The decline was registered in higher prices and the rate at which
currency exchanged for hard money. Exactly when the depreciation began was always doubtful, as was its rate at a given moment,
for the effect of depreciation could not be isolated from other factors
that influenced the demand for specie or affected local prices given
for commodities and services. Moreover, the value of Continental
money varied considerably from one place to another, the discount
usually being greater in Pennsylvania and the middle colonies than
in areas removed from the seat of the federal government. With
these reservations noted, the following table, compiled from the
books of a Philadelphia merchant, may be taken as indicative of
the general course of depreciation.[18]

18. Bezanson, *Prices During the Revolution,* 17, 25-30. This table is to be
found in many places, including *ibid.,* 65, where it is set forth more fully and

DEPRECIATION OF OLD CONTINENTAL CURRENCY
(Currency Required to Purchase $1.00 Specie)

1777		1778		1779		1780	
January	1.25	January	4.00	January	8.00	January	42.50
April	2.00	April	6.00	April	16.00	April	60.00
July	3.00	July	4.00[19]	July	19.00	July	62.50
October	3.00	October	5.00	October	30.00	October	77.50

1781

January	100.00
April	167.50

Congress was at first reluctant to support its currency by the use of economic controls. Most members were enlightened in political economy and would not have disputed the "Hacknied Maxim, that Trade Must alwais Regulate itself"[20]—at least they would have agreed that it ought to. In the fall of 1776, Congress recommended state action against monopolizers, but it was not until early the next year, when depreciation was an ominous fact, that the states were asked to make Continental currency legal tender. When proceedings of a convention of New England states were submitted early in 1777, Congress gave price regulation a mild endorsement and suggested that similar conventions be held in the middle and southern states. However, neither at this time nor any other time was it supposed that economic controls could by themselves sustain the value of Continental money.[21]

Eventually, the visible ruin of its currency stiffened Congress's attitude. Resentful of being overcharged and humiliated, Congress lashed out against profiteers who accumulated wealth "by every

against other tables. Bullock, *Finances of the United States,* 133, offers this and several other tables adapted from official scales of depreciation drawn up by the states.

19. The course of depreciation was temporarily reversed in 1778 by the optimism created by the French alliance.

20. This frequently quoted phrase belongs to John Armstrong. Armstrong to Joseph Reed, Jan. 24, 1780, Burnett, ed., *Letters,* V, 14.

21. *Journals,* VI, 915, VII, 35, 111, 121, 124. See Benjamin Rush, Diary, Feb. 14, 1777, Burnett, ed., *Letters,* II, 250-53.

means of oppression, sharping, and extortion." In its endorsement of regulations adopted by a second convention in the summer of 1777, Congress recommended sweeping regional agreements to fix the value of all services and commodities except imported military stores. A further resolution invited the states to pass laws authorizing and regulating the seizure of hoarded goods by state or Continental officers. Shortly afterwards, Congress passed a drastic resolution asking the states to enact general confiscation laws which would cover all goods useful to the army. To regulate retail trade more effectually, it was suggested that the states limit the number of retailers and compel them to operate under licenses.[22] These resolutions mark the beginning of a general resort to confiscation and forced collections which, along with futile efforts to enforce tender laws, fix prices, maintain embargoes, and stop profiteering, eventually made all classes of the population feel the hard fist of governmental authority.[23]

Congress at the same time tried to persuade the states to levy taxes. This point had not been pressed during the transition to independence, but early in 1777 Congress formally resolved that the states should sink their quotas of Continental money already issued and raise additional funds to meet current federal expenses—in such amounts as they thought "most proper in the present situation of the inhabitants." Congress grew bolder as the Articles of Confederation was drafted and its own status became better defined. The first formal requisition was adopted in November 1777. The states were asked to deliver $5,000,000 during the following year, and each was assigned a definite quota of this sum. The Articles of Confederation prescribed land values as the rule for determining each state's share of the common expenses; but since it was impossible to assess land during the war, the quotas were based on estimated population. Thus began the requisition system, which be-

22. *Journals*, IX, 957, 1043.
23. In June 1778, when depreciation was temporarily halted, Congress recommended the lifting of price controls, but the next year again gave support to price fixing. *Ibid.*, XI, 472, 569, XV, 1289. On economic controls see Richard B. Morris, "Labor and Mercantilism in the Revolutionary Era," Richard B. Morris, ed., *The Era of the American Revolution* (N.Y., 1939), 76-139; Oscar and Mary Handlin, "Revolutionary Economic Policy in Massachusetts," *Wm. and Mary Qtly.*, 3rd ser., 4 (1947), 3-26.

came the constitutional mode of raising federal revenue under the Articles of Confederation.[24]

By this time five million dollars was a minor sum. In a vain effort to halt depreciation, Congress was soon voting requisitions that ran into scores of millions. By the end of 1779, they totalled $65,000,000, and it had already been announced that beginning in 1780 the states would be expected to remit $15,000,000 a month. Congress had also committed them to a general withdrawal of Continental currency at the rate of $6,000,000 annually over a period of eighteen years.[25] Had these requisitions or any great part of them

OLD MONEY REQUISITIONS TO 1780

November 22, 1777	$ 5,000,000
January 4, 1779	15,000,000
May 21, 1779	45,000,000
October 7, 1779	30,000,000[26]
	$95,000,000
January 4, 1779	$ 6,000,000 annually[27]

STATE CREDITS TO 1780

Credits on requisitions as of September 1, 1779	$ 3,027,560
Credits for drafts drawn by Congress on the states and for withdrawals of federal currency	9,870,015
	$12,897,575 (currency)
State credits on the books of the federal departments, reduced to specie value. Date uncertain, but probably before 1780. Less than	$ 881,641 (specie)
State payments credited in specie, date uncertain, but probably before 1780	$ 61,696 (specie)

24. *Journals,* VII, 35, IX, 955.
25. *Ibid.,* 955, XIII, 21, 25, XIV, 626, XV, 1147, 1150.
26. Payments were to begin February 1, 1780, and continue at the rate of $15,000,000 a month until the following October 1. All but the first two payments were superseded by the requisition of March 18, 1780.
27. This requisition was superseded by the requisition of March 18, 1780.

been paid before paper money was moribund, the results might have been beneficial; however, payments credited to the states were small.[28]

Entries on the federal Treasury books by no means do justice to the contributions of the states. The state governments were engaging in their own military operations, as well as assuming heavy expenses for the United States in such matters as recruiting soldiers, raising militia, and maintaining fortifications. The figures show most plainly, however, that as long as Congress managed to pay its way with paper money, it received little financial support from the states.

During the course of the war, Congress developed a considerable secondary revenue from the sale of loan certificates (government bonds). The first loan of $5,000,000 was offered at 4 percent interest in October 1776 and was the first of a continuing series.[29] As the certificates were struck in sums of no less than $200, it is evident that they were intended to be an investment security rather than a circulating medium. Agencies were established in each state to handle the business, and the officers in charge of them became the local financial agents of the federal government. Loan officers not only sold certificates, but received and disbursed public money, paid Congress's drafts out of their funds, and sold bills of exchange which Congress drew on its agents abroad.

Although much was expected from the early loans, they proved disappointing. Four percent was no incentive, apparently, when money yielded higher returns in trade. Congress considered raising the interest; however, a few southern members objected on the grounds that loan certificates would become concentrated in the commercial states, to the detriment of their own constituents when the debt was repaid. Others prophesied that loan certificates would degenerate into merely another circulating medium—of a particularly objectionable kind, since they would draw interest. But Congress finally decided it would have to bid higher to get loans and in February 1777 raised the interest to 6 percent.[30]

28. *Journals*, XV, 1053; *American State Papers, Finance*, I, 54, 55, 59-62. The specie value of state payments on requisitions and drafts was small. Most of the payments were in 1779, when depreciation was far advanced. According to my calculations, $12,897,575 currency represented no more than $776,000 specie.

29. *Journals*, V, 845. The bonds were called "loan office certificates" in contemporary references to them.

30. William Hooper to Robert Morris, Feb. 1, 1777, Burnett, ed., *Letters*, II, 232; Thomas Burke, Abstract of Debates, Feb. 8, 1777, *ibid.*, 240-42; *Journals*, VII,

Loans offered a way of obtaining income without recourse to ruinous currency emissions, and Congress was disposed to make every effort to increase them. In 1777 the American commissioners in France received a secret grant of two million livres from the French government, with the assurance that it would be annually renewed. Expecting that remittances of American products would pay for supplies purchased in France, they conceived of using the grants as security for domestic loans in America, proposing to Congress that the interest on loan certificates be made payable in bills of exchange drawn on American credits in France.[31] Bills of exchange were readily negotiable in American ports at their value in hard money. It was possible that such a security would boost domestic loans to the category of a major revenue.

One argument against this rosy idea sprang out of those prudential considerations that Americans never lost sight of, even amidst the clash of arms. It was said (before the French alliance) that to increase the foreign debt was unwise—in case of default it would provoke French intervention in America. Another objection was that the scheme would give too much profit to merchants and speculators. The need to break through the vicious circle of currency emissions and depreciation was so compelling, however, that Congress voted to pay interest in bills of exchange on all previous loans and on all new loans subscribed to before March 1, 1778.[32]

Six percent interest paid in the equivalent of specie was a real inducement. By the time the loan offices began functioning in 1777,

---

158. A resolution of January 14, 1777, authorized acceptance of state paper money for loan certificates—presumably a concession to the southern states, where, it was said, Continental currency was not as abundant as elsewhere. The resolution was repealed, November 19, 1778. *Ibid.*, 37, XII, 1147.

31. Franklin, Deane, and Lee to the Committee of Secret Correspondence, Jan. 17, 1777, Wharton, ed., *Diplomatic Correspondence*, II, 248-51. The commissioners understood that France would always pay bills drawn for the interest on loan certificates, whatever other aids were furnished; however, they were thinking of a domestic loan of only $5,000,000. Franklin complained afterwards when asked to pay bills beyond the interest on loan certificates, saying this was all he had bargained for. See Franklin and Deane (Lee) to Committee of Foreign Affairs, May 25, Sept. 8, 1777, *ibid.*, 324, 389-90; Commissioners at Paris to Committee of Secret Correspondence, Nov. 30, 1777, and Franklin to Samuel Huntington, May 31, 1780, no. 248, Miscellaneous, Envelope no. 5, Foreign Affairs Section, National Archives; Arthur Lee's Journal, Feb. 16, 1778, R. H. Lee, *Life of Arthur Lee* (Boston, 1829), 395-96.

32. James Lovell to Oliver Wolcott, Aug. 21, 1777, and Henry Laurens to John Lewis Gervais, Sept. 5, 1777, Burnett, ed., *Letters*, II, 461, 477-78; *Journals*, VIII, 724.

Continental money was down to at least 1.25 to 1 of specie; by March 1778, when Congress voted to pay interest in bills of exchange, the rate was 5 to 1. Paper money was accepted at face value in the purchase of loan certificates; the real interest was therefore 7½ percent to 30 percent—payable, not in paper money, but in the equivalent of specie.

Besides giving a high premium on loans, Congress sacrificed important sums abroad. Bills of exchange drawn for interest payments up to March 1782 amounted in the whole to an estimated $1,664,400 specie. Had this sacrifice of foreign assets spurred the purchase of loan certificates in the United States, it would have been worthwhile; but it produced meager results. The specie value of loans made between September 9, 1777, when the proposition was advanced, and March 1, 1778, when Congress withdrew it, was only $832,000.[33] The sacrifice was to little purpose.

Some affluent individuals were aware of the bargain. After the deadline of March 1, 1778, had passed, Robert Morris tried to invest $40,000 in loan certificates drawing interest in bills of exchange. Unable to buy more than $8,000, he reported that the owners knew their value and were not selling. English investors were curious and asked Franklin about them.[34] The American public, however, was not greatly interested, and during the six-month duration of the

33. *American State Papers, Finance,* I, 12, 147. See *Journals,* XIX, 403. The sum of $3,330,731 subscribed during this period has been reduced to specie value by the following method: I have used the table of depreciation of old Continental currency (p. 32) and applied it to the table of loan office subscriptions to March 18, 1780 (p. 38), as given in the Auditor General's statement cited in note 37. The total figure given in that statement falls short of the Treasury figures of 1790 by about $20,000,000 currency. This sum has been estimated at 75 to 1 on the assumption that most of it was subscribed after March 18, 1780, or was being subscribed in South Carolina and Georgia in 1780. Although inexact, the method should not be far wrong, and it allows us to use the Auditor General's statement, the only breakdown of loan subscriptions according to short time intervals that has been found. Depreciation is calculated on the total amount subscribed in each six months period at mid-point.

34. Morris was acting as William Bingham's agent. Morris to Bingham, Mar. 10, May 5, Oct. 5, 1778, Robert Morris Papers, 1778-1783, Lib. Cong. (hereafter cited Morris Correspondence, Lib. Cong.); Samuel Wharton to Franklin, London, Mar. 23, 1778, Franklin Papers, VIII, 186, Amer. Philos. Soc. Robert Morris bought loan certificates for French investors in 1779, both those bearing interest in bills of exchange and those that drew interest only in paper money. Buffault and Company in account with Robert Morris, 1779, Holker Papers, IX, 1710, Lib. Cong. On European investment in loan certificates at this time, which, it should be said, was not important, see John Adams to Vergennes, June 20, 1780, Wharton, ed., *Diplomatic Correspondence,* III, 805.

offer, the rate of new subscriptions was hardly greater than before. The obvious reason for this lack of enthusiasm was that no interest was actually paid in bills of exchange during the period in which the offer stood. Congress's promise seemed insubstantial except to those who knew of the funds in France; also, of course, there was ample reason to doubt the pecuniary integrity of a government whose financial position was already collapsing.

Unwilling any longer to sacrifice more of its foreign income to a vain purpose, Congress withdrew the premium after six months. Certain other schemes for stimulating domestic loans were sounded in 1778 and 1779, including one loan of which the principal was to be repaid in such a manner as to guarantee the subscriber against depreciation.[35] Such novelties were never operative and had little, if any, effect upon the volume of loans.

LOAN OFFICE RETURNS
(Currency Values)

Complete table (1790)[36]		*Incomplete table (1780)*[37]	
Interest Payable in Bills of Exchange:		*Interest Payable in Bills of Exchange:*	
To Sept. 1, 1777	$3,787,900	To Sept. 10, 1777	$4,011,544
Sept. 1, 1777 to		Sept. 10, 1777 to	
March 1, 1778	3,459,000	March 1, 1778	3,330,731
Interest Payable in Paper Money		*Interest Payable in Paper Money*	
March 1, 1778 to		March 1, 1778 to	
close of loans		Sept. 1, 1778	4,675,113
(1781)	59,830,212	Sept. 1, 1778 to	
	$67,077,112	March 1, 1779	8,024,188
Specie certificates		March 1, 1779 to	
issued in 1781,		Sept. 1, 1779	13,347,833
deducting those		Sept. 1, 1779 to	
canceled and		March 18, 1780	13,169,826
registered	$112,704		$46,559,235

35. *Journals*, XIV, 717-20, 772, XVII, 567-69.

36. *American State Papers, Finance*, I, 27. All statements of loan subscriptions vary somewhat; those of the early 1780's because of incomplete returns, the later ones because certificates were being entered at the federal treasury and there changed into the "registered debt."

37. This report of the Auditor General, July 1, 1780, gives the only close

Loan certificates were the security of the moneyed investor. Those bought with depreciated currency before March 1, 1778, gave an excellent return. Of all forms of the federal debt, they were the type of security most likely to remain in possession of the original holder until funded. Their value stayed relatively high until 1782, when Congress discontinued payment of interest, and even after that they sold at higher rates in the market than other forms of Continental obligations. "Those who lent . . . [Congress] the Paper Money . . . until March, 1778, fix'd their Property and prevented its depreciation."[38]

Loan certificates taken out after March 1, 1778, had a different character. They drew interest only in paper money, and the actual return on investment was therefore negligible; yet about $60,000,000 currency was subscribed before loans ceased in 1781. Some purchasers may have hoped Congress would decide to pay interest on these too in bills of exchange;[39] however, the main reason for the large subscription was that merchants acquired certificates in the course of business, without deliberate investment. When they could not collect immediately from government officials who bought their goods, they accepted payment in loan certificates rather than wait for money whose value steadily declined. Thus, a great number of the subscriptions issued after March 1778 did not represent bona fide loans,

---

breakdown of subscriptions that I have found. It is in the Franklin Papers, LIV, 75, Amer. Philos. Soc.; a less complete version is in Papers of the Continental Congress, no. 12, 90, Foreign Affairs Section, National Archives. Hereafter cited as Papers of Cont. Cong. The total of $46,000,000 falls short of the treasury figures of 1790 by some $20,000,000 (currency) and results from the absence of any figures for Georgia, incomplete returns from other areas up to March 18, 1780, and the exclusion of later subscriptions. Internal evidence, plus a comparison with another schedule of subscriptions as of 1790–broken down according to states—makes it fairly certain that most of the shortage represents certificates taken out in 1780 and 1781. Despite its incompleteness, I have used it in calculations in the chapter because it seems fairly reliable for the period it covers and its listing of subscriptions at six-month intervals makes it possible to calculate the actual specie value of loan subscriptions.

38. "Of the Paper Money of the United States," Smyth, ed., *Writings of Franklin*, IX, 233. Price quotations are scarce during the war, but see Elias Boudinot to Lewis Pintard, Aug. 6, 1781, Boudinot Papers, II, f. 80, Hist. Soc. of Pa., for an offer of $100, presumably specie, for a $300 certificate; and John Jeffrey to Jeremiah Wadsworth, Feb. 17, 1783, Wadsworth Papers, box 134, Conn. Hist. Soc., for a report that loan certificates dated 1777 were discounted only a third in purchase of West Indian commodities and dry goods.

39. Cf. Robert Morris to William Bingham, May 5, 1778, Morris Correspondence, Lib. Cong.

but were paid out by the government in purchase of supplies.[40] Although the certificates drew interest only in paper money, they remained a "very vendible commodity" and held their value better than an equivalent sum in paper money. In a transaction dated September 7, 1780, when Continental money was about 75 to 1, loan certificates dated November 20, 1779, sold at 24 to 1.[41] For this reason, foreigners bought loan certificates when it was not convenient for them to invest their returns from commodity shipments in land or goods. American merchants acquired them for similar reasons and as a mere convenience in remitting money.[42] They were a kind of mercantile currency.

Another source of Congressional income during the Revolution was foreign loans. Before 1780 they involved a small amount of money compared with the total cost of the war, and since none of the income was spent within the United States during this period, except what was drawn to pay interest on loan certificates, they did not contribute to the solution of financial problems at home. The real importance of the early loans and subsidies was that they opened French arsenals and warehouses, providing a quick supply of critical materials.

FOREIGN AIDS TO 1780
(Specie Values)

France:

Government:[43]

1777 Subsidy	2,000,000 livres
1778 Loan	3,000,000
1779 Loan	1,000,000

6,000,000 livres

40. The point will be discussed in the next chapter.

41. Elias Boudinot Papers, II, f. 74, Hist. Soc. of Pa.

42. Informing a Bordeaux merchant about American conditions, Silas Deane told him that in the event he could not make up a full return cargo, he could invest in loan certificates. "You can always pass those Notes when you want to lay out your money." Deane to Janze, Dec. 29, 1777, Charles Isham, ed., *The Deane Papers* (19-23 [1887-91]), N. Y. Hist. Soc., *Collections* II, 292. Hereafter cited as *Deane Papers*. See Edward Bancroft to John Holker, Mar. 13, 1780, Holker Papers, IX, 1659, Lib. Cong.; Robert Morris to Jonathan Hudson, Feb. 23, 1779, Robert Morris Papers, Folder A, Public Records Division, Pennsylvania Historical and Museum Commission, Harrisburg.

43. Franklin, Deane, and Lee to Committee of Secret Correspondence, Jan.

Beaumarchais:[44]

| Supplies, 1777 and 1778 | 5,107,594 livres | |
| Repaid through June 1780 | 552,110 | 4,555,484 livres |

Farmers-General:[45]

Tobacco contract in 1777	1,000,000 livres	
Repaid through 1779	153,230	846,770 livres
(Total French Aid)		11,402,254 livres	$2,111,528

Spain:[46]

1777 Subsidy	187,500 livres	
1778 Loan	187,500	
		375,000 livres	$69,444

---

[17], 1777, Wharton, ed., *Diplomatic Correspondence*, II, 248-51; Foreign Treaties and Contracts, Papers of Cont. Cong., no. 135. The American commissioners receipted for three millions, although one million was in fact paid to Beaumarchais. See Secretary of Congress to Franklin, May 15, 1786, Burnett, ed., *Letters*, VIII, 361-62; Franklin to Charles Thomson, June 18 and Jan. 25, Franklin to Grand, July 11, 1786, Smyth, ed., *Writings of Franklin*, IX, 517-18, 553-55, 527-28.

44. This figure is Robert Morris's estimate in 1782, after deducting $1,167,250 allowed for interest. Beaumarchais's commission is not included. Accounts of Beaumarchais, submitted June 3, 1782, Morris Correspondence, Lib., Cong. On June 5, 1779, Congress gave 2,400,000 livres in bills of exchange payable with interest in three years. These he immediately negotiated. *Journals*, XIV, 690-93. Congress made further remittances in bills of exchange and cargoes amounting to over 338,000 livres through 1781, and the next year paid to Beaumarchais's account 2,544,000 livres in bills of exchange, which included the sums granted in 1779. Before the end of the war, payments thus aggregated 3,434,439 livres, about $636,000, besides two additional cargoes of unsettled value. Excluding charges for interest and commissions, these payments left a balance against Beaumarchais's actual delivery of cargoes of something less than 1,673,155 livres, or $466,653.

45. Foreign Treaties and Contracts, Papers of Cont. Cong., no. 135, I.

46. Arthur Lee's accounts, dated Jan. 1, 1779, Wharton, ed., *Diplomatic Correspondence*, III, 15. As to the first sum's being a subsidy, see *ibid.*, II, 290-91, 292-95, 308. These amounts received from Spain do not figure in later accounts. It must be assumed that they were settled by shipments of cargoes and payments to individuals through whom the Court dealt.

Holland:[47]

Private loans
through 1779   80,000 florins $32,000

                      (Total Foreign Aid) $2,212,972

(An additional floating debt to individuals in Europe was estimated in 1783 at 3,000,000 livres.)[48]

These sums do not accurately represent the volume of supplies which Congress received from Europe. A trade was waged by European and American merchants on private account, unconnected with loans or subsidies. Commodities sometimes were shipped directly to the United States, but more often they were sent to the West Indies and then ferried to the mainland.[49] Congress bought such cargoes from merchants in the United States, paying with paper money. The committees of Congress assigned to foreign procurement often made similar purchases or bought goods themselves in the West Indies and Europe, trying whenever possible to make payment by remitting cargoes of American products which they had bought with Continental money. Transactions of this nature were financed out of domestic resources.

Closely involved in foreign dealings were the incidental cash revenues and actual commodities which accrued to the government as its share of prize cargoes captured by privateers or Continental vessels of war. The money value of this income cannot be estimated, but it provided a degree of support. Another trickle of income came from the national lottery which Congress started in November 1776. Sales moved slowly, and although the lottery functioned throughout the war, depreciation consumed most of the income.[50]

We can now estimate the real or specie value of federal income during the first five years of war:

47. Franklin to Committee of Foreign Affairs, May 26, 1779, and Franklin to Jay, Oct. 4, 1779, *ibid.*, III, 188-89, 361-62.

48. *Journals*, XXIV, 285.

49. Louis Leonard de Lomenie, *Beaumarchais and His Times* (N.Y., 1857), 278, surmises that French merchants other than Beaumarchais got subsidies from the French Court in order to give aid to America. The booming war trade in the West Indies is described in J. Franklin Jameson, "St. Eustatius in the American Revolution," *Amer. Hist. Rev.*, 8 (1902-3), 683-708.

50. See *Journals*, VI, 959, VIII, 619, IX, 775, X, 24. XIII, 441, XV, 1225.

FEDERAL INCOME TO 1780

(Specie Values)

Continental Currency[51]

1775	$ 6,000,000
1776	17,300,000
1777	4,530,000
1778	11,695,000
1779	5,964,000

$45,489,000

Loan Certificates[52]

To March 1, 1778	$ 2,437,301
March 1, 1778 to March 1, 1779	2,506,143
March 1, 1779 to March 18, 1780	988,607

$ 5,932,051

State Credits[53]

On requisitions ($3,027,650 currency, as stated in 1779), specie value uncertain, but suppose at 8 to 1 $ 378,456

51. Specie value has been calculated on the basis of the scale of depreciation on p. 32, figuring depreciation on each emission at midpoint between the date it was authorized and the date of the next emission. In addition to the income from old Continental currency, Congress derived $530,740 (estimated on the basis of a 3 to 1 depreciation) from the new emission money authorized in 1780.

52. In addition to these sums, Congress realized an estimated $266,666 from about $20,000,000 (estimated at a depreciation of 75 to 1) in loan certificates issued from March, 1780 to the close of loans. A further sum of $112,704 was derived from so-called specie certificates issued in 1781 to pay debts.

It is a measure of Bullock's orthodoxy in the sound money doctrines of the nineteenth century that whereas he calculates the real depreciation of income derived from Continental currency, he accepts the official scale of depreciation in calculating the income received through loan offices. The official scale vastly overstated the income. My method of calculation is described in note 33.

53. Whenever the mention of dates permitted reduction to actual specie value, I have used the table of depreciation on p. 32. Otherwise, as in the case of state credits on the books of federal departments, I have accepted the Treasury's computation of depreciation. *American State Papers, Finance,* I, 54, 59.

State payments of federal drafts, also state cancellations of Continental money	397,522	
Payments of specie, probably before 1780	61,696	
State credits on the books of the federal departments probably before 1780, considerably less than	881,641	
	$1,719,315	
(Total Domestic Income)		$53,140,366[54]

Foreign Aids[55]

France	$2,111,528	
Spain	69,444	
Holland	32,000	
(Total Foreign Income)		$2,212,972
(Total Federal Income to 1780)		$55,353,338

Emerging from these figures is the fact that paper money provided the sinews of war in the first five years of the Revolution, and that other incomes were distinctly secondary to it. Foreign loans, although more important after 1780, had "little to do with the business."[56] The burden was borne at home; indeed, currency finance sustained the war and survived in an attenuated form until the moment of victory. Only after the French and American forces captured Cornwallis at Yorktown did foreign loans and state payments become important.

Through most of 1778 Continental money held steady at 5 or 6 to 1 of specie, but at the close of the year it began slipping badly. By the next spring the exchange was 16 or 20 to 1, and Congress was expending enormous sums. In May 1779 it was reported that dis-

54. This sum falls far short of estimated expenses, which at $20,000,000 a year amounted to at least $80,000,000 by the end of 1779. The discrepancy was represented by a floating certificate debt, which will be discussed in Chapter 4.

55. See the table on p. 40.

56. Elbridge Gerry's recollection, Feb. 10, 1790, Joseph Gales, comp., *The Debates and Proceedings in the Congress of the United States ...* (Wash., 1834), I, 1216-17. Hereafter cited as Annals of Congress.

bursements in the Quartermaster and Commissary departments alone were running at the rate of $200,000,000 a year.[57] It was already too late to expect much from requisitions; had all the Continental money in existence been drawn in by the states and paid to Congress within the year, it would not have sufficed to meet current expenses.

Congress struggled to find a way out. One alluring idea would have compelled citizens to buy loan certificates with paper money on pain of the money's being declared worthless. This scheme had the virtue of simplicity, and it was within Congress's power to accomplish. In April 1778 Congress contemplated forcing the conversion of $20,000,000 currency into loan certificates; within a few months the sum being considered had grown to $46,500,000, nearly the whole amount of currency issued up to April 1778.[58] Congress in the end shrank back from an undisguised forced loan, and the scheme which it finally adopted left the citizens an alternative. Under the pretense that two emissions, totaling $41,500,000, had been counterfeited, Congress declared them void. The holders were given the option of exchanging bills of these emissions for other bills or subscribing them at the loan office. It was hoped, of course, that most of the money would be offered on loan. However, as long as Continental currency passed in trade, most of the people who brought in voided bills preferred to exchange them for other bills rather than loan certificates. Congress's plan to wipe out part of the paper money did not produce the expected results. It was said to have astonished the people and destroyed confidence in the government.[59]

After France became actively engaged in the war, there was some prospect of a large foreign loan, and various schemes to exploit this possibility were explored. One committee proposed drawing bills of exchange on France for twenty-five million livres and selling them in the United States for paper money—a measure calculated to revive the currency. Another idea was to enter the government into competition with the profiteers by using its foreign credits to purchase European goods, then selling them to the American people,

57. *Journals*, XIV, 561. Expenses in these two departments were said to have been $5,400,000 in 1776, $9,270,000 in 1777, and $37,200,000 in 1778.
58. *Ibid.*, X, 322, XII, 929, 1073.
59. Emissions of May 20, 1777, and April 11, 1778. *Ibid.*, XII, 1223-24, XIII, 20-21; Thomas Burke to the Governor of North Carolina, Dec. 20, 1778, Burnett, ed., *Letters*, III, 542; "Free-holder," *Providence Gazette*, Oct. 26, 1782.

presumably at current prices.[60]   All such projects were somewhat
visionary in view of Franklin's repeated advice that the United States
had little more credit in France than would support the activities
of the American commissioners in Europe and meet drafts for the
interest on loan certificates. Congress finally admitted that its schemes
were premature.   Henry Laurens was appointed as a special agent
to solicit a Dutch loan, and Congress made no immediate effort to
tap its prospective reservoir of foreign credit beyond drawing bills
for £100,000 sterling each on Laurens and on John Jay, who was in
Spain seeking aid.   It was expected that these bills could be sold in
the United States for $20,000,000 currency.[61]

Nothing that Congress did in 1779 arrested the decline of its currency.   So rapid was the course of depreciation that it was nearly
impossible to estimate the cost of the next campaign. Unacquainted
with twentieth-century examples of currency depreciation, members
of Congress took the unimaginative position that if much more paper
money was issued, it would become worthless.   The situation seemed
to call for drastic measures.

Finally, Congress made the momentous decision to stop issuing.
On September 3, 1779, a limit of $200,000,000 was set; when that
amount was in circulation emissions were to cease.   Since $160,000,000
had already been issued, only a narrow margin remained.   The rate
of expenditure was so enormous that it was only a matter of weeks
before the principal means of supporting the war must be laid aside.[62]
But it was a rational act of great courage and proceeded, as Madison
observed, from the firmest conviction that "to continue to emit *ad
infinitum* was ... more dangerous than an absolute occlusion of the
press."[63]

The stoppage of paper emissions not only signalized a new phase
in the prosecution of the war, but it heralded a change in the relationship between Congress and the states.   As long as paper money
lasted, it allowed Congress to assume and discharge the main burdens
of the war, conferring upon the central government a power and
freedom of action out of character with its constitutional position
under the Articles of Confederation.   The decline of paper money

60. *Journals,* XIV, 900, XV, 1174; Papers of Cont. Cong., no. 26, I, 57.
61. *Journals,* XV, 1196, 1209, 1232, 1299, 1404.
62. *Ibid.,* XV, 1019. Congress did not count $41,500,000 declared void.
63. Burnett, ed., *Letters,* V, 427.

brought a reduction in status. "In a word, Sir," the North Carolina delegates informed their governor, "the Exertions of Congress are no longer competent; and, unless the states exert themselves, the Cause is utterly lost."[64] At the lowest ebb of its resources, Congress fell back upon the sovereign states and tried to pass on to them the burden of supporting the war.

64. North Carolina delegates to the Governor of North Carolina, Feb. 29, 1780, *ibid.*, 55.

3

Return to the States

*"This Currency, as we manage it, is a wonderful Machine.
It performs its Office when we issue it; it pays and clothes
Troops, and provides Victuals and Ammunition; and when
we are obliged to issue a Quantity excessive, it pays itself
off by Depreciation."*

—Benjamin Franklin to
Samuel Cooper, 1779.

THE first product of the attempt to switch support of the war
from Congress to the states was the system of specific supplies.   In
the past, Congress had always purchased supplies through its own
agents; now the states themselves must provide whatever they could.
They had never paid requisitions in money, and Congress therefore
decided that the best plan would be to obtain requisitions from
them which were payable in the actual goods needed by the army.
Late in 1779 Congress asked certain states to deliver flour and wheat.
It found this scheme so attractive that on February 25, 1780, it
adopted a general requisition asking delivery of such commodities
as beef, pork, rum, flour, and tobacco.   For the immediate future, at
least, specific supplies were regarded as the mode of supplying the
army.[1]

The new system had certain advantages.   Prices, even of country
produce, were so high that all the Continental money in existence
would scarcely have bought provisions for the next campaign.   It

1. *Journals*, XV, 1311, 1371, 1377, XVI, 196, XVIII, 1011.   A final specific
supply requisition was adopted in November 1780.

was possible that the elimination of competitive buying between federal and state agents would bring prices down.[2] However, the states, if they chose, had the power to bypass the market entirely—merely by levying taxes payable in commodities. Still hoping to revive Continental currency, Congress theorized that if the army could be supported by specific requisitions until the states complied with the heavy money requisitions of the previous year, state taxes would reduce the Continental currency in circulation and raise its market value. "We are now at the very pinch of the game," wrote William Ellery, a Rhode Island delegate. "If we can but supply our army a few months without further emissions of money, the game is our own. We then can at our leisure . . . appreciate our currency."[3]

Another attractive feature of the new system was that it promised a solution to federal administrative problems. Congress had long tried without success to achieve some degree of order and economy· The expenses of its supply departments were out of control, and it was the general consensus, both in and out of Congress, that the waste and fraudulent misuse of funds had added greatly to the cost of the war. An undated report, probably written in the fall of 1779, put the case for specific supplies in the strongest language: "On the present Mode you have 1 Man in the Staff for every fighting Man in the Field . . . You will not continue these Departments on Commission, if you do they will ruin you . . . You cannot trust them upon Salaries for they will do Nothing and a failure will ensue . . . Congress cannot supervise the People employed in the Staff Departments, the several States can do it better, and they will do it."[4] Under the new system the states were to raise and deliver supplies, leaving to federal officers only the duty of receiving and transporting them to the army. Happily contemplating the eventual dismantling of its purchasing department, Congress reorganized the Quartermaster and Commissary services to conform with the new arrangement.[5]

2. See Timothy Pickering to the New Jersey legislature, about Oct. 20, 1780, Pickering Letterbooks, Revolutionary War Manuscripts, no. 126, 161, Natl. Arch.; North Carolina Delegates to the Governor of North Carolina, Feb. 29, 1780, Burnett, ed., *Letters,* V, 55.

3. Ellery to the Governor of Rhode Island, Dec. 21, 1779, Burnett, ed., *Letters,* IV, 545.

4. Papers of Cont. Cong., no. 26, I, 131.

5. *Journals,* XVII, 615, 723, XVIII, 1109; Victor L. Johnson, *The Administration of the American Commissariat During the Revolutionary War* (Phila., 1941), 161-65. See President of Congress to the Several States, Feb. 26, 1780, Burnett.

During the year or two in which specific requisitions operated, they proved no more than a stopgap arrangement. Without money for purchasing, the states had to collect or seize the bulk of the supplies from their citizens, and their deliveries to Congress awaited the seasons. Frequently the goods were not available in time and quantity to suit the needs of the army, and the quality was often poor. Congress was unable to discontinue purchases by its own officers or realize any significant economies in administration. With all its faults, however, the system produced crude results in an emergency, for specific supplies provisioned the army in the last campaigns of the war.[6]

Under the stress of poverty, Congress, in 1780, attempted to unload further responsibility on the states by turning over to them the pay of the army, both arrears of salary and pay due for current service. It was also decided to compensate the troops for previous losses sustained from receiving pay in depreciated currency. Accordingly, Congress asked the states to assume all sums due to their soldiers in the Continental army—an act later regretted by exponents of strong central government because it relinquished a vital element of the sovereignty they wished to invest in Congress. But in 1780 there was no remedy; Congress did not have the money. How long the states were to continue paying their troops was not stipulated, but most of them acted on the assumption that they would be indefinitely responsible.[7] Massachusetts, Connecticut, Rhode Island, New York, New Jersey, Maryland, Virginia, North Carolina, and South Carolina not only provided for depreciation, but carried forward the settlement to include pay for varying periods of service in 1781 and 1782. The sums involved were large, representing the

---

ed., *Letters*, V, 51; Ephraim Blaine to Thomas Sim Lee, Apr. 5, 1780, and Blaine to Chaloner, and White *et al.*, Apr. 5, 1780, Blaine Letterbook, 1780-1783, Ephraim Blaine Collection, Lib. Cong.

6. Timothy Pickering to Deputy Quartermasters, Dec. 16, 1780, Pickering Letterbooks, Revo. War Mss., no. 123, Natl. Arch.; Robert Morris to Franklin, Nov. 27, 1781, Wharton, ed., *Diplomatic Correspondence*, V, 16. New York and New Jersey were said to have furnished their whole quotas under the requisition of February 25 by July 1780. Ezekiel Cornell to the Governor of Rhode Island, June 30, 1780, Burnett, ed., *Letters*, V, 246.

7. *Journals*, XIV, 975; XV, 1335; XVI, 344. Depreciation pay was restricted to troops enlisted for three years or the duration of the war. Congress later limited the period for which the states should be responsible for current pay to August 1, 1780. See *ibid.*, XVII, 726, XXIV, 93.

bulk of several years' pay to the men enlisted for three years or the duration of the war. Specie was seldom involved in these transactions. The states gave their soldiers "military" or "depreciation" certificates, which in most cases remained the largest item of state debts after the Revolution.[8]

A final evolution of policy was to involve the states as guarantors of a new federal currency. Because Congress controlled no sure revenues, Continental money had always lacked the security then understood to be basic to currency finance: that the power to tax be joined with the power to emit.[9] Not wholly in despair of regaining the use of money, Congress came forward in 1780 with a plan for a new currency. It was to be underwritten by the federal government but issued and redeemed by the states.

Under the plan of March 18, 1780, Congress revalued "old" Continental money at 40 to 1 of specie, a rate above its current value. The states were called upon to tax this money out of existence at the rate of $15,000,000 per month. Their deliveries of the old currency to Congress would release the new emission for use. Each $40 of the old money brought in and canceled would release $2 of the new bills, of which four-tenths would go to Congress and the remaining six-tenths to the state which delivered it. The new emission was to be girded and supported with all the resources that Congress could bring to bear. Doubly guaranteed by the pledge of both state and federal governments, bills of the new emission were also to draw 5 percent interest, payable in bills of exchange.[10] Congress asked the states to make them legal tender.

This act constituted a virtual repudiation of the old money, reducing its legal value at a single stroke from $200,000,000 to $5,000,-000.[11] The whole amount was to be retired in approximately thir-

8. E. James Ferguson, "State Assumption of the Federal Debt During the Confederation," *Miss. Valley Hist. Rev.*, 38 (1951), 408-9.

9. See "Tribunus," *Worcester Magazine*, 3 (May 1787) , 380. "When the Continental money was issued," wrote Robert Morris in 1782, "a greater confidence was shown by America, than any other people ever exhibited. The general promise of a body not formed into, nor claiming to be a Government, was accepted as current coin and it was not until long after an excess of quantity had forced on depreciation that the validity of these promises was questioned." *Journals*, XXII, 434.

10. *Journals*, XVI, 262-67. The interest was never paid in bills of exchange.

11. The repudiation aroused no particular indignation, since the "evident injustice" of calling in the money at its nominal value was acknowledged. The keynote of John Adams' famous defense of the measure was that "the public has

teen months and its place taken by $10,000,000 in new bills, which, presumably, could be kept from depreciating since the total amount would not be in excess of the needs of the economy. The change to a new currency would have the additional virtue of raising an income of $10,000,000 specie, to be shared by Congress and the states. Congress's portion would in some measure relieve its financial stringency, and it was supposed that the new money would be employed by the states in lieu of state emissions.

The act of March 18 was not a hopeless plan. It corresponded with known and accepted practice. The repudiation could not be supposed to have inspired confidence; yet Continental currency immediately rose in value. Robert Morris was optimistic: "Continental money," he wrote, "will never be of less value than it is now." From Congress's standpoint, much depended on the success of the plan; it was a last effort to make a paper currency work. "All the resource we have is the new money," one member commented. "If that should not freely circulate, or should it speedily depreciate, we shall be at our wits' end."[12]

While alternatives were being tested, Congress fell upon hard times. During the winter of 1779 the army lived mainly by impressments. Specific supplies eventually afforded some relief, but during preparations for the campaign of 1780 there was an absolute dearth of money at the federal Treasury. Urgent needs of the Quartermaster and Commissary departments were met by drawing drafts on the states. Every few days Congress parceled out a million dollars or so among different states, drawing on each according to its presumed ability to pay or its proximity to where funds were needed. From December 1779 through June 1780, drafts amounted to approximately $40,000,000. Mindful of their responsibilities now that Congress was feeble, the states made unusual efforts to discharge the drafts. They accepted and eventually paid $35,000,000 and in later months discharged nearly $2,000,000 more. They also tried, with-

its rights as well as individuals." Adams to Vergennes, Paris, June 22, 1780, Wharton, ed., *Diplomatic Correspondence*, III, 809-16.

12. Robert Morris to Jonathan Hudson, Apr. 25, 1780, and Thomas McKean to the President of Pennsylvania, Aug. 29, 1780, Burnett, ed., *Letters*, V, 126n, 346. Morris reported in May that imported goods had fallen in price. Morris to Hudson, May 2, 1780, Robert Morris Papers, Folder A, Penn. Hist. and Museum Commission. The improvement in the value of Continental money was generally observed.

out much effect, to implement the plan of March 18. The states appear to have withdrawn about $2,000,000 in old money through January 1781, releasing about $40,000 in new bills for the use of Congress.[13] However, their whole contribution in 1780 amounted to considerably less than a million dollars in specie and did no more than ease the most critical situations.

Desperately in need of funds, Congress at length fell to corrupting the loan offices. Among the various types of paper employed by Congress, loan certificates had always been regarded as a special obligation involving the honor and integrity of the nation, for the buyers were presumed to have ventured their money in a patriotic spirit. Had it been widely known that loan certificates were paid out directly to vendors of high-priced goods and services, the esteem in which they were held would have been qualified. This issue was raised in 1778 when Congress learned that Ephraim Blaine, a commissary officer, had contracted with a merchant for the delivery of goods with the understanding that payment be made in back-dated loan certificates which drew interest in bills of exchange. Refusing the merchant's request for payment, Congress observed that all creditors might justly claim similar payment, with the result that loan certificates would be degraded to the status of another circulating medium. Always in difficulty, Congress was often driven to make statements for the record, and this was one of them. It was common knowledge among members of Congress that loan certificates were being issued for supplies.[14]

When federal agents ran short of money, they frequently gave loan certificates in payment to merchants, who accepted certificates rather than wait for money whose value would decline before they got it. The procedure was simple. The federal agent presented a warrant against federal funds presumably on hand in the loan office. When no funds existed, the loan officer issued a certificate to the

13. *American State Papers, Finance,* I, 58-62. Harlow, "Some Aspects of Revolutionary Finance," *Amer. Hist. Rev.,* 35 (1929-30), 67, writes that there was nothing available to show that returns from state taxation were "appreciable" before 1781.

Through June 1781, when Continental money ceased to circulate except in the south, the states were credited with an additional $29,000,000 in withdrawals, which entitled Congress to $580,000 in new bills. By this time the bills were no better than 4 or 5 to 1 of specie.

14. *Journals,* XII, 1241.

agent in his name, and the agent endorsed it over to the merchant.[15] According to the informed testimony of Jeremiah Wadsworth, this practice was common as early as 1776 or 1777, and it continued without official sanction on an increasing scale.[16] Finally, late in 1779, Congress itself resorted to loan certificates when nothing else was at hand to make essential purchases or pay urgent debts. Reluctant to degrade the securities, Congress resisted to the last, but eventually it became impossible to deny aid to General Benjamin Lincoln in South Carolina, and payment of his drafts in loan certificates was authorized.[17] Throughout the dismal winter of 1780-81, securities were used in emergencies. The largest disbursements were authorized when it became necessary to place the fragments of Continental credit behind the fugitive government of South Carolina. Governor Rutledge's bills, amounting to some $2,300,000 currency, were declared payable in loan certificates.[18]

The specific authorizations entered in the journals of Congress were only a fraction of the securities issued for supplies in 1780. The whole system of loans, it appears, was converted to the payment of current debts. Reports disclosed that only a small amount of actual money was coming into the loan offices—scarcely more than

15. The loan officer entered the amount of the warrant as a cash payment in purchase of loan certificates and in another book recorded that he had paid out so much cash in discharge of a warrant.

16. Wadsworth's comment, Feb. 16, 1790, *Annals of Congress*, I, 1237-39. Elbridge Gerry recalled at this time that supplies during the Revolution were paid for in Continental money or "in loan-office certificates issued some time after the purchase."

In May 1778, Henry Laurens talked about the "taking up loan Office Certificates for raising Money." Burnett, ed., *Letters*, III, 247. In January 1778, the Commercial Committee paid debts with loan certificates or negotiated certificates to pay debts. *Ibid.*, 38. William Ellery tried hard in the spring of 1778 to get an advance of loan certificates to the state of Rhode Island as compensation for debts contracted for the Union. *Ibid.*, 12, 103, 217. See also Johnson, *Commissariat*, 61-63; Robert A. East, *Business Enterprise in the American Revolutionary Era* (N.Y., 1938), 41. In 1780 and 1781 loan certificates were being issued for the interest arising on loan certificates. See Wharton, ed., *Diplomatic Correspondence*, IV, 793; William Duane, ed., *Extracts from the Diary of Christopher Marshall* (Albany, 1877), 243-44.

17. *Journals*, XVI, 74, 136, 166, 173, 280. See Elbridge Gerry to William Hunt, Jan. 6, 1780, Madison to Jefferson, Mar. 27, 1780, Burnett, ed., *Letters*, V, 3-4, 96-99. Nearly $2,000,000 of Lincoln's drafts were paid in loan certificates. *Journals*, XXIV, 365.

18. *Journals*, XVI, 289, 319, 339, 402, XVII, 495, 533, 562, 571, XVIII, 832, 903, XX, 493, 511; Papers of Cont. Cong., no. 139, 379.

would meet the interest on money already loaned. Yet according to the books, large sums were being received on loan—approximately $30,000,000 from September 1779 until the offices closed in 1781.[19] Much of this amount undoubtedly represented loan certificates issued for supplies rather than money loaned to the government.[20]

This conclusion is reinforced by the fact that a new emission of loan certificates offered in 1781 went almost entirely to pay debts. Late in 1780, Congress authorized $1,000,000 in "specie certificates" which in theory were to be sold for hard money; but when the notes were ready for sale, Congress allowed them to be issued in discharge of current federal debts. Soon the Board of Treasury reported that few notes would be issued except in settlement of debts. Only a small number of the certificates were released, something more than $112,000 specie but their use reflects the general procedure.[21] Issued as cash, loan certificates were thrown into the breach caused by the failure of paper money.

Foreign aid furnished scant relief during 1780. The only fountain of credit abroad was the French Court, and American funds there were largely committed to the activities of the American commissioners in Europe and the payment of bills of exchange drawn for the interest on loan certificates.[22] Late in 1779, as we have seen, Congress struck bills for £100,000 sterling on John Jay, who was in Spain, and Henry Laurens, who was scheduled to visit Holland in

19. *Journals*, XVII, 563, 675, XIX, 400. This necessarily rough calculation is based on the Auditor General's statement of 1780, in Franklin's Papers, LIV, 75, Amer. Philos. Soc.; also under date of Feb. 18, 1780, in Papers of Cont. Cong., no. 12, 90. It is in general agreement—allowing for different time intervals covered and more complete returns—with another statement of loan subscriptions, dated July 16, 1782, in *ibid.*, no. 137, I, 709.

20. Members of the House of Representatives in 1790 well recalled that extensive use of loan certificates had been made in purchase of supplies. See remarks by Samuel Livermore and Elias Boudinot. *Annals of Congress*, I, 1185, 1238; and letters by "An Original Holder" and by a "merchant," *Daily Advertiser* (N.Y.), Feb. 18 and 22, 1790.

When Pennsylvania assumed federal securities in 1785, she made provision for "loan-office certificates, received by any citizen . . . in lieu of money." Mitchell and Flanders, eds., *Statutes of Pennsylvania*, XI, 461. Subscriptions of loan certificates reported in Pennsylvania were very large from September 1779 through 1781, over half of the $30,000,000 noted above being subscribed in that state— the seat of the federal government.

21. *Journals*, XVII, 803, XX, 447, 484, 579; *American State Papers, Finance*, I, 27.

22. In August 1780, Congress prepared bills of exchange on France for $456,- 000 specie to pay interest on loan certificates. *Journals*, XVII, 689.

quest of a loan.[23]   But Congress scarcely dared cash these bills, knowing their payment was dubious.   They were carefully hoarded and
used only in emergencies.   The greater portion was finally deposited
without being cashed in the "bank" of Pennsylvania, an association
formed in 1780 to advance supplies to Congress.[24]

From time to time other bills were drawn on France; the *Journals*
record some $215,000 specie drawn on Franklin, aside from bills to
discharge interest on loan certificates.   However, of all foreign bills
authorized by Congress during this period, it appears that $93,000
specie was still uncashed as the year closed.[25]   Congress longed to
abuse its credit with France, but Franklin's protestations of in-
solvency and the discouraging attitude of the French minister made
it seem unwise to draw too heavily on funds that had only a prospective existence.   In September the French minister said plainly
that a bill for £40,000 sterling would be refused, to which a member
of Congress added: "We have not the least shadow of promise that
a Bill for £20 on any power in Europe would be paid."[26]

Worst of all, Congress endured the slow agony of watching its
new currency fail.   The plan of March 18, 1780—the final effort to
make currency finance work—was destined to fall victim to one massive fact which Congress had not sufficiently taken into account.

23. Laurens's departure was delayed several months; then he was captured on
his voyage.   Adams took over his negotiation and the responsibility of paying
the drafts.   *Journals,* XVII, 534.

24. The Board of Treasury was instructed to place in the bank a sum not to
exceed £150,000 sterling to guarantee the associators against loss.   *Ibid.,* 548-50.

25. Drafts on Franklin recorded in the *Journals* amount to some $204,000
specie and £2,500 sterling.   Sterling at this time exchanged at the rate of £1 to
$4.45.   As to unexpended funds, see *Journals,* XVIII, 1144.

26. Ezekiel Cornell to the Governor of Rhode Island, Sept. 2, 1780, Burnett,
ed., *Letters,* V, 353-55; Luzerne to the President of Congress, Sept. 1, 1780,
Wharton, ed., *Diplomatic Correspondence,* 44; *Journals,* XVII, 713.

4

Mass Expropriation

"It's taken for granted that the farmer is to be deprived of his horses at this busy time of ploughing for winter's grain. O wretched rulers! O monstrous directors of our State! . . . O glorious Whigs for magistrates!"

"Had our government by their officers exerted the authority that they have used with some degree of cruelty on the poor farmers by taking their horses out of their ploughs, &c., they might have collected a great number of useless yet valuable ones today and yesterday on the race ground."

—Christopher Marshall's
Diary, July 24, 25, 1780.

ONE important source of federal income during the Revolution is almost unknown to history. The role played by certificates has escaped notice, mainly because the record of their existence was dissipated in the obscurity of state accounts and does not figure largely in the federal documents upon which scholars have usually relied. But as the money revenues of Congress dwindled in the later stages of the war, certificates became the chief means of sustaining the army.

Certificates were drafts which federal officers drew upon their respective departments. They were issued by all the departments in lieu of money, but the Quartermaster and Commissary departments used them in overwhelming numbers. At first merely hand written notes, they later became printed forms. From the beginning they were connected with impressment.

As early as December 1776, Congress authorized Washington to impress goods and services; this power was renewed from time to time.   Washington and other commanders delegated their authority to subordinate officers and agents in the Quartermaster and Commissary departments.   Although a legal basis for impressment existed, all evidence suggests that it was a mere formality.   Continental officers conducted impressments from the earliest stages of the war, and it is clear that Congress and its staff simply asumed that impressments were justifiable in any emergency.[1]   "Now my sweet scolding Jeremiah," wrote Quartermaster General Thomas Mifflin, to Jeremiah Wadsworth in October 1776, "be pleas'd to impress for the public Service all such Teams as you want. . . . If the Inhabitants will hire their Teams at reasonable Rates you will not I dare say proceed to impress—If they refuse to aid you you are to impress without Loss of Time."   Wadsworth had already been instructed by Hugh Hughes, an assistant quartermaster general, to hire or impress such teams and forage "as may be necessary to answer the purposes of your department, and for so doing this [letter] shall be your sufficient Warrant."[2]   The general attitude of Congress was expressed by a committee report which declared that "Congress, the Board of War, and the Commanders of every army, from the nature of their charges, must necessarily have and exercise a power to order Impresses of Carriages and other Articles in cases of *extraordinary Emergency*." But, the report continued, "every possible attention should be paid to the Laws of States and the Rights of Individuals."[3]

Since impressments caused trouble with state authorities, Congress avoided a formal endorsement of them so far as possible; but it carefully refused to prohibit them, urging only that federal officers secure the cooperation of local officials.   In December 1777 Congress asked the states to pass laws authorizing and regulating Continental impressments.[4]

1. See *Journals*, VI, 826, 56, 75, 144.   Washington continued to grant impress warrants to Clement Biddle through 1780.   See the Washington Correspondence with Clement Biddle, I, folios 8, 15, 19, 21, 22, 23, 26, 28, 30, Clement Biddle Papers, Hist. Soc. of Pa.

2. Mifflin to Wadsworth, Oct. 12, 17, 1776, and Hughes to Wadsworth, Oct. 16, 1776, Jeremiah Wadsworth Papers, box 124, Conn. Hist. Soc.

3. *Journals*, X, 273.   The allusion to the right of impressment was scratched out of the reply to Pennsylvania's complaint.

4. *Ibid.*, VII, 56, 75-78, 144-47, IX, 1042.   See also XII, 974, 979, 1177.

Although early in the war impressments fell mainly on disaffected persons, they were soon executed upon patriots and loyalists alike. "Since the year 1776," recalled Elbridge Gerry in 1780, "Congress have not been able to Supply the *Officers* of the Staff with the Sums required by them for making their purchases." Even when federal procurement officers had money, they were often obliged by their instructions to pay no more than "reasonable" prices or those fixed by state authority. If the owners of goods would not sell or refused to accept legislated prices, their goods were confiscated, and they received certificates.[5]

After Continental money began its rapid descent in 1779, prices rose so high that the funds given to public officials evaporated immediately. From this time forward, military operations in the field were supported almost entirely by impressments, sometimes levied by the states, sometimes by federal officers. Great quantities of provisions were taken by the army during the winter of 1778-79, and the next winter "the army was in such extremity for want of provisions that the Commander in Chief was reduced to the sad alternative, either to suffer it to disband, or to collect supplies by military force."[6] The middle states bore the brunt in 1779 and 1780. Writing in 1782, Timothy Pickering, the quartermaster general, said that the cash expended by federal officers in the middle states was *"but as the dust of the ballance."* In New York, he claimed, one hardly met a man who was not a public creditor for services or supplies rendered the army. "The business of my department in all the posts in this state and in Jersey, when the army has been there, has been effected almost wholly by persuasion and impress." As early as 1780 it was

5. Gerry to James Lovell, Aug. 14, 1780. Burnett, ed., *Letters*, V, 326-27. The letters passing between Ephraim Blaine, deputy and later commissary general, Oct. 1777, are full of allusions to the shortage of cash and impressments, sometimes with and sometimes without the offer of payment in paper money. Blaine Letterbook, 1777-1779, Lib. Cong.

6. For 1778-79, see *Journals*, XIII, 275-79; for 1779-80, see *ibid.*, XIX, 410. Accepting the post of quartermaster general in March 1778, Nathanael Greene wrote of the large claims already outstanding against the department. Greene to Henry Laurens, Mar. 26, 1778, Nathanael Greene Papers, Clements Library, Ann Arbor. In October 1779, Jeremiah Wadsworth, then commissary general, was informed that the assistants of one of his deputies were a million dollars in debt, besides which they had not paid for grain and 3,000 head of cattle recently purchased. Jacob Cuyler to Wadsworth, Oct. 14, 1779, Wadsworth Papers, box 129, Conn. Hist. Soc.

reported that citizens of Pennsylvania alone held $20,000,000 in cer-
tificates, and those of New York and New Jersey equal amounts.[7]

Wherever the armies went they littered the country with certificates. When the war moved to the south, the governor of Virginia complained that the American as well as the British army,
"lived on free quarter, & ravaged the Country from one end of it
to the other." "Nor," he added, "is there one of the staff departments,
that has had any money from Congress that I know of, since the
War has been in the South."[8] "I never saw a country so loaded with
certificates as the state of Virginia," wrote Timothy Pickering in
March 1781. Everything in the state had been impressed, even
"breakfast & dinners" for officers and soldiers. It was useless for the
people to object, observed Pickering, because the soldiery had the
force.[9]

Continental impressments merged with seizures conducted by
state authorities. As their own currencies failed, the states were
driven to a use of violence which soon became normal procedure,
rising in scope and intensity during periods of crisis. Preferably,
goods were seized from the disaffected or those who violated the
laws against hoarding and profiteering. Virginia declared in 1778
that any one who bought country produce for resale was an engrosser
and his goods liable to seizure. The governor was authorized to
seize all grain and flour purchased by any forestaller, engrosser, or
monopolizer. In Maryland, the same year, upon information that
speculators were buying up the scanty grain crop, the legislature
directed justices of the peace to seize grain for the United States. The
justices were instructed to summon for questioning persons suspected

7. Pickering to Major Richard Claiborne, Jan. 16, 1782, Pickering Letterbooks,
Revo. War. Mss., no. 83, Natl. Arch.; *Journals,* XVIII, 1175-77. See *ibid.,* XVI, 271,
XVII, 441, 455.

8. Benjamin Harrison to Robert Morris, Mar. 20, 1782, Robert Morris Papers,
N.Y. Pub. Lib. Pickering wrote that Colonel Finnie, who had charge of Quartermaster affairs with Greene's forces from Aug. 1780 to Dec. 31, 1780, drew absolutely no money from the department, to Pickering's knowledge. Pickering to
Edward Carrington, June 29, 1786, Pickering Letterbooks, Revol. War Mss., no.
88, Natl. Arch. There are numerous allusions to this situation in William P.
Palmer and H. W. Flourney, eds., *Calendar of Virginia State Papers and Other
Manuscripts* (Richmond, 1875-93), *State Papers,* II, 110, 194, 292, 542, III, 30, 37;
see also Jared Sparks, ed., *The Diplomatic Correspondence of the American Revolution* (Boston, 1829-30), XI, 434, 486.

9. Pickering to the President of Congress, Mar. 30, 1781, Pickering Papers,
XXXIII, 331, Mass. Hist. Soc.

of cornering the supply of salt: If their responses were unsatisfactory, their goods were to be confiscated.[10] Pennsylvania directed its justices, upon complaint, to seize grain, flour, and salt which appeared to have been acquired in violation of the anti-monopoly laws. The Pennsylvania authorities were to set the price of the seized goods, then deliver them to Continental agents. New York's more drastic law required persons to sell to the army all ordinarily marketable goods in their possession above what they needed for personal use. The state also authorized federal officers to apply to local justices for the purpose of seizing any flour, meal, or wheat purchased by the owner for resale. Because farmers were withholding wheat from market, the legislature declared the whole crop of the preceding year subject to confiscation, limited only by family need.[11]

As the crisis deepened in 1780, the states close to the scene of action, unable to render financial aid, devoted their full authority to the procurement of supplies for the Continental army. With scant regard for the welfare of the people, the New York legislature in March 1779 authorized the governor to appoint agents to purchase or seize any flour in the state and hand it over to Continental agents. The procedure was typical of New York's legislation for the duration of active warfare. An act of February 1780 directed the state assessors to inquire how much wheat, above the amount necessary for subsistence, was held by individual citizens. The surplus was to be confiscated and paid for with certificates. In the months that followed, other impressments were extended to articles of military supply.[12]

In November 1779 Maryland empowered the governor to grant Continental officers, acting through local justices, the right to seize any provisions for sale at higher than legal prices. All goods above

10. William Hening, ed., *The Statutes at Large, Being a Collection of All the Laws of Virginia* (Richmond, 1821), IX, 581-83, 584-85, X, 142, 157-59; the act was extended the next year. For Maryland, see the session laws, published currently, Oct. sess., 1778, ch. VIII. The act was continued into 1780. *Ibid.,* July sess., 1779, ch. XVII; Nov. sess., 1779, ch. XVIII.
11. Mitchell and Flanders, eds., *Statutes of Pennsylvania,* IX, 421; *Laws of New York, 1777-1801,* 1st sess., ch. 34; 2nd sess., ch. 5.
12. *Laws of New York, 1777-1801,* 2nd sess., chs. 21, 32; 3rd sess., chs. 1, 4, 34, 41, 67, 69, 74; 4th sess., chs. 6, 8, 42. In discussing state impressments, I have taken New York, Pennsylvania, Maryland, and Virginia as examples. These will stand for the middle and southern states, but are less representative of the New England states which were unvisited by the enemy after the opening phases of the war.

family need were also subject to confiscation under this act, which was later extended to teams and drivers, vessels and their crews. Commissioners were appointed in each county to impress transport. Nearly all such purchases, whether accomplished by "persuasion" or impress, were paid for with certificates.[13]

Pennsylvania was often accused of being laggard in prosecuting the war, and indeed her legislation did not rise to the sweeping grants of executive authority which other states enacted. But in 1780 Pennsylvania assigned county officials the task of impressing the specific supplies required by Congress and then peremptorily declared all sheep, cattle, and salted provisions in the state subject to seizure.[14]

As the campaigns moved into the south, the government of Virginia assumed dictatorial power. In May 1780 commissioners were appointed in each county to seize or purchase provisions at adjudicated prices, payable in certificates; all goods above family need were declared forfeit on these terms. The next year, on the eve of the Yorktown campaign, the governor was given unlimited power to produce the resources of the state. He was authorized to put Virginia's procurement services entirely at the disposal of Continental officers.[15]

In its last years the war was supported by a general levy on the inhabitants, justified by the principle that "those who are nearest to where the scene of action is to be, must expect to give up everything they have which is wanted for the enterprize."[16] The line between purchases and impressments was vague and unmeaningful. When federal or state agents had money, the owners of goods were sometimes paid in cash, but as time went on money payment gave way to the wholesale employment of certificates. Whether certificates were issued by Continental agents or state officials was purely fortuitous; impressments mingled inextricably with state collections of

13. *Maryland Session Laws,* Nov. sess., 1779, chs. XVII, XXXII, XXXIV.

14. Mitchell and Flanders, eds., *Statutes of Pennsylvania,* X, 176, 214.

15. Hening, ed., *Statutes of Virginia,* X, 233-37, 309-15, 326-38, 341-45, 413-16, 426. Federal officers testified to the great contributions of both Virginia and Maryland to the Yorktown campaign. Charles Stewart and Ephraim Blaine to Col. William Davies, Yorktown, Nov. 8, 1781, *Cal. Va. State Papers,* II, 587; Ephraim Blaine to Robert Morris, Nov. 27, 1781, Letterbook, 1780-1783, Ephraim Blaine Papers, Lib. Cong.

16. Major Richard Claiborne to Col. Davies, Sept. 15, 1781, *Cal. Va. State Papers,* II, 439.

specific supplies.[17]   This situation prevailed until the end of active warfare.   Although Congress obtained important foreign loans beginning in 1781, the Yorktown and subsequent campaigns were conducted by impressments and the issue of certificates.[18]

It is impossible to say how many certificates were issued.   Aside from those put out by the states, the certificates issued by federal officers must have approximated, in nominal amount, the entire sum of Continental currency.   Early in 1781, before the Yorktown campaign, an estimated $95,000,000 was outstanding in the Quartermaster and Commissary departments—and this did not include certificates issued in the Carolinas and Georgia.[19]   Although much of the federal certificate debt was absorbed by the states, the adjusted specie value of unredeemed federal certificates at the close of the war was over $3,723,000 specie.[20]

Not all certificates represented forced collections.   Many patriots gave their goods willingly, especially since they were often compensated, if they gave cheerfully, by an allowance of far more than the goods were worth.   The officers who were "compelled to the melancholy duty of plundering their fellow-citizens endeavor[ed] by the sum of their certificates to compensate for the manner of taking as well as for the value of the thing taken."[21]   Before 1780, however, federal certificates were almost a total loss to the holders; they fre-

17. Federal officers, for example, were given state certificates to dispense in Virginia and Connecticut. Although issued for federal purposes, state certificates remained a financial obligation of the state. As to Virginia, see Answer to Certain Queries . . . enclosed in a letter from J. Ambler, Feb. 8, 1783, Madison Papers, III, 76, Lib. Cong.

18. The Correspondence of Timothy Pickering, who succeeded Greene as quartermaster general makes plain just how little money was available or southern campaigns. "You have often asked for money," he wrote to Major Richard Claiborne, his deputy in Virginia. "I can scarcely get enough to support my own expenses & am every day running into debt to my friends." July 1, 1781, *Cal. Va. State Papers*, II, 194. Pickering informed a newly appointed deputy commissary of purchases that "the *purchase* of forage will probably seldom happen, from want of money. . . . A warrant of impress, I fear, will be for the most part your only resource." Pickering to William Keefe, Aug. 26, 1781, Pickering Letterbooks, Revol. War Mss., no. 82, Natl. Arch.

19. *Journals*, XIX, 165.

20. *American State Papers, Finance,* I, 239.

21. Robert Morris to the President of Congress, Aug. 28, 1781, Wharton, ed., *Diplomatic Correspondence*, IV, 676. A writer recalled in 1790 that prices paid in certificates were four times the value of services or commodities rendered. Letter dated New York, Jan. 28, in the *Providence Gazette*, Feb. 6, 1790. This was an exaggeration, but it was generally acknowledged that certificates, like other forms of Continental obligations, represented excessive charges.

quently lacked details of the transaction or were issued by officers without competent authority. Persons who applied for payment were shunted from one office to another. It was not easy for an ordinary citizen to secure payment from a distant central government; in any case, Congress had no money. The certificates bore no interest, and while the holders waited for payment, the nominal sums expressed on the notes declined in real value as paper money depreciated. As early as March 1779, Quartermaster and Commissary certificates were reported selling for a "trifle"—if any purchasers could be found.[22]

By 1780 few inhabitants of the middle states, which were already glutted with certificates, would accept them unless under duress. President Reed of Pennsylvania said that farmers refused to plant crops in excess of their own needs because the surplus was confiscated.[23] Bloodshed, so it was said, attended the collection of forage in New Jersey. When the war shifted southward, troops marching into Virginia seldom saw a wagon that had not been stripped of wheels or gear. Teamsters working under compulsion committed sabotage or deserted. Horses were scarce, and local men could not be induced to help find them.[24] Although most people exhibited a remarkable degree of patience— a fact attested by Continental officers whose onerous duty was to put them under imposition—it is not surprising that impressments inspired a growing disgust with the government.

The massive certificate debt foredoomed Congress's efforts to restore its currency. With their pockets full of Quartermaster and Commissary notes, the people refused to pay state taxes levied for Continental purposes unless certificates were accepted. New York began receiving them for taxes in February 1780, and it was not long before New Jersey and Pennsylvania asked Congress to accept them in discharge of Continental requisitions. Congress yielded to the extent of taking them for old money requisitions adopted prior to the act of March 18, 1780. Shortly afterwards it passed a special requisi-

22. *Journals*, XII, 1099, XIII, 275. See Johnson, *Commissariat*, 83-84, 88-93.
23. William B. Reed, *Life and Correspondence of Joseph Reed* (Phila., 1847), II, 224.
24. Timothy Pickering to John Hancock, Nov. 20, 1780, Revol. War Mss., no. 123, Natl. Arch.; *Cal. Va. State Papers*, I, 559, II, 308, 439, 531, III, 113.

tion of $3,000,000, payable in certificates reduced to specie value.[25] The object was to provide an outlet for certificates and at the same time preserve the requisition of March 18 for the essential task of withdrawing Continental currency.

It was politically impossible, however, for the states to refuse to accept certificates for any taxes, especially when impressments were still putting them into the hands of their people. And since state taxes returned certificates, the mass of outstanding Continental currency remained untouched. Even with good intentions, the states found it difficult or impossible to comply with the procedure set forth in the plan of March 18, and, as they could not withdraw the old currency, they could not realize the expected income from the emission of new bills.[26] They were under a powerful temptation to issue the new bills without complying with Congress's plan, or simply to emit state currency to pay their expenses.

Congress was thoroughly aware that the continuing use of certificates cut across its vital projects. "In vain have we endeavoured to obtain a knowledge of the amount of these certificates, or how far they have been reduced," ran an address to the states in 1781, "and they continue to obstruct every plan which hath been devised for restoring public credit and supporting the war." Nevertheless, Congress could not afford to give them up. A committee observed that while they might be productive of evil, they might also "under . . . pressing necessities have a happy tendency by answering the purposes of money.[27]

By the end of 1780 the plan of March 18 was dead. Only a small part of the old currency had been sunk. By June 1781, when the

25. *Laws of New York, 1777-1801*, 3rd sess., ch. 35; *Journals*, XVI, 271, XVII, 441, 455, 462-64, 782.

26. A memorial from the New York legislature to the Continental Congress, Feb. 5, 1781, illustrates the difficulties of the states: "The Servants of Congress having given in Payment for the far greater Part of the Purchases made by them only Certificates and these Purchases having been made under the compulsory Laws [passed by the state]. . . . We were compelled . . . to enact that the Certificates should be received in Payment for Taxes, hence every Person altho' he has none of his own finds Means to obtain these Certificates, they being of much less Value than Money and we do not collect by Taxes in Currency a Sum sufficient to defray the Expense of Management." Abraham Yates Papers, N.Y. Pub. Lib. See also New Jersey's memorial to Congress, printed in the *Journals* under date of November 24, 1780, XVIII, 1087, and David Jameson to James Madison, Aug. 10, 1780, William C. Rives Collection, Madison Papers, box 10, Lib. Cong.

27. *Journals*, XIX, 37, XVII, 760.

whole quantity was to have been retired, the states were credited
with withdrawals of $31,000,000, which was not enough to arrest
depreciation or permit the use of a significant amount of the new
bills.[28]   Pennsylvania and New Jersey at length authorized their
executives to fix the legal value of federal currency at its real market
value.   In December, Pennsylvania put the value of Continental
money at 75 to 1.   Within a couple of months the rate was 125 to
1.[29]   When the new bills were issued, they never passed equal to
specie but were regarded only as $40 in Continental money; the
old money remained the standard, and by April 1781, it was 150 to 1
or lower.[30]   At this point it passed out of circulation, first in the
middle colonies, later in New England and the south.   It was "viler
than the Rags" on which it was printed, seldom used in trade, and
valued at purely speculative rates of 500 to 1 and lower.[31]

When the currency expired in the spring of 1781, not a murmur
was heard.   There was general relief that it was quietly "interred in
its grave."   Men of property rejoiced that tender laws were a thing
of the past, and the people were grateful that its departure left no
incubus of debt.   Its immense service to the cause of American liberty
was duly acknowledged.   "Common consent has consigned it to rest
with that kind of regard, which the long service of inanimate things
insensibly obtains from mankind," wrote Thomas Paine.   "Every
stone in the bridge, that has carried us over, seems to have a claim
on our esteem, but this was a corner-stone and its usefulness cannot
be forgotten."[32]

28. How many of the new bills were actually issued is impossible to say. A
report of 1785 alludes to $4,408,000 as the total become *issuable,* at which time
some $88,000,000 had been withdrawn under the act of March 18.   State of
Accounts of the Several States with the United States, November 1, 1785, U. S.
Finance, Lib. Cong.   Later payments would raise the total become issuable.   See
American State Papers, Finance, I, 58-59.   However, the states did not issue all
to which they were entitled, nor did Congress.   Congress drew on the states
for $1,592,222, as its share of the new emission, but these were drafts and there
is no assurance that they were paid by emission of new bills.   *Ibid.*

29. Mitchell and Flanders, eds., *Statutes of Pennsylvania,* X, 249; Jesse Root to
William Williams, Jan. 29, 1781, Burnett, ed., *Letters,* V, 545-46.

30. Abraham Clark to Josiah Hornblower, Oct. 31, 1780, Burnett, ed., *Letters,*
V, 435-36.   See also Robert Levere Brunhouse, *The Counter Revolution in
Pennsylvania, 1776-1790* (Phila., 1942), 95.

31. For various comments see Burnett, ed., *Letters,* VI, 79-83, 142, 151.

32. "Letter to the Abbé Raynal (1782)," Philip S. Foner, ed., *The Complete
Writings of Thomas Paine* (N.Y., 1945), II, 228.

Congress's problems were greatly simplified. Any further ventures in paper money were hopeless. Not out of choice but as a recognition of fact, Congress gave up the plan of March 18, recommended the repeal of tender laws, and began making requisitions in specie. Old money requisitions were useless so far as revenue was concerned; hence nothing was lost when Congress at last agreed to accept certificates in discharge of the requisition of March 18, 1780. This and all previous "old money" requisitions became a mere device for draining off currency and certificates.[33]

Depreciation had wiped out a mass of paper which would otherwise have been a debt. Approximately $226,000,000 in currency, from which Congress derived a real income of over $40,000,000 specie, had shrunk to almost nothing. The loss was carried by the people of the nation as money depreciated in their hands—a process sometimes considered as a form of taxation in rough proportion to ability to pay.[34] Eventually the dead mass of currency was drawn in by the states. A good part of it was scattered or destroyed, and in 1790 only about $6,000,000 remained in the hands of individuals.[35]

Quartermaster and Commissary certificates shared in some degree the fate of paper money. Those issued before August 1780 bore no interest, and they merited no more consideration from Congress than a suggestion that the states receive them for old requisitions. Until the states began making provision for them—they began this by 1780—the certificates lay on the owner's hands. Eventually, when his state acted, the owner had the privilege of paying his taxes with them. In August 1780 Congress declared that certificates reduced to their actual value in terms of specie might be redeemed with new emission money. Meanwhile, at the instigation of Quartermaster General Timothy Pickering, Congress embarked on a new policy of

33. *Journals*, XIX, 266-68, XX, 523-25, XXI, 1087, 2090-92. It appears that no interest was ever paid in bills of exchange on the new emission money. Little, if any, interest was paid at all. See *ibid.*, XIX, 266-68, 352, XX, 591-93; Samuel Osgood to John Lovell, July 10, 1781, Burnett, ed., *Letters*, VI, 141. After March 1782, no bills of exchange were drawn for interest arising on any portion of the domestic debt.

34. Franklin was one of those who took an easy view of the matter. Smyth, ed., *Writings of Franklin*, IX, 234. See James Wilson's comment, in Madison's Notes of Debates, *Journals*, XXV, 867; and Robert Morris's comment, in Wharton, ed., *Diplomatic Correspondence*, VI, 660.

35. Elliot, "Funding Systems," *House Doc. No. 15*, 28th Cong., 1st sess., 1843-44, II, 12. This figure represents nominal, not specie value. Currency was funded at 100 to 1 of specie.

issuing certificates stated in specie values and bearing interest until paid.[36]   Finally, when Congress was in process of abandoning paper money and tender laws, certificates were included in a general promise to pay all Continental debts at their actual value.[37]   In the general financial settlement after the Revolution, they were merged in the body of federal debts. By this time the states had redeemed most of them.

Currency and certificates were the "common debt" of the Revolution, most of which at war's end had been sunk at its depreciated value.[38]   Public opinion did not view contracts as sacred and tended to grade claims against the government according to their real validity.   Paper money had the least status; the mode of its redemption was fixed by long usage.   If depreciation occurred in spite of adequate taxes voted to redeem the money, the fault lay in the general community, or the war was responsible.   In any case, the holder had no exemption from the general misfortune, and he was expected to abide the ordinary processes by which money was redeemed.[39]   Although the holder of a Quartermaster or Commissary certificate merited a little more consideration, because he had rendered a public service, it was presumed that he had taken his profit.

Loan certificates, on the other hand, were "preferred securities" and received the most favorable treatment within Congress's means. In 1780, shortly after the virtual repudiation of Continental currency, Congress reduced outstanding loan certificates to their specie value according to a table of depreciation which presumably registered the actual specie value, from time to time, of the money with which the certificates had been purchased.   Loan certificates were greatly overrated in the process.   The "liquidated" (reduced to specie) value of a $200 certificate issued before September 1, 1777,

36. *Journals*, XVI, 363, XVII, 463-65, 761, 782-83, 784-85; Pickering to the President of Congress, Aug. 12, 1781, Pickering Letterbooks, Revol. War Mss., no. 126, Natl. Arch.

37. *Journals*, XIX, 266.

38. Historians have been impressed by the small size of the debt remaining from the Revolution. See Harlow, "Aspects of Revolutionary Finance," *Amer. Hist. Rev.*, 35 (1929-30), 67-68. The answer is that scarcely a dollar was paid off at full value. See a letter dated New York, July 31, 1790, in the *Providence Gazette*, Aug. 7, 1790.

39. There is an interesting exposition of currency finance doctrine in the *Votes and Proceedings of the House of Delegates of the State of Maryland* (n.p., n.d.), Nov. 25, 1791. More accessible is John Adams's famous defense of the repudiation of March 18, 1780. Wharton, ed., *Diplomatic Correspondence*, III, 809-16.

was, for example, put at $200, whereas the real value of the purchase money was anywhere from $65 to $100.[40] Similarly, loan certificates purchased after March 1, 1780, were liquidated at the rate of 40 to 1, whereas the value of the money with which they were purchased was, at that time, 60 to 100 to 1 and lower.

Other provisions were equally favorable. Congress continued to draw bills of exchange for the interest on loan certificates taken out before March 1, 1778; moreover, the interest was paid on the face value of securities issued up to that date, even though, according to the Continental scale, currency depreciation had begun February 10, 1777. Most significantly, however, Congress assigned no functions to the states, either in paying the interest on loan certificates or redeeming the principal. Whereas the common debt had been freely relinquished to the states, Congress reserved the preferred debt for the federal government.

Loan certificates were held mainly in the commercial states by merchants and other men who had money to invest.[41] High in public esteem, they were to become the cornerstone of the domestic "public debt," which in the years ahead was to be the source and inspiration of movements to strengthen the powers of Congress under the Articles of Confederation.

40. *Journals,* XVII, 567-69. Webster's table of depreciation, which has been used in this study, gives a ratio of 3 to 1, on September 1, 1777; Bezanson, *Prices During the Revolution,* 65. Abraham Yates recalled that currency was actually worth one-half its face value when the loans started. Article dated Feb. 24, 1786, Abraham Yates Papers, N.Y. Pub. Lib.

41. This subject will be treated below. See East, *Business Enterprise,* 41n. Hamilton remarked in 1783 that at least four-fifths of the domestic debt was held in states from Pennsylvania northward. Henry Cabot Lodge, ed., *Works of Alexander Hamilton,* 2nd edn. (N.Y., 1904), IX, 342. So far as loan certificates are concerned, the figures for 1790 as to original issue bear him out. Ninety percent of the loans were subscribed originally in states north of Maryland. Three states—Massachusetts, Connecticut and Pennsylvania—held 66 percent of the total. Pennsylvania alone had over one-third. *American State Papers, Finance,* I, 239. But original concentration was increased by transfers which Madison observed as early as 1783 had been constant into Pennsylvania. *Journals,* XXV, 915n.

5

Business, Government, and Congressional Investigation

"It seems to me the present oppert'y of improving our Fortunes ought not to be lost, especially as the very means of doing it will contribute to the Service of our Country at the same time."

—Robert Morris to Silas Deane,
August 11, 1796

A NORMAL aftermath of war is the exposure of the inefficiency and graft that occurred in waging it. Among the wars of the United States, the Revolution was notable for a general public awareness of the sins of administration. The common opinion was that government officials were corrupt. More responsible than anything else for this feeling was the fact that procurement services were staffed with merchants who remained in private trade. The ordinary person found it hard to believe they did not take advantage of their position, and it is still hard not to think so. Certainly an arrangement which allowed a merchant to transfer his business into the administration and conduct it as his official duty would not now be tolerated.

It should be borne in mind, however, that such practices were less shocking in a time when the concept of a distinct professional functionary of the state had not emerged, except, perhaps, in the military service. Administrative tasks having to do with money or commerce were usually assigned to merchants, who were but half-servants of the government. Their status must be described in terms of the contemporary development of mercantile capitalism.

Commercial enterprise in the eighteenth century was only beginning to acquire an institutional character. The typical American merchant was still a solitary adventurer who performed the whole range of functions involved in the movement and marketing of goods, acting as banker, shipper, wholesaler, retailer, and sometimes as insurer. There had been only a partial development of that regularity in the economic world which allows business to be conducted impersonally. Merchants of the era still proceeded on the basis of personal acquaintance and trust.[1]

The key figure in mercantile affairs was the commission agent, usually seated at a port or market, who handled transactions placed in his hands by correspondents. His function was to take care of his patrons' business as though it were his own, buying or selling for them to the best advantage. He was also a bill broker, and was expected to advance short-term credit to his more trusted principals by accepting bills of exchange which they drew on him. His most valuable asset—indeed the most valuable asset of any merchant in an era when business was intensely personal—was a reputation for honesty and a scrupulous discharge of commitments. Some merchants were primarily commission agents, but all merchants of consequence acted as agents for one another.

The structure of business relationships was shot through with a conspiratorial element. A big merchant had numerous agents or correspondents in distant places whom he patronized, and they in turn gave him preference when they had business in his area. Such contacts were often expanded into temporary partnerships confined to a single venture or a series of related speculations. A big merchant, however, usually formed more permanent partnerships which had the qualities of a firm or concern. In any case, most of his business ties remained a closely guarded secret. His affairs were therefore complicated and obscure, projected through a network of hidden personal connections and fostered at every turn by mutual patronage.

1. Several studies of mercantile practice are: Baxter, *House of Hancock;* East, *Business Enterprise;* Margaret E. Martin, *Merchants and Trade of the Connecticut River Valley, 1750-1820* (Northampton, Mass., 1939), Smith College Studies in History, XXIV; Lucy Sutherland, *A London Merchant, 1695-1774* (London, 1933).

A shorter version of this chapter appeared in the *Wm. and Mary Qtly.*, 3rd ser., 16 (1959), 293-318.

The specialized skill of merchants was indispensable to Congress during the Revolution because they alone had the knowledge and the connections required to execute the government's commercial business. The chief positions in the Quartermaster and Commissary departments were given to prominent traders, such as Joseph Trumbull and Thomas Mifflin. Robert Morris dominated the Congressional committees in charge of foreign procurement. Lesser positions concerned with raising supplies were nearly all handed over to merchants or commercial firms.

These merchants felt no obligation to give up their own affairs; nor was it expected of them. They thought of themselves as commission agents and the government as their principal—in fact, their position *was* like that of a commission agent. They received commissions rather than salaries; they acted in their own names and incurred debts for which they were personally liable; and they were also expected to make occasional advances of their own money for public purposes.[2]

Retaining all the freedom appropriate to a private status, they did not hesitate to mingle the government's business with their own. They bought goods from themselves or their partners and employed their own ships in public service. They used public wagons to carry private commodities, mixed public and private goods in overseas shipments. They engaged the government as a shareholder in privateering cruises and, alternatively, allotted themselves shares in voyages fitted out with public money. Certain other practices, unthinkable today, illustrate the essentially private character of public office. Government agents sometimes sold public goods in the civilian market to raise funds to buy other goods they thought more urgently needed. In guarding against personal loss arising from debts incurred in behalf of the government, public officials were known to seize and hold goods which they had purchased as representatives of the government. Once a federal officer apparently reimbursed himself by taking over and selling a prize cargo brought in by a government vessel.[3]

2. See Edward Channing, *A History of the United States, 1700-1861* (N.Y., 1905-25), IV, 114n.

3. For examples, see Timothy Pickering to Robert Morris, Mar. 13, 1783, and Pickering to Col. Udney Hay, May 31, 1783, Pickering Letterbooks, Revol. War Mss., no. 86, Natl. Arch.; Franklin to John Ross, Apr. 22, 1780, Smyth, ed., *Writings*

Not only did these men remain in private trade, but they pursued their official duty almost without supervision. Overseas procurement was administered until 1781 by committees of Congress whose functions overlapped and whose membership constantly changed.[4] Merchants who dominated these committees either did the work themselves—and usually by themselves—or assigned it to agents whom the various committees appointed at different ports or sent out on special missions. In domestic procurement the same casual arrangements were the rule. The "civil executive departments" connected with the army—Quartermaster, Commissary, Clothier, Hospital, and Marine—were supervised, though not administered, by shifting committees or boards consisting of members of Congress and appointed officers. In charge of each department was a single executive officer, such as the quartermaster general, but in practice he neither controlled his organization nor was responsible for it. He did not appoint his subordinates, and, in the absence of a bureaucratic system, it was not possible for him to direct the inferior agents who swarmed over the country.[5] They acted on their own initiative in the manner of commission agents. With public money in hand and a task to perform, they sallied forth to accomplish it by their own devices.

Their freedom of action was not seriously hampered by the necessity of keeping accounts. During the whole course of the war, very few large accounts involving foreign procurement and the disposition of foreign loans were ever inspected, let alone settled. A show was made of regular examination in the five executive departments, but even if the examining officers had known more than they did about bookkeeping, the vagaries of war and the fluctuations of the currency would have made it impossible to maintain a rigorous system. At the end of the war, nearly all the officers who had handled public money or property departed with their accounts unsettled, and the process of bringing them to book stretched on for a full

---

of *Franklin*, VIII, 59-60; Robert Morris to William Bingham, Apr. 21, Morris Correspondence, Lib. Cong.

4. See Jennings B. Sanders, *Evolution of the Executive Departments of the Continental Congress, 1774-1789* (Chapel Hill, 1935), 3-5.

5. Congress in 1778 gave Jeremiah Wadsworth, the new Commissary General, and Quartermaster General Nathanael Greene the power to appoint their leading deputies, but as most of their staff was held over from previous administrations, the reform accomplished little.

decade. In the absence of effective checks on financial activities during the war, a wide field existed for the cultivation of private advantage by means that ranged from comparatively innocent forms of nepotism down to outright peculation and fraud. Fear of exposure was a deterrent in some degree, but honest merchants were restrained primarily by loyalty to professional standards and a regard for their own reputations.

An administration weak in authority at the top and staffed below with small capitalists chasing their fortunes allowed ample scope for empire-building. Merchants viewed it as no breach of propriety if, as public officers, they were linked in a dozen secret partnerships with persons who sold goods to the government. Except when plainly detrimental to the public cause, it was deemed legitimate for an officer to throw business to his partners or appoint them to subordinate positions. Merchants who dispensed official patronage had an opportunity to sponsor their own firms and extend their professional ties.

Any ethical problem was resolved according to the mercantile code. Merchants always denied using government money for their own purposes—that was unethical—and when they bought their own goods for public use, they felt obliged to defend the price as reasonable: they were executing the government's business as faithfully as that of a private client. Otherwise, as long as in their own judgment they did not betray the government's interests, they felt free—in fact duty-bound—to hew to the line marked out by self-interest. Robert Morris, who had an exalted sense of the dignity of his vocation, once observed to his partner, Silas Deane, that some persons would think "private gain is more our pursuit than Public Good . . . however I shall continue to discharge my duty faithfully to the Public and pursue my Private Fortune by all such honorable and fair means as the times will admit of, and I dare say you will do the same."[6]

Despite the robust courage with which Morris and his generation of merchants faced down an ethical problem which would have

6. Morris to Deane, June 29, 1777, *Deane Papers*, II, 77-84. Ruminating on this subject, Deane later wrote: "Though an honest merchant will never deviate from the path of honor and justice to promote his interest, yet it can never be expected of him to quit the line which interest marks out for him." Deane to Jonathan Williams, Sept. 24, 1781, *ibid.*, 474-75.

baffled a trained moralist, their virtue was not highly regarded outside their own ranks. Men of property and sophistication might, it is true, take the attitude that self-interest moved the world, and when merchants served the country one had to expect a certain amount of skulduggery. But most Americans were gripped by agrarian prejudices and scarcely considered the practice of trade an honorable vocation. As reports of venality poured in from every side, the stereotype of the virtuous merchant became less convincing. What good were the wisest institutions, thundered John Adams from Europe, "when almost every public department . . . is filled, as I am informed, with men of rapacious principles, who sacrifice the common weal to their private emolument."[7] The Virginia planter Richard Henry Lee countered the disciples of economic self-interest: "I know there are Mandevilles . . . who laugh at virtue, and with vain ostentatious display of words will deduce from vice, public good! But such men are much fitter to be Slaves in the corrupt, rotten despotisms of Europe, than to remain citizens of young and rising republics." The attitude of the general public was best expressed in the simple persuasion that "he who increases in wealth in such times as the present, must be an enemy to his Country, be his pretentions what they may." It was always difficult, as a member of Congress once said to a Quartermaster officer, to explain to the people why public officers should remain in private trade.[8]

The merchant whose career owed most to the fertile linkage of public office and private business was Robert Morris, who became a member of Congress in 1775 and helped raise supplies for both Congress and the state government of Pennsylvania. Soon after American ports were opened to foreign trade, he was appointed to the Secret Committee of Trade and became its chairman. Already a big merchant, the active partner in the reputable Philadelphia firm of Willing and Morris, he rose during the Revolution to become possibly the richest and certainly the most famous merchant in the country. His energy spilled over into politics, which most merchants eschewed, and his capacity for leadership thrust him into high

7. Adams to Cushing, Dec. 15, 1780, Wharton, ed., *Diplomatic Correspondence*, IV, 194.
8. Lee to Henry Laurens, June 6, 1779, Ballagh, ed., *Letters of Richard Henry Lee*, I, 61-64; William Whipple to Josiah Bartlett, May 21, 1779, Burnett, ed., *Letters*, IV, 222-23; Henry Marchaunt to Nathanael Greene, date obscure, 1778, Greene Papers, Clements Lib.

positions. A controversial figure about whom legends clustered, he pursued fortune with audacity, attaining the heights of wealth and reputation, ending at last in debtors' prison. But he had played a primary role in the world of business and in the development of the nation. The myth still persists that Robert Morris financed the Revolution out of his own pocket. If it is rather the other way around—that the Revolution financed Robert Morris—he was nevertheless one of the great men of his time.

The Secret Committee which Morris headed in 1776 was the chief agency in the purchase of foreign goods, which the committee bought overseas or from merchants who imported them.[9] As overseas purchases could not be made with Continental money, the Committee dealt in the remittance of goods, buying tobacco and other American products, and shipping them abroad. Along with the Secret Committee of Correspondence, whose primary duties lay in the diplomatic field, it shared with other Congressional agencies—the Marine Committee and the Admiralty Board—a general supervision over the Continental navy and the sale of prizes brought in by privateers and Continental warships.[10] A single agent residing in the United States or abroad sometimes represented all these committees at once, buying and selling goods for them, disposing of prizes, taking orders from each of them, as well as from their individual members. It was a most informal and flexible system which left much to personal initiative.

The Secret Committee had unusual discretionary powers. Because aid was expected from technically neutral countries, the committee's activities were kept secret even from Congress, which neither supervised its operations nor examined its accounts. The committee delegated to its own agents the authority to manage Continental business. To a very large degree, the individual members of the committee were free to carry on as they saw fit, restrained only by the need to produce results and the prospect of one day having to display their accounts.

9. *Journals*, II, 255, III, 426; William Whipple to John Langdon, May 20, 1776, Burnett, ed., *Letters*, I, 459. The best modern treatment of Robert Morris as a business figure is Clarence L. Ver Steeg, *Robert Morris, Revolutionary Financier* (Phila., 1954). The best older work is William G. Sumner, *The Financier and the Finances of the American Revolution* (N.Y., 1891).

10. Consult Charles Oscar Paullin, *The Navy of the American Revolution* (Chicago, 1906), 93-100, 104-7.

Morris gained such an ascendancy over this committee, as well as the Secret Committee of Correspondence, that he became the virtual manager of foreign procurement. Most of the other members were leagued with him in commercial enterprises, and for the sake of concealment much of the committee's business was conducted by the firm of Willing and Morris under its own name. Only the book-keeping entries separated the company's affairs from those of the government. Morris's predominance in everything relative to foreign procurement was well illustrated when news arrived that France would definitely give aid to America: the committee did not think it necessary to inform Congress, since Morris served on all the essential committees and would be able to take appropriate action. "I well know," wrote his associate, John Langdon, "that almost the whole of the business must pass thro' your hands."[11]

Not surprisingly, the committee laid out a large share of its funds in contracts with Morris and his associates. From 1775 to 1777, at a time when the value of Continental money was nearly equal to specie, it expended over $2,000,000, and payments of $483,000, nearly a fourth of all disbursements, went directly to the firm of Willing and Morris. An additional $80,000 was advanced to the firm in 1775 before the committee was active. With his partner, John Ross, Morris also shared in another contract for $90,000, and was connected with five other members of the committee in the so-called "Indian Contract," which involved $200,000. He may also have shared in other disbursements, for he had close business relationships or partnerships with several merchants who got contracts.[12]

A perquisite of his office was the use of government money to float his private enterprises. How much he converted to his own use is impossible to know, for if private ventures were successful, money could be replaced and a misapplication of funds would very likely leave no trace. It should be said that an officer in Morris's position would, in the normal course of events, sometimes owe the

11. Memorandum, Oct. 1, 1776, Wharton, ed., *Diplomatic Correspondence,* II, 150-51; John Langdon to Robert Morris, Feb. 18, 1777, Morris Correspondence, Lib. Cong.

12. State of the Accounts of the Secret and Commercial Committees . . . Office of Accounts, May 27, 1789, Arthur Lee Papers, Houghton Library, Harvard Univ. In 1777 the Secret Committee of Trade was superseded by the Commercial Committee, which disbursed $1,300,000. Morris received $80,000 directly and probably shared in $283,000 which the committee charged against the importation of West Indies and European goods.

government money and thus have the use of public funds to conduct his private trade; at other times the government might be in debt to him. It is clear, however, that Morris took an improper advantage of his position. He diverted at least $80,000 to his own purposes and did not replace it. Twenty years later, after his accounts had finally been settled, he executed two bonds for $93,000 which he still owed to the government. Eighty thousand dollars of this represented money given him under the Indian Contract of 1776 for the purpose of buying and forwarding goods to Europe in payment of supplies to be purchased there. The goods were not sent, but he did not return the money.[13] In the early stages of the war, $80,000 was a capital large enough to be the making of a mercantile fortune.

Morris's official position enabled him to build a commercial empire in the public service. As head of the Secret Committee, he was in the enviable position of negotiating with himself or his associates. His partners ranged from New Orleans and the West Indies to Europe. They were likely to supply the tobacco, rice, and indigo which the committee bought for exportation; frequently they owned the ships in which the cargoes were dispatched, and, when goods arrived at their destinations, Morris partners or correspondents usually handled them. As the French merchant, Théveneau de Francey, once explained to his patron, Beaumarchais, Morris kept the government's business in the hands of persons with whom he was *de moitie*.[14] Except in New England, his influence and his concerns were ubiquitous.

One of his key partners was William Bingham, who was sent out in 1776 as American commissioner to Martinique. It was an important assignment, for this island, along with Cape François in Santo Domingo (where Morris set up his agent, Stephen Ceronio, with a committee appointment) and the Dutch island of St. Eustatius, were

13. Outstanding Debtors (undated, but about 1791), doc. 28,793, War Records Section; Outstanding Debtors, Oct. 26, 1793, doc. 29,304, Treasury Department, Comptroller's Office; Late Government Balances Struck on the Treasury Books (undated, but 1789 to about 1791), ser. 392, Record Group 53, Fiscal Records Section; Personal Debtors Accounts (undated, but about 1795 through 1797), ser. 393, Revolutionary and Confederation Governments; all in Natl. Arch. Rufus King to Robert Morris, Apr. 15, 1791, Rufus King Papers, 1788-1792, N.-Y. Hist. Soc.

14. Théveneau de Francey to Beaumarchais, July 31, 1778, John Bigelow, *Beaumarchais the Merchant, Letters of Théveneau de Francey, 1777-1780* (N. Y., 1870), 10.

way stations for considerable American trade with Europe.[15] Before his departure for Martinique, Bingham formed a general partnership with Morris. In the next two years their trading voyages were numerous and, from all appearances, profitable, although it may be doubted whether fortune would have smiled so warmly if they had not had the advantage of official position. Bingham operated partly, at least, on money which Morris advanced him out of committee funds, and at a time when ships were expensive and crews were scarce, they freely employed public vessels to transport private cargoes.[16] Such Continental ships of war as the *Hornet,* the *Wasp,* the *Independence,* the *Sachem,* and the *Reprisal* plied back and forth, their holds containing the firm's goods, and their captains acting under orders of Robert Morris, head of the Secret Committee. There is no indication that the partners charged themselves for freight. A part of the goods in which they traded were undoubtedly sold to the Secret Committee of Trade, the Clothier General, or other government purchasers; but many of the goods consisted only of articles for the civilian market.[17]

The vigor of their private operation stands in contrast with the conduct of public business lying outside the scope of their personal interests. Morris and Bingham found the money, ships, and cargoes for their ventures but were apparently unable to do as much when private ends were not involved. The debts Bingham contracted in the course of official business at Martinique remained unpaid because the Secret Committee failed to remit goods which could

15. Ceronio to Morris, Jan. 14, 1778, Morris Correspondence, Lib. Cong. On Bingham's career at Martinique, see Bingham to Committee of Foreign Affairs, Apr. 13, June 29, 1779, Territorial Papers, Florida, I, Foreign Affairs Section, Natl. Arch.; Papers of Cont. Cong., no. 90, I, 33-39, 69-71; Lovell to Bingham, Apr. 16, 1778, Wharton, ed., *Diplomatic Correspondence,* II, 553; Ver Steeg, *Morris,* 15-16; Margaret L. Brown, "William Bingham, Agent of the Continental Congress in Martinique," *Penn. Mag. of Hist. and Biog.,* 61 (1937), 54-87.

16. In September 1776, Morris sent Bingham bills of exchange which he later divulged were the property of the Secret Committee. When Bingham cashed bills for £1,000 sterling, Morris instructed him to enter them in his public account and take them off their private account so there would be no record. Morris promised to settle for the bills with the committee. Willing, Morris and Company to Bingham, Sept. 27, Oct. 26, 1776, Apr. 25, 1777, Morris Correspondence, Lib. Cong.

17. Willing, Morris (Swanwick) and Co. to Bingham, June 3, July 24, Sept. 14, 24, 27, Oct. 20, Nov. 7, 8, Dec. 3, 6, 1776, Feb. 1, 16, Apr. 25, 1777, *ibid.* Lists of Continental vessels and their commanders may be found in *Journals,* IV, 293, VI, 861; and in Robert Morris to the Commissioners at Paris, Dec. 21, 1776, Wharton, ed., *Diplomatic Correspondence,* II, 231-38.

be sold to meet his obligations. In Europe the American commissioners repeatedly complained that they received no cargoes shipped on public account and therefore could not pay their debts. A clue to the situation may lie in a remark Morris dropped shortly after Bingham's arrival at Martinique. There was a problem of raising money on the island to put the firm in operation, and Morris notified Bingham that a certain cargo would be sent on private rather than public account, "as we want to throw Funds into your hands."[18] When a choice could be exercised, it would appear that personal concerns sometimes got priority over those of the government.

Bingham was the hub of an expanding network of Morris affiliates. His tie with Morris linked him with numerous firms in Virginia and the Carolinas which often supplied the commodities sent as remittances to the West Indies and Europe on both public and private account.[19] In Williamsburg, Benjamin Harrison, Jr., was a Morris partner and the agent of the Secret Committee, as well as paymaster of the Continental army in Virginia. His offices were convenient for speculative purposes; he was able to get the cooperation of state authorities in obtaining vessels and crews, and as paymaster he handled large sums of public money which became the basis of a brokerage business. Morris at Philadelphia and David Stewart at Baltimore, as well as other agents, bought Virginia state money locally at discounts ranging from 2 to 5 percent. The money was sent down to Harrison, who got rid of it at par in the course of his official duties.[20] At New Orleans, the agent of the Secret Committee

18. Willing, Morris and Co. to Bingham, Oct. 20, 1776, Morris Correspondence, Lib. Cong.

19. Such firms were Benjamin Harrison, Carter Braxton, Jenifer and Hooe, J. H. Norton and Samuel Beal of Virginia, Hewes and Smith of North Carolina, John Dorsius of Charleston, and John Wereat in Georgia. See the Willing and Morris correspondence cited in note 17, also Morris and Swanwick to Samuel Beal, Mar. 6, 1776, Morris Correspondence, Lib. Cong.; Thomas P. Abernethy, *Western Lands and the American Revolution* (N.Y., 1937), 172; East, *Business Enterprise*, 159-60; Ver Steeg, *Morris*, 14-22.

20. Harrison also sold drafts on Morris at Philadelphia, payable in Continental money, for which he received Virginia currency at a discount. Such a brokerage business would have been unexceptionable if conducted by wholly private persons, for state money was usually discounted at a distance. Conducted by public officers, it aroused suspicion; moreover, the Virginia authorities thought that even a 2 percent discount tended to depreciate state currency. They would have been more disturbed if they had known that the partners got as high as 5 percent. Benjamin Harrison, Jr., to Willing, Morris and Company, May 17, 24, June 2, 7, 15, 29, July 6, 1776, Morris Correspondence, Lib. Cong. See Abernethy, *Western Lands*, 159-60.

was another Morris partner, Oliver Pollock, who at the time of his appointment in June 1777 was handling Willing and Morris trade with enemy ports. Under color of Spanish registry, and in his own name, he managed one end of a commerce reaching from New Orleans and the British West Indies to New York City and London. One link in this trade was Charles Willing, a Morris correspondent in the British Island of Barbados.[21]

In Europe the leading agents of the committee were nearly all Morris partners. This select group included Silas Deane, who was sent over in 1776 as the committee's chief representative. Other partners whom the committee sent to Europe on specific missions were John Ross and Samuel Beal. Several of the foreign firms designated as committee agents at specific posts were Morris's regular European correspondents: Samuel and J. H. Delap of Bordeaux, Andrew Limozin at Le Havre, and Clifford and Teysett of Amsterdam.[22] On the fringes of this expanding network were more recent connections which Morris partners like Deane and Ross made with such European capitalists as LeRoy de Chaumont, procurer of supplies for the French army, and John Holker, who later became agent for the French navy in America—a commission he exercised in partnership with Morris. Thus Morris drove his enterprises to the limits of government dealings abroad.

The career of Silas Deane—the Secret Committee's first agent in Europe—is central to the unfolding story of American procurement and affords intimate details of the life of a government purchaser. He was eventually recalled to face a Congressional investigation into corrupt practices, but none of his accusers could prove that he had

21. Willing, Morris, and Company to Bingham, Apr. 25, June 20, 1777, Morris Correspondence, Lib. Cong. On Pollock, see James A. James, ed., *George Rogers Clark Papers, 1771-1781* (Springfield, 1912), III, Ill. State Hist. Lib., *Collections*, VIII; Oliver Pollock Case, George Rogers Clark Papers, Draper Mss., 43j1-43j133, State Hist. Soc. of Wis. (microfilm collection of the Ill. Hist. Survey, Champaign, Ill.); Letters and Papers of Oliver Pollock, Papers of Cont. Cong., no. 50, Foreign Affairs Section, Natl. Arch.; Clarence V. Alvord, ed., *Kaskaskia Records, 1778-1790* (Springfield, 1909), Ill. State Hist. Lib., *Collections*, V.

22. For some of Morris's dealings with Ross, see State of the Accounts of the Secret Committee . . . , Arthur Lee Papers, Houghton Lib., and the correspondence cited in note 43 below. On Beal, see Willing, Morris and Co. to Samuel Beal, Mar. 6, 1776, Morris Correspondence, Lib. Cong. On foreign connections, see Willing, Morris (Swanwick) and Company to Bingham, Mar. 6, June 3, Sept. 14, 27, 1776, *ibid.*

violated the prevailing standards of official conduct. In the opinion of his defenders—now as then—he was the victim of a political attack.

Deane was a Connecticut merchant of middling circumstances, a small capitalist who aspired to become a big one in those speculative times. Early in 1776 he accepted the committee's appointment to Europe, hoping to gain admission into the select company of first-rank merchants and take part in large operations. His assignment was to obtain loans in France and buy military supplies for Congress. He was also party to the "Indian Contract," which Morris and five other members of the Secret Committee made with the committee. Under this contract, Deane was to buy goods to the amount of $200,-000, on credit if possible, while the other partners were to use committee money to buy and ship American products to pay the debts he contracted in Europe. Before his departure, Deane formed a general partnership with Morris in the hope of becoming a satrap in the expanding Morris empire.[23]

Deane later confessed that although pecuniary motives had little bearing on his acceptance of the commercial agency, he could not be blind to the fact that his large expenditures in Europe would establish his credit there and obtain for him "no small degree of consideration in the mercantile world."[24] Not long after his arrival, such Morris associates as Clifford and Teysett of Amsterdam and Messrs. Delap of Bordeaux gave him a share in ventures for which they supplied the capital. Delap contributed the ship and cargo for a voyage in which Deane and Morris each had a third interest. This venture was

23. Deane had himself been an early member of the Secret Committee and had received government contracts. Under the Indian Contract of 1776, the partners in America, including Deane, got 5 percent commission on money they disbursed. Deane got another 5 percent on money he disbursed in Europe. Congress bore all risks. Deane's initial capital consisted of Willing and Morris drafts on British mercantile houses, most of which were not honored when, according to Morris, they were stopped by the British ministry. Naval Committee to Deane, Nov. 17, 1775, Secret Committee to Deane, Mar. 1, 1776, Deane to Mrs. Elizabeth Deane, March 1776, Morris to Deane, Aug. 11, Oct. 4, 1776, Messrs. Delap to Deane, Dec. 31, 1776, *Deane Papers*, I, 90-92, 116-18, 119-23, 172-77, 305-6, 434; Barnabas Deane to Deane, Oct. 18, 1775, Secret Committee to Deane, Mar. 2, 1776, *The Deane Papers: Correspondence Between Silas, His Brothers and Their Business and Political Associates, 1771-1795*, Conn. Hist. Soc., *Collections*, 23 (1930), 10-11, 19. On Deane's earlier career and the background of his mission to Europe, see Charles J. Hoadley, "Silas Deane," *Penn. Mag. of Hist. and Biog.*, 1 (1877), 96; Papers Appertaining to the Silas Deane Claim, Amer. Philos. Soc.

24. Deane to Morris, Sept. 10, 1781, *Deane Papers*, IV, 455.

a failure. However, Deane soon arranged a profitable voyage financed by LeRoy de Chaumont. Morris and Deane were each committed for 50,000 livres, and each realized a profit of 38,000 livres without having advanced any money.[25] But Deane struggled in all his ventures against the handicap of a small capital. Although Morris reminded him from Philadelphia that there never had been "so fair an oppet'y of making a large Fortune."[26] Deane had no money to engage in large operations himself and was dependent upon the patronage of his associates.

Even Morris counted on operating with European capital. He urged Deane to form a syndicate of French and Dutch houses to make shipments to America in which he and Deane would be given a share.[27] He suggested Thomas Walpole in Britain, Chaumont in France, and the firm of LeGrand, which had branches in both France and Holland. A combination of these important houses, he believed, might well absorb the entire indirect trade between Britain and America being conducted through neutral countries. Deane received the plan enthusiastically and was soon urging his friends, the Messrs. Delap, to join a syndicate which he claimed would include the principal firms in France and Holland.[28]

Whatever notions the American public might have entertained, merchants considered trade with Britain as a fact of economic life. That British goods would find their way to the United States was in their view a law of nature, and as merchants their allegiance to self-interest left them no alternative but to assist the process. The British government itself connived at the trade, which was accomplished merely by transferring ownership and registry of vessels to make it ap-

25. Silas Deane in Account Current with Robert Morris, Nov. 12, 1779, Silas Deane Papers, Conn. Hist. Soc.; Deane to Messrs. Delap, Nov. 13, 1776, to Morris, Jan. 6, 1777, Chaumont to Morris, Jan. 7, 1777, Deane to Morris, Oct. 1, 1777, to Simeon Deane, Oct. 12, 1777, to Beal, Feb. 17, 1778, to Ross, Mar. 23, 1778, statement of Morris, pub. Jan. 9, 1779, *Deane Papers,* I, 354-57, 448-49, 450-51, II, 161-63, 185-86, 367-68, 422-23, III, 259-66.

26. Morris to Deane, Aug. 11, 1776, *Deane Papers,* I, 172-77.

27. Morris to Deane, Aug. 11, Sept. 12, 1776, Deane to Morris, Sept. 30, 1776, *ibid.,* 172-77, 232-37, 286-87. Morris proposed the same scheme to Thomas Morris and John Ross.

28. Thomas P. Abernethy, "Commercial Activities of Silas Deane in France," *Amer. Hist. Rev.,* 39 (1933-34), 478-79. See Richard Henry Lee to Robert Morris, Dec. 24, 1776, Stan V. Henkel, comp., *Catalogue, No. 1183* (Phila., n.d.), 29-30; Deane to Morris, Dec. 12, 1776, Morris Correspondence, Lib. Cong.; Deane to Messrs. Delap, Dec. 14, 1776, *Deane Papers,* II, 421-23.

pear they belonged to partners who were citizens of other countries.[29]
Americans in Europe, who were often intimate with British merchants, did not scruple to enter this commerce. Franklin's grandnephew, who acted as American agent at Nantes, was sponsored by
English friends as agent for British merchants in the West Indies.
Franklin's grandson and secretary, William Temple Franklin, engaged
in ventures with British merchants, and John Ross owned a vessel
listed under British registry.[30] The indirect trade between Britain
and America was so well developed by 1778 that Franklin had to
answer complaints of the French ministry that the commerce was as
great as before the war. When John Laurens went abroad in 1781
to obtain the first large loan France gave to the United States, he
could find no better way of spending the money than to purchase
British goods in Holland. The same year John Adams wrote from
Europe that British customs receipts were steadily increasing because
of the American trade. He claimed that American merchants could
readily obtain a credit from London merchants, whose slogan was:
"Let us understand one another and let the governments squabble."[31]

The league envisaged by Morris and Deane was a natural growth
in the commercial world of the times—a system of mutual patronage
which, in this case, was to include their associates and "friends," and
finally, the friends of their friends. It is doubtful whether an organized coalition was ever achieved. However, a loosely-knit alliance

29. Deane, on his first voyage to Europe, had sailed as supercargo on a Morris
vessel. Arriving in the West Indies, he dispatched it to trade with a British
port under false registry. Deane to Morris, May 8, 1776, Morris Correspondence,
Lib. Cong. On the attitude of the British government, see John Vaughan to
William Temple Franklin, Nov. 11, 28, 1778, Franklin Papers, CI, 75, Amer.
Philos. Soc.; John Reynolds to Franklin, Apr. 14, 1778, John Vaughan to Benjamin
Franklin, Oct. 22, 1778, *ibid.*, IX, 44, 68.

30. Benjamin Vaughan to William Temple Franklin, Dec. 29, 1778, *ibid.*, CI,
87. Edward Bancroft to John Holker, Mar. 13, 1780, Holker Papers, IX,
1659, Lib. Cong.; John Ross to Deane, Jan. 3, 20, 1778, Deane Papers, Conn. Hist.
Soc.; Ross to Deane, Jan. 15, 1778, *Deane Papers*, II, XX, 331-32. Ross asked
Franklin to issue him a passport which would protect a cargo of British manu-
factures destined for America. His argument was that the trade was going on
anyhow and it would be cheaper to ship directly rather than by way of neutral
countries.

31. Franklin's Memoranda, July 6, 1778, Wharton, ed., *Diplomatic Correspondence*, II, 639-40; Franklin to Vergennes, Jan. 18, 1782, Smyth, ed., *Writings of
Franklin*, VIII, 362-64; Silas Deane to William Duer, June 14, 1781, *Deane Papers*,
IV, 424-29; John Adams to the President of Congress, June 26, 1781, Wharton,
ed., *Diplomatic Correspondence*, IV, 521.

seems to have existed until 1779, when it included the important John Holker, then intendant for the French navy in America.[32]

Deane brought his brother Simeon to Europe in 1777, hoping to gain for them both a foothold in the tobacco trade, which produced the best remittances from America. He persuaded European merchants to advance Simeon the money to ship goods to the United States. Fortunately, he was able to provide a thirty-six gun frigate, recently purchased for the American government, to escort a ship carrying one of Simeon's important cargoes.[33] With the proceeds of his ventures Simeon founded the house of Simeon Deane and Company in Petersburg, Virginia. The company soon became affiliated with other Virginia and Maryland houses, and Silas Deane, who owned a half-interest, urged his friends to patronize the house. Robert Morris promised to throw business to the Virginia firm, and some of Deane's other acquaintances consigned cargoes to Simeon or gave him shares in their ventures. In 1779 Simeon was one of a society that included Morris, Chaumont, and Holker—no mean advancement in the commercial world![34]

Meanwhile, Silas pursued his career in Europe. Although he vacated his commercial position after being made a political commissioner at the French court, his new post involved the disposal of French loans to the United States and allowed scope for commercial activity. His official position gave him many advantages. He was privy to the sailing arrangements of many ships; when government cargoes did not completely load outgoing vessels, he shipped private goods. Within reasonable limits, he could hasten or delay the voyages of Continental warships to afford convoy for vessels with private goods aboard. He and other Continental agents also had wide latitude in disposing of prizes taken by American privateers and ships of war. Since France maintained a technical neu-

32. Simeon Deane to John Holker, Mar. 22, Apr. 20, 1779, *Deane Papers*, Conn. Hist. Soc., *Collections*, 23 (1930), 143-46, 146-47. See Sumner, *Financier*, I, 226.

33. Deane to Jonathan Williams, Dec. 18, 1777, Deane Papers, Conn. Hist. Soc.; Deane to Capt. Fogg, Jan. 4, 1778, to Messrs. Delap, Feb. 3, 1778, *Deane Papers*, II, 305-6, 351-52; Worthington C. Ford, ed., *The Letters of William Lee* (Brooklyn, N.Y., 1891), 346-52.

34. Agreement signed by Silas Deane and Simeon Deane, Dec. 22, 1777, Simeon Deane to John Holker, Mar. 22, Apr. 20, 1779, *Deane Papers*, Conn. Hist. Soc., *Collections*, 23 (1930), 124, 143-46, 146-47; Robert Morris to Silas Deane, Dec. 29, 1777, *Deane Papers*, II, 293-97.

trality in the war, sales had to be conducted secretly, and prizes brought a mere fraction of their value. The American officers sometimes made private sales to themselves or their partners, and they seem to have had a rather free choice of whatever prizes were available. Their conduct was usually defensible: Deane and other agents could argue that they had caused the American government no loss or injury. He, no less than his associate John Ross, was prepared to say that he consulted the public interest "at least" as much as his own.[35] Once or twice, however, Deane came close to indiscretion.

Upon his first arrival in France, he had asked for the power to issue privateering commissions, and had been refused. Instead, the Secret Committee of Correspondence directed him to buy vessels on public account and send them out as Continental ships of war.[36] Under cover of these instructions, Deane used public money to buy several vessels which were commissioned as Continental cruisers. Their voyages, however, were organized on the basis of shares divided between the United States and private individuals.

Two expeditions under command of Captain Gustavus Cunningham achieved a certain notoriety.[37] Cunningham's second voyage, and probably the first, involved the United States as joint sponsor with the firm of Ephraim Cunningham and Company, of which the captain was a member. Another share in the expedition belonged to William Hodge, whom Deane sent with some 90,000 livres of public money to purchase and dispatch the ships.[38] It seems entirely possible that Deane originally had an interest in this venture. Ultimately the United States owned a half interest, but it cannot be

35. Ross to Deane, Jan. 26, 1778, Deane Papers, Conn. Hist. Soc.
36. Harrison, *et al.*, Committee of Secret Correspondence to Franklin, Deane, and Lee, Dec. 21, 1776, Wharton, ed., *Diplomatic Correspondence,* II, 226-31. The commissioners did not have the authority to issue privateer commissions until after France joined the war. This point came out in Congress's investigation of Deane.
37. Cunningham, or Conyngham, as his name was sometimes written, appears to have been a privateer commander for Carter Braxton and associates. Carter Braxton to Capt. Cunningham, Dec. 14, 1776, Papers of Cont. Cong., no. 44, I, 17-20. On this and other ventures, consult Abernethy, "Commercial Activities of Silas Deane in France," *Amer. Hist. Rev.,* 39 (1933-34), 477-85.
38. It is not clear whether the United States paid the whole cost of the expedition; however, it is worthy of note that in Deane's many defenses of his conduct relative to this episode, he said nothing about private contributions toward the voyage.

said how much of this represented an original interest or a later assignment of shares.[39]

The voyages were unfortunate. Prizes captured during the first cruise were confiscated by French authorities, and the second expedition was long detained in port, mired in heavy expenses from which it had to be rescued by applications of public money. At last the ship sailed, but its captures did not pay the expense of its refitting. At this point, Deane turned over the public's share in the vessel to John Ross and William Hodge without requesting payment or an estimate of the ship's value. In discussing this transaction with Deane, Ross prudently asked him to get the prior consent of Arthur Lee, who was the one commissioner at Paris unfriendly to Deane. Deane did not mention the affair to Lee. The upshot of the second Cunningham voyage was that a ship bought and equipped largely at Continental expense fell into private hands, and the implication was that shares were shuttled between private parties and the government according to the prospects of profit. The criticism aroused by these tangled maneuvers was sharpened because the cruises seriously compromised French neutrality and brought protests from the French court.[40]

Another venture of the same kind was an even greater fiasco. Robert Morris obtained a privateer commission in the United States for one of his ship captains, Thomas Bell, whom he sent to launch a cruise from the Continent. Morris and John Maxwell Nesbitt of Philadelphia each contributed £1,000 sterling toward the cost of the expedition. It was proposed that Deane and Thomas Morris form the rest of the company. (Thomas Morris was Robert's half-brother, who replaced Silas Deane as the committee's chief representative after Deane went to the French court.) The plan was agreed upon, and

39. The distribution of shares is discussed in Deane to John Ross and William Hodge, Dec. 2, 1777, *Deane Papers*, II, 263-64; William Carmichael's testimony, Sept. 30, 1778, Burnett, ed., *Letters*, III, 439-40.

40. The details may be found in Carmichael's testimony, Burnett, ed., *Letters*, III, 439-40; Ford, ed., *Letters of William Lee*, I, 226n; Papers of Cont. Cong., no. 31, 1-2, 3-4; *Deane Papers*, II, 61-63, 89-91, 213-19; Wharton, ed., *Diplomatic Correspondence*, II, 226-31, 375, 376-82, 768-73; Ross to Deane, Dec. 16, 1777, Jan. 10, 1778, Deane Papers, Conn. Hist. Soc.; Ballagh, ed., *Letters of Richard Henry Lee*, II, 11-26; Charles O. Paullin, ed., *Outletters of the Marine Committee and the Board of Admiralty* (N.Y., 1914), II, 51, 52, 70-71; William Bingham to the Committee of Foreign Affairs, Mar. 27, 1779, Territorial Papers, Florida, I, Foreign Affairs Section, Natl. Arch.

Deane brought Beaumarchais into it, as well as the redoubtable
Captain Cunningham. It appears that Deane also intended giving
a share to the United States.[41]

The expedition never got under way. The promoters were
tricked and defrauded in their efforts to buy a ship and, after spending a good deal of money, were forced to give up the attempt to find
a suitable vessel for Captain Bell. When it became clear that the
venture would produce only losses, Thomas Morris attempted to
escape by juggling entries in his public and private accounts. First,
he demanded of Deane that the money he had paid toward Bell's
expedition be shown on Deane's books as having been paid on public
account. Deane would have none of this. Undaunted, Morris tried
to recoup in another way. A Willing and Morris cargo had arrived
at his port, part of it sent on public account and part assigned to
the payment of Robert Morris's share of the Bell expedition. Thomas
Morris seized the cargo and refused to send on to Deane the funds intended for the Bell expedition. He made the excuse that 90,000 livres
he had previously sent to Franklin and Deane on public account had
in fact been a payment toward the Bell venture; he therefore had a
right to appropriate all the money from the sale of the Willing and
Morris cargo. Left without funds to pay the bills of the Bell expedition, Deane apparently fell back upon Beaumarchais, who bailed
him out.[42]

On another occasion, Deane found different means of succor.
His associate John Ross had bought a vessel in behalf of Deane,
Robert Morris, and himself, as well as a certain Captain Green, who
was to be its commander. It was a heavily armed ship, built like a
war vessel. Ross had picked it up cheap at a forced sale, without
reflecting enough on the fact that its previous owners had gone
bankrupt. As neither Ross nor Deane had funds to launch a privateering cruise at the moment, they planned to lease the vessel to

41. Robert Morris to Deane, Jan. 31, 1776, *Deane Papers*, I, 475-79; Deane to
Morris, Aug. 23, 1777, Morris Correspondence, Lib. Cong.; Carmichael's testimony,
Sept. 30, 1778, Burnett, ed., *Letters*, III, 433-35.

42. Thomas Morris to Deane, Apr. 22, May 3, 1777, Deane to Beaumarchais,
Aug. 9, 1777, Pliarne, Penet, and Co. to Deane, Sept. 27, Oct. 11, 25, 1777,
Deane to Messrs. Pliarne, Penet, and Co., Oct. 2, 1777, Deane Papers, Conn. Hist.
Soc.; Deane to Robert Morris, Aug. 23, 1777, Beaumarchais to Robert Morris,
June 3, 1782, Account of Beaumarchais, Morris Correspondence, Lib. Cong.;
Deane to Pliarne, Penet, and Co., Oct. 5, 1777, to Capt. Bell, Dec. 2, 1777, *Deane
Papers*, II, 190-91, 262-63.

the United States for the purpose of shipping home a cargo of goods which Ross had bought for the government. They expected to make their profits from a return shipment of tobacco.

The ship was a white elephant. Its armament and gear were so extensive that little space remained for freight. Leasing the vessel to the United States would not return them enough to pay expenses unless they charged freight rates which could not be justified. Falling into debt by reason of his outlays on the vessel, Ross at last suggested to Deane that they sell it to the United States. All the expense could then be made a public charge. Deane consented, whereupon Ross offered the proposition in a formal letter to the commissioners at Paris. Deane, acting for the commissioners, wrote a formal acceptance, again without consulting Arthur Lee. The vessel no doubt made a suitable cruiser for the United States, and the transaction was doubly fortunate in that it got Ross and Deane out of their predicament.[43]

Although it may appear that Deane was unlucky in many of his mercantile ventures, he was fortunate in his stock speculations—a kind of activity more culpable in the contemporary view than any of his other transactions. As a commissioner at Paris he had access to state secrets, which presumably gave him an advantage in the British market, where stock values fluctuated with the course of the war. He was accused of stock speculation at the time, and although historians have repeated the charge, it is probably correct to say that the evidence has thus far been unsatisfactory, for it has rested upon hearsay and the testimony of outsiders.[44] But there is explicit proof that he did engage in speculation as charged: one of the few significant items in his papers that has escaped publication is a statement of accounts dated February 1778 which shows profits of 20,000 livres arising from his share of transactions in British stocks con-

43. Ross to Deane, July 26, Aug. 11, 17, Dec. 16, 1777, Jan. 26, 1778, Deane Papers, Conn. Hist. Soc.; Deane to Ross, Dec. 1, 8, 18, 1777, Feb. 1, 11, 1778, Ross to Deane, Feb. 5, 1778, *Deane Papers*, II, 259-60, 268-69, 280-81, 349-50, 361-63, 356-57.

44. Deane's close friend was Edward Bancroft, a British spy whom he and Franklin unsuspectingly took into their employ. Bancroft made frequent trips across the English Channel, and it was said that these trips were linked with stock speculations in which Deane participated, the principal associate in Britain being Thomas Wharton. See Carl Van Doren, *Secret History of the American Revolution* (N.Y., 1941), 62-63; Abernethy, *Western Lands*, 185, 206-7; and Julian P. Boyd, "Silas Deane: Death by a Kindly Teacher of Treason," *Wm. and Mary Qtly.*, 3rd ser., 16 (1959), 165-87, 319-42, 515-50.

ducted through the Amsterdam firm of Hornica, Fizeau and Company.[45] This speculation was probably executed on the basis of Deane's foreknowledge of the Franco-American alliance, agreed to January 7 and signed February 6, 1778.

It is somewhat unfair to single out Deane for misconduct on this account. Among those most assiduous in accusing him of prematurely disclosing the alliance were Arthur and William Lee, who also served as American commissioners in France. Arthur Lee was a planter who did not speculate, but his brother William was a merchant who did. William attempted to capitalize on his knowledge of the approaching alliance, and his ventures were on a large scale. If he succeeded in carrying them through, they must have topped Deane's best efforts.[46]

Despite obstacles in the way of his rise to fortune, Deane felt a growing confidence in his future as a merchant. When France joined the war he began to think of casting loose from public office, which he said was taking too much of his time. His connections were so well established and his grasp of commercial affairs was so extensive that, as he informed Robert Morris, he thought he could serve his country better in a private station. Like all ambitious American merchants in Europe, he was allured by the rich potentialities of a tobacco contract with the Farmers General. However, his views of retiring from office coincided with those which his critics held for quite different reasons. In December 1777 Congress summoned him back to America to answer charges.[47]

Patronage afforded means of rapid advancement in the public service, but it also fostered conspiracies against the individual who obtained a favored post. Deane's troubles had begun early in his mission when Thomas Morris appeared as a rival in the Morris em-

45. Mr. Grand's account, Mar. 26, 1778, Deane Papers, Conn. Hist. Soc. It was rumored in Paris that Franklin had advised John Holker in December to buy goods on the strength of France's joining the war. Deane denied that Franklin had done so, but assured one of his associates that war seemed imminent. Deane to Limozin, Dec. 29, 1777, *ibid.*

46. Lee to Thomas Rogers, Dec. 8, 18, 1777, to T. Adams (Edward Browne), Jan. 12, Feb. 26, 1778, Ford, ed., *Letters of William Lee*, I, 284-86, 300, 341-43, 368-70. For samples of the accusations against Deane, see Richard Henry Lee to the Editor of the *Penn. Packet,* Aug. 17, 1779, Ballagh, ed., *Letters of Richard Henry Lee,* II, 125-30; Arthur Lee to the Committee of Correspondence, Aug. 7, Sept. 9, 1777, Wharton, ed., *Diplomatic Correspondence,* 679-80, 704-5.

47. Deane to Robert Morris, Jan. 4, 1778, to Simeon Deane, Jan. 15, 1778, *Deane Papers,* II, 307-8, 332-35; *Journals,* IX, 1008-9.

pire. Thomas, who was being pushed by his masterful relative, succeeded Deane in the commercial agency and took his station at Nantes, the chief port in France for the American trade. Henceforth, Thomas rather than Deane, was to handle Secret Committee business and the company affairs of Willing and Morris. Imparting this news to Deane, Robert Morris softened the blow by declaring his hope that Deane and Thomas would join forces in private ventures. In any case, Morris expressed confidence that Deane's new position as political commissioner would afford plenty of commercial opportunities.[48]

In spite of the alleged honor of his new appointment, Deane was not pleased with the turn of affairs. Presumably, however, there was enough business for everyone, and he was willing to cooperate with Thomas Morris and John Ross, another Morris partner roaming Europe for the Secret Committee. But Thomas Morris was an alcoholic with whom it was very hard to cooperate. He and Deane soon parted ways when Morris refused to hand over funds which the Secret Committee had sent Deane to discharge public contracts.[49] The feud was deepened by Deane's association with Franklin's grandnephew Jonathan Williams, whom Deane helped to establish as a rival commissioner to Thomas Morris. Williams had settled in Nantes, at the invitation of his great uncle; the benevolent Franklin proposed to start his relative in a mercantile career by giving him official business. Although Thomas Morris was the designated American agent at Nantes, he was incompetent, and Deane and Franklin soon entrusted all their affairs to Williams.[50]

While Thomas Morris and Williams contended for the American business at Nantes, Thomas sank deep into debauchery, allowing all his financial affairs to slip into the hands of his French partners, Pliarne, Penet and Company and J. Gruel—a firm of du-

48. Robert Morris to Deane, Sept. 12, Oct. 4, 23, 1776, *Deane Papers*, I, 232-37, 305-6, 331-32; Committee of Secret Correspondence to Deane, Oct. 1, 1776, Wharton, ed., *Diplomatic Correspondence*, II, 161.

49. Deane to Robert Morris, Dec. 4, 1776, to Secret Committee, Jan. 10, 1777, *Deane Papers*, I, 399-402, 455-56.

50. On Franklin's early connection with Williams, see Williams to Franklin, Feb. 6, 8, Mar. 1, 4, 11, Apr. 8, June 23, 1777, Franklin Papers, XXXVII, 51, 52, 63, 64, 68, 80, 96, Amer. Philos. Soc. Through September 1778, Williams disbursed some 2,600,000 livres on official business and was employed by the commissioners for a year or two longer. Papers and Documents furnished by Jonathan Williams, and The Negotiation in Europe of Money Matters, undated, Samuel Osgood Papers, N.-Y. Hist. Soc.

bious reputation. The commissioners at Paris complained of his conduct to the Secret Committee, but they clashed with the formidable Robert Morris, who believed his brother to be the victim of a plot to force him out of the agency in favor of Williams. Confronted by the accusations against Thomas, Robert Morris swore that if he could be certain of his brother's innocence, "all the Commissioners at Paris should not remove him."[51] But Thomas's past record gave reason to suspect that the charges were not groundless, and Robert Morris instructed John Ross to investigate. Ross arrived at Nantes, found the agency's affairs in chaos, and asked Thomas to resign. The younger Morris refused but was so unequal to his duties that he finally turned over all the public business to Jonathan Williams. A few days later he died, but not before he had been dismissed from the firm of Willing and Morris by his brother, who had learned the truth.[52]

The downfall of Thomas Morris might have enhanced Deane's prospects if it had left him to deal only with Ross and Williams. He had very happy business relations with them and was on intimate terms with the venerable Franklin, who let him handle all commercial business. But Deane had made an implacable foe of Arthur Lee, the third commissioner at Paris and a man of bitter and paranoic disposition. On the strength of early conversations with Beaumarchais in London, Lee believed the supplies to be furnished America through Beaumarchais were a gift from the French Court. When Deane then took over the negotiation and contracted for repayment, Lee perceived a conspiracy to defraud the United States. Never engaging in trade himself, he was shocked by the unabashed commercialism and self-promotional atmosphere in the Continental service abroad. Lee was disturbed by Deane's intimacy with Franklin, who as agent for a Pennsylvania land company had lobbied against

51. The quotation is from Robert Morris to Deane, June 29, 1777, *Deane Papers*, II, 77-84. See Deane to Williams, July 4, 1777, Morris to Franklin and Deane, July 24, 1777, Deane to Morris, Oct. 1, 1777, *Deane Papers*, II, 87, 98, 159; Thomas Morris to Deane, July 12, 1777, Deane Papers, Conn. Hist. Soc.

52. John Ross to Deane, July 19, 1777, Thomas Morris to Deane, Sept. 15, 1777, Deane to Robert Morris, Oct. 1, 1777, Robert Morris to Henry Laurens, Dec. 26, 1777, *Deane Papers*, II, 94-97, 137, 159, 243-54; Willing and Morris to Thomas Morris, Dec. 20, 1777, Thomas Morris to Jonathan Williams, Dec. 5, 1777, Jonathan Williams to Thomas Morris, Dec. 25, 1777, to the Commissioners of the United States, Dec. 6, 1777, Franklin Papers XLVII, 97, VII, 131, XXXVII, 123, 124, Amer. Philos. Soc.

Virginia's interests before the war.   Before long, he regarded them
both as conspiring with the Morris interests to usurp the leading
positions in the Continental administration and bleed the government for their own advantage.[53]

In June 1777 he was joined by his brother William Lee, who
had been appointed to share the commercial agency at Nantes with
Thomas Morris.   William, sometimes called "Alderman" Lee because he had not resigned his position as an alderman of London,
had given up a mercantile career in Britain to accept the appointment—a sacrifice for which he vainly claimed credit.   When he arrived in Paris, he was frostily received by Deane and Franklin.   It
seemed to Lee that they obstructed his taking over his new position, and he promptly adopted all his brother's suspicions.   He was
determined to expose corruption in the American agency at Nantes,
but he found after reaching the city that he could not begin his
duties.   Jonathan Williams was handling most of the public business at the port.   Thomas Morris, still lingering on, jealously kept
all the papers relating to his commercial agency in a strong box.
The most William could accomplish was to seize Morris's papers
after his death and rush them off to Paris.   Arthur and William
Lee had great expectations of these papers, which included private
documents of the firm of Willing and Morris.   They hoped to find
evidence to incriminate all their enemies, not only Deane and Franklin, but Robert Morris himself.[54]   Deane and Franklin defended their
actions as vigorously as the Lees attacked them, and the rupture
among the American commissioners was soon complete.   Everyone
connected with the government service in Europe was forced to take
sides.   John Adams, when he arrived, said he had never seen anything to match the vituperation with which the quarrel was waged.[55]

Nourished by factionalism, the squabble in Europe assumed the
dimensions of a major political trial which divided Congress into

53. The ill-humored quarrel is spread out at length in the correspondence
of Arthur and William Lee, Richard Henry Lee, Henry Laurens, Deane, and
Franklin.   See the long discussion in Wharton, ed., *Diplomatic Correspondence*,
I.

54. William Lee was nominated by the Secret Committee in January 1777,
but did not try to assume his duties until July; this was followed by a further
delay.   See Deane to Jonathan Williams, Mar. 15, 1778, *Deane Papers*, II, 408.
His commercial appointment lapsed when Congress appointed him political commissioner at Vienna and Berlin, May 9, 1778.

55. See Adams to Richard Henry Lee, Aug. 5, 1778, to Elbridge Gerry, Dec.
5, 1778, Wharton, ed., *Diplomatic Correspondence*, II, 677-79, 848-50.

hostile camps and precipitated a struggle for control. Charges and countercharges crossed the Atlantic, reinforcing lines of division already existing. The Lees were protagonists of the "Adams-Lee junto," which had long been opposed to Robert Morris, John Dickinson, and the Livingstons of the middle states. Lines were not closely drawn on all issues, but rivalry existed, ready to spring forth. To the proud and influential Lee family, the ascendancy of Robert Morris and Benjamin Franklin marked a drift of power into unfriendly hands.[56]

Meanwhile, Congress was wracked by a series of domestic scandals which, coinciding with the Deane-Lee imbroglio, nearly demoralized the federal government. Official business at home was conducted in much the same way as abroad. Although Quartermaster General Timothy Pickering may have exaggerated when he surmised that the federal debt was nearly doubled as a result of malfeasance in public administration, he expressed the general opinion. There were grounds for such suspicion when speculation was so widespread that even combat officers engaged in it. In justice to them, it should be said that they had good reason to speculate, for as Continental money sank in value their salaries became worthless. They compensated themselves somewhat by a lavish consumption of military stores; nevertheless, an officer who merely attended to his duties usually found himself in debt for his own maintenance.[57]

Benedict Arnold is an example, though an extreme one, of a speculating combat officer. Before his treason he was court-martialed on charges of misbehavior as commander of the American forces reoccupying Philadelphia after the British evacuation in 1778. There were valuable imported goods in the city, and Washington ordered him to suspend private trade until Continental agents had an opportunity to buy them. Although Arnold had an agreement with his aide Major Franks to purchase imported goods, there is no proof that Franks made any purchases while the suspension was in effect. However, Arnold had another arrangement with James Mease, the

56. Abernethy, *Western Lands,* 169-72, 205.

57. Pickering to Governor Trumbull, Dec. 25, 1780, Pickering Letterbooks, Revol. War Mss., no. 123, Natl. Arch. No system could work, said Pickering, if officers were not adequately paid. "They will find means to help themselves; and thus a thousand irregularities & abuses are introduced." *Ibid.* For a further comment, see Friedrich Kapp, *Life of John Kalb, Major-General in the Revolutionary Army* (N.Y., 1884), 137-43.

Clothier General, who was an official purchaser. The two men agreed to share in all goods Mease bought in excess of the army's needs, and he apparently took care to buy in excess, for he was later condemned by Congress for forcing large quantities of goods from the people of Philadelphia and converting them to private use.[58]

Arnold engaged in other exceptionable ventures. He had partners in Philadelphia, including two New York traders who had come down to buy goods before the British evacuation. Arnold gave them a pass to move a cargo out of the city and thereby avoid forced sale to Continental agents; later, he sent two brigades of Continental wagons to bring the goods back. In return for a 50 percent interest, he intervened in a court suit involving ownership of a captured British vessel. In 1779 he carried on speculations with partners in British-held New York and in the south.[59] The ease with which unethical behavior could escape detection appears from the fact that proof of Arnold's flagrant misconduct was beyond reach of the military court which tried him, and he escaped with a reprimand.

Other high-ranking officers, particularly those in the civil executive departments—Quartermaster, Commissary, Clothier, Hospital, and Marine—engaged in trade without overstepping legal bounds. An instance is that of General Nathanael Greene, scion of a Rhode Island mercantile family, who rose to the rank of major-general in the army before accepting the post of Quartermaster General in March 1778. He considered this position a step down in his career and thought it only proper that he should refurbish his commercial affairs, which his duties as a combat officer had forced him to neglect.

When Greene entered the Quartermaster service, he moved the family interests in with him and soon created a complex of interlocking governmental and private interests. As a condition of accepting the appointment, he insisted that Congress name as his chief assistants two business partners, Charles Pettit and John Cox, with whom he operated an iron foundry and conducted other enterprises. Already he had formed a general partnership with Pettit, the

58. The Arnold case is reviewed in Van Doren, *Secret History,* 172-75, 251-56. See *Proceedings of a General Court Martial for the Trial of Major General Arnold* (N.Y., 1865). There were complaints about Mease early in 1778, which he airily dismissed as the chronic grumbling to be expected against public officers. James Mease to Dana, Jan. 30, 1778, Papers of Cont. Cong., no. 31, I, 44-46.

59. Van Doren, *Secret History,* 175-76. The partners were Robert Sherwell of Philadelphia and James Seagroves and William Constable of New York.

life of which was to be coextensive with his term of office. He had
minor connections with Ephraim Bowen of Rhode Island, an officer
in the department, and engaged in privateering ventures with Samuel
A. Otis of Boston, who had dealings with both the Quartermaster
and Clothier departments.[60] He was a partner in the firm of Barnabas Deane and Company, which also included Commissary General
Jeremiah Wadsworth. He had an interest in Jacob Greene and
Company, and he was or became the business partner of another
relative, Griffin Greene.[61]

It was Griffin who proposed a highly dubious piece of business.
He asked Nathanael to lend him public wagons to haul goods
through Connecticut, New York, and New Jersey. The purpose
was to evade state restrictions on the movement of goods and to
escape state taxation; the stamp of the United States exempted goods
from such regulations. Griffin justified his proposal on the grounds
that Thomas Mifflin, the former Quartermaster General, had not
scrupled to turn a profit this way. If Nathanael had no objection
to the plan, Griffin was prepared to suggest other projects of the
same ethical caliber.[62]

It cannot be assumed that Nathanael agreed to this unethical
proposal. Yet sometime afterward, rumors circulated in New England that brigades of Continental wagons loaded with flour bought
at public expense had arrived in Boston, where the goods were sold
and the wagons dispatched southward with private goods. Greene's
name was linked with the incident. Rumors of this kind damaged
his reputation and were sufficiently widespread to claim the attention of Congress, where an opinion grew, as Greene observed, that
he was "making a fortune too rapidly."[63] It was in part owing to

60. Greene to the Treasury Board, Apr. 6, 1779, Pettit to Greene, May 5,
1779, Jan. 17, June 11, July 19, Aug. 12, 1780, Feb. 8, 1783, Bowen to Greene,
Feb. 9, 1779, Greene to Bowen, Jan. 22, 1779, Jacob Greene and Co. to Greene,
Feb. 14, 1779, Otis to Greene, Aug. 30, Sept. 7, 1779, May 14, 1780, Greene to
Otis, Sept. 17, 1779, Greene Papers, Clements Lib.
    61. Estimate of the State of Barnabas Deane and Co.'s Affairs, Sept. 1, 1780,
Estimate of the Property of Barnabas Deane and Co. exhibited June 1783,
Barnabas Deane to Greene, Jan. 5, 1784, Greene in Account with Jeremiah
Wadsworth, 1783, signed Sept. 5, 1785; Greene to Ephraim Bowen, Jan. 22, 1779;
Accompt of the State of Stock gained since the Commencement of the Company
of Jacob Greene and Co., July 1779; all in *ibid.*
    62. Griffin expected to pay the hire of the wagons. Griffin Greene to Na-
thanael Greene, May 24, 1778, *ibid.*
    63. Ephraim Bowen to Greene, June 13, 1779; Henry Marchaunt to Greene,

censure on this score that he resigned in 1780 to take command of the southern army.

Greene's activities were at least as innocent as those of the other high-ranking officers in the civil executive departments. His predecessor, Thomas Mifflin, had doled out government business to his brother and to his mercantile associates in Philadelphia.[64] Jeremiah Wadsworth, the Commissary General, was one of the greatest merchants in the country. The Clothier General, James Mease, was a flagrant speculator. Dr. William Shippen, head of the Hospital department, was a dealer in hospital supplies. Except for Timothy Pickering, who was not in trade, the heads of departments and virtually every minor officer in the procurement services were merchants who, it was said, scrambled into government employment to make a fortune.[65]

The life of a procurement officer was admittedly hard, complicated, and unpleasant, especially in the upper echelons. Among themselves, the officers complained of the unrequited service they gave their country. With two years as Quartermaster General behind him, Timothy Pickering wrote: "I have found the office, as I expected, full of anxiety, of toil, of difficulty and vexation; and in all respects more arduous beyond comparison, than any other office with which I have ever been acquainted."[66] His sacrifice went largely unrecognized by the general public, for it was a fixed notion that procurement officers never resigned because they were making too much money.

This feeling was understandable. The people endured much from public officials and from the authority of government during the Revolution. When their goods were confiscated or put up for sale at regulated prices, they suffered the added injury of suspicion that the enforcing officer was converting the goods to his own profit. Public officers were privileged to move through state economic controls which

---

date obscure, 1778; Griffin Greene to Nathanael Greene, Oct. 8, 1780; Greene to the Treasury Board, Apr. 6, 1779; all in *ibid.*

64. Kenneth R. Rossman, *Thomas Mifflin and the Politics of the American Revolution* (Chapel Hill, 1952), 49-51. Judging from this study, Mifflin left few records displaying his commercial activities.

65. See William Shippen's comment on purchasing officers in a letter to Richard Henry Lee, June 22, 1779, Burnett, ed., *Letters*, IV, 282.

66. Pickering to the President of Congress, Dec. 4, 1782, Pickering Letterbooks, Revol. War Mss., no. 85, Natl. Arch.

were vigorously applied to other persons. When merchants acting as agents for the United States or the French forces were allowed to buy wheat in the countryside and export it through state embargoes, it was always suspected—often with reason—that more than the stipulated quantity had been bought and that a part of the goods were privately owned. The state governments repeatedly complained to Congress about the activities of federal officers.

Multiplying reports of fraud and waste in the administration gave Congress the utmost concern. It could hardly be disputed that needless expenditure vastly increased the expense of war and contributed to the decline of Continental currency. After 1778 Congress talked constantly of such reforms as putting officers on salary rather than commission and giving department heads more authority over their subordinates. But not much could be done. Congress's own lack of money, the rapid fall of the currency, the uncontrolled resort to the issue of certificates, the inadequacy of accounting procedures, the loose organization of all branches of the administration, the engagement of public officers of every rank in private business, and the disorder of war itself—all contributed to the defeat of reform.

As Congress vainly explored ways of solving its problems, it was rocked by a series of scandals touching nearly every department head. In June 1778 members were appalled at the disclosure of expenditures in the Quartermaster department during the preceding year, when the army had been badly supplied. General Washington was directed to investigate the conduct of former Quartermaster General Mifflin and his subordinates. Reporting on this matter nearly a year later, a committee of Congress introduced further information: at a time when the army had been in extreme want, public wagons were hauling private goods to New York and New England. The main culprit was said to be a Deputy Quartermaster General who was still in office. Mifflin was not directly incriminated, but on the strength of this and other evidence, he was court-martialed, though not convicted.[67]

So disturbed was Congress that its wrath was sometimes too quick to fall. In August 1778, a Commissary officer, Cornelius Swears, confessed to misdeeds and implicated Colonel Benjamin Flower, who was Commissary General of Military Stores. Swears said Flower had

67. *Journals*, XI, 591-92, XII, 1245-46, XIII, 106-7.

not inspected his accounts properly. Congress at once ordered the Board of War to arrest Fowler and hold him in strict confinement, but the two active members of the Board, Timothy Pickering and Richard Peters, thought him an honorable man and, because he was ill, protested against his being held in close confinement. Congress roundly denounced them for insubordination and made them enforce his detention. Ironically, Flower was placed under arrest by General Arnold, who was soon to be the object of a more justifiable investigation. The charges against Flower proved groundless, and he was released.[68]

The Hospital department came under heavy fire in 1779 and 1780, though it had been a target for criticism almost since its inception. The department had long been stewing in rivalries and conspiracies. As a result of accusations brought mainly by Dr. John Morgan, a discharged officer of the department, and by Dr. Benjamin Rush, the Director General was court-martialed in June 1780 and accused—among other things—of appropriating hospital stores and selling them for his own profit while soldiers were dying for want of them. The evidence was not sufficient to maintain the extreme charge against Dr. William Shippen, but it was proved that he had speculated in commodities normally used in hospitals, such as wine and sugar, at a time when they were badly needed by the Hospital department. Shippen admitted as much, but merely said that his speculations had not been inconsistent with the duties of his office. The military court exonerated him, but his reputation was stained.[69]

Congressional censure also fell upon the respective chiefs of the Quartermaster and Commissary departments, Nathanael Greene and Jeremiah Wadsworth. The expenditures in their departments were ruinous and seemed not to produce commensurate results. In two campaigns before his resignation at the close of 1779, Wadsworth had disbursed $79,000,000; Greene had spent about the same amount over a similar period. These figures took no account of an enormous issue of certificates.[70]

68. *Ibid*, XI, 741-43, 761-63, 769, 831-34;Timothy Pickering to the President of Congress, Aug. 4, 8, 1778, Pickering Papers, V, 91, 93, Mass. Hist. Soc.

69. The Shippen affair is recounted at length in James E. Gibson, *Dr. Bodo Otto and the Medical Background of the American Revolution* (Springfield, Ill., 1937), especially pp. 228, 246-98.

70. *Journals*, XVI, 398-99, XVII, 716; Account, undated, extending to May 1780, Greene Papers, Clements Lib.

Congress continued to ask for an account of expenditures and an itemization of certificates which had been issued, but neither Wadsworth nor Greene could get the information from their deputies. Both felt Congress's requests were unreasonable, claiming that the paper work was impractical under war conditions. Greene flatly declared that his department could not be run like the "plain business of a common storekeeper."[71] Neither he nor Wadsworth would accept responsibility for the crimes of their subordinates, many of whom they had not appointed. They insisted that they had no means of controlling them. There was much truth to their argument, and Congress would no doubt have taken a more lenient view if money had not been flowing through their departments at a rate which in late 1779 and early 1780 approached $200,000,000 a year.[72]

Confessing at last that the job was too much for it, Congress tried to saddle the states with the task of regulating its departments. In July 1779, the state governors were authorized to put Continental officers under surveillance and, on proof or even the suspicion of misbehavior, to replace them with state appointees. Shortly afterwards Congress adopted the system of specific supplies, under which the states were asked to deliver actual goods instead of paying requisitions in money. The intention was to eliminate federal purchases and the abuses connected with them. Congress then set about reorganizing the Quartermaster and Commissary departments, reducing personnel and tightening procedures.[73]

A variety of other expedients were mulled over, and all of them reflected Congress's suspicion of its own administrative staff. It was suggested that Quartermaster and Commissary officers be specifically forbidden to have a personal interest in vehicles or vessels hired to

71. Greene to the President of Congress, June 19, 1780, George Washington Greene, *The Life of Nathanael Greene* (Boston, 1890), II, 288-92. See also Greene to a committee of Congress, July 14, 1779, *ibid.*, 304-8, and the Greene Papers in the Clements Library under dates of May and July 1780.

72. Greene to the President of Congress, Mar. 25, Dec. 12, 1779, June 19, 1780, Greene, *Greene*, II, 158-59, 259-63, 288-92; Greene to the President of Congress, Apr. 27, 1779, Greene Papers, Clements Lib.; *Journals*, XIV, 944-45, XVII, 656-58.

73. *Journals*, XIV, 812-13, and see X, 139-40; Margaret Burnham MacMillan, *The War Governors in the American Revolution* (N.Y., 1953), 117-18, 199-200. The Commissary department was reorganized piecemeal. For the Quartermaster department, see *Journals*, XVII, 615-35. Congress was unable to discontinue Continental purchasing until Financier Robert Morris began supplying the army by contract in 1781 and 1782.

transport supplies. Every barrel of flour, beef, or pork should be marked with the full name of the deputy who purchased it. All deputies should be required to make detailed monthly reports to the state governors. Officers appointed to act as federal purchasers by the state governors should be obliged to take an oath to reveal frauds or abuses which they knew or suspected to exist in the Continental departments. In January 1780, Congress sent a committee of its members to the main army camp with the authority to conduct investigations on the spot, discharge unneeded personnel, stop excessive rations, abolish posts, and revamp procedures.[74]

Such open declarations of suspicion aroused the bitter resentment of the higher officers in the departments, who felt they were being pilloried. There was talk of mass resignation, and a few men left the service. Wadsworth took the first opportunity to resign and thus escaped serious trouble, and Greene frequently expressed his wish to do so, saying that fifty times his present pay would not induce him to serve another campaign.[75] But he stayed on and suffered the ignominy of legislative censure.

Greene's difficulties arose mainly because he was unwilling to give Congress a statement of expenditures. Although he was known to be in private trade, there was less question of his integrity than of his refusal to submit accounts. It did not improve his relations with Congress that he plainly resented criticism and took the haughty tone of a high military officer who had put aside his true career to accept an unwanted post. His pretentions were offensive to Congress, whose republican principles were quickly touched by any signs of military arrogance.[76]

It is illustrative of the general atmosphere prevailing in the federal administration that Greene interpreted criticism as the work of a conspiracy against him led by Thomas Mifflin, who was himself not

74. *Journals*, XIV, 812-15, XVI, 75-76. The staff of the Board of Treasury was enlarged in January 1780 to bring about a quicker settlement of the accounts of discharged officers. Congress discussed the feasibility of not allowing officers to resign until they presented their accounts. *Ibid.*, XVI, 95-96.

75. See Greene to Nehemiah Hubbard, July 21, 1779, Greene to John Collins, Aug. 18, 1779, to Charles Pettit, Aug. 18, 1779, Charles Pettit to Greene, Feb. 3, 1780, John Cox to Greene, Feb. 4, 1780, Greene Papers, Clements Lib.; Nehemiah Hubbard to Governor Trumble, [Trumbull], Aug. 2, 18, 1779; Peter Colt to Royal Flint, Nov. 28, 1779, Wadsworth Papers, box 129, Conn. Hist. Soc.; *Journals*, XV, 1200.

76. *Journals*, XIV, 695, XVII, 501-2; Greene to Joseph Reed, Apr. 25, 1780, Reed, *Reed*, II, 281-82.

absolved of charges of misbehavior. When Greene received the first
draft of a new organizational plan for his department and saw that
no positions had been created for his two business partners, Cox and
Pettit, he resigned in a huff in the midst of the campaign, announcing
that he would issue no more orders and giving Congress ten days to
name his successor.[77] His resignation was accepted at once—apparently much to his chagrin. Congress only debated whether to
dismiss him from the army. But Greene had his defenders, among
them General Washington, who warned that an impairment of
Greene's rank would demoralize the officer corps.[78] No action was
taken.

It was in this disturbed era of scandal, which shattered the morale
of Congress and spoiled the faith of many patriots in their own cause,
that the Deane-Lee controversy rose to its climax. Silas Deane, who
arrived back from Europe in July 1778, immediately requested a
hearing, but feeling ran so high that Congress could not decide to
proceed with his examination. He was kept waiting for months while
his accusers held the floor. Eventually he published his side of
the case in a Philadelphia newspaper, and the whole controversy
spilled into print, all the protagonists rehearsing their charges and
countercharges in imaginative detail. Thomas Paine entered the
lists against Deane and Morris with such abandon that he had to
resign as secretary of the Committee of Foreign Affairs when the
French minister complained that he had disclosed secret information. The Lees and the Laurenses pressed the attack, however, and
they were countered by Robert Morris, Gouverneur Morris, and
Deane.[79]

The attack on Deane had always been indirectly aimed at Robert
Morris, and at one point Morris was forced to reveal his business
dealings with Deane. While technically accurate, his account was

77. Reed to Greene, Feb. 14, 1780, Greene to Reed, Aug. 29, 1780, Reed,
Reed, II, 265-67, 241-43; Greene to the President of Congress, July 26, 1780,
Greene, *Greene*, II, 314-16; *Journals*, XVI, 293-311, 364, 398-99, XVII, 522, 579-
80.

78. Washington to Joseph Jones, Aug. 13, 1780, Greene Papers, Clements Lib.;
Greene, *Greene*, II, 320-24; *Journals*, XVIII, 686, 690-91, 697, 715-16, 783.

79. For widely contrasting versions of the Deane-Lee controversy, see the ac-
counts in Burnett, ed., *Letters*, III, xxxii-xxxv, and IV, xix-xxi; Wharton, ed.,
Diplomatic Correspondence, I; Ver Steeg, *Morris*, 23-25; David Duncan Wallace,
The Life of Henry Laurens . . . (N.Y., 1915), II, 305-28; Abernethy, *Western
Lands*, 182-87, 212-15.

spare, to say the least, and conveyed little of the complexities of their relationship. It implicated Morris in nothing that was not common practice, and yet the mere proof of a business connection wrung from him under pressure was sufficient to whip up popular feeling. The legislatures of both Virginia and Maryland passed laws forbidding their delegates in Congress to engage in any sort of private trade.[80]

Morris was frequently investigated. On one occasion he was charged with shifting ownership of a cargo from private to public account, after the ship which carried it had been captured by the enemy, in order to throw the loss on Congress.[81] Although eagerly pressed, the charge was proved false. He was investigated by Philadelphia committees and accused of violating the state anti-monopoly laws. He cleared himself of one charge by showing that his actions had been within the laws against forestalling. In disproof of another accusation, he established that he had been acting as agent for John Holker, procurer of supplies for the French navy.[82] His enemies frequently demanded an examination of the accounts of the Secret Committee of Trade. As Morris was the only person who could possibly arrange them, he was asked to put them in order. Retiring from Congress, he took the papers home and kept them for over six months. When the delay at length gave rise to criticism, he simply returned them saying that he could do nothing with them. The statement was undoubtedly true enough, for the accounts were wholly incomplete and, in any case, useless without a painstaking correlation with the many other accounts to which they were related. The process of settling them required many years of labor after the

80. "To the Public," [by Morris], Jan. 9, 1779, Common Sense's reply to R. Morris, Jan. 12, 1779, *Deane Papers*, III, 259-66, 266-72; *Maryland Session Laws*, May sess., 1779, ch. 42, July sess., 1779, ch. 2; Hening, ed., *Statutes of Virginia*, X, 113.

81. See Ver Steeg, *Morris*, 22-23.

82. Robert Morris to Committee of Complaints, June 28, 1778, *Henkel's Catalogue, No. 1183*, 34-35; Morris to William Herpham, Chairman of the Committee of Complaints, June 17, 1779, Morris to ———, July 2, 1779, Robert Morris Papers, N.Y. Pub. Lib.; Morris to Timothy Matlack *et al.*, June 26, 1779, Morris Correspondence, Lib. Cong.; Philadelphia Committee to Robert Morris, pub. July 24, 1779, Deane to Simeon Deane, July 27, 1779, Answer of Robert Morris, pub. Aug. 6, 1779, *Deane Papers*, IV, 19-22, 22-24, 34-40; Daniel of St. Thomas Jenifer to the Governor of Maryland, May 24, 1779, Burnett, ed., *Letters*, IV, 232-33; Samuel MacLane to Caesar Rodney, May 27, 1779, George H. Ryden, ed., *Letters To and From Caesar Rodney* (Phila., 1933), 303; Brunhouse, *Counter Revolution in Pennsylvania, 1776-1790*, 71.

war. Yet Morris's inability to arrange them gave apparent substance to the accusations against him.[83]

The Deane affair continued to hang over Congress until August 1779. Congress listened to the testimony of William and Arthur Lee, William Carmichael, Ralph Izard, and others, permitting Deane only to submit written answers to the charges. Enough was heard to prove one or two irregularities and, when spun out by the Lees, to suggest a thousand others. Not much could be actually proved, since Deane had left his accounts in Europe. Underlining its suspicions, Congress refused to grant his claim for commissions and merely gave him leave to depart, presumably to return to France and bring forward his accounts.

The Deane affair had unsavory aspects, and its results were destructive. It laid bare to public view the selfish bickering that disgraced the American service abroad; at one point a committee of Congress listed the offenses of which each of the foreign commissioners had been accused and suggested that all of them be recalled.[84] Neither Arthur Lee nor anyone else gained credit for his part in it. The only beneficial result to the nation was the recall of Arthur Lee and Silas Deane and the placing of American affairs overseas in the hands of John Adams and John Jay. At home, the controversy excited the deepest animosities without resulting in any important administrative reforms or constructive alterations in the balance of power in Congress. The rancor it left was for years the underlying basis of Congressional division on questions which might better have been considered on their own merits.

The revelation of widespread corruption in the federal service at home also left a residue. It contributed heavily to the perilous demoralization of the country in 1780, when the American cause seemed on the verge of disaster. Its echoes were still heard many years later when the foes of Hamilton's funding program damned the speculators who had profited from the country's distress.

83. Wallace, *Life of Henry Laurens*, 329-30; "To the Public," Jan. 9, 1779, *Deane Papers*, III, 259-66; John Penn to Morris, Feb. 4, 1778, Henry Laurens to Morris, Jan. 11, 1779, Morris to Laurens, Jan. 11, 1779, Laurens to Morris, July 8, 1779, Burnett ed., *Letters*, III, 70-71, IV, 25-28, 28-33, 303-6; *Journals*, XIII, 173.

84. *Journals*, XIII, 362-68. Richard Henry Lee perceived in this suggestion a maneuver of the opposition. To Francis Lightfoot Lee, Apr. 26, 1779, Ballagh, ed., *Letters of Richard Henry Lee*, II, 49-51.

The fault, of course, lay in an administrative system which failed to distinguish between public and private functions. The two were merged in the normal duties of officers who served their country by pursuing their commercial vocations. Administrative positions existed, in a sense, to be exploited, and it was inevitable that they should be abused. The people were never content with this state of affairs, nor would they accept the reasoning by which merchants justified it, and after the Revolution, procedures were changed. The army was supplied by contract rather than direct purchases by government officers. In 1789 the first conflict of interest law was passed in the process of organizing the Treasury department. By this and subsequent legislation the intercourse between business and government has not been entirely terminated, as we have cause to know, but at least they have been legally divorced.

PART II

NATIONALIST ASCENDANCY
1781-1783

"The Confederation . . . gives the power of the purse too entirely to the State Legislatures. It should provide perpetual funds, in the disposal of Congress, by a land tax, poll tax, or the like. All imposts upon commerce ought to be laid by Congress, and appropriated to their use. For, without certain revenues, a Government can have no power. That power which holds the purse-strings absolutely, must rule."

—Alexander Hamilton to
James Duane,
September 3, 1780.

6

Counterrevolution in Finance

*"Individuals are now alarmed for the Publick Safety who
have for years past been Employed in amassing wealth."*

—John Sullivan to
George Washington,
January 29, 1781.

THE dismal state of public affairs in 1780 delivered the political initiative to conservative spokesmen, who had been in eclipse since the early phases of the Revolution. When the approaching break with Britain portended radical alterations in the *status quo*, a faction supporting a strong government and the preservation of the existing order had emerged.[1] The drastic measures which popular state governments employed to prosecute the war confirmed the views of those who had such leanings, but there was no opportunity to direct the course of public affairs until the apparent failure of the war effort in 1780. The emergency brought men of conservative temper to the fore in several important states; soon they were to dominate Congress. The aims and motives of this group, which we shall call the *Nationalists,* were similar even in detail to those of the Federalists who later drafted the Constitution and enacted Hamilton's funding program. Such Federalists as Washington, Hamilton, and Madison played a role in the earlier movement, whose presiding genius was the great merchant, Robert Morris.

1. See Edmund S. and Helen M. Morgan, *The Stamp Act Crisis* (Chapel Hill), 15-19. The full exposition of the subject is in Merrill Jensen, *The Articles of Confederation* (Madison, 1940).

The war for independence reached its nadir in 1780, when it was doubtful whether the nation would continue the struggle. British armies swept through the south virtually unopposed, while General Gates fled at Camden, and Benedict Arnold was exposed as a traitor. Congress and the state governments were nearly destitute. The Continental army eked out an existence by impressments and was sometimes in danger of having to disband for lack of supplies. Many persons thought of "abandoning the cause, not from disaffection, but from despair," while others pondered ways of reaching an "accommodation" with the enemy.[2]

Civilian morale was at low ebb. The nation had been too long at war, and much of the enthusiasm of 1776 had worn off, giving way to indifference, preoccupation with gaining wealth, and, in some quarters, a contempt of the American government. The old patriot Christopher Marshall, offended by most of what he saw, stayed in his house, and mourned the "abomination of the times." Good Whigs, viewing the passion for making money, wondered whether they did not merit a share in the profits of this "diabolical war."[3] Military officers resented the fortunes acquired by men of their own social standing in civilian life. The common people raged against profiteers and government officers. Farmers counted their certificates and felt a sense of injustice. In some states, notably Pennsylvania, political rivalries crippled the administration. The Deane-Lee affair continued to boil up in Congress with each new disclosure of corruption or waste in the federal service. The time was ripe for a change in leadership.

It was understandable that the impetus came from the propertied class. Especially in the middle states, it was the common people and the backcountry farmers, rather than the aristocracy, who supported the leadership of Congress. New England and Virginia had always dominated major Congressional policies, and although the Adamses and the Lees could scarcely be called radical in their social ideas, the measures they advocated were radical in their effects. By promoting the overthrow of colonial governments, pushing through in-

2. "Dissertation on Government," Foner, ed., *Writings of Paine*, II, 397; John Adams to Cushing, Dec. 15, 1780, Wharton, ed., *Diplomatic Correspondence*, IV, 193-95.

3. Duane, ed., *Christopher Marshall's Diary*, July 24, 25, 1780, Apr. 12, 1781; Richard Peters to Robert Morris, Aug. 28, 1780, *Henkel's Catalogue, No. 1183*, 96-97.

dependence against the will of the aristocratic leaders of the middle colonies, and drafting a federal constitution which reserved sovereignty to the states, Congress gave scope and encouragement to the social changes that came with the Revolution.[4]

Congress's financial measures also suited the tastes of the common people, whose views ran to such measures as paper money, legal tender, price-fixing laws, embargoes, and anti-monopoly legislation. Paper money was unavoidable, and it was the usual practice of governments to legislate in economic matters; nevertheless, propertied men believed that the weight of restriction fell mainly upon them. They burned with resentment at their subordination to radical committees. In an age when the tenets of laissez-faire were increasingly accepted as natural law, they considered themselves the victims of class legislation.

Dissatisfaction with the existing political order was most prevalent in the propertied class, but by 1780 the idea of strengthening the central government was supported by a considerable and diversified body of opinion. Four years before, this would have been unthinkable. With Britain as their example, most patriots of 1776 had conceived of central government as at best an oppressive force and by its nature a check upon self-rule. Although Congress emerged as an agency for prosecuting the war, the revolutionists had no intention of laying the foundations of a strong central government. Freedom from Britain signified to most Americans that each state would henceforth be free to conduct its affairs without hindrance.

The Articles of Confederation expressed this Revolutionary emphasis upon defense of local rights against central authority. The Articles were designed to safeguard liberty; the Union was a league of states, presided over by a dependent Congress. Its authority was limited in many ways, but of all the restraints devised to forestall usurpation of power, the denial to Congress of the right to tax was the most fundamental. No maxim of political philosophy was so widely accepted in Revolutionary times as that the "power which holds the purse-strings absolutely, must rule."[5] Popular control of taxation was deemed the very foundation of representative government and the only protection of the rights of the citizens. Under

4. Jensen's *Articles of Confederation* analyzes the party conflict in Congress.
5. Hamilton to Duane, Sept. 3, 1780, John C. Hamilton, ed., *The Works of Alexander Hamilton* (N.Y., 1851), I, 154.

the Articles of Confederation the states remained in a position to
check arbitrary proceedings by withholding revenue from Congress—
just as the states' own citizens could similarly curb the states' power.
Agreement on this principle was so nearly universal that although
proponents of stronger government took part in drafting the Articles
of Confederation, they never proposed that Congress should be given
authority to collect taxes.

That a weak central government was a handicap in waging war
was acknowledged and accepted as a calculated risk. The extent of
the risk was not appreciated, however, during the first few years of
the Revolution. Until paper money was exhausted, the limitations on
Congress's powers were not thoroughly tested. "It was easy times to
the government while Continental money lasted," and Congress proceeded with its affairs without depending on the states.[6] Late in
1779 the decision to stop emissions signalized the virtual end of this
resource and exposed to full view the weakness of Congress under
the Articles of Confederation.

The ensuing crisis in public affairs led many to re-examine the
postulates of their thinking and to wonder whether "political and
civil Liberty can be enjoyed amidst the Din of Arms, in their utmost
platonic Extent."[7] The violence wrought by popular governments
upon their own citizens suggested new approaches to a definition
of liberty. There was also some realization that the active support
of propertied men must be enlisted to maintain the war. "While
the war was carried on by emissions . . . the poor were of equal
use in government with the rich," mused Thomas Paine. "But when
the means must be drawn from the country . . . unless the wealthier
part throw in their aid, public measures must go heavily on."[8] People whose partisanship was not unshakable began listening to conservatives who spoke less of liberty and more about the need for
financial stability and strong government. Also, because paper money
and tender laws were evidently futile, there was less objection to a

6. The quotation is from Thomas Paine's "Dissertation on Government,"
Foner, ed., *Writings of Paine*, II, 397.
7. J. M. Varnum to the Governor of Rhode Island, Apr. 2, 1781, Burnett, ed.,
Letters, VI, 41-42.
8. Thomas Paine to Joseph Reed, June 4, 1780, Foner, ed., *Writings of
Paine*, II, 1186. Joseph Reed echoed this idea in a letter to Washington, June
5, 1780, Reed, *Reed*, II, 209-10.

trial of the conservative formula of sound money and unrestrained private enterprise.

The swing in popular sentiment produced conservative majorities in several important states, notably Massachusetts, Pennsylvania, and Virginia. New delegates altered the composition of Congress. The Adams-Lee alliance was fractured at the northern end by the advent of Oliver Wolcott of Connecticut, John Sullivan of New Hampshire, and Ezekiel Cornell and James Mitchell Varnum of Rhode Island. Richard Henry Lee left Congress, and the Virginia delegation was guided until 1783 by Theodorick Bland, Joseph Jones, and James Madison, who joined with Daniel Carroll and John Hanson of Maryland to give the southern states a conservative representation.[9]

The change of personnel was only partly responsible for the shaping of new policies: the old methods had failed, and there was scant prospect of reinvigorating them. It no longer seemed possible for Congress to discharge the responsibility it had assumed. After he had arrived in Philadelphia, almost every delegate favored enlarging Congressional powers. Even New Englanders, alert to the slightest portents of despotism, were disgusted with the ineffectiveness of the federal system and admitted that practical affairs sometimes required actions not described in the "political catechism" of good republicans.[10]

A new harmony was soon visible in Congress. Conservatives began saying this was the best Congress since the first and that "party intrigue" and "old prejudices" were being dispelled by "mild spirits" and "sensible men" who put the nation's welfare above factional advantage. Writing from Philadelphia, Samuel Huntington, the President of Congress observed: "There Seems a Spirit rising in this part of the Country to exert themselves in the common cause greater than I have Seen for Some years." But this new unity, although it owed something to the pressure of adversity, had a partisan basis. Two years later Joseph Reed remarked that the old Whigs were disappearing from public life. "Most of those who were

9. Merrill Jensen, "The Idea of a National Government During the American Revolution," *Pol. Sci. Qtly.*, 53 (1943), 366-72; Benjamin Harrison to Hamilton, Oct. 27, 1780, Hamilton, ed., *Works of Hamilton*, I, 192-93.

10. Samuel Adams to Samuel Cooper, Nov. 7, 1780, James Warren to Samuel Adams, Dec. 4, 1780, Connecticut Delegates to the Governor of Connecticut, Jan. 16, 1781, Burnett, ed., *Letters*, V, 440, 488n, 536-37.

much distinguished, and known in times of our greatest difficulty," he lamented, "are now in private stations."[11]

The revisionist group which was to rule Congress until the end of the war was conservative, mercantile, and nationalist in its aims. The group was strongest in the middle states, where it incorporated elements of the displaced colonial aristocracy. Independence had caused a breach in the social order, and, as one observer declared, the previously dominant classes aspired to a pre-eminence which the people now refused to grant them. Moreover, the Revolution had cut the aristocratic classes loose from the security of the British connection, with only their own resources to depend on. A propertied minority, they felt perpetually menaced in the presence of an agrarian majority. Many of them were fundamentally Tories, but even those who sincerely backed the Revolution felt that the experiment in liberty had got out of hand. Lamenting the absence of "public Checks upon the reserved licentiousness of the People," they considered themselves as living under mob rule. They sought security in the establishment of a central government which would protect property and minority rights.[12]

The war itself created another group which was vitally concerned with the enlargement of federal powers—the "public creditors." Up to 1783, the public creditors consisted of the holders of loan certificates, who alone received interest on their securities from the federal government.[13] Eager to assume responsibility for the loan certificate debt, Congress refused to surrender any part of it to the

11. Samuel Huntington to Rev. James Cogswell, July 22, 1780, *ibid.*, 285; Reed to Nathanael Greene, Mar. 14, 1783, Reed, *Reed*, II, 394. See the correspondence of Theodorick Bland, Joseph Jones, Ezekiel Cornell, Benjamin Harrison, John Sullivan, James Duane, and others in Burnett, ed., *Letters*, V, 347, 396, 397, 442, 477, 521, VI, 7; Benjamin Harrison to Hamilton, Oct. 27, 1780, Hamilton, ed., *Works of Hamilton*, I, 192-93.

12. James Mitchell Varnum to Horatio Gates, Feb. 15, 1781, Burnett, ed., *Letters*, V, 571; Charles Lee to Robert Morris, June 16, 1781, *Henkel's Catalogue, No. 1183*, 143-44; Jensen, "Idea of a National Government," *Pol. Sci. Qtly.*, 53 (1943), 378-79. Gouverneur Morris analyzed this interest in national government as early as 1774; a central government for the colonies would "restrain the democratic spirit." Jared Sparks, *Life of Gouverneur Morris* (Boston, 1832), I, 27.

13. Other securities constituted a floating debt until "liquidated," i.e., examined and restated in terms of specie value, whereupon Congress considered itself bound to pay interest on them. After the war, the various types of paper issued to soldiers, farmers and government officers were all liquidated. They then became part of the "public debt."

states. Unfortunately, there were insufficient funds to honor this commitment, and in 1780 Congress was obliged to suspend payment of the interest due in paper money. Interest payable in bills of exchange was continued until March 1782, when it too was stopped. Long before the final default the public creditors were lobbying for increased federal powers.[14] Since creditors were likely to be propertied men residing in states north of Maryland, they were in part identical with the aristocracy of the middle states which desired strong central government on other grounds. Drawn from the same powerful and influential ranks of the population were the enlightened merchants of the time, who, along with many intellectuals, regarded a powerful national state as a positive good.[15]

Grimly satisfied that paper money was approaching its destined end, the Nationalists proposed a clean sweep of such radical paraphernalia as tender laws, price regulation, embargoes, and anti-monopoly laws. Once this "detestable tribe" of restrictions was put away they predicted that the country would find new sources of vigor in the self-interested actions of private men.[16]

As "correct principles" were applied in the economic sphere, the Nationalists hoped to inject authority and some degree of managerial efficiency into the government. During 1780 and 1781, the outlines of their policy materialized in acts of Congress. The army was reorganized along lines recommended by Washington. The "militia system" of short-term enlistments was discarded in favor of enlistments for three years or the duration of the war. A significant step was taken when officers who served to the end of the war were promised pensions for life—an act offensive to republican thought, especially in New England where it aroused anxiety that a military caste take root in America.[17]

14. See "Original Documents; a Hartford Convention in 1780," *Mag. of Amer. Hist.,* 8 (1882), pt. 2, 688-98; George Bancroft, *History of the Formation of the Constitution of the United States* (N.Y., 1882), I, 14-15.
15. Robert A. East, who discusses this point, notes that in 1780 merchants for the first time formed voluntary organizations to support Congress. *Business Enterprise,* 208-9, 322-25.
16. See Robert Morris to the Governors of the States, Dec. 19, 1781, Wharton, ed., *Diplomatic Correspondence,* V, 58-59.
17. Hamilton formulated Nationalist policy in a remarkable letter to James Duane, Sept. 3, 1780, Hamilton, ed., *Works of Hamilton,* I, 150-68. See Hamilton to Isaac Sears, Oct. 12, 1780, Lodge, ed., *Works of Hamilton,* IX, 224.

Another triumph over "prejudice" was scored in the reorganization of the federal administrative departments. Fearful of delegating authority, Congress had hitherto given executive functions only to committees of its own members or to mixed boards made up of members and hired officials. The system was inefficient but persisted until late in 1780, when a sufficient retreat from republican principles took place to permit the establishment of separate executive departments. War, foreign affairs, naval matters, and finance were placed under the direction of individuals, not members of Congress. As the future showed, the forebodings of those who then opposed such extensive delegation of authority were to some extent justified. There was greater efficiency, but the heads of departments wielded an influence that threatened for a time to reduce Congress to a secondary role. Congress entered a phase of "executivism," in which the federal assembly was to a considerable degree dominated by the men appointed to manage its affairs.[18]

These reforms appeased the conservative instinct for authority and efficient management. They were but peripheral, however, to the one reform upon which all else depended. This related to finance.

Any real effort to strengthen the central government, restore its financial solvency, and rationalize federal administration had to begin with settling adequate revenues upon Congress. Requisitions had been unproductive; in any case the Nationalists opposed them in principle because they could not in the nature of things afford a basis for centralized authority. Unable to admit this point too openly, they usually argued the less dangerous point that the requisition system was and always would be faulty because it could not supply Congress with an assured income which would support its credit. In contracting foreign and domestic loans, they said, Congress had to act as a responsible agent; but without an income subject to its sole control, it could not really guarantee payment to its creditors. The only thing that would do was a federal tax.

Early in 1781 a proposal for a federal tax was offered to the states. Congress had been mulling over various schemes of finance for nearly a year and at length resolved to ask for an "impost," or import duty, of 5 percent on goods imported into the country. A special minister was being sent to Europe at this time in quest of

18. Sanders, *Executive Departments*, 2-5.

loans, and it was supposed that they would be more easily obtained if Congress could guarantee security in the form of a revenue subject to its sole control. As orginally conceived, therefore, the impost was to provide an income to discharge foreign loans. In its final wording, however, the resolution did not restrict the income to the discharge of loans then being sought, but instead pledged it to the payment of the interest and principal of all debts contracted during the war, both domestic and foreign. The power to collect this revenue was to be coextensive with the existence of the federal debt—in other words, permanent.[19]

That the impost was designed to be a permanent addition to Congress's powers was further confirmed by the wording of the resolution. An early draft had asked the states to "pass laws granting" the duty to Congress. This phrase was changed to "vest a power in Congress." Equally significant was the failure to specify whether the states or Congress were to control the collectors. Wary of reviving memories of the disputes with Britain, Congress did not spell out an arrangement under which federal collectors would act within the states, but the subsequent history of the impost leaves no doubt that collection was to be by federal officers.[20]

A few members thought that the impost could be disguised as a simple revenue measure. Then it would become effective after ratification by nine states. The states, however, at once recognized it as an amendment to the Articles and ratified it only on condition that it be approved by every state in the Union. The impost had a long road to travel, but as one state after another endorsed it in 1781 and 1782, its chances of adoption seemed good. Congress waited eagerly to try new powers.

As the Nationalists in Congress formulated their objectives, they discovered their leader in Robert Morris. He embodied in his person the constituent elements of the Nationalist group, and his genius was to shape their movement. A rich merchant and security holder, he had married into an aristocratic family. As a member of Con-

19. *Journals*, XVIII, 1033-36, 1141, 1157-64, XIX, 102-3, 110-13. The resolutions of the Hartford Convention were laid before Congress while the impost was being considered and may have been responsible for the change. One of the main resolutions adopted at the convention was a demand for a federal tax to enable Congress to discharge the loan certificate debt.

20. See Madison to Edmund Pendleton, May 29, 1781, Burnett, ed., *Letters*, VI, 103-4.

gress he had associated himself with the conservative faction in Pennsylvania, refusing to vote for the Declaration of Independence. His aims were primarily mercantile rather than political, but in the acrimonious party battle that developed in Pennsylvania during the war, he became an acknowledged leader of the conservative faction which fought the radical Constitutionalists for control of the state.[21]

In the spring of 1781, when Congress began selecting the men to head its administrative departments under the new plan, Morris was the inescapable choice for the Department of Finance. Congress had need of an executive whose personal standing and credit would bolster its weak directives. Morris had a mastery of Continental business that was virtually unsurpassed, and his fortune was one of the greatest in the country. Above all, he had the confidence of the mercantile and propertied interests whose aid was vital to the prosecution of the war.

When tendered his appointment, Morris made two stipulations. He required that Congress expressly sanction his continuance in private business while holding office—undoubtedly a rejoinder to the criticism of his previous service with the federal government. This demand was not hard for Congress to accept, but Morris's second condition aroused grave misgivings. He claimed the right not only to appoint all officers in his own department, but also to dismiss any officer in any branch of the government who handled public property. Only in this way, said Morris, could he cleanse the stables of federal administration.[22]

The terms implied that Morris's authority would penetrate every branch of the administration and even the army. Congress deliberated more than a month and once voted down the proposition, but "Mr. Morris was inexorable, Congress at [his] mercy," and at length his stipulations were met.[23] Actually, Congress had for years leaned ever more definitely towards granting decisive authority to its executive officers. The Congress of 1781 went the whole distance.

21. James Wilson, reflecting on conservative gains in Pennsylvania in 1781, said he had not the least doubt that Morris could be elected President of the state if he desired. Wilson to Silas Deane, Jan. 1, 1781, *Deane Papers*, IV, 270-73.

22. For the correspondence and Congressional action, see Wharton, ed., *Diplomatic Correspondence*, IV, 297-99, 330-33, 412-14; *Journals*, XIX, 180, 255, 263, 287-89, 290-91, 326-27, 337-38, 429, 432-33, XX, 455-56, 499.

23. Joseph Reed to Nathanael Greene, Nov. 1781, Reed, *Reed*, II, 374-75; Sanders, *Executive Departments*, 128-31.

Morris soon possessed the greatest influence of any man in the country except, perhaps, George Washington. Whatever the subject under consideration in Congress—whether military matters, foreign affairs, or relations with the states—the main problems usually related to finance. Morris was expert and full of expedients. Under the spell of its own helplessness, Congress all but relinquished the initiation of policy to the Financier. His formal powers were increased. In the name of economy, the Department of Marine was placed under the Financier; the Board of Admiralty and the several navy boards were abolished and their functions transferred to the Office of Finance. All the proceeds of foreign loans were placed in his hands, and he was given discretionary power to import or export goods on the account of the United States. He was authorized to supply the army by contract and to dispose of specific supplies by sale to private individuals. In recognition of the fact that negotiations with foreign nations mainly concerned loans and material aids, he was empowered to correspond with the foreign ministers of the United States; thus diplomatic functions were added to his chores. After the lapse of a few months, General William Irvine wrote that "the most trifling thing can not be done in any department but through Mr. Morris."[24]

Not long afterward, one of Morris's detractors observed that since his appointment the business of Congress had been extremely simplified. "Mr. Morris having relieved them from all business of deliberation in executive difficulty with which money is in any respect connected . . . they are now very much at leisure to read despatches, return thanks, pay and receive compliments &c. For form's sake some things go thither to receive a sanction, but it is the general opinion that it is form only."[25]

Morris's personal influence was strengthened by the appointment of his friend and business associate, Robert R. Livingston, as Secretary of Foreign Affairs. Gouverneur Morris, who was not a relative but a close friend, became Assistant Financier. General Philip J. Schuyler was a candidate for the post of Secretary of War, and it was said that if he were named to the office, Morris and his associates

24. *Journals*, XX, 597-98, 721, 734, XXI, 943, 1070; Sanders, *Executive Departments*, 134-35; Irvine to Col. Walter Stewart, Aug. 26, 1781, Col. Walter Stewart Papers, N.-Y. Hist. Soc.

25. Joseph Reed to Nathanael Greene, Nov. 1, 1781, Reed, *Reed*, II, 374-75.

would hold the chief positions in all the executive departments. As
it was, Richard Peters, a friend who had once begged Morris for admission into the "privateer circle," served as active head of the Department of War for a lengthy period before General Benjamin Lincoln took over.[26]

His enemies were alarmed at what they considered his overween-
ing ambition and continued to make snide allusion to his remaining
in private trade, but Morris's conduct of the Office of Finance leaves
no doubt that his personal goals were couched in the larger purpose
of effecting reforms which he deemed beneficial to the country. Announcing his appointment to friends, he took high ground: "Pressed
by all my friends, acquaintances, and fellow-citizens, and still more
pressed by the *necessity,* the *absolute necessity* of a change in our
moneyed system to work salvation, I have yielded, and taken a load
on my shoulder." In his letter accepting the position, he informed
Congress: "It is not from vanity that I mention the expectations
which the public seem to have formed from my appointment."[27]
Although such effusions were discounted, they had considerable validity, for Morris considered himself, and was in fact, the leader of a
party with a definite program of action.

Like the class of progressive merchants with whom he was associated, Morris had scant sympathy with agrarian tradition. For
him the goal of the Revolution was the creation of a national state
which would rise to "power, consequence, and grandeur." This idea
was inseparably joined with the conception of a political regime
which would foster business enterprise and at the same time leave
business free of restrictions. Morris was accustomed to define liberty
primarily in economic terms. "It is inconsistent with the principles
of liberty," he argued, "to prevent a man from the free disposal of
his property on such terms as he may think fit." He looked forward
to the moment when, by the removal of all economic restraints, the
people would be put in possession of "that freedom for which they
are contending."[28]

26. See Sanders, *Executive Departments,* 15, 103; Richard Peters to Robert
Morris, Aug. 28, 1780, *Henkel's Catalogue, No. 1183,* 96-97.
27. Morris to Philip Schuyler, May 29, 1781, to President of Congress, May
14, 1781, Wharton, ed., *Diplomatic Correspondence,* IV, 458, 412-14. See also
Morris to John Jay, June 5, 1781, *ibid.,* 470-71.
28. Morris to the Governors of the States, July 25, Dec. 19, 1781, *ibid.,* IV, 601-
4, V, 56-59; Sumner, *Financier,* II, 26-27.

Freedom of trade, however, was but part of his goal. Like many of the Revolutionary generation, he was imbued with the idea that the United States was standing on the threshold of its development. With Gouverneur Morris he believed that "Nothing remained but Vigor Organization & Promptitude to render this a considerable Empire."[29] He and his associates admired the commercial and industrial progress of European nations, particularly Great Britain. Anticipating a similar development in the United States, they could scarcely wait to experiment with the magical properties of commercial banks and marine insurance companies. They were deeply impressed by the sheer power of British public finance, which had withstood the shocks of two costly wars, and they contrasted the sound fiscal policy of Britain with the vagaries of public finance in America. To them the Revolution meant a break with the agrarian past and the growth of commercial and industrial enterprise in the United States—a process in which they hoped to play a significant role.[30]

Democracy was no part of the pattern. In their private letters, Morris and his associates avowed their contempt for the people and their impatience with popular government. They ascribed the behavior of the common people to such motives as passion, greed, and an incapacity to generalize above limited experience. They complained that popular governments were slow and perverse in action, distracted by petty conflicts of interest. "There is no *order* that has a will of its own," wrote Hamilton. "The inquiry constantly is what will *please,* not what will *benefit* the people." Arrogating to themselves a higher knowledge of natural law and public affairs, they dismissed their political foes as men of diminutive intellect and paltry motives, "vulgar souls whose narrow optics can see but the little circle of selfish concerns." They considered themselves

29. Governeur Morris to Matthew Ridley, Aug. 6, 1782, Matthew Ridley Papers, box 1, Mass. Hist. Soc.

30. See Morris to the Governors of Massachusetts, etc., July 27, 1781, to the President of Congress, Sept. 30, 1784, Wharton, ed., *Diplomatic Correspondence,* IV, 606-9, 821-22; Morris to Willink, Staphorst and Co., July 25, 1783, Feb. 12, 1784, Official Letterbook E, 821-22, Official Letterbook F, 429-32, Morris Correspondence, Lib. Cong. As to Morris's interests in banks and marine insurance companies, see East, *Business Enterprise,* 23-25; Sumner, *Financier,* II, 21; Joseph S. Davis, *Essays in the Earlier History of American Corporations* (Cambridge, Mass., 1917), II, 35.

men of "patriotic mind seeking the great good of the whole on enlightened principles."[31]

Morris and his associates were quite aware that the United States was a singularly democratic country and that the majority of people did not subcribe to their aims. As Superintendent of Finance, Morris set himself the task of "doing that infinite variety of things which are to be done in an infant government, placed in such delicate circumstances that the people must be wooed and won to do their duty to themselves and pursue their own interest." He proposed to draw by degrees "the bands of authority together, establishing the power of Government over a people impatient of control, and confirming the Federal Union . . . by correcting defects in the general Constitution."[32]

He proposed first of all to demonstrate managerial efficiency, showing what might have been accomplished had "Continental men" not held the reins. "Regularity" was to be introduced into fiscal affairs: henceforth federal requisitions on the states were to demand specie, not paper money. Federal officers were to keep orderly accounts and submit periodic reports. At the first opportunity, Morris intended to bring about a settlement of Congress's accounts with individual citizens and the states. When the government knew what its debts were and the amount of its income, a basis would exist for rational planning.

These reforms were preliminary to the restoration of "public credit," and he hoped to initiate the process by keeping his own administration solvent. Morris was most earnest about this because his personal affairs as a merchant were mingled with his official engagements, and for the sake of his own finances it was essential that he pay the bills he contracted as Financier. To sweep aside the clutter of the past, he refused to pay federal debts contracted before January 1, 1782, which he considered the effective date of his administration. From that date forward he accepted responsibility, intending to prove that the government could remain solvent if correct administrative methods were employed. Economies could be

31. Hamilton to Morris, Aug. 13, 1782, Lodge, ed., *Works of Hamilton*, IX, 269-80; Morris to Hamilton, Aug. 28, 1782, Wharton, ed., *Diplomatic Correspondence*, V, 673-75.

32. Morris to Franklin, Sept. 27, 1782, Wharton, ed., *Diplomatic Correspondence*, V, 771-75.

expected from the discharge of superfluous personnel and supplying the army by contract. Morris planned to expand government funds by creating a bank and by utilizing in behalf of the government all the anticipatory devices customary among merchants.

Such fiscal reforms were the proper work of a financial administrator and of sufficient importance to have absorbed Morris's whole energy. They were but instrumental, however, to his larger goal of recasting the structure of the Union. Illustrative of Morris's methods were his plans for the Bank of North America, which he submitted to Congress three days after taking office. On the ground that the Bank would aid his conduct of the finances, he requested a federal charter of incorporation. As outlined to Congress, the main function of the Bank was to hold government funds, make loans to the government, and discount its notes. Morris contended that by the sale of shares to individuals, the Bank would draw private capital in support of the government's operations.[33] Although these services were sufficient justification of the Bank's existence, they were but the beginning of Morris's designs. The Bank was to be capitalized at only $400,000 specie; Morris hoped to increase its capital to the extent that much of the private wealth in the country would be invested in its stock. Its circulating notes would then provide a medium of exchange for the entire nation. He intended to bring about an early retirement of all federal and state currencies, replacing them with bank notes, and thereby put an end to the evils of agrarian paper money.[34] Thus enlarged, the Bank would become a citadel of the Union. Morris advised John Jay of his desire to "unite the several States more closely together in one general money connexion, and indissolubly to attach many powerful individuals to the cause of our country by the strong principle of self-love and the immediate sense of private interest."[35]

The same interweaving of financial and political reform is evident in Morris's plans for dealing with the federal debt. In one aspect, the debt represented potential capital for business develop-

33. Morris to President of Congress, May 17, 1781, *ibid.*, IV, 421; *Journals*, XX, 519; Sumner, *Financier*, II, 26-27.

34. See Morris's letters to Hamilton, John Jay, Franklin, and his circular to the states, Wharton, ed., *Diplomatic Correspondence*, IV, 439-40, 494-95, 562-65, 574-75.

35. Morris to Jay, July 13, 1781, *ibid.*, 563. See also Morris to Franklin, July 13, 1781, *ibid.*, 568-69.

ment. Morris once told Congress that if the debt were properly funded—that is, if the payment of interest and principal was secured by adequate revenues—the market value of securities would rise, causing wealth to flow "into those hands which could render it most productive." Deposited in the Bank of North America and other financial institutions, the revitalized securities would constitute backing for a national system of currency and credit. "A due provision for the public debts would at once convert those debts into a real medium of commerce."[36] Pursuant to these ends, Morris proposed in 1782 that existing federal securities be taken in exchange for new securities, which would be backed by (as yet nonexistent) federal taxes. Like Hamilton at a later date, he had to refute the notion that a discrimination be made between original and present holders. Needless to say, Morris advocated acceptance of all securities at full value without discrimination.

The economic functions of a public debt went hand in hand with its political uses. Invigorated by the establishment of federal taxes and held by propertied men in all parts of the country, the public debt would be a bond of union. "It is . . . an advantage peculiar to domestic loans," he explained to Congress, "that they give stability to Government by combining together the interests of moneyed men for its support and consequently in this Country a domestic debt would greatly contribute to that Union, which seems not to have been sufficiently attended to, or provided for, in forming the national compact."[37]

Morris's plan of action anticipated the major features of the later Federalist program. As the leader of the first conservative movement in national politics, he addressed himself to his task.

36. *Journals*, XXII, 436; Robert Morris, *A Statement of the Accounts of the United States During the Administration of the Superintendent of Finance, 1781-1784* (Phila., 1785), ix.
37. *Journals*, XX, 429-47.

Reign of the Financier

"To you, who are acquainted with republican governments, it is unnecessary to observe on the delays which will arise, the obstacles which will be raised, and the time which will be consumed, in placing the revenue of America on a proper footing."

—Robert Morris to John Jay,
July 4, 1781.

IT WAS important to Morris that he score an outstanding success in the fiscal duties of his office, not only as a display of his own virtuosity, but as a demonstration of the reforms which he advocated. The time was propitious, for he took over his post as the last major campaign of the war was under way. His energetic conduct of the Office of Finance contributed to the defeat of Cornwallis but was scarcely a decisive element in the victory. The troops were moved and fed much as before, by supplies from the states and impressments in the field. After Yorktown, a military force had to be maintained until the spring of 1783, but the emergency was over. Morris's administration was associated with the return to peace. His role was to close off the era of war finance and to struggle toward a balanced budget, to rationalize financial administration, and to deal with the legacy of the Revolution.[1]

His chances of executing reforms in financial administration were better than those of the boards that preceded him. Except for a short interval, his administration did not bear the strain of large-

1. Morris hoped to be an American Necker. Morris to Silas Deane, June 7, 1781, *Deane Papers*, Conn. Hist. Soc.

scale warfare, and he could choose his methods without having to act under the compulsion of military necessity. Morris also bene-fited from receiving his income mainly in hard money, with which more could be accomplished. But it was the reduction of military expense that gave him his opportunity. Continental troops and militia in service shrank from 90,000 in 1776 to about 45,000 in the years from 1777 through 1780, then dwindled to 29,000 in 1781, 18,000 in 1782, and 13,000 in 1783. There were no major campaigns the last two years. Previously, expenses had been estimated as high as $20,000,000 specie annually. Excluding sums received and ex-pended in Europe, Morris managed for more than three years on a real income of about $6,700,000.[2] His superb abilities contributed greatly to his success, but circumstances made it possible.

His greatest asset was foreign loans.[3] During the whole course of the war to the beginning of 1781, French gifts and loans had been only 6,000,000 livres through 1779; an additional 4,000,000 in 1780; 846,000 livres which the United States received from the Farmers General; and 4,555,000 in supplies from Beaumarchais, a total of 15,400,000 livres—about $2,852,000. During the first year of his ad-ministration, Morris received from France $1,000,000 more than the sum of all French grants and loans up to that time. Just before he took office in 1781, the Court agreed to a loan of 4,000,000 livres for the year, and a great deal more was soon forthcoming. Congress had sent a special minister, John Laurens, to France to solicit aid. On the eve of his arrival, Franklin bestirred himself to get a free gift of 6,000,000 livres. (Laurens was identified through his brother Henry with the anti-Deane faction in Congress.) But Laurens man-aged to improve upon Franklin's feat. Although he may have "brusqued" the French ministry too much, as Franklin let it be known, he obtained a concession of great importance.[4] He persuaded

2. These figures are derived from an analysis of his accounts. Statements of the Financial Affairs of the late Confederated Government of the United States from February 1781, to September 1789, compiled and collated with the public records by Michael Nourse ... ; and Statement of the Receipts and Expenditures (1791); both in United States, Finance Mss., Lib. Cong.

3. The best treatment of this whole subject in its technical details is an un-published doctoral dissertation, Robert R. La Follette, The American Revolu-tionary Foreign Debt and Its Liquidation (George Washington Univ., 1931). The contracts for both French and Dutch loans may be found in Papers of Cont. Cong., no. 135, I.

4. Vergennes to Luzerne, Feb. 14, 1781, Franklin to the President of Congress,

the Court to pledge repayment of a loan to be opened in Holland for the United States, and the Court agreed to advance immediately the amount of the loan—10,000,000 livres.[5]

Not all of the money received from France was available for expenditure within the United States. Franklin retained 4,000,000 livres and, in order to meet the interest on loan certificates and pay a large sum which Congress had granted Beaumarchais, he arbitrarily held up another 1,500,000 which had been earmarked for shipment to America. Laurens himself laid out over 2,000,000 livres for military supplies.[6] Delivery of the sum which France agreed to advance in anticipation of the Dutch loan was delayed when Laurens indiscreetly made his purchases in Holland. Most of the goods were of British origin. Irritated by his failure to patronize home industry, the Court refused at first to advance the sum of the loan to the United States. The prospects of obtaining it were dubious, for in spite of the French guarantee, Dutch capitalists would not touch United States securities offered in Holland. At last, in November 1781, the French government entered into a contract with the Estates General of Holland by which both governments underwrote the loan.[7]

Much of the income from France in 1781 was therefore consumed in Europe, leaving only a minor fraction to support Morris's domestic expenses. Nevertheless, French aid had been generous—20,000,000 livres in a single year, amounting to $3,700,000. It was enough to meet American obligations abroad, purchase an overstock of clothing and other military supplies, and leave more than a million dollars for disposal within the United States. It furnished the initial capital for Morris's enterprises.

Mar. 12, 1781, John Laurens to the President of Congress, Mar. 20, 1781, Franklin to Carmichael, Aug. 24, 1781, Wharton, ed., *Diplomatic Correspondence*, IV, 256, 281-84, 317-21, 659-61; Franklin to William Jackson, July 6, 1781, Smyth, ed., *Writings of Franklin*, VIII, 276-79.

5. John Laurens to the President of Congress, Apr. 9, 1781, Vergennes to John Laurens, May 16, 1781, Wharton, ed., *Diplomatic Correspondence*, IV, 355-56, 418-19. The amount of the loan was 5,000,000 guilders ($2,000,000), which France computed at 10,000,000 livres ($1,850,000)—the amount received by the United States. French assumption of the charges on the loan and temporary remission of interest more than made up for the difference.

6. Vergennes to John Laurens, May 16, 1781, *ibid.*, 418-19.

7. Silas Deane to William Duer, June 14, 1781, *Deane Papers*, IV, 424-29; Franklin to Morris, July 26, 1781, Smyth, ed., *Writings of Franklin*, VIII, 289-91; Adams to Franklin, Dec. 6, 1781, Franklin Papers, XXIII, 101, Amer. Philos. Soc.; Contract of July 16, 1782, with France, Papers of Cont. Cong., no. 135, I, 1-23.

From this high point, French loans dwindled to 6,000,000 livres in 1782 and a final loan of 6,000,000 in 1783—a total of $2,200,000. After payments which had to be made in Europe were subtracted, there was not much surplus for expenditure at home, and by the fall of 1782 Morris was feeling the pinch. Then loans in Holland came to the rescue. Still the bourse of Europe in the eighteenth century, Holland was patronized by all the great powers. The American commissioners abroad had long sought entry into this money market without success. Franklin started a loan there in 1778 through a banker nominated by Chaumont, but although the French Court guaranteed payment of the interest, the loan failed after realizing only $32,000. The project was kept alive by an upstart Dutch merchant, John de Neufville, who was eager to speculate in the poor credit rating of the United States; however, his terms were too high and the American commissioners did not trust him. Prospects were still poor in 1781 when John Adams looked over possibilities. Dutch capitalists were simply unwilling to take the risk.[8]

Their attitude changed only when it became certain that the United States would gain independence. The loan of 1781, backed by the French government, had not established the United States on the list of regular borrowers in Holland, but in 1782 John Adams negotiated the first loan which the United States obtained on the strength of its own credit.[9] The amount was 5,000,000 guilders ($2,000,000), which became available as the sale of bonds progressed and money accumulated in the hands of the Dutch syndicate promoting the loan. Over $650,000 was realized by November 1782, after which the sale of bonds continued at a moderate pace.[10] As

8. Franklin, Adams, and Lee to the President of Congress, Sept. 17, 1778, Franklin to Vergennes, Mar. 17, 1779, to Dumas, Mar. 18, 1779, to the Committee of Foreign Affairs, May 26, 1779, to Dumas, July 26, 1780, John Adams to the President of Congress, Nov. 17, 25, 1780, Jan. 15, 1781, Wharton, ed., *Diplomatic Correspondence*, II, 722-25, III, 84-85, 86-87, 186-94, IV, 11-12, 155-56, 160-62, 234; Neufville to Franklin, July 13, 1780, Franklin Papers, XIX, 20, Amer. Philos. Soc.; Neufville to Congress, July 28, 1779, Acc. 161, no. 248, env. 6, Foreign Affairs Sec., Natl. Arch.; Franklin to Vergennes, Sept. 20, 1780, Smyth, ed. *Writings of Franklin*, VIII, 139-40.

9. Contracts for the Dutch loans may be found in Papers of Cont. Cong., no. 135, I.

10. Wilhelm and Jan Willink *et al.* to Robert Livingston, Aug. 16, 1782, John Jay to Congress, May 26, 1783, Acc. 161, no. 248, env. 4, 5, Foreign Affairs Sec., Natl. Arch.

this source dried up, Adams got another loan of 2,000,000 guilders ($800,000) in 1784, which, as he said, saved the honor of the Financier's bills, allowing Morris to quit his post in November 1784 with his debts paid. The balance which the United States then had on the books of Nicholas and Jacob Van Staphorst at Amsterdam was rising towards $200,000.[11]

Although foreign loans were Morris's mainstay, he also managed to extract more money from the states than anyone had before. The states had begun making larger contributions to the federal cause in 1780. Their assistance continued through 1781 in the form of specific supplies and the assumption of federal debts, but they also paid more on money requisitions—over $2,000,000 specie during Morris's administration. These payments did not represent old paper money or useless certificates dumped on Congress; they were in such form that Morris could apply them to current expenses. At least $730,000 consisted of specie or redemption by the states of paper instruments which Morris issued from the Office of Finance.[12]

Minor revenues came from other sources. The progressive dismantling of the military establishment produced war surpluses which Morris converted into cash whenever possible. He sold a large quantity of imported clothing for which there was no longer a need and disposed of federal buildings, land, horses, wagons, and ships. In addition, the surrender of Cornwallis produced a quantity of military spoil.[13]

Morris also engaged in so-called commercial negotiations, exporting and importing goods for the United States and selling public supplies on the civilian market.[14] As part of his official duties, he

11. It reached this point in January 1785. Adams to President of Congress, Mar. 2, 1784, Wharton, ed., *Diplomatic Correspondence*, VI, 783; United States in account current with Nicholas and Jacob Van Staphorst, Papers of Cont. Cong., no. 145, 215-19.

12. The states were credited with $730,000 on the specie requisition of 1781. A General View of Receipts and Expenditures . . . , Papers of Cont. Cong., no. 137, III, 319, 337, 636-37; Receipts and Expenditures (1791), Statements of the Financial Affairs of the late Confederated Government, United States, Finance Mss., Lib. Cong.

13. The army was so abundantly supplied with clothing after 1781 that Morris sold shipments arriving from Europe. Franklin to Jonathan Williams, Mar. 23, 1782, to Morris, Mar. 30, 1782, Smyth, ed., *Writings of Franklin*, VIII, 400-1, 401-4.

14. Most of this business seems to have been conducted by Morris's partner and agent, John Swanwick. See Diary in the Office of Finance, July 17, 1783, Morris Correspondence, Lib. Cong., hereafter cited as Official Diary.

speculated in bills of exchange and in the paper money of Pennsylvania.[15] After the surrender of the British garrison at Yorktown, he entered into an arrangement whereby merchants of the town sold their stock of goods to the United States, receiving payment in tobacco which they were allowed to export to New York City under special license.[16]

Negotiations of this kind were instrumental to the conduct of financial business and lent flexibility to his operations, but except for the speculation in Pennsylvania currency, which netted a clear $32,000, they appear to have added little to his basic income. This came from foreign aids, state payments, and, in a much smaller degree, from the sale of federal property. Revenues available to the Financier for expenditure within the United States from the time he entered upon his duties to November 1, 1784 were:

	(specie values)
1. State payments:[17]	$2,190,734
2. Foreign aid:	4,182,845
3. Other incomes, perhaps	330,000
	$6,703,579
(Expenditures in 1781 before Morris assumed direction of finance.)	1,200,000 [18]

It was generally acknowledged that Morris employed his funds to the greatest effect and achieved long-overdue economies in admin-

15. Morris to Franklin, July 21, 1781, Official Letterbook A, 196-200, Statement of the Accounts of the United States during the Administration of Robert Morris, *ibid.;* State of the Account of . . . Robert Morris as agent for Pennsylvania . . . May 4, 1785, John Nicholson to President John Dickinson, May 17, 1785, An Account of the Proceeds at the Requisition Prices, Post-Revolutionary Papers, XVI, 10, 43, XVII, 67, Division of Public Records, Penn. Hist. and Museum Commission; John Agnew to John Nicholson, Jan. 9, 1783, Records of the Comptroller General, Prothonotaries Account, Cumberland County, *ibid.;* Ver Steeg, *Morris,* 69-71.

16. See Morris to Clark, May 30, 1782, Wharton, ed., *Diplomatic Correspondence,* V, 448-54; Official Diary, Jan. 31, 1783, Morris Correspondence, Lib. Cong.

17. This does not include a wide variety of state contributions, such as specific supplies, state payment of federal troops, and the assumption of federal debts.

18. Morris's total receipts are given as $8,177,000, but part of them represent loans from the Bank of North America and private individuals which Morris repaid. Other items were mere bookkeeping entries. The calculation is based upon Receipts and Expenditures (1791), and Statements of the Financial Affairs of the late Confederated Government, United States, Finance Mss., Lib. Cong.

istration. All previous efforts to reduce costs had made little headway against the rank growth of the federal bureaucracy. The basic problem had been lack of enough money and of the right kind of money. Without specie, federal officers had to pay paper money prices, which were always raised in anticipation of future currency depreciation, and when they had no funds at all, as was often the case, they had to buy on credit at still higher prices. Lack of money also forced the government to employ costly and inefficient procedures. All services in logistical support of the army were swollen with personnel. Soldiers taken from the lines served as carpenters, cooks, and blacksmiths at a multitude of posts where they only occasionally had jobs to perform. The government had no money to hire men as they were needed, and therefore maintained an excessive staff. Similarly, it would have been cheaper to supply the army by contract and let private merchants raise and transport provisions rather than maintain the personnel and equipment which the government required to perform the same tasks. But the government was in no position to offer terms which contractors would accept.[19]

Morris was able to introduce constructive reforms. He was not, as were his predecessors, obliged to throw all system, all method, to the winds in an effort to repel the enemy. Great authority was centered in his hands: like none of the boards which preceded him, he could enforce and carry out an executive policy. Finally, he had enough hard money to place some phases of government operations on a specie basis.

As a result of reductions in both the Quartermaster and Commissary staffs begun in 1780, the bureaucracy had already shrunk considerably when Morris took office. At his suggestion, the Department of Marine was eliminated as a separate agency and placed under the Office of Finance. Several expensive navy boards were abolished. The Hospital department, frequently reorganized, was reorganized again at the Financier's instigation. The former Clothier General's department, now inactive, was absorbed by Morris.[20] As soon as the Yorktown campaign ended, Morris undertook a survey of the Quartermaster department with the willing cooperation of its

19. The Timothy Pickering Letterbooks during the years 1781 to 1783, especially Pickering to Col. Hugh Hughes, July 12, 1781, Pickering to General McDougall, Jan. 14, 1782, Revol. War Mss., nos. 82, 83, Natl. Arch.
20. Ver Steeg, *Morris*, 109.

chief, Timothy Pickering, his ardent admirer. They found it possible to abolish a large number of military posts which were no longer
necessary, partly because the war had subsided, partly because they
were made superfluous by Morris's new contracts for supplying the
army. Numerous posts were dismantled with scant regard for the
anguish of those afflicted by the loss of their sinecures.[21]

The outstanding novelty which Morris introduced into administrative procedure—and the reform for which he had highest hopes—
was supplying the army by contract. This method promised to
obviate the need for a large federal staff. Presumably, all transactions would be reduced to a single negotiation between the Financier and private individuals who would take responsibility and
exact only a reasonable profit for their pains. Federal accounts
would be simplified, the possibility of fraud reduced, and the government relieved of a mass of petty details. Morris proposed to
award contracts on the basis of competitive bidding to ensure the
lowest cost to the government.

He was eager to try the system, and introduced it on a limited
scale during the rush of the Yorktown campaign. The first contracts were restricted to Pennsylvania, where control of the state's
paper money gave him a ready means of making payments to the
contractors, but early in 1782 he invited bids for supplying com-
ponents of the army stationed in New York and New Jersey. By
1783 contracts were the principal mode of supplying Continental
forces everywhere but in the deep south.

They did not work without trouble, particularly in the first year,
for there were frequent complaints about the quality of rations and
failure of delivery. Morris tried to adjust the army's differences
with the contractors, but was himself soon at odds with them in
consequence of falling behind in his payments. Late in 1782 he had
to break off the main agreement with Sands, Livingston and Company (a virtual syndicate of contractors for the army in New York)
when the company refused to go further on a credit basis. Morris

21. Pickering to Col. Hugh Hughes, July 12, 1781, to Aaron Forman, Dec.
13, 1781, to Jabez Hatch, Dec. 18, 1781, to Ralph Pomeroy, Dec. 19, 1781, Pickering Letterbooks, Revol. War Mss., no. 82, Natl. Arch.; Pickering to Major Richard
Claiborne, Jan. 16, 1782, to Robert Morris, Feb. 19, 1782, *ibid.*, no. 83, Pickering
to Col. Carrington, July 12, 1782, to Major General Lincoln, Aug. 9, 1782, *ibid.*,
no. 85.

accepted an offer from Wadsworth and Carter at a higher figure. It had become evident that the advantages expected from competitive bidding were almost nullified by the paucity of bids and by the propensity of merchants to join forces and establish a community of interests. An element of nepotism also tinged the contracting system; some, though not all, of the undertakers proved to be partners or ex-partners of Morris. John Holker, Walter Livingston and Morris's protégé, William Duer, were among those who received contracts.

By 1783 the system was operating smoothly and continued without interruption until the disbandment of the army. There were few complaints from the troops, and Morris maintained his payments to the contractors. The prices they charged were high, sometimes considered excessive, but the reduction of governmental functions unquestionably produced an over-all saving.[22]

The introduction of contracts was a bold, successful feat and one of the least criticized acts of Morris's administration. The only real objection was that they were not applied everywhere. Complaints were heard from the south, where, except for a brief interval, the army was maintained on the old basis. The contrast to the orderly regime which Morris built up in the north was unmistakable. Greene's army lived on a hand-to-mouth basis without money, relying upon scanty deliveries of specific supplies, otherwise subsisting by impressments. The southern states were exhausted and disorganized, but Morris spared Greene little money and required him as a precautionary measure to put none of it in the hands of officers who had not plainly accounted for sums which they had already received.[23] This was about all the system possible under circumstances which had once been general over the country.

By economizing his resources to the utmost, Morris hoped to achieve something new in federal affairs—a balanced budget. Ultimately, by habituating the country to a solvent and efficient administration, he proposed to repossess for the United States the "inestimable jewel" of public credit. To maintain the solvency of his own administration he found it necessary first to close the door against the mass of pre-existing claims which had always engulfed the cur-

22. This discussion of contracts is based on the full account in Ver Steeg, *Morris*, 106-8, 141-52, 159-66. Cf. *Journals*, XXIV, 397-98.

23. Morris to Greene, Dec. 19, 1781, Official Letterbook B, 245-52, Morris Correspondence, Lib. Cong.

rent revenues of the federal government. Morris simply disowned past debts. He refused to pay claims originating before January 1, 1782, which he considered the effective date of his office. "It was necessary," he wrote later, "to draw Some Line between those Expenditures for which I should be answerable, and those which had already been incurred . . . [otherwise] I could have done nothing." This policy was rigidly enforced. Staff officers were told to adhere to it on pain of dismissal. The Financier's rule was that current revenues must be applied only to current expenses.[24]

Inevitably, the rule was adjusted to the situation. Some claims were allowed which did not meet the requirements, while others which did were excluded. The most important exception to the general principle was Morris's refusal to pay the army. The soldiers and officers received virtually nothing in 1781 and 1782, and not until the moment of their discharge in 1783 did Morris feel obliged to give them anything. His attitude was that army pay had to come out of requisitions: the states had not complied with Congress's requests, so the troops could not be paid. This executive policy relieved him of an expense of at least $3,500,000 specie a year, and was necessary to maintain solvency in other areas.[25] However, he paid the salaries of administrative personnel in order to maintain their efficiency and loyalty. This discriminatory policy in deciding whom to pay was characteristic of his administration. In general, he preferred to make payments which would benefit his associates, both in and out of the government, and preserve his standing with the mercantile community. He promptly discharged in specie the considerable sums owed to his former partners, John Ross and William Bingham, even though their claims predated his

24. Morris to Pickering, Sept. 2, 1782, Papers of Cont. Cong., no. 137, Appendix, 301; Timothy Pickering to Col. Hughes, Jan. 4, 1782, to Col. Hughes, Mar. 21, 1783, Pickering Letterbooks, Revol. War Mss., no. 83; Pickering to Col. John Chandler, Feb. 7, 1783, to Major Richard Claiborne, May 17, 1783, *ibid.*, no. 86. So that a clean break could be made with the past, Morris proposed to substitute Le Coulteux for Le Grand as banker for the United States in France. Morris also tried to wriggle out of paying Beaumarchais the sums Congress had granted him. Morris to Franklin, June 8, 1781, May 23, 1782, Franklin Papers, V, 23, VI, 27, Univ. of Pennsylvania; Franklin to Morris, Aug. 12, 1782, Smyth, ed., *Writings of Franklin*, VIII, 580-84.

25. For various estimates of army pay, see Papers of Cont. Cong., no. 137, II, 199-203, 319, 337, 451, 669-71; *ibid.*, no. 12, 55; report of Jan. 28, 1783, *ibid.*, no. 141, 1.

administration and there was some doubt about the validity of Bingham's claim. Morris replied to criticism merely by saying that his settled policy was to pay all debts to individuals contracted abroad.[26]

In this and other cases claims which he paid had no more intrinsic merit than a hundred others. There were, in fact, many shades and degrees of preference. Some claims had a higher rating because Morris or his principal officers had given their personal word in promising payment. As Morris said afterwards, no strict rule was followed: "The Doctrine then in use was that every pressing occasion must receive a Part of its Demands out of such Funds as could be found, and when the Treasurer could not ward off the Pressure of various Claimants who obtained Warrants, the temporary Discretion of the higher Powers determined the Preference of Payment according to their Idea of the existing Necessity."[27]

However manipulated by the "higher Powers," this policy raised a barrier which protected Morris's revenues against immediate submergence by past debts. On the ground thus preserved he carefully began the reconstruction of public credit. His major problem was the credit rating of the federal government, whose financial reputation had been shattered. His solution was to build the credit of his own administration as distinct from that of Congress and, in doing so, to make the utmost use of private credit drawn from sources outside the government. The first of these sources was his own fortune and private reputation, which he deliberately placed behind his acts as Financier. "My personal Credit," he wrote, "has been substituted for that which the Country had lost."[28] His second resource was the Bank of North America, which he founded as an adjunct to his office. Both Morris and the Bank were enmeshed in the functions of the government; yet they had independent standing in the mercantile world, and this inspired a confidence that would not have been accorded to the government.

26. Ver Steeg, *Morris*, 78; Observations on Mr. Bingham's Accounts, items 162, 163, Arthur Lee Papers, Houghton Lib.; Morris to President of Congress, Nov. 14, 1782, Papers of Cont. Cong., no. 137, II, 1-24; Morris to Franklin, Dec. 4, 1781, Franklin Papers, V, 78, Univ. of Penn.

27. Morris to Charles Pettit (copy), Jan. 20, 1784, placed after a letter from Pettit to Nathanael Greene, Mar. 6, 1784, Greene Papers, Clements Lib.

28. Morris to Benjamin Harrison, Jan. 15, 1782, Morris Correspondence, Lib. Cong.

Morris focused his attempt to establish the credit of his administration on an effort to launch and sustain a new series of paper instruments. This paper was of two kinds: "Morris's notes," and the notes
of the Bank of North America. Both were freely employed in public
business and closely associated with the person and office of the
Financier. Technically, they were distinct from one another; both,
in fact, were the Financier's paper.

Morris's notes were issued in denominations ranging from $20
to $100 specie. They were at first mere drafts drawn against him-
self or John Swanwick, who was Morris's partner, unofficial cashier
to the Office of Finance, and federal tax receiver for the state of
Pennsylvania. The form of these notes later became more elaborate:
besides being signed by Morris they were watermarked "United
States." They were payable at periods of thirty to sixty days, sometimes longer. Morris guaranteed them in both his public and private
capacity. Their security was his personal ability to direct payment
out of government funds and, failing that, his private assets as a
merchant.[29]

The Bank of North America was the first commercial bank in
the United States. Morris tried to establish it as soon as he received
his appointment as Financier. Congress endorsed his plan in principle, but he could not raise private subscriptions for $400,000—the
capital necessary to begin operations. Although he wrote everywhere, "Gentlemen of monied interest" would not invest, and he
finally used government funds to put the bank in business.[30] Approximately $462,000 in hard money had arrived from France, and
Morris subscribed $254,000 of it on behalf of the government. Pledges
for the remaining amount needed to complete the Bank's capital

29. See Morris to Receivers for the several States, Aug. 29, 1782, Official Letterbook D, *ibid.*; Ver Steeg, *Morris,* 87.

30. *Journals,* XX, 519, 545, 548; Wharton, ed., *Diplomatic Correspondence,*
IV, 565-68. Morris tried to draw in the members of the Bank of Pennsylvania,
an association which he and others had formed the previous year to buy rations
for the federal army and, incidentally, to undermine the radical government of
Pennsylvania. It is uncertain whether his plan succeeded. For details see Plan
for establishing a Bank in Pennsylvania, Papers of Cont. Cong., no. 20, II, 87-92;
Washington to Reed, July 4, 1780, President Reed in Council to Washington,
May 17, 1781, Reed, *Reed,* II, 220-22, 300-6; *Journals,* XVII, 548-50, XX, 688;
Sumner, *Financier,* II, 23, 29; Morris to President of Congress, June 21, 1781,
Official Letterbook A, 43, Morris Correspondence, Lib. Cong.; Morris to Don
Diego Jos. de Navarro, July 7, 1781, Papers of Cont. Cong., no. 137, I, 188-93,
197-209, 213; Ver Steeg, *Morris,* 68-69.

were secured from private individuals, and Congress granted a charter of incorporation. The president was Morris's erstwhile partner, Thomas Willing, and at least four other members of the original board of directors had been connected with the Financier in business.[31]

The primary function of the Bank was to make short-term loans to the government. Morris disbursed bank notes in the course of official business, and these were redeemed over the Bank's counter at fixed dates in the future. The Bank also advanced money to merchants who obtained contracts from Morris for supplying the army. A further service was to discount the personal notes which Morris received from individuals when he sold them bills of exchange or surplus government property. Undeniably, the Bank was a most useful institution. Morris said afterwards that he could not have done without it. Its loans to the government during his administration exceeded $1,200,000.[32]

This figure does not represent loans at any one time; it is the total of smaller advances which the government was continually repaying. Actually, the Bank's usefulness was limited, since most of its capital was public money. Unable to extend long-term credits, it could do little more than anticipate the government's income for a few weeks ahead. Its advances appear to have run only $50,000 to $165,000 above the amount of the government's investment.[33]

The Bank's greatest contribution was to lend flexibiltiy to Morris's operations. The use of its notes allowed him to anticipate revenues and still maintain the mode of cash payments. Whenever bank notes or his personal notes were taken up and redeemed by the states, they were not presented to him for payment, and he was

31. *Journals*, XX, 597-98, XXI, 1185, 1187-90; Morris, *Statement of the Accounts*. Morris discusses the bank in his introduction to these published accounts. See Ver Steeg, *Morris*, 84-86. Sumner gives as the leading shareholders, presumably in 1783: Robert Morris, 95 shares; William Bingham, 95; John Swanwick, 71; William Smith, 50—all closely associated with the Financier—Jeremiah Wadsworth, 104; John Carter, 98. Sumner, *Financier*, II, 28-29.

32. Ver Steeg, *Morris*, 116-17; Morris, *Statement of the Accounts*.

33. The calculation is in Elliot, "Funding Systems," *House Doc. No. 15*, 28th Cong., 1st sess., 1843-44, II, 91n. There is little material on the activities of the Bank in this early period. Late in 1782 Morris sold the government's shares, and its connection with the government terminated with Morris's resignation in 1784. See Ver Steeg, *Morris*, 178-9.

so much specie ahead. By employing notes in lieu of hard cash, he conserved the specie at his disposal—it had greater utility employed to back a note issue than if directly expended. Finally, the reputation which the Bank gained for sound practice obtained a credit with the mercantile community which was valuable to his administration.

Morris put all the assets which he and the United States government could command behind bank notes and his personal notes. Nevertheless, he still had to exhaust the arts of fiscal management to preserve the credit of his paper, particularly his personal notes, in a country habituated to currency depreciation. Morris was extremely careful to avoid any implication that his notes were less valuable than specie. Federal officers were forbidden to pay more in notes than the specie prices of goods, and Morris threatened to take the difference out of their salary if they did. They were merely to offer his notes, not urge them upon people, lest too much pressing raise doubts as to their value. Better that public business come to a halt, declared Morris, than his notes depreciate. In areas where they had in fact depreciated, he stopped issuing them, and once, in a matter of purchasing ox teams in 1782, he ordered his subordinates to accept no discount even if it meant that the army did not take the field.[34]

This incident suggests how greatly his hand was strengthened by the recession of war. Previous administrators could not have taken such a position. Nonetheless, considering the disrepute of all paper instruments and the universal habit of promoting depreciation by anticipating it, Morris's ability to keep up the value of his paper was a striking accomplishment. Bank notes passed at par with specie in Philadelphia, and there is no indication that they were discounted elsewhere beyond the normal rate for paper circulating at a distance from its place of origin. Morris's personal notes usually passed at par in the middle states. In New England and the lower south,

34. Pickering to Col. Jabez Hatch, Mar. 26, 1782, to Col. Hughes, Mar. 26, 1782, Pickering Letterbooks, Revol. War Mss., no. 83, Natl. Arch., Pickering to General Lincoln, May 27, 1782, to Col. Jabez Hatch, June 19, 1782, *ibid.*, no. 85; Pickering to Mr. Andrew Dunscomb, Sept. 5, 1782, *ibid.*, no. 84; Morris to Edward Carrington, Apr. 25, 1782, Official Letterbook C, 214-19, Morris Correspondence, Lib. Cong.

where his influence stretched thin, it would appear that a discount of 15 or 20 percent was exceptional.[35]

As a financial administrator Morris was supremely competent, even brilliant. He did not restore the credit of the central government, but he established his own, paid the debts for which he assumed responsibility, and quit his office in November 1784 with a balance of $22,000 in the Treasury. He displayed zeal and ability in rationalizing procedure, economizing revenue, and maximizing his resources. His methods were often disliked, but friend and foe alike conceded that his administration was singularly able. In June 1783, an investigating committee which included Arthur Lee and Stephen Higginson, certainly no friends of Morris, reported:

In examining the reforms which have been made in the public expenditures, the attention of the committee was necessarily called to the expenditures of former years . . . In comparing these expenditures with the present, and making every allowance for the difference of times and circumstances, the committee are of opinion, that the order and economy which has been introduced since the establishment of this office, has been attended with great savings of public money, as well as many other beneficial consequences.[36]

Samuel Osgood, who wished to see Morris dismissed, said that it was unwise and untrue not to admit that he had saved the United States a great deal of money: "I lay it down as a good general maxim that when a person is to be attacked, it is wise not to endeavor to depreciate his real merit." James Madison recalled in 1790, with some exaggeration, that Morris "with 5,000,000 Dlrs. carrd. on the War to more effect, paid & clothed a large army & rendered more Services than his Predecessors in Office had done for 4 times the Amot."[37] The finest tribute, however, was an inverse reference in the *Providence Gazette,* in whose pages Morris's name was the symbol of corrupt wealth and centralized tyranny. "Plain Dealer" was in-

35. This discount was reported at various times in 1782 and 1783. Pickering to General Washington, Apr. 23, 1782, Pickering Letterbooks, Revol. War Mss., no. 83, Natl. Arch.; John Chaloner to Peter Colt, Aug. 13, 1782, to Jeremiah Wadsworth, Oct. 18, 1782, Chaloner and White Letterbook, Hist. Soc. of Pa.; Ver Steeg, *Morris,* 116-19.

36. *Journals,* XXIV, 397-98.

37. Osgood to Stephen Higginson, Feb. 2, 1784, Burnett, ed., *Letters,* VII, 432. Madison is quoted in John Constable to Thomas Truxton, Mar. 7, 1790, William Constable Letterbooks, 1782-1790, Constable-Pierrepont Papers, N. Y. Pub. Lib.

veighing against Congress's request for a federal impost, which he said portended the beginning of big, expensive government. He considered it necessary to explain, however, that the present economy in federal affairs was not typical of centralized governments. Conditions before Morris took office were more typical. The present economy, he said, resulted from the "peculiar genius and temperament" of the Financier.[38]

Impressive though it was, Morris's competence in fiscal administration left a smaller mark on the country's future than his acts as a party leader. It was in the realm of political and constitutional development that his contributions are most significant. Never for a moment was he so submerged in the details of his office as to forget that he was building a system. His every decision was determined by whether or not a particular policy would yield block or mortar for the institutional foundations of an effective central government. By acting continuously on the assumption that Congress would evolve into a strong government, and thereby committing Congress and, to a lesser extent, the states to policies based on that assumption, he contributed to the eventual triumph of Federalism.

Morris had nothing but scorn for the constitutional mode of raising revenue by requisitions—his entire hope and expectation was to secure federal taxes and thereby give Congress the sinews of power. Meanwhile, he tried to organize the requisition system in such a way as to enhance Congress's position within the Union.

Requisitions had always operated under the dominance of the states, which were addicted to particularist methods involving the use of local currency and paper instruments. Since they dealt so largely in paper money and certificates, the states found it more convenient to pay Congress's debts in their own way or to assume and execute federal functions upon their own citizens, than to remit specie to Congress. In any case, they preferred their own devices, and when they raised money in compliance with requisitions, they often disbursed it themselves for federal purposes. The loan officer—Congress's financial agent—was a state appointee, who could not usually resist the demands of local authority. It often happened, therefore, that the states raised and spent considerable sums in behalf of the

38. "Plain Dealer, No. XI," *Providence Gazette,* May 10, 1783.

federal government, for which they sometimes got credit on requisitions; but Congress never saw the money and had no chance to control its expenditure. Although the procedure had the merit of expediency, since the states could act more effectively upon their people than Congress, it deprived Congress of income and the power of spending its own money.

All this was anathema to Morris. He demanded hard money revenues for Congress or the payment of requisitions in the paper instruments which he issued from the Office of Finance. In compliance with his views, Congress dropped all "facilities" from its requisition of 1781, refusing to accept specific supplies or Quartermaster and Commissary certificates. Contemptuous of specific supplies, Morris was even more rigidly opposed to the acceptance of Quartermaster and Commissary certificates on requisitions because they represented merely the cancelation of past debts and constituted no present income. At his insistence, Congress stripped the proposed requisition of all features except a bare demand for the enormous sum of $8,000,000 specie, payable in hard money or the Financier's paper. For the next year Morris suggested $9,000,000 specie. This was high policy, befitting his conception of the dignity which he hoped to confer upon Congress.[39]

Morris also fought to establish exclusive federal control of money raised by the states in compliance with requisitions. Soon after he assumed office, various states began paying the salaries of their troops for the years 1781 and 1782, a period when the soldiers were receiving no pay from Congress. Morris refused to countenance this procedure. He announced that such payments would be considered as gifts for which the states would receive no credit on requisitions. They must pay the money to Congress, said Morris, and Congress would then pay the troops. There must be "one common Treasury, replenished by the common contribution of all according to established Principles." Congress backed his stand in this matter. Transmitting its decision to the federal tax receivers, Morris remarked: "You will consider this Act as an Additional Evidence of the firm

39. *Journals*, XXI, 1090-91; Morris accepted specific supplies on special occasions in discharge of the specie requisitions of 1781, notably in the case of South Carolina where the goods were channeled directly to Greene's army, which Morris did not otherwise support.

Determination of our Sovereign to persevere in those Systems which they have adopted."[40]

The state-appointed loan officers were unreliable instruments of centralized authority, and Morris soon relieved them of important functions, leaving them only clerical duties connected with old debts. He put the financial business of his administration in the hands of a newly created staff of officers, the tax receivers, who took charge of all money paid to Congress by the states. Usually residents of states other than the one in which they served, the tax receivers were appointed by Morris and acted under his orders. They did not handle a large volume of money, and their duties and commissions were small, but Morris gave them extra commissions. He was gearing an administrative system for the time when Congress would collect its own taxes. Meanwhile, he employed the receivers as his personal agents to lobby with state legislatures and inspire favorable publicity for his measures. They were detested in many states as "licensed" spies.[41]

Specie revenues, centralized receipts and disbursements, a federalized corps of administrators—all this was groundwork for the establishment of a national government. It proved to be premature. Little was to remain after Morris retired from office in 1784. Congress, reacting against one-man rule, returned supervision of its finances to a Treasury board. The tax receivers were eliminated. Specie requisitions proved to be impractical, and Congress slid back into acceptance of state-oriented finance. In one respect, however, Morris built permanently. The legacy which he and the Nationalist Congress bequeathed to the cause of national government was the appropriation of the Revolutionary debt for the federal government. The details of this action belong to a later chapter but its significance must be indicated here.

40. Morris to the Governor of Rhode Island, June 26, 1782, Wharton, ed., *Diplomatic Correspondence*, V, 524; *Journals*, XXIII, 624-26, 629-31; Morris to Daniel of St. Thomas Jenifer, Mar. 12, 1782, Official Letterbook C, 97-99, Morris's report on the New Jersey memorial, Sept. 27, 1782, Morris to Receivers of the several states, Oct. 5, 1782, Official Letterbook D, 231-34, 277-78, Morris Correspondence, Lib. Cong.

41. See Morris to Hamilton, June 4, 1782, Official Letterbook C, 384; Morris to George Abbot Hall, Jan. 18, 1782, Official Letterbook B, 325-26; Morris to Ezekiel Cornell, Nov. 29, 1782, Official Letterbook D, 422-23; Morris to Thomas Tillotson, June 22, 1783, Official Letterbook E, 382-83; all in Morris Correspondence, Lib. Cong.

The public debt was vital to the strategy of centralization. As long as it belonged to Congress it was a potential bond of union. It gave rise to an economic motive for supporting the central government; its existence justified the demand for federal taxes. From Congress's standpoint, possession of the debt was especially important at the end of the war, when military necessity could no longer be pleaded as a reason for strengthening the central authority. Only the obligation of Congress to discharge the debt remained to justify the request for enlarged powers.

The way in which Morris and the Nationalists proposed to deal with the public debt violated the letter and spirit of the Articles of Confederation. Under the Articles, the common charges of the war, including the expenses of the federal government, were to be paid by requisitions, and the same procedure applied to debts. It was expected that Congress would ascertain the amount of the debt and draw up a requisition assessing a certain proportion of it upon each state. As the states paid the requisition, Congress would discharge the debt.

Morris and the Nationalists took the position that the debt could be paid only by federal taxes, levied and collected by Congress. Their argument was that the debt represented an obligation of Congress rather than the thirteen states. Morris discerned an implied contract between Congress and the public creditors which could only be validated if Congress had perfect control of the revenue to pay them. It did not matter that Congress had possessed no power of taxation when the debts were incurred. The creditors, he said, had trusted the Union, not the states. The obligation to them could not be fulfilled unless the Articles of Confederation were amended. In short, the existence of the public debt implied a federal power of taxation.[42]

This line of reasoning became fashionable in Congress during the Nationalist ascendancy, but it presumed a condition that did not exist, and while the request for a federal tax awaited unanimous ratification, the states began to take independent action, proceeding in ways that were feasible under existing circumstances and consonant with the Articles of Confederation. As we have seen, they

42. Morris to the Governors of Massachusetts, *et al.*, July 27, 1781, to President of Congress, Aug. 28, 1781, Wharton, ed., *Diplomatic Correspondence*, IV, 608-9, 674-75.

made inroads on the army debt, assuming pay due to their troops in 1781 and 1782. They steadily absorbed the Quartermaster and Commissary debt, taking up the certificates from their citizens in payment of taxes.

There were foes of the Nationalists in every state, who thought in terms of solutions that were compatible with the existing political system. They extenuated the failure of requisitions during the war. When the war drew to a close and requisitions were still unproductive, they sometimes admitted that the system would not work, but their alternative was separate action by the states. They supposed—and their solution was quite feasible—that when the whole amount of the debt had been determined, Congress would apportion it among the states, declaring each one responsible for a certain share, a money sum, and allow each to redeem its quota in its own way, acting so far as possible upon its own citizens.[43]

Another possibility which entailed no revision of the Articles of Confederation was the redemption of debt by the sale of western lands. Although Congress could have no firm title until the states with claims to western lands ceded them to the United States, it was widely expected that the federal government would fall heir to a great tract west of the Alleghenies. Its value could not be estimated, but there was vague confidence that it would be enough to sink the foreign debt and probably the domestic debt as well.

Morris recognized a "fatal tendency" at work. He scouted rumors that the public debt would ever be divided among the states; this, he said, implied a principle of disunion which would be ruinous to the nation. Congress must pay the debt out of the revenue from federal taxes. Morris likewise discounted western lands as a means of debt redemption. Sold for public securities, they would bring almost nothing, for the common people could not afford to buy them, and moneyed men would abstain from so remote a speculation. In any case, he argued, western lands would never provide the regular and certain revenues needed to pay interest and discharge the principal of the debt. There was no substitute for federal taxes.[44]

As Morris defended Congressional ownership of the debt and the necessity of federal taxes, he moved to consolidate the mass of

43. Morris to the Governors of Massachusetts, *et al.*, July 27, 1781, *ibid.*, 608.
44. Morris to the President of Congress, Aug. 28, 1781, July 29, 1782, *ibid.*, 674-75, V, 632-34.

certificates and other claims left over from the Revolution in such a way that they would be a clear obligation of Congress. Under his prodding, Congress early in 1782 began the settlement of its accounts with individuals. Claims of all sorts were "liquidated," i.e., inspected, given a formal money value, and entered on Congress's books as an interest-bearing debt. The result was that most of the remaining debts of the Revolution (except what the states had already absorbed) were consolidated as an obligation of the federal government. The "public debt," which originally included just loan certificates, grew by accretion. The remnant of the Quartermaster and Commissary debt was assumed by Congress, along with the extensive claims of the discharged army.

This action undoubtedly forestalled an early assumption of the Revolutionary debt by the states. It preserved an economic interest in an extension of Congressional powers and committed the country to a course of action predicated on a revision of the Articles of Confederation. In the years after 1783, when the Nationalists succumbed to the disintegrative tendencies of the postwar era, it kept alive the movement for national government.

8

The Aristocracy Suppressed

"I sometimes almost lament that the Aristocracy in 1783 was suppressed."

> —Stephen Higginson to
> Samuel Osgood,
> Feb. 21, 1787.

THE germ of a national government had materialized by 1782, but it required a quickening flow of revenues. Without federal taxes there could be no bank nor loyal public creditors, no evolution of Congress into an effective central government. A beginning had been made in the impost resolution of 1781. It became the central purpose of Morris's administration to secure its adoption. "The political existence of America," said Morris, "depends on the accomplishment of this plan."[1]

The impost was no more than an entering wedge to establish the principle of federal taxation. Its estimated yield was only $500,000 a year, perhaps a million in time of peace. Although this amount was sufficient to pay interest on the federal debt in 1781, it was inadequate for the enlarged debt which the Nationalists assumed in the closing years of the war; nor did the expected income allow for administrative expenses or the interest on foreign loans. Morris intended to sponsor taxes on polls, property, and commodities, but the impost had to come first.[2]

1. Morris to Nathaniel Appleton, Apr. 16, 1782, Wharton, ed., *Diplomatic Correspondence*, V, 311-12.
2. *Journals*, XXII, 439; Morris to the President of Congress, Aug. 28, 1781, to Franklin, Nov. 27, 1781, *ibid.*, IV, 675, V, 16; Morris to the Speaker of the Assembly of Pennsylvania, Feb. 13, 1782, to the President of Congress, Feb. 27, 1782, Official Letterbook C, 12-13, 60-62, Morris Correspondence, Lib. Cong.

From the Office of Finance, he launched a barrage of correspondence, flaying the delinquent state legislatures in language that often bordered on insult and sometimes rose to the imperious tone of a sovereign addressing his subjects. They must ratify the impost: victory was impossible without foreign loans, and these were unavailable until Congress was in a position to guarantee repayment out of its own incomes. "Let us apply to borrow where we may, our mouths will always be stopped by the one word, security." Carrying this argument to its logical extreme, he wrote: "He . . . who opposes the grant of such revenue . . . labors to continue the war, and, of consequence to shed more blood, to produce more devastation, and to extend and prolong the miseries of mankind."[3]

Morris's plea that the impost was necessary as a war measure was forceful, but it lost much of its urgency when he managed to obtain foreign loans without the tax. He deliberately understated and tried to conceal the amount of aid being received from abroad, but the fact was that, under his astute management, it was enough to support the limited campaigns after Yorktown. Although he still warned that the hope of the enemy was in the "derangement of our finances," his arguments were vitiated in the spring of 1782, when changes in the British ministry forecast peace.[4]

This made it necessary for Morris to shift the emphasis and represent the impost, not as a war measure, but as a fund to discharge the debts of the Revolution. The public debt (still confined at this period to loan certificates) was a sacred obligation. The public creditors, of whom widows and orphans formed a major component, had suffered from the criminal negligence of the nation. Aside from the moral obligation to pay them, Morris intimated that the Republic would be politically insecure until these individuals were reconciled to its existence by receiving the money owed them. The impost was therefore vital to national welfare on grounds of public policy. With it, the nation would possess the "inestimable jewel"

3. Morris to the Governors of the States, Jan. 3, 1782, to the President of Congress, Feb. 11, 1782, Wharton, ed., *Diplomatic Correspondence,* V, 85, 153.

4. In May 1782, Morris told Congress that he had withheld information of the latest French loan out of concern that the states would relax their efforts. Morris to the President of Congress, May 27, 1782, *ibid.,* 442-43. See Morris to Franklin, Nov. 27, 1781, and compare the tone of his public communications, *ibid.,* 26, 423-24.

of public credit. Without it, the Union would be a coterie of weak, impoverished states.[5]

Convinced, as he was, that the state legislatures were generally immune to all considerations of honor and sound policy, Morris must have doubted the effect of his arguments. However, he had more than verbal supplications at his command. Entrenched at the strategic center of the federal government and wielding an enormous personal influence, he was able, in some degree, to manipulate men and events.

When Morris took office in 1781, the impost had seemed well on the road to an early adoption. He was content to bide his time and withhold proposals for other federal taxes. By 1782, with peace in sight and the impost still pending, he recognized a state of emergency. War provided the most favorable auspices for the realization of the Nationalist program; peace would jeopardize it. Accordingly Morris began to marshal his forces. While he continued to harry the state legislatures with unabated vigor, he tried to bully Congress into compliance with the details of his larger program, and, at the same time, reach out from the Office of Finance to rally conservative and creditor support in the states. From July or August 1782 until the following spring, Morris and his close associates pressed to accomplish their program before peace was declared.

In May 1782, Morris prevailed upon Congress to send special delegations of its members to plead with those legislatures which had not ratified the impost. When the Congressional delegation arrived in New York, Governor Clinton called the legislature into special session. Alexander Hamilton, who was Morris's tax receiver in that state, hastened to Poughkeepsie, where he almost certainly drew up a series of resolutions which his father-in-law, Philip Schuyler, introduced into the Senate. The resolutions called for enlarging Congress's powers of taxation and proposed a general convention to revise the Articles of Confederation. They were agreed to by both houses and sent to Congress.[6]

5. Morris to the Governor of Rhode Island, Dec. 29, 1781, to the President of Congress, July 29, 1782, *ibid.*, 77, 623-24.
6. Morris to the Governors of the States, May 16, 1782, to the President of Congress, May 17, 1782, *ibid.*, 423-24, 426; *Journals*, XXII, 289; Bancroft, *History of the Constitution*, I, 37-38; Morris to Hamilton, July 22, 1782, Official Letterbook D, 33, Morris Correspondence, Lib. Cong.; Hamilton to Morris, July 13, 1782, to Governor Clinton, July 16, 1782, to Morris, [July] 22, 1782, Hamilton, ed., *Works of Hamilton*, I, 286, 287, 287-89.

Meanwhile, Morris had stirred up public creditors throughout the country by discontinuing all interest payments on loan certificates. The previous year he had stopped the practice of paying interest by the issue of loan certificates in lieu of money. Morris observed at the time that his order had caused "much clamor" among the creditors and would likely cause more; but he wanted to impress upon them that their loss resulted from the failure of states to grant the impost. "I must direct . . . those who are injured to those who have done them wrong." To Franklin he had confided his "well-grounded expectation that the clamors of the public creditors would induce the states to adopt the impost."[7]

The greater part of the loan certificate debt still drew interest in bills of exchange on France. Morris now hoped to discontinue this mode of payment, not only because it drained his foreign credits, but also because he hoped to mobilize the creditors behind federal taxes by reducing them to complete dependence on Congress's domestic revenues. With this purpose in view, he requested in an official letter that the French government honor its promise (given early in the war) to pay all bills of exchange drawn for interest on loan certificates without deducting the amount from money currently loaned by France to the United States. He informed Franklin privately, however, that he wished to "remove the load from France to ourselves." It would be better if "the people were taught to look at home for the basis of national credit." France shortly renounced any obligation to pay bills in excess of current American funds in France. Imparting this news to Congress, Morris advised that no more bills be drawn and that future payment of interest on loan certificates should be made contingent on the establishment of federal taxes.[8]

As the news of his recommendation leaked out, anxious public creditors began visiting the Office of Finance. Morris suggested that they form an organization to protest the stoppage of interest, declaring that their only hope lay in the establishment of federal taxes—

7. Morris to the Governors of the Several States, Oct. 19, 1781, to Franklin, Nov. 17, 1781, to the Governors of the States, Jan. 3, 1782, Wharton, ed., *Diplomatic Correspondence*, IV, 793-94, V, 16, 85.

8. Morris to Franklin, Nov. 27, 1781, to the President of Congress, May 27, 1782, *ibid.*, V, 17, 442-43; Report of Resolutions respecting Loan Officers Accounts, June 12, 1782, Report to Congress . . . June 26, 1782, Official Letterbook C, 415-16, 449-50, Morris Correspondence, Lib. Cong.; *Journals*, XXII, 365.

and not the impost alone, for it was insufficient; other taxes were necessary. He advised them to press such views on members of Congress and organize public creditors in the various states to oust members of state legislatures who opposed federal taxes. The Philadelphia creditors soon held a meeting at which they decided to memorialize Congress and write the creditors in other states. A committee drew up a petition to Congress which, after the customary allusions to widows, orphans, and patriots, registered a protest against the discontinuance of interest payments and underscored the necessity of funding the public debt by federal taxes. Congress promptly referred the memorial to the Financier for a report.[9]

Morris had not been altogether satisfied with the outcome of the creditors' meeting: feeling had run high, and gentlemen had not been able to suppress their sense of outrage. He summoned the creditors' committee to the Office of Finance and warned them against the use of threatening or violent language; they must not let it appear that their sole concern was their own payment. They should speak not merely as holders of loan certificates, but rather make "one Common Cause with the whole of the public Creditors of every kind to unite their Interest so that they might be able to have influence on all the Legislatures in the several States."[10] It was imperative that the existing public creditors be aligned with the creditors-to-be, who would emerge as Congress settled other categories of the Revolutionary debt; only in the name of the entire Revolutionary debt was it justifiable to plead for federal taxes beyond the impost. Concluding his interview, Morris assured the Philadelphia creditors of his full support and promised to make a report in favor of federal taxes adequate to the entire debt.

The letter which the Philadelphia committee sent to creditors in other states revealed the Financier's hand. It emphasized that some general plan, other than requisitions, was necessary to fund the debt. Since the impost alone was inadequate, Congress must be instructed in its duty to sponsor additional federal taxes. The creditors could help by petitioning Congress as individuals and as organized

9. Official Diary, June 25, 28, 1782, Morris Correspondence, Lib. Cong.; Portfolio 146, no. 12, Broadside Coll., Rare Books Div., Lib. Cong.; *Journals*, XXII, 373n; *Penn. Gazette,* July 5, 1782; *Penn. Packet,* July 6, 1782.

10. Official Diary, July 9, 10, 1782, Morris Correspondence, Lib. Cong.; John Taylor Gilman to Josiah Bartlett, July 9, 1782, Benjamin Huntington to Andrew Huntington, July 13, 1782, Burnett, ed., *Letters,* VI, 380-81, 382.

groups; and whenever Congress requested such taxes, the creditors must do everything in their power to ensure support by the states.[11]

Morris soon reported to Congress on the creditors' petition. In an elaborate treatise on the public debt—the most systematic exposition of his ideas he ever committed to writing—he reminded Congress that the impost was inadequate and that federal taxes on polls, property, and commodities were necessary. Alluding to the petition, Morris declared that he rejoiced to see this "numerous, meritorious and oppressed body of men . . . beginning to exert themselves."[12]

The Philadelphia creditors were continuing their exertions. After petitioning Congress, they memorialized the Pennsylvania legislature, complaining that while other states were assuming such federal obligations as army pay and Quartermaster and Commissary certificates, Pennsylvania had done nothing but remit money to the federal Treasury; thereby she discriminated against her own citizens. If Congress did not pay them, the creditors asked that the state do so and withhold the money from Congress.

The Pennsylvania legislature notified Congress of its objection to the stoppage of interest. When this did not prevent Congress from accepting Morris's recommendation, Pennsylvania delivered an ultimatum: Unless means were quickly found to pay the interest on the public debt, the important state of Pennsylvania would assume payments due to her own citizens. To the extent that she did so, she would divorce herself from the general financial system of Congress. Fully appreciating the threat, Congress could still do no more than advance another plea for the impost and pass a special, temporizing requisition for $1,200,000, which allowed the states to fulfill their quotas by paying interest directly to public creditors.[13]

New York public creditors now joined the action, holding a meeting at Albany in September, presided over by Philip Schuyler. Hamilton was again present, and although he had no specific instructions

11. Portfolio 146, no. 12, Broadside Coll., Rare Books Div., Lib. Cong.

12. The report is in *Journals*, XXII, 429-46. Morris sent copies of it to his tax receivers for their information. Morris to the Receivers of the several States, Sept. 12, 1782, Official Letterbook D, 190, Morris Correspondence, Lib. Cong.

13. Portfolio 142, no. 12, Broadside Coll., Rare Books Div., Lib. Cong.; *Journals*, XXII, 447-48, XXIII, 539-40, 545, 553-55, 564, 586, XXIV, 99-105; Madison's Notes of Debates, *ibid.*, XXIII, 850, 860-62; Morris to Loan Officers . . . Sept. 9, 1782, Official Letterbook D, 182, Morris Correspondence, Lib. Cong.; *American State Papers, Finance*, I, 147; Madison to Edmund Randolph, Dec. 19, 1782, Burnett, ed., *Letters*, VI, 559-60.

from Morris, he was sufficiently aware of the Financier's mind to advise a creditors' committee to demand the establishment of federal taxes. The meeting proposed a state convention to take some kind of unified action, and a committee was appointed to correspond with creditors in other parts of the country with a view to holding a national convention.[14]

Besieged by creditors and goaded by its grimly determined Superintendent of Finance, Congress settled down to an almost continuous discussion of methods of funding the enlarged debts it would hold after the war. A grand committee agreed in principle on the necessity for federal taxes on land, polls, and whiskey; but each of these proposals was voted down on the floor. Divergence of interest among the states prevented agreement on any specific tax beyond the impost, and Congress was disposed to wait for its adoption before proceeding further. Since, by the late summer of 1782, all the states had given their consent except Rhode Island, the impost seemed on the verge of success. Scarcely conceiving that a negative reply was possible, Congress peremptorily asked the state legislature for an immediate decision.[15]

The circumstances were less propitious than Congress imagined, however, for recent elections had brought the "country party" to power, and Rhode Island's previous delegates to Congress, who had favored the impost, were being replaced by men who soon became its ardent foes—David Howell, Jonathan Arnold, and John Collins. It was Howell who almost singlehandedly wrecked the impost of 1781. Arriving at Philadelphia, he found everybody in favor of it, whereupon he set himself to oppose it, countering the official propaganda from his seat in Congress. When Congress alluded to Rhode Island's willfulness in blocking a necessary reform, Howell congratulated the legislature for standing alone as the last defender of liberty. When Morris declared that foreign loans could not be had without the impost, Howell enlarged upon the aid being obtained without it.

14. East, *Business Enterprise*, 107; Joel Munsell, ed., *Annals of Albany* (Albany, 1850), 282; Hamilton to Morris, Sept. 4, 28, 1782, Hamilton, ed., *Works of Hamilton*, I, 306-7, 309-11; Morris to Hamilton, Sept. 5, Oct. 16, 1782, Official Letterbook D, 175, 314-15, Morris Correspondence, Lib. Cong.; Hamilton to Morris, Oct. 9, 1783, Lodge, ed., *Works of Hamilton*, IX, 296.

15. *Journals*, XXII, 439, XXIII, 545-47, 551-53, 564-71, 604-6, 643-45; North Carolina Delegates to the Governor of North Carolina, Oct. 22, 1782, Burnett, ed., *Letters*, VI, 516-18.

He argued that Rhode Island was expected to surrender the advantage she derived from her trading position, while other states had not been willing to cede claims to western lands.[16]

Howell was in Congress when Rhode Island was asked for an immediate answer. Rising to the challenge, he and his colleague Jonathan Arnold advised the legislature not to yield. It was "clear as the Meridian sun," that the impost, once granted, would be a permanent accession. The Rhode Island delegates outlined a process by which Congress would grow huge by feeding on revenue. Larger expenses would soon make it necessary to adopt other federal taxes, such as those which were even now being proposed, after which "the bond of Union to use the phrase of the Advocates of these Measures, would be complete. And we will add the Yoke of Tyranny fixed on all the states, and the Chains Rivotted."[17]

Moved by these arguments, the Rhode Island legislature unanimously rejected the impost. Congress, unwilling to accept the decision as final, appointed a commission of its members to travel to the state and make a special appeal. Armed with concessions intended to take off various objections raised by the legislature, the commission left Philadelphia, heading north. Not far along the way, one of the delegates happened to mention that before leaving the city he had received a letter from a friend saying that Virginia had repealed its grant of the impost. The commission returned to Philadelphia, where other letters verified the report. Dumbfounded, Congress abandoned the mission.[18]

The wrath of Congress fell upon David Howell, and an attempt was made to disgrace him. Howell had written a personal letter which dwelt on the success of American loans in Europe. He expressed his satisfaction that American credit had not been bolstered by such devices as the impost, lest there be a temptation to contract too large a debt. "Posterity," he commented, "when they feel the

16. Allan Nevins, *The American States During and After the Revolution, 1775-1789* (N.Y., 1924), 226-27. See the letters of David Howell and the Rhode Island delegates from July 1782 on, in Burnett, ed., *Letters.*

17. Rhode Island Delegates to the Governor of Rhode Island, Oct. 15, 1782, Burnett, ed., *Letters,* VI, 503-7.

18. *Journals,* XXIII, 770-72, 783-84, 788-90, 798-810, 811-12, 831; Madison's Notes of Debates, *ibid.,* 860-62, 864, 871-72; Madison to Edmund Pendleton, Dec. 30, 1782, Burnett, ed., *Letters,* VI, 569-70; Bancroft, *History of the Constitution,* I, 44.

Weight of Debt . . . transmitted on them, will admire at its Extent and rejoice it went no further."[19]   His remarks were published in a newspaper and eventually called to the attention of Congress.   Since the contents of the letter implied access to information supposedly secret, a resolution was adopted to investigate the authorship.   Though "visibly perturbated," Howell at first said nothing, but when the inquiry was pursued, he declared himself the author, saying only that his remarks were substantially correct.   His confession did not prevent a formal vote of censure, unanimous except for the Rhode Island delegates.[20]

When Howell went to the Office of Finance to get extracts from Franklin's correspondence which would show the truth of his statements about foreign loans, Morris would disclose nothing without a specific order of Congress—it was a "delicate affair."   Howell nevertheless managed to obtain copies of letters of the Secretary of Foreign Affairs, along with extracts from Congress's journals, which he forwarded to Providence.   The Rhode Island legislature completely vindicated Howell and his fellow delegates, declaring its sense of the "meritorious Services rendered to this state, and to the Cause of Freedom in General, by the firm and patriotic conduct of the . . . Delegates; particularly in their strenuous Exertions to defeat the Operations of Measures which this State considered as dangerous to the public liberty."[21]

Rhode Island's action jolted the Nationalists, who realized that time was running out and that they would soon lose "that great friend to sovereign authority, a foreign war," without having won their minimum objective.[22] Morris declared that as a patriot he would desire a continuation of the war until the government was strengthened and the people got used to paying taxes. Washington, although he described himself as not one who would wish the war to continue

19. Howell to John Carter, Oct. 16, 1782, Burnett, ed., *Letters*, VI, 509.

20. *Journals*, XXIII, 770, 791-93, 812, 813-19, 821-22; Madison's Notes of Debates, *ibid.*, 863-64, 867, 868; Jonathan Arnold to the Governor of Rhode Island, Dec. 6, 1782, Burnett, ed., *Letters*, VI, 555-56.

21. Resolution of Feb. sess. 1783, State Papers of New Hampshire and Rhode Island, 1775-1788, Papers of Cont. Cong., no. 64, Lib. Cong.

22. Gouverneur Morris to General Greene, Dec. 24, 1781, Sparks, *Gouverneur Morris*, I, 239-40.   There is a remarkable letter on this general subject from Gouverneur Morris to Matthew Ridley, Aug. 6, 1782, Ridley Papers, box 1, Mass. Hist. Soc.

"till the Powers of Congress—or political systems—and general form of Government" were perfected, nevertheless felt that the fruits of victory would be lost if Congress was not given more power. Madison observed early in 1783 that the following months would determine whether "prosperity and tranquility, or confusion and disunion" would result from the Revolution.[23]

Convinced that affairs had reached a crisis, the Nationalists in Congress were in a mood for drastic action, and they welcomed the long expected arrival of a delegation from the main army, encamped at Newburgh on the Hudson River. Discontent had long smoldered in the army. Feeling had lately run so high that Washington had been afraid to leave camp to spend the winter at Mount Vernon. Although the inactive troops were better supplied than ever before, their mood was explosive. Officers and men of all ranks were soured by lack of pay and were especially bitter because administrative personnel had continued to draw salaries while they had not. Many officers had spent their personal funds to keep up the appearances of their rank, and with the end of the war saw themselves impoverished and without careers, while men of their own station had grown wealthy in civil life.[24] Scarcely any of the officers could look forward to a career in the service because the peace time establishment was certain to be inconsiderable, nor could they expect to bask in the preferment of their countrymen. Most of the troops at Newburgh were from New England, where anti-military traditions were strong, and the citizens were likely to view discharged officers with

23. Robert Morris to Matthew Ridley, Oct. 6, 1782, *Henkel's Catalogue, No. 1183*, 41; Washington to Dr. William Gordon, Oct. 23, 1783, Worthington C. Ford, ed., *The Writings of George Washington* (N.Y., 1889-93), X, 103-4. See Washington to Governor Harrison, Mar. 4, 1783, to Arthur Lee, Mar. 29, 1783, to Tench Tilghman, Apr. 24, 1783, John C. Fitzpatrick, ed., *The Writings of George Washington . . .* (Wash., 1931-44), XXVI, 183-85, 265-66, 358-59; Hamilton to John Laurens, Aug. 15, 1782, Lodge, ed., *Works of Hamilton*, IX, 280-81; Duane to Hamilton, Feb. 17, 1783, Madison to Edmund Randolph, Feb. 25, 1783, Burnett, ed., *Letters*, VII, 45-46, 58; Luzerne to Vergennes, Feb. 6, 1783, Bancroft, *History of the Constitution*, I, 293-94; Hartley to Franklin, Oct. 4, 1782, Wharton, ed., *Diplomatic Correspondence*, V, 797; Greene to Reed, Apr. 23, 1783, Reed, *Reed*, II, 395.

24. Rufus King's relation of a conversation with William Duer, 1788, Charles R. King, *Life of Rufus King* (N.Y., 1894), I, 621-22; Washington to Joseph Jones, Dec. 14, 1782, to General William Heath, Feb. 5, 1783, Fitzpatrick, ed., *Writings of Washington*, XXV, 430-31, XXVI, 185-88; Henry Knox to Benjamin Lincoln, Dec. 20, 1782, Samuel F. Drake, *Life and Correspondence of Henry Knox* (Boston, 1873), 77; Madison's Notes of Debates, *Journals*, XXV, 852.

disparagement or even contempt.[25]   What aroused the bitterest emotion of both officers and men, however, was the prospect of being cheated out of the money actually due them for their services.   They were afraid that when the war was over their just claims would be ignored by a country at peace.   In January 1783 three officers of high rank, headed by General Alexander McDougall, presented a statement of army grievances to Congress.   It was a formal and strongly worded remonstrance, demanding some immediate pay for both officers and men, else "fatal consequences" were likely to ensue.   Believing that it could expect nothing from the country if its claims were ignored until after disbandment, the army requested a general settlement of accounts, in which all claims for pay, rations, forage, clothing, and other items should be given a money value and entered to the credit of individuals.[26]

The most controversial demand of the army related to officers' pensions.   In 1780 Congress had succumbed to an ultimatum from its military officers and granted those who remained in service for the duration of the war a life pension of half their regular pay. This action was taken over the objection of the New England states, where pensions were regarded as the foundation of a military caste.[27] The officers at Newburgh were aware of popular sentiment on this point, and as a conciliatory measure they proposed that their pensions be commuted into a cash sum.   Their memorial did not stipulate whether they expected to be paid by Congress or by the states; it merely asked Congress to determine the cash equivalent of the pensions and "point out a mode" of payment.   Unquestionably, the majority of the officers expected to be referred to their states for payment.   Indeed, the officers of the Massachusetts line had already

25. Samuel Parsons informed General McDougall in September 1783 that discharged Connecticut officers were applying for a grant of land from New York, as they were unable to remain in Connecticut, "without Honor." If New York refused asylum, he said, the officers would have no other way of avoiding "daily Insults" and "contemptuous malignant Neglect" than to settle farther west. Parsons to McDougall, Sept. 20, 1783, Alexander McDougall Papers, N.Y. Pub. Lib.

26. The petition is in *Journals*, XXIV, 291-93.   An earlier version is in Washington Papers, CCXIII, 90-91, Lib. Cong.

27. "That the Alternative offered to the then Congress was—either to have no Army . . . or to grant the half pay—are facts of unquestionable notoriety."   Paraphrase of an address of the Connecticut Assembly, Papers of Cont. Cong., no. 20, I, 345-47.   Every delegate from Massachusetts, Connecticut, Rhode Island and New Jersey voted in the negative.   *Journals*, XVIII, 958-62.

applied to their state for a commutation of pensions, but the legislature deferred action, not knowing what Congress would decide on
a matter which was essentially federal in nature.[28]

The presentation of the army's grievances rekindled the hopes of
the Nationalists surrounding Robert Morris, for it promised to re-
cruit another legion to their cause. Their first maneuver was to align
the army with the public creditors and the Nationalists in Congress.
In private conversations, the army delegates were made to feel that
the great majority of Congress was "rather pleased . . . at the address's coming on," but they were told it was an error to propose
that the officers be directed to their states for payment of the commuted pensions. Congress would oppose this move and take no
action on pensions, at least until all hope of obtaining federal taxes
was at an end. Morris sharpened the point in an interview by warn-
ing that until federal taxes were operative the army could expect
little in the way of pay. Seeing how the land lay, the army delegates
kept silent as to what sources of payment they wished or expected
and in their formal interview with a committee of Congress enlarged
upon the need for federal taxes, assuring the committee that the
army favored an expansion of Congressional powers. Reporting
back to Newburgh on their progress, the delegates inquired of the
officers at camp what they thought of joining with Congress and the
public creditors in a drive for federal taxes.[29]

With the army being recruited as a pressure group, men closely
associated with the Financier began creating an atmosphere of crisis,
reviving memories of Cromwell's Roundheads, who, in an analogous
situation during the Puritan Revolution, had turned on Parliament

28. On the prospect of payment by the states, see Benjamin Lincoln to Wash-
ington, Oct. 14, 1782, Ford, ed., *Writings of Washington*, X, 93n; Lincoln to Knox,
Dec. 3, 1782, Knox to Lincoln, Mar. 3, 1783, Knox Papers, X, 29, XI, 176, Mass.
Hist. Soc.; Knox to Lincoln, Dec. 20, 1782, to McDougall, Feb. 21, 1783, Drake,
Life of Knox, 77, 78-79; Gouverneur Morris to General Greene, Feb. 15, 1783,
Sparks, *Gouverneur Morris*, I, 250-51; Arthur St. Clair to Major General Mc-
Dougall, Colonel Ogden and Colonel Brooks, Jan. 5, 1782, McDougall Papers,
N.Y. Pub. Lib. On the action in Massachusetts, see Col. Brooks to Knox, Sept. 26,
Oct. 17, 1782, Knox to Lincoln, Nov. 25, 1782, Samuel Osgood to Knox, Dec. 4,
1782, Knox Papers, X, 13, 60, 123, 130, Mas. Hist. Soc.
29. General McDougall to Henry Knox, Jan. 9, 1783, General McDougall and
Colonel Ogden to Knox, Feb. 8, 1783, Burnett, ed., *Letters*, VII, 14n, 35n; Sparks,
Gouverneur Morris, I, 250-51; *Journals*, XXIV, 43-44, 48; Madison's Notes of
Debates, *ibid.*, XXV, 847-55, 857. See Samuel Osgood to Henry Knox, Dec. 4,
1782, Burnett, ed., *Letters*, VI, 553.

and subdued it when an attempt was made to disband them without pay. Assistant Financier Gouverneur Morris spread reports that the army had secretly decided to stand against the country until its demands were met. "The army have swords in their hands," he darkly observed to John Jay. "You know enough of the history of mankind to know much more than I have said, and possibly much more than they themselves yet think of." Writing to Henry Knox, who was stationed at Newburgh, he advocated the alliance of the army with the creditors: "The army may now influence the Legislatures, and if you will permit me a Metaphor from your own Profession after you have carried the post the public Creditors will garrison it for you." He also sounded out General Greene, preparing him for the crisis.[30] Hamilton, now a member of Congress, corresponded with General Washington, taking pains to inform him that the army would "subsist itself to procure justice to itself." In conversation with members of Congress, Richard Peters, who was on the Board of War, and Hamilton reported that a decision had already been taken at camp to resist disbandment—a public declaration to this effect would soon be made. Affairs were so far advanced, they said, that plans were actually being formed to supply the army after the declaration was published.[31]

Rumors flew about Philadelphia that "a most violent political storm" was brewing, that the army would overthrow Washington and replace him with a "less scrupulous guardian of their interests," that the army was "ripe for annihilating [Congress]." Madison, who was not in the inner councils of the Morris group, wrote: "The opinion seems to be well founded that the arms which have secured the liberties of the country will not be laid down until justice is secured." Arthur Lee, now in Congress, viewed the turmoil from a different angle. "Every Engine is at work here," he informed Sam Adams, "to obtain permanent taxes .... The terror of a mutinying Army is played off with considerable efficacy."[32]

30. Gouverneur Morris to John Jay, Jan. 1, 1783, to General Greene, Feb. 15, 1783, Sparks, *Gouverneur Morris*, I, 249, 250-51; Gouverneur Morris to General Knox, Feb. 7, 1783, Burnett, ed., *Letters*, VII, 34n. See Gouverneur Morris to Matthew Ridley, Jan. 1, 1783, Ridley Papers, Mass. Hist. Soc.

31. Hamilton to Washington, Feb. 7, 1783, Lodge, ed., *Works of Hamilton*, IX, 310-13; Madison's Notes of Debates, *Journals*, XXV, 906-7; Madison to Edmund Randolph, Feb. 13, 25, 1783, Burnett, ed., *Letters*, VII, 44, 57-58.

32. Bancroft, *History of the Constitution*, I, 296-97, 300; Madison to Edmund

Perversely, the army remained quiet. Although emotion ran high, the officers were the influential element at Newburgh, and they had been committed by their leaders—Washington, Henry Knox, and Secretary of War Benjamin Lincoln—to await the results of the petition to Congress. It became necessary, therefore, for the Nationalists to move their crisis from Philadelphia to Newburgh. Colonel Brooks, one of the army's deputies to Congress, returned to camp in February allegedly to prepare the officers for some "manly, Vigorous Association with the other public Creditors," but he was lukewarm in executing his mission. Colonel Walter Stewart was more determined. Said to be a "kind of agent" from certain persons in Congress and the federal administration, he arrived in camp about March 8. Rumors quickly spread: it was universally expected that the army would refuse to disband; the public creditors would stand with the troops; many members of Congress favored a display of force; the army could expect the aid of the Financier. According to the reputed statement of William Duer, who was an intimate of Robert Morris, when Morris was asked how the army could be fed when opposed by the country, he replied, "I will feed them."[33]

Hamilton endeavored to coach General Washington in the role allotted to him. Washington's unmatched prestige was one of the Nationalist's greatest assets, a fact of which they were thoroughly aware. The problem was to guide the army's discontent into constructive channels: "This," wrote Hamilton, "Your Excellency's influence must effect." Hamilton advised him to act discreetly in the forthcoming crisis. Washington must not forfeit the army's confidence by opposing any action it might take, but neither should he espouse the army's case too openly, or he would lose the confidence of the civilian population. At the moment of "extremity," he would

---

Randolph, Feb. 13, 25, 1783, Arthur Lee to Samuel Adams, Jan. 29, 1783, Burnett, ed., *Letters*, VII, 44, 57-58; Joseph Jones to Washington, Feb. 27, 1783, Fitzpatrick, ed., *Writings of Washington*, XXV, 431n; Brutus to [Knox], Feb. 12, 1783, Knox Papers, XI, 120, Mass. Hist. Soc. See Von Steuben to Knox, Feb. 25, 1783, Brutus to Knox, Feb. 27, 1783, *ibid.*, 160, 165.

33. Henry Knox to General McDougall, Feb. 21, Mar. 12, 1783, Drake, *Life of Knox*, 78-80; John Armstrong, Jr., to General Gates, Apr. 29, 1783, Burnett, ed., *Letters*, VII, 155n; Rufus King's relation of a conversation with William Duer, 1788, King, *Life of King*, I, 621-22; Bancroft, *History of the Constitution*, I, 93-94; Horatio Gates to John Armstrong, Jr., June 22, 1783, *ibid.*, 318; Washington to Joseph Jones, Mar. 12, 1783, to Hamilton, Mar. 12, 1783, Fitzpatrick, ed., *Writings of Washington*, XXVI, 213-16, 216-18.

then be able to "guide the torrent and to bring order perhaps even good, out of the confusion." Lest there be any doubt about the goal of all this effort, Hamilton reminded him: "The Great desideratum at present is the establishment of general funds . . . in this the influence of the army, properly directed, may cooperate."[34]

Morris wheeled his big guns into line by announcing his resignation. In a dramatic message to Congress, he said that recent events made him doubt whether public credit would ever be established. To increase the debt while the prospect of paying it diminished, he said, did not comport with his ideas of integrity. He gave Congress until the end of May to produce a comprehensive plan for paying the debt; otherwise he would quit his office. "I will never," he concluded, "be the minister of injustice."[35]

His resignation and the words in which it was couched were widely condemned, particularly when, without the consent of Congress, he published his letter of resignation in the *Pennsylanvia Packet*. He was attacked in the press for having dealt a "mortal blow" to what remained of public credit and betraying his trust as finance minister. Even Madison, who was an unwavering Nationalist, wished that Morris's attackers had "less handle" for the purpose. But among the mercantile and conservative classes of the middle states, the resignation apparently had its calculated effect. It was a denunciation of current policy by the great champion of strong government and sound money.[36]

Morris's strategy was to force Congress into an aggressive position. He had given up striving for such fractional gains as the impost and was now determined to push through a schedule of federal taxes which would support the increasing debt and provide the basis for a vigorous central government. The initial action had to come

34. See Hamilton to Schuyler, Feb. 18, 1782, Lodge, ed., *Works of Hamilton*, IX, 235-36; Greene to Hamilton, Jan. 10, 1781, Hamilton, ed., *Works of Hamilton*, I, 204; Hamilton to Washington, Feb. 7, 1783, Burnett, ed., *Letters*, VII, 33-35. See Madison's Notes of Debates, *Journals*, XXV, 907.

35. Morris to President of Congress, Jan. 24, 1783, Wharton, ed., *Diplomatic Correspondence*, VI, 228-29.

36. Morris to President of Congress, Feb. 26, 1783, *ibid.*, 266; *Journals*, XXIV, 151; Madison's Notes of Debates, *ibid.*, XXV, 916-20; *Penn. Packet*, Mar. 4, 1783; "Lucius," *Freeman's Journal*, Mar. 5, 12, 1783; Arthur Lee to Sam Adams, Mar. 5, 1783, Madison to Edmund Randolph, Mar. 11, 1783, Burnett, *Letters*, VII, 69; Hamilton to Washington, Apr. 9, 1783, Lodge, ed., *Works of Hamilton*, IX, 334-35; Bancroft, *History of the Constitution*, I, 300.

from Congress in the form of a resolution to be submitted to the states for ratification.

Congress had been discussing federal taxes for months without being able to agree on anything more than the impost. This failure arose in part from conflict of interest among the states, but it also proceeded from a timidity felt even by those members who thoroughly approved of an extension of Congressional powers. They knew the views of their constituents. There was a gap between what most members of Congress believed to be necessary and what they knew the states would approve.

Morris soon indicated what he had in mind: He proposed an ultimatum to the states. Asserting the doctrine of implied powers, he declared that under the Confederation as it existed, the states were absolutely obliged to comply with any federal plan for dealing with the debt. *"The Right of Congress is perfect and the Duty to pay is absolute."* Congress should set a definite date, perhaps a year hence, on which the public debt would be due for payment. If the states did not pay their quotas of the debt, they would have to submit to the collection of federal taxes within their border—not only the impost, but whatever taxes were necessary to discharge their quotas.[37] It was clearly impossible that the states could pay their quota on the debt within a year; Morris's real purpose was to push Congress into a bold demand for a full schedule of federal taxes, sufficient to fund the whole debt. As the price of his continuance in office, he was asking Congress to throw caution to the wind and try to cram federal taxes down the throats of the state legislatures by an assertion of authority. Morris might have been suspected of having lost touch with reality had it not been for the developing army conspiracy. His report was delivered just two days before the climax of events at Newburgh.

The inner details of the Newburgh conspiracy are obscure, irrecoverable, and probably not important. Undoubtedly, some of the officers at camp were adventurers who disliked the prospects of a

37. Morris to President of Congress, Mar. 8, 1783, Wharton, ed., *Diplomatic Correspondence*, VI, 277-81. For examples of the Nationalists' advocacy of implied powers, see Hamilton to Governor Clinton, Feb. 24, 1783, Lodge, ed., *Works of Hamilton*, IX, 313-22; Madison's Notes of Debates, Jan. 28, 1783, *Journals*, XXV, 870-75; Hamilton to Duane, Sept. 3, 1780, Hamilton, ed., *Works of Hamilton*, I, 150 *et seq.*

return to civilian life and therefore were not averse to fishing in troubled waters. There were jostlings for priority and plots within plots. The major plot, however, was to rally the army as a pressure group. Events at camp were precipitated by the Nationalists as part of a studied effort to organize maximum force behind their program. Public creditors, Congress, the Financier, and the army would stand in line confronting the nation. Washington was to be the mediator in the crisis.

On March 10, 1783, two addresses were circulated at camp. One was an announcement of a meeting in which the petition to Congress would be discussed. The meeting had not been authorized by the Commander-in-Chief and was therefore against regulations; the implication was that it involved casting off Washington's leadership and taking some drastic action. The second address was a pamphlet, probably written by John Armstrong, Jr., sitting in the tent of General Gates. It had a high, dramatic tone and played expertly on the emotions of the officers. The army, it said, had been neglected during the war and would be abandoned with the advent of peace. "If this be your treatment while the swords you wear are necessary for the defense of America, what have you to expect from peace." The officers were urged to discard the "milk and water" style of their previous supplications and unite in a manly declaration that they would resist disbandment until they had obtained justice.[38]

This appeal, with its telling allusions to the "wounds, infirmities and scars" which were all that the officers would carry with them into ignoble retirement, threw the whole camp into an acute state of tension. Washington was very disturbed. In order to forestall the unauthorized meeting, he called an official session of the officers' council. Another address then appeared in camp; its contents are interesting in view of the outlines of the conspiracy as it appears to have been hatched in Philadelphia. The anonymous author took the line that Washington secretly favored strong action and that his purpose in calling an official session was to give additional weight to any declaration by putting it through regular channels. Fear of

38. Horatio Gates to John Armstrong, Jr., June 22, 1783, Bancroft, *History of the Constitution*, I, 318; Rufus King's relation of a conversation with William Duer, 1788, King, *Life of King*, I, 621-22. All documents relative to the Newburgh affair are printed in *Journals*, XXIV, 294-311.

Washington's disapproval should not deter the officers from acting boldly and independently at the official meeting.

The meeting was "exquisitely critical." General Gates, a moving spirit in the conspiracy, was president of the council, and many of the officers had allowed their tempers to rise to the point of explosion. Washington, however, managed to keep the meeting under control. He first assured the officers that as their leader he would support them in any decision, but he emphasized the practical difficulties, as well as the disgrace, of any attempt to stand against the country. They must not lose confidence in Congress, which was well disposed toward them, but like all public bodies disrupted by conflicts and slow to act. Eventually, he had no doubt, "compleat justice" would be done.[39]

Although it is doubtful whether this speech was convincing to all the officers present, Washington had the advantage of rank. In the presence of the Commander-in-Chief nobody had the courage to speak out against him. General Gates looked on helplessly while the meeting capitulated to moderation. A committee headed by General Knox, who was Washington's close ally, left the room and shortly returned with a number of resolutions which affirmed the army's loyalty to Congress and expressed hope that its requests would be acted upon before its disbandment. Another resolution voiced abhorrence of the ideas contained in the addresses lately circulated in camp. Hardly anyone spoke on the resolutions except the three members of the committee which drew them up. One gathers that a number of officers, including Timothy Pickering, departed in a rage. Under no illusion that the crisis was dispelled, Washington hurried a record of the proceedings to Congress, urging immediate satisfaction of the army's demands.[40]

39. King, *Life of King*, I, 621-22; *Journals*, XXIV, 306-10. Timothy Pickering wrote a detailed account of the meeting for his subordinate, Samuel Hodgdon, in a letter of Mar. 16, 1783, Pickering Papers, XXXIV, 145, Mass. Hist. Soc. See Brig. General Rufus Putnam's Examination of Certain Anonymous Papers, Mar. 15, 1783, "To the Officers of the Army," Mar. 15, 1783, Knox Papers, XIII, 22, XII, 22, *ibid.*

40. *Journals*, XXIV, 310-11. Pickering was incensed at what he considered Washington's feeble support of the army's case. Later, he indulged in sarcastic remarks about Washington's farewell address to the troops. See Pickering to [probably Samuel Hodgdon], Nov. 5, 1783, Pickering Papers, XXXIV, 256, Mass. Hist. Soc.; *Boston Magazine*, Dec. 1783; John Armstrong, Jr., to General Gates, May 30, 1783, Burnett, ed., *Letters*, VII, 175n.

Congress had already made some progress. The Financier had been instructed to settle army accounts, including those for back pay and rations; Morris had given this job to John Pierce, the Paymaster General. He had also taken stock of his resources and discovered that he could present the army with a month's pay, delivered to the officers in Morris's notes and doled out in cash to enlisted men at the basic rate of fifty cents a month for privates.[41] However, the question of pensions had become mired in the larger debate over a general funding program. Morris's adherents wanted to merge the commuted pensions with other federal debts and pay them all by means of federal taxes, whereas the foes of centralization wished to refer the officers to their states for payment.[42]

Washington's urgent communication from Newburgh prompted a quick decision in favor of the Nationalists. The officers were granted five years' full pay in lieu of pensions. The officers of any state line, acting collectively and within a limited time, might elect to receive payment from their states; otherwise, they would receive federal securities. The difficulties put in the way of applying to the states were such that the effect of the measure was to add the commuted pensions to the growing body of the federal debt and join the officers with the other public creditors. Since under Morris's direction, the other debts to the army were also converted into federal securities, the whole army debt passed to the federal government.[43]

This was all the Nationalists were able to accomplish. They failed in their most important objective, which was to commit Congress to an endorsement of a full schedule of federal taxes. The debate continued from January to April, and although most of the members were half-convinced that Congress had some kind of implied powers under the Articles of Confederation, they shrank from a decisive test of authority. "The generality of the members," wrote Madison, "are convinced of the necessity of a continental revenue . . . .

41. Morris to the Paymaster General, Mar. 15, 1783, Official Letterbook E, 167-70, Official Diary, Jan. 17, 1783, Morris Correspondence, Lib. Cong.; Morris to General Washington, Jan. 20, 1783, to Paymaster General, Jan. 20, 1783, Washington Papers, CCXIV, 80, 81, Lib. Cong.

42. *Journals,* XXIV, 145-51, 154-56, 178-79, 330-31; Madison's Notes of Debates, *ibid.,* XXV, 911-12, 916, 918; Richard Peters to Horatio Gates, Mar. 5, 1783, William Floyd to the Governor of New York, Mar. 12, 1783, Burnett, ed., *Letters,* VII, 67, 72-73.

43. *Journals,* XXIV, 206-10; Madison's Notes of Debates, *ibid.,* XXV, 926.

The extent of the plan however compared with the prepossessions of their constituents produces despondence and timidity." Arthur Lee remarked with satisfaction: "The Confederation is a stumbling block to those who wish to introduce new, and I think arbitrary systems."[44]

Although most members of Congress could agree on the impost, the consent of Rhode Island, Virginia, and Massachusetts was considered dubious. A land tax gave rise to many complexities: the New England states desired a uniform rate based on acreage, since land values were high in New England, whereas the southern states, which had large tracts of thinly populated and uncultivated land, wanted to base the tax on land values. A nearly insoluble question was whether Congress or the states should make the assessments. A poll tax was easy to administer, but unpopular in some states, and the constitution of Maryland prohibited it; there was also a question as to whether slaves should be taxed. An excise was considered hard to administer and repugnant to popular traditions, especially if collected by federal officers. Finally, every consideration of a specific tax brought up differences between the landless states and those with claims to western lands. Rather than accept any sacrifice entailed in the operation of a particular tax, the landless states suggested western lands as an alternative source of revenue, demanding the cession of all western claims to Congress.[45]

Opinion varied about how federal taxes ought to be collected. Intransigent Nationalists like Morris and Hamilton deemed taxes collected by state officers no better than requisitions and not worth contending for. Their opponents argued that collection by federal officers would project too much Congressional influence into the states. Nothing was said at this time about legal enforcement, but it must have occurred to minds like those of Hamilton and James Wilson that federal collection would entail federal law and federal courts.

The debate continued in the shadow of the developing Newburgh conspiracy. Hamilton and James Wilson demanded federal taxes, collected and administered by Congress. They tried to open Congress's sessions to the public, so the creditors of Philadelphia could influence the proceedings. Arthur Lee, the Rhode Island dele-

44. *Journals*, XXIV, 126-27; Madison to Edmund Randolph, Feb. 4, 1783, Arthur Lee to James Warren, Feb. 19, 1783, Burnett, ed., *Letters*, VII, 31, 51.
45. Madison discusses these issues in his Notes of Debates, *Journals*, XXV, 866-962.

gates, and a few other members fought against any federal tax, even the impost, as long as the Morris group dominated Congress. Tiring of the argument, Stephen Higginson of Massachusetts criticized the Nationalists for their refusal to accept any other mode of paying the debt than federal taxes, whose ratification by the states must be a slow and dubious process during which the creditors would remain unpaid. "The truth is," he said, "they are so very desirous of carrying the impost, that they are willing to hazard much, rather than give over the pursuit."[46]

Before the Newburgh affair reached its climax, the less intransigent Nationalists became convinced that they could not establish any federal taxes beyond the impost. On the evening of February 20, a session was held in the lodgings of Thomas Fitsimmons attended by Nathaniel Gorham, Hamilton, Richard Peters, Daniel Carroll, and Madison. The conversation ended in a general agreement to limit Congress's request to the impost and obtain additional funds by asking the states to commit long-term taxes to federal purposes.[47] Hamilton dissented.

This compromise, however, was the basis for the funding requisition of 1783—Congress's postwar plan for dealing with the public debt. As first drafted, it was an omnibus bill, containing several provisions relative to the financial relationship between the states and the Union; but the heart of the plan was its revenue features. Congress once more asked the states to grant the impost, modifying the terms to eliminate some of the states' objections. Though removable by Congress, the collectors were to be appointed by the states, and the duration of the grant was limited to twenty-five years. The second major feature of the bill was the request for supplementary (state) taxes, sufficient to raise $1,500,000 annually, and appropriated to the federal government for twenty-five years.[48]

Morris was scornful of the bill when it was submitted for his opinion. Having published his resignation, he was in no mood for

46. *Journals*, XXIV, 140, XXV, 198-202, 313-15; Madison's Notes of Debates, *ibid.*, XXV, 901, 937, 952; Stephen Higginson to Theophilus Parsons, Apr. 7, 1783, Burnett, ed., *Letters*, VII, 123-25. See Higginson to General Knox, Feb. 8, 1787, *ibid.*, 123n.

47. *Journals*, XXIV, 144n, 170-74; Madison's Notes of Debates, *ibid.*, XXV, 906-7, 909, 920-22; Joseph Jones to Washington, Feb. 27, 1783, Burnett, ed., *Letters*, VII, 60-61.

48. *Journals*, XXIV, 170-74, 188-92, 195-261 *passim*, XXV, 920-62 *passim*.

compromise. It was on this occasion that he proposed his ultimatum to the states—either to pay their share of the debt immediately or submit to federal taxes. Later, after he had consented to remain in office beyond the date set for his retirement, he asked Congress to publish a special declaration that his staying on was not to be construed as tacit approval of the funding requisition.[49]

If the Newburgh conspiracy had not misfired, Congress might have taken a stronger position. As it was, a majority of the members accepted the funding requisition. A few extremists on both sides opposed it: Arnold and Collins of Rhode Island, Higginson of Massachusetts, and Hamilton of New York voted in the negative. The Rhode Island delegates wanted all the collectors to be state officers; Higginson believed that the plan was a waste of time; Hamilton deemed it so inferior that he would not put his name to it.[50]

But any possibility of manipulating the army had disappeared. After the crisis at Newburgh, it became politically inert. The responsible military leaders had always urged moderation. Although Morris upbraided him for it, General Lincoln opposed the alliance with the public creditors, and General Knox stayed close to Washington's side. Many of the officers, it was said, were aghast when they recollected how they had nearly ruined themselves.[51]

Washington had grown increasingly suspicious of the Nationalists in Congress. He accused them of using the discontented officers as "mere puppets" to secure their ends. He attributed Congress's delay in granting commutation of officers' pensions to the Nationalists' refusal to accept any mode of payment other than federal taxes. He criticized Morris for not arranging to give the troops some pay, even funds from the states rather than Congress. Although Washington was a firm Nationalist, his primary allegiance was to the army, and in the last analysis he believed that its claims were superior to those of any other creditors. He was convinced that the outburst at camp

49. Morris to the President of Congress, May 1, 3, 1783, Wharton, ed., *Diplomatic Correspondence*, VI, 399-403, 405.

50. Rhode Island Delegates to the Governor of Rhode Island, Apr. 23, 1783, Alexander Hamilton to the Governor of Rhode Island, May 14, 1783, Burnett, ed., *Letters*, VII, 147-49, 165-66.

51. Official Diary, Apr. 23, 1782, Morris Correspondence, Lib. Cong.; John Armstrong, Jr., to General Gates, Apr. 22, 29, 1783, Burnett, ed., *Letters*, VII, 150n, 155n.

was hatched in Philadelphia and gave credence to rumors that Robert and Gouverneur Morris were at the bottom of it.[52]

Hamilton, to whom his recriminations were often directed, replied that the Nationalists were the true friends of the army, but that the soldiers' interests could be secured only by the establishment of federal taxes. He did not contradict the allegations against Robert and Gouverneur Morris, except to say that he himself might be accused of playing a deep game. It was no secret that he had tried to align the army with the public creditors. "The men against whom the suspicions you mention must be directed," he declared, "are in general the most sensible, the most liberal, the most independent and the most respectable characters in our body, as well as the most unequivocal friends of the army, in a word they are the men who think continentally."[53]

The arrival of peace rapidly dissipated all remaining intrigues within the army. Shortly after the outbreak at Newburgh, a vessel put into Philadelphia with news that the preliminary articles of peace had been signed. Congress proclaimed the cessation of hostilities on April 11 and four days later ratified the peace agreement. Since the peace was not definitive, Congress entertained the notion of keeping the troops together in case Britain should renew hostilities; but the army began to disintegrate. Men enlisted for the duration of the war cried out against their officers. Mutinies occurred in the southern army, and most of it was disbanded. Except for the troops under Washington's immediate command and the garrison at West Point, the army rapidly declined as an organized force, and there was soon little possibility of countering an enemy thrust if one had been made. Keeping the remnants of the army together only increased expense and invited disorder. What might be expected was indicated when the noncommissioned officers of the Connecticut line presented Washington with a petition demanding half-pay pensions for themselves.[54]

52. Washington to Theodorick Bland, Apr. 4, 1783, to Hamilton, Apr. 16, 22, 1783, Fitzpatrick, ed., *Writings of Washington*, XXVI, 293-96, 323-26, 350-53; Rufus King's relation of a conversation with William Duer, 1788, King, *Life of King*, I, 621-22; Louis C. Hatch, *The Administration of the American Revolutionary Army* (N.Y., 1904), 163-64; Madison's Notes of Debates, *Journals*, XXV, 926.

53. Hamilton to Washington, Mar. 17, Apr. 11, 1783, Hamilton, ed., *Works of Hamilton*, I, 345-49, 355-59.

54. Washington to the President of Congress, Apr. 18, 1783, to Hamilton, Apr. 22, 1783, Fitzpatrick, ed., *Writings of Washington*, XXVI, 330-34, 350-51; Morris

Congress intended to give full satisfaction to the army's requests before sending it home, but was confronted with a dilemma. The two remaining subjects of the army's petition upon which action had not been completed were pay and the settlement of accounts. Both would entail considerable delay, but neither officers nor men wanted to remain in service, and, as Morris pointed out, the longer they were kept together the greater the expense to the government and the less chance of affording them any pay. Finally, on May 26 Congress directed Washington to grant furloughs; within a month the army virtually melted away.[55]

Some time previously Congress had decided that three months' pay would be an appropriate gift to the departing soldiers. Morris, the final authority in such matters, had said there was no money for the purpose, but that the necessary $600,000 to $750,000 could be raised by a paper anticipation, that is, by issuing Morris's notes. Since the notes were tinged with a personal obligation, he would have to stay on as Financier until they were redeemed. Congress was willing that he should remain, but Morris, uncertain whether he wished to, dickered with Congress about the precise conditions. Thus matters stood until General Lincoln arrived from camp with the announcement that the officers were tired of the delay and would accept their pay in mere orders on the tax receivers in the various states "for the payment of which they [were] . . . willing to run the Chance." Morris was also shown a letter from Washington, who warned that unless he fell in with the officers' suggestion or pointed out an alternative, he would lose the friendship of the army. Morris then agreed to issue his notes for three months' pay and remain in office under the express condition that he should be disassociated from Congress's financial plans; his functions would be restricted to running his department and redeeming his notes.[56]

---

to a Committee of Congress, May 15, 1783, Official Letterbook E, 299-304, Morris Correspondence, Lib. Cong.; John Armstrong, Jr., to General Gates, Mar. 22, May 29, 1783, Burnett, ed., *Letters,* VII, 146n, 160n.

55. *Journals,* XXIV, 270, 364-65; Timothy Pickering to John Pickering, June 18, 1783, Pickering Papers, XXXIV, 215, Mass. Hist. Soc.

56. Washington to Robert Morris, Apr. 9, 1783, to Hamilton, Apr. 22, 1783, Fitzpatrick, ed., *Writings of Washington,* XXVI, 309, 351-52; Morris to Bland, Apr. 14, 16, 1783, to a Committee of Congress, May 15, 1783, to the President of Congress, July 18, 1783, Official Letterbook E, 221-22, 265-66, 299-304, 422-29, Morris Correspondence, Lib. Cong.; Bland to Morris, Apr. 16, 1783, Papers of Cont. Cong., no. 137, II, 661; *Journals,* XXIV, 283-85; Morris to the President

Morris's bargaining with Congress and the time required to print and sign the notes caused such delay that it was almost too late to send them to camp before the troops departed. They did not arrive until June 7, five days after Washington had issued general orders that the army was to be furloughed home; as a result, several detachments left without receiving pay.[57] Many of the soldiers who remained had already forfeited their rights. In the preceding weeks the contractors for the army had sent a large supply of goods to camp and solicited purchases on credit. When Morris's notes arrived, soldiers signed them over to the contractors at a discount—so it was said—of 40 percent to 50 percent. Those who withstood the temptation and managed to carry away their pay in Morris's notes had to accept a discount of at least 20 percent when they cashed them.[58]

The soldiers thus received a pittance of their pay, and the army was disbanded with no settlement of its accounts. Early in January, Congress had instructed Morris to undertake the settlement; he had made Paymaster General John Pierce responsible for the business, but little was accomplished. Morris finally explained that Congress's resolution did not give him the proper authority to act and also that state payments to their lines complicated the settlement. Congress quickly gave him the authority he desired, but by this time most of the troops had gone home.[59] Actually, the settlement of army accounts was destined to be the work of years, requiring ex-

---

of Congress, May 1, 3, 1783, Wharton, ed., *Diplomatic Correspondence*, VI, 399-403, 405-6.

57. Morris to the President of Congress, July 18, 1783, Official Letterbook E, 422-29, Morris Correspondence, Lib. Cong.; *Journals*, XXIV, 447-51; John Pierce to Morris, July 23, 1783, Papers of Cont. Cong., no. 137, II, 717-18.

58. On the transactions with the contractors, see Unsigned to Chaloner and White, June 22, 1783, Chaloner and White Letterbook, Hist. Soc. of Pa.; Sumner, *Financier*, II, 35; "The Tablet," *Gazette of the United States*, Feb. 20, 1790; "For the Advertiser," *Daily Advertiser* (N.Y.), Feb. 22, 1790. On the depreciation of Morris's notes, see John Chaloner to Peter Colt, Aug. 13, 1783, Chaloner and White Letterbook, Hist. Soc. of Pa. The notes issued to the troops were due for payment late in 1783 and in early 1784. Morris paid them by drawing bills on American funds in Holland. Five hundred and thirty thousand dollars of these bills were being protested in March 1784 for lack of funds. However, the Dutch loan of 1784 raised the money for their redemption and enabled Morris to retire in November with his accounts paid. Morris to the President of Congress, Mar. 17, 1784, Papers of Cont. Cong., no. 137, Appendix, 345-51.

59. Report to Congress respecting settlement of army accounts, June 22, 1783, Morris to Paymaster General, July 8, 1783, Official Letterbook E, 383-85, Morris Correspondence, Lib. Cong.; Circular Letter to [the New England States and New Jersey], Apr. 12, 1783, Washington Papers, CCXIX, 30, Lib. Cong.

amination of state records all over the country. There never had been a possibility of gratifying the army's desire for a settlement before disbandment.

Under these casual and ignominious circumstances, the Continental army melted away. Its behavior through all the years of war and the hardships of disbandment had conformed to the ideal of a republican army. Most of the common soldiers—at least those of Massachusetts, which comprised the bulk of the forces—were boys in their teens who had enlisted for the bounty. Except for a few embittered officers and a core of hardened veterans who were accustomed to a soldier's life, they were content merely to go home.

The tide of Nationalist influence subsided with the end of the war. There was now less reason for increasing federal powers.[60] The intransigent Hamilton retired in disgust, having, as he said, "no future views in public life." Madison declined to serve out his term. Other members whose entry into Congress began with the Nationalist upswing in 1780 were forced into retirement because the Articles of Confederation restricted their terms to three consecutive years. Their successors were on the whole less ardent in pursuing those "catholic arrangements" which the Nationalists deemed vital to the country's welfare.[61] Morris stayed on for a year, but disassociated himself from a Congressional policy which he despised. Robert R. Livingston resigned as Secretary of Foreign Affairs and accepted a high court position in New York.

The new order was dramatized by the physical removal of Congress from Philadelphia. When, in the late spring of 1783, the state government would not disperse a crowd of armed soldiers in front of its chambers, Congress haughtily retired to Princeton, later to Annapolis. The adversaries of Morris and the Nationalists welcomed Congress's delivery from the clamors of public creditors and the sinister influence of wealth and aristocracy. Stephen Higginson said

60. See Washington to Rev. William Gordon, July 8, 1783, Fitzpatrick, ed., *Writings of Washington*, XXVII, 49-50; Hamilton to John Jay, July 25, 1783, Hamilton, ed., *Works of Hamilton*, IX, 381-82.

61. Hamilton to Governor Clinton, May 14, 1783, Madison to Edmund Randolph, June 3, 1783, Samuel Osgood to Stephen Higginson, Feb. 2, 1784, Burnett, ed., *Letters*, VII, 165-66, 178, 430; Irving Brant, *James Madison, the Nationalist, 1780-1787* (N.Y., 1948), 285. See Proposed Resolution of Hamilton for a Convention, June 30, 1783, Hamilton, ed., *Works of Hamilton*, II, 269-75, and a fuller version in Hamilton Papers, V, 582-85, Lib. Cong.

that at Princeton he could carry motions in which but one man would support him in Philadelphia. According to Samuel Osgood, the removal destroyed "Systems which would finally have ended in absolute Aristocracy." Even David Howell was pleased to recognize some "very amiable characters" among his colleagues and could no longer discern the least trace of "poisonous influence."[62]

Morris was harassed by investigations. A committee reopened the case of Silas Deane's accounts and the activities of the early Secret Committee. Asked to explain once more his connection with Deane, Morris replied that technically speaking, "the Superintendent of Finance has no official Knowledge of the private concerns of Mr. Robert Morris." Nonetheless, he did not neglect to defend himself, and nothing was proved to his discredit.

He came under fire again when Congress discovered that he had instructed his tax receivers to give priority to the redemption of his personal notes and pay them in specie. It was alleged that the discharged troops were ignorant of the special status of Morris's notes and were selling them at a discount to speculators. The implication was that Morris was speculating in his own notes. He angrily replied that his instructions to the tax receivers had never been secret, and he defied anyone to prove that he was speculating in his notes either directly or through third parties.[63] No one came forward with proof of this allegation or the related charge that he had purposely delayed issuing his notes to the furloughed troops until the contractors (it was implied that he was in partnership with them) had set up their stores at camp.[64] Morris could still declare, as at the

62. Stephen Higginson to Nathaniel Gorham, Aug. 5, 1783, Samuel Osgood to John Adams, Dec. 7, 1783, David Howell to the Governor of Rhode Island, Dec. 24, 1783, Osgood to Stephen Higginson, Feb. 2, 1784, Burnett, ed., *Letters*, VII, 251-52, 378-81, 398, 430-31.

63. Information to the Public relative to the Notes signed by the Superintendent of Finance, Aug. 16, 1783, Morris to Mr. Lee, Oct. 4, 11, 1783, Official Letterbook F, 52-53, 153-55, 167-69, Morris Correspondence, Lib. Cong.; Report of the Committee to whom was referred the motion of Mr. Higginson (July 11, 1783), Papers of Cont. Cong., no. 20, I, 43-44; *Journals*, XXIV, 441-42, 477-79, 480-83; Morris to the President of Congress, July 15, 1783, to the Governors of the States, July 28, 1783, Wharton, ed., *Diplomatic Correspondence*, VI, 550-51, 611.

64. Unsigned to Chaloner and White, June 22, 1783, Chaloner and White Letterbook, Hist. Soc. of Pa.; Sumner, *Financier*, II, 35. Morris wrote that his zeal in behalf of the army had greatly cooled "in consequence of allegations against him spread by military persons." Morris to the Paymaster General, Aug. 12, 1783, Wharton, ed., *Diplomatic Correspondence*, VI, 644.

time of the Deane-Lee affair: "I have never failed to get the better of my Enemies in the day of Trial." Nevertheless, Congress issued a directive obliging him to publish in the newspapers that his notes were given priority by the tax receivers.[65]

Although there is no evidence that Morris was speculating in his notes, his close business associates availed themselves of the opportunity. John Holker, his partner in a number of enterprises, formed an agreement in October with the main army contractor, Daniel Parker and Co., to purchase Morris's notes, which were then passing at 10 percent discount. Acting in behalf of Le Couteulx and Co., Morris's banker and agent in Europe, Holker was to supply Daniel Parker and Co. with £10,000 to make the purchases.[66] Rumors of such activities did not allow Morris's enemies to forget that he was in private trade. In addition to the charge that he speculated in his personal notes, he was accused of rigging the terms under which public vessels were sold to enable his partners to buy them cheaply. He had to take special precautions to avoid charges of complicity when it was discovered that two public ships had arrived in port— one of them a privileged vessel bearing the preliminary articles of peace—with unexplained cargoes of private goods.[67]

Morris had, in fact, given nearly all his attention to public affairs while he was Superintendent of Finance. Except for speculations in bills of exchange, which he apparently carried on in person, it appears that he left his private concerns to the management of partners.[68] The ventures in which he was directly or indirectly engaged were small compared with the spectacular operations of his early public career. Yet the odor of private commerce lingered over his administration. If nothing else, the use of his personal notes and

65. Morris to Franklin, Sept. 18, 1779, Franklin Papers, XV, 199, Amer. Philos. Soc.; *Journals*, XXIV, 430-32, 477-79.

66. Contract between John Holker in behalf of Le Couteulx and Co. and Daniel Parker and Co., Phila., Oct. 14, 1783, Holker Papers, XXII, 5848, Lib. Cong.

67. John Chaloner to Jeremiah Wadsworth, Oct. 18, 1783, Chaloner and White Letterbook, Hist. Soc. of Pa.; Stephen Higginson to Arthur Lee, undated, [Oct.], 1783, Amer. Hist. Assn., *Annual Report*, 1 (1896), 713; Morris to President of Congress, May 1, 1783, Papers of Cont. Cong., no. 137, II, 403-13; Official Diary, Apr. 29, 1783, Morris Correspondence, Lib. Cong.

68. Ver Steeg, *Morris*, 187-88; Morris to Luzerne, Dec. 27, 1781, Morris to Le Coulteulx and Co., Dec. 27, 1781, Morris Correspondence, Lib. Cong.

his connection with the Bank of North America could not fail to excite suspicion.

Morris realized that his usefulness was over. In March 1784, he wrote: "I think it is necessary for America that I should quit my office . . . the People will I hope more easily beleive when they hear Truth from some other Quarter."[69] Morris probably did not realize how truly he had spoken. His leadership had given energy and direction to the Nationalist movement but had also imposed upon it the limitations implicit in his personality and background. Morris never relinquished the role of the big merchant: his regime had an aura of patronage and conspiracy appropriate to a mercantile house. He operated through henchmen and built up an official staff bound to him by personal ties. His public acts were obscurely mixed with his private affairs.

The power and influence which he acquired were enough in themselves to alarm a people deeply suspicious of authority. Even those who were in general sympathy with his views sided against him in the belief that his unavowed purpose in strengthening the central government was to aggrandize himself and share all positions of honor and profit with his friends. Stephen Higginson, a conservative Massachusetts merchant, wrote in 1783 that the impost, if adopted, would augment "particular, individual influence & not Congressional." There is no doubt that opposition to the impost in Massachusetts, as well as in Virginia and Rhode Island, was in some degree inspired by distrust of the Financier. After the Nationalist influence subsided in Congress, Higginson wrote that if Morris would also resign, Congress might then be safely trusted with the impost.[70]

It may be significant that Morris, who was so ready with proposals, never marshaled his forces in support of a general convention to amend the Articles of Confederation. The idea was brought up repeatedly after 1780 by prominent men and in the resolutions of state

69. Morris to George Olney, Mar. 24, 1784, Official Letterbook G, 60-62, Morris Correspondence, Lib. Cong.

70. Higginson to Samuel Adams, May 20, June 20, 1783, Samuel Osgood to Stephen Higginson, Feb. 2, 1784, Burnett, ed., Letters, VII, 166-67, 184, 430-36. Alexander Gillon is an unreliable witness because his hatred of Morris was intense; however, he wrote in 1783 that Morris was so unpopular in the southern states that if they ratified the impost he thought they would stipulate that the income be kept out of Morris's hands. Gillon to Arthur Lee, undated, 1784, Arthur Lee Papers, Houghton Lib.

legislatures and conventions. Morris, already in the seat of authority, apparently chose to drive toward his goals by wielding the power in his hands.[71]

The underlying weakness of the Nationalists under Morris was lack of conservative support in New England and the south. Morris himself was thoroughly identified with the middle states, and his opponents were frequently actuated by sectional bias. Thus, his propensity for peopling the government with cronies and business associates was interpreted as an attempt to establish the predominance of the middle states in the Union. The ghost of the Deane-Lee affair fluttered over his administration. His unreconciled foes of that controversy, which had been rooted in sectional antagonism, remained his severest critics. Reviving the tone of old accusations, they alleged that Morris and the Nationalists had consented to accept French terms in the peace negotiations, thereby betraying the interests of New England and the south.[72] Stephen Higginson, one of those who perceived an attempt of the middle states to dominate federal affairs, wrote triumphantly in 1784: "Their schemes are now entirely defeated; their web is broken, which they have with so much art and industry been for several years spinning."[73]

During the whole of the Nationalist ascendancy, there was a strong, latent resistance in both New England and the south—a resistance which remained uncrystallized only because the Nationalists' schemes proved abortive. In December 1782, on the occasion of Congress's duel with the Rhode Island legislature, a committee of Congress drew up an ordinance for executing the impost. The publication of this, as well as Congress's letter to Rhode Island, which contained an assertion of Congress's alleged powers under a liberal construction of the Articles of Confederation, aroused much adverse comment. A member of the Massachusetts Senate cried out that an

71. Stephen Higginson commented in 1787 that he had urged Madison and others in 1783 to promote an amending convention if they wanted to strengthen Congress but they had demurred. Higginson to General Knox, Feb. 8, 1787, Burnett, ed., *Letters*, VII, 123*n*.

72. Arthur Lee to Samuel Adams, Aug. 12, 1781, *Deane Papers*, IV, 447-48; Thomas McKean to Samuel Adams, July 8, 1781, Samuel Osgood to John Adams, Dec. 7, 1783, Burnett, ed., *Letters*, VI, 139, 379-81; Sanders, *Executive Departments*, 95-96.

73. Higginson to Thedorick Bland, Jan. 1784, Charles Campbell, ed., *The Bland Papers* (Petersburg, Va., 1840, 1843), II, 113-15. See Elbridge Gerry to Samuel Adams, Mar. 4, 1784, Samuel Adams Papers, Houghton Lib.

Englishman must have written the ordinance. Dr. William Gordon wrote that it had excited the resentment of everyone who had seen it and that the impost, under the terms by which Congress meant to enforce it, would have broken the Union, for the northern states would never have submitted. The same sentiments were reported in Virginia. In 1783 the Massachusetts legislature, while ratifying the impost as it was presented in the funding requisition of 1783, entered a formal complaint against Congress's action in enlarging the federal debt and forcing all creditors to look to the central government for payment.[74] The basis for this kind of objection was sectional feeling and local particularism.[75]

Beneath party opposition and sectional feeling, however, there was also a genuine apprehension that a strong Union under the auspices of high government men such as Morris and his associates would establish the rule of an "Aristocratical Junto." Samuel Osgood described a real problem for conservatives when he explained to John Adams, who was in Europe, why the impost had failed: "If you were here, you would find it very difficult to establish Funds that would not have a Tendency to destroy the Liberties of this Country."[76] Morris's views on government and society were not shared by the majority of Americans, but aside from this, his public career too often exhibited a highhanded, somewhat unscrupulous disposition to strike boldly and crudely at his main objectives with whatever means came to hand, without much regard for the opinions and legitimate interests of those who presumed to differ with him. As one of his critics said, Morris never thought it necessary to secure the confidence of the people.[77]

74. William Gordon to General Gates, Feb. 27, 1783, Horatio Gates Papers, XVI, N.Y. Pub. Lib.; Joseph Jones to Madison, June 14, 1783, Madison Papers, IV, Lib. Cong.; Stephen Higginson to Arthur Lee, undated, [Oct.], 1783, Amer. Hist. Assn., *Annual Report*, 1 (1896), 711-12.

75. See, for example, a similar objection in a set of resolutions presumably drawn up by the conservative George Mason of Virginia. "The Address and Instructions of their Constituents" [Fairfax County, Va.], May 30, 1783, Kate Mason Rowland, *Life, Correspondence and Speeches of George Mason* (N.Y., 1892), 48-52.

76. Samuel Osgood to John Adams, Jan. 14, 1783, Burnett, ed., *Letters*, VII, 414.

77. Samuel Osgood to John Adams, Dec. 7, 1783, *ibid.*, 379.

PART III

POSTWAR ERA

"These states by themselves are sheltered from a foreign invasion; but the government, though just, cannot be sure of being obeyed without having at its disposition the means of coercion.... These observations on the powerlessness of the government do not prevent me from recognizing that the people of this country are in general happy; that the tribunals have a sufficient authority; that there is room for all the world; that abundance reigns; that the most unlimited toleration does not engender the smallest religious dispute; that union and peace reign in families; and that the government is not faulty, except with regard to several great objects of internal administration and to those of foreign policy...."

—Chevalier de la Luzerne to Vergennes, Aug. 4, 1782.

9

Settlement of Individual Accounts

"Affairs were so complicated that it was hardly possible to say who was at Fault."

—Robert Morris to the President
of Congress, 1784.

UNTIL 1782 the only segment of the ill-defined mass of federal debts which Congress formally acknowledged as its responsibility was loan certificates. They alone comprised the "public debt" which exponents of centralization hoped would one day afford cement to the Union. Whether Congress or the states were responsible for other federal debts was an unresolved question. But in the closing years of the war, the Nationalists asserted Congress's right to pay all debts contracted by the federal government during the war. Under an act of February 1782, Congress undertook the conversion of "unliquidated" federal debts into a "liquidated" public debt. Commissioners were appointed to travel among the states and inspect the claims of civilians, most of which arose from debts of the Quartermaster and Commissary departments. The commissioners verified claims and revalued them in specie if they were stated in terms of depreciated currency. For balances due they issued "final settlement certificates" amounting to over $3,700,000.[1] Similarly, Congress in 1783 took over the claims of the Continental army. Under the supervision of Paymaster General John Pierce, army accounts were ad-

1. Henceforth, all figures are in specie values unless otherwise stated.

justed, and about $11,000,000 in final settlement certificates (Pierce's notes) were issued to the troops. Finally, Congress settled the accounts of officials who had handled public money or property during the war. This process, which stretched on for a decade after 1782, produced a small crop of final settlement certificates. Congress thus converted unliquidated federal debts into the public debt—which already included loan certificates. The effect of the consolidation was to raise the public debt from $11,000,000 (the value of loan certificates) to more than $27,000,000.

Before Congress could liquidate its debts many of them were absorbed by the states, in which case they became a state obligation and were not added to the public debt.[2] State assumption had begun in 1780, when a destitute Congress tried to rid itself of burdens. In April of that year, Congress asked the states to compensate their lines in the Continental army for back pay not received and to make up losses which the troops had suffered from having been paid in depreciated currency. In compliance with this request, the states settled the accounts of their lines and issued state certificates for balances due. Large sums were involved, and since the certificates were usually given a preferred status, i.e., not absorbed by taxes but set at interest, they made up a very considerable part of the debt which most states carried through the remaining years of the Confederation. Of Virginia's debt of $2,766,000 in 1792, certificates issued to its Continental line accounted for $1,754,000. Pennsylvania's debt in 1787 was something over $1,845,000, including $721,000 that remained of $1,673,000 originally issued to her line.[3] New York's debt of about $387,500 in 1790 included $135,000 in pay and depreciation certificates; $175,000 had already been redeemed through sales of land. In Massachusetts, military certificates outstanding in 1786 amounted to $833,000, but this was only a minor fraction of an inflated debt of $5,400,000 with which the state saddled herself at the end of the war.[4]

2. The following discussion is based on my article, "State Assumption of the Federal Debt During the Confederation," *Miss. Valley Hist. Rev.*, 38 (1951), 404-24.

3. *Journals*, XVI, 344-45; *Cal. Va. State Papers*, V, 431; *American State Papers, Finance*, I, 31. Pennsylvania's total debt is exclusive of the assumption of the debt of her citizens. On state assumption of the public debt, see Chapter 11. Statement of the Finances of Pennsylvania, Nov. 7, 1787, portfolio 147, no. 4, Broadside Coll., Rare Books Div., Lib. Cong.; *Minutes of the . . . General Assembly of Pennsylvania* (printed currently), Nov. 12, 1787.

4. New York's total debt excludes public securities assumed by the state.

Although Congress intended to resume payment of military salaries after August 1, 1780, the Financier chose to apply funds to other purposes; accordingly, for varying periods of service in 1781 and 1782 the states continued to pay their troops in certificates and occasionally in money. South Carolina carried the process furthest, issuing state certificates for all debts due to her line.[5] The Nationalists recognized a divisive tendency and tried to refuse the states credit for such payments; but this stand could not be maintained, and in 1784 a Congress of altered political character approved any settlements which the states had made with their lines.[6] Thus the states sank part of the debt which would otherwise have been due to the Continental Army.

During its period of great weakness in 1780, Congress had also asked the states to withdraw old Continental currency and accept Quartermaster and Commissary certificates in their taxes. The states absorbed nearly $120,000,000 in currency, which had a specie value of perhaps $1,200,000. They also withdrew Quartermaster and Commissary certificates, possibly $10,000,000 (currency), for which they received credit on old requisitions. Most of them felt obliged to extend additional relief to their citizens by converting Quartermaster and Commissary certificates into state debts. New York and New Jersey gave their citizens state notes in exchange for these federal certificates. Connecticut was said to have assumed $640,000 and Maryland to have paid an estimated $266,000 to holders of certificates.[7]

State assumption of Quartermaster and Commissary certificates went furthest in the south. There, the last campaigns of the war were fought when neither Congress nor the states had effective money and the troops were supported by impressments. More often than in the earlier campaigns, impressments were conducted by state

Statement of Certificates due the citizens of New York now funded, Jan. 1788, James Duane Papers, box 7, N. Y. Pub. Lib.; *Daily Advertiser* (N.Y.), Jan. 18, 1790; item in Alexander Hamilton Papers, IV, 436, Lib. Cong. On Massachusetts, see *Acts and Laws of the Commonwealth of Massachusetts [1780-1805]* (Boston, 1890-98), "1786-87," 143.

5. Journals of the House of Representatives of the State of South Carolina, Feb. 22, 1783, Microfilm Collection of Early State Records, A. 1b, Reel 20, Lib. Cong.; Charles G. Singer, *South Carolina in the Confederation* (Phila., 1941), 63, 65.

6. *Journals*, XXIII, 624-26, 629-31, XXVII, 506, XXVIII, 261.

7. Ferguson, "State Assumption," *Miss. Valley Hist. Rev.*, 38 (1951), 406-7.

agents, but Continental officers were also at work.[8] Whether a citizen got a state or a federal certificate was purely fortuitous.

Virginia's case stands out clearly and is typical of the Carolinas and, to a lesser extent, Maryland. Virginians were overloaded with both state and federal certificates. When the state got around to paying debts after the war, she did not distinguish between the two kinds of certificates; the people insisted that both be accepted for taxes. The county courts liquidated, i.e., examined and adjusted to specie value, all certificates or other claims. The people who presented them got state notes in exchange. These notes were rapidly absorbed by taxes, which included a special "certificate tax," estimated to return $546,000 annually to the state treasury. From 1782 through 1785 it appears that Virginia redeemed $3,250,000 in certificates and was then able to discontinue the special tax. The state thus "paid" claims which otherwise would have survived to become part of the public debt. As a result of her action, the public debt arising from Quartermaster and Commissary certificates was extremely small—only $171,000.[9]

The pattern was similar in the Carolinas. A delegate to Congress from North Carolina complained that in New England all the costs of the war were evidenced by federal securities, whereas in the south they had become a charge against the states. A committee of the legislature reported in 1788 that North Carolina had "assumed to her citizens the payment of claims for supplies and services rendered the United States, of the same nature with those assumed in other states by Congress." In North Carolina the federal debt arising from Quartermaster and Commissary certificates was only $8,695.[10]

South Carolina went to even greater lengths. Commissioners were appointed in 1783 to receive claims of any nature whatsoever against either Congress or the state government. When the claims had been

8. Congress was trying to rely upon state deliveries under specific supply requisitions.

9. Board of Treasury report, June 12, 1786, Papers of Cont. Cong., no. 139, 219; *American State Papers, Finance,* I, 239. In settling her account with the United States, Virginia listed $2,745,000 in warrants sunk by state taxes after January 1, 1781; these were either federal certificates or state certificates issued for federal purposes. *Cal. Va. State Papers,* V, 393.

10. Richard Dobbs Spaight to the Governor of North Carolina, Apr. 30, 1784, Burnett, ed., *Letters,* VII, 509; Ferguson, "State Assumption," *Miss. Valley Hist. Rev.,* 38 (1951), 407; *Journals of the House of Commons of the State of North Carolina* (published currently), Dec. 6, 1786, Dec. 2, 1788.

verified, the people who submitted them received state "indents." Nearly all war debts, including Commissary and Quartermaster certificates, were taken over by the state. The public debt originating in Commissary and Quartermaster certificates was only $65.[11]

As a result of the active assumption of Quartermaster and Commissary certificates by southern state governments, their citizens owned little of the public debt arising from this source. Only $264,000 out of a national total of $3,761,000, a mere 7 percent, was held in the states from Maryland to Georgia. This debt was lodged almost entirely in states north of Maryland, the greatest concentration occurring in New York, New Jersey, and Pennsylvania, which together had 83 percent. New York alone had over 31 percent.[12]

This sectional imbalance increased the disparity between general holdings of public securities in the south and the rest of the nation, since the south was also deficient in other forms of public debt. The three major categories of the debt were: loan certificates, the war bonds of the Revolution, of which a mere 10 percent were originally issued in states from Maryland to Georgia; final settlement certificates issued by federal commissioners to civilians, of which, as we have just seen, the south had only 7 percent; and the final settlement certificates which John Pierce issued to the Continental army. These three kinds of securities comprised the great bulk of the public debt after its consolidation, amounting to $25,400,000. The south held only $4,170,000, or 16 percent, of the total, whereas its proportion of the white population in 1790 was 38 percent.[13]

The consolidation of the public debt which Congress undertook in 1782 proved to be a long and complicated process, giving rise to many disputes. Some phases of it were never completed. Over

11. Thomas Cooper and David J. McCord, eds., *The Statutes at Large of South Carolina* (Columbia, 1836-41), IV, 679-80; Alexander S. Salley, *Accounts Audited of Revolutionary Claims Against South Carolina* (Columbia, 1935), I, 3-4; *American State Papers, Finance,* I, 239. Claims for supplies and services rendered, and service in the militia or Continental line were lumped together and a certificate issued to the claimant for the total. See Alexander S. Salley, *Stub Entries to Indents Issued in Payment of Claims Against South Carolina Growing Out of the Revolution* (Columbia, 1917), books R-T.

12. Computations are based on a Statement of the Liquidated and Loan Office Debt, Receipts and Expenditures, 1784-1787, Papers of Cont. Cong., no. 141, I, 361, and the Treasury report of 1790, *American State Papers, Finance,* I, 239.

13. *A Century of Population Growth from the first census of the United States to the twelfth, 1790-1900* (Wash., 1909), 47.

the course of years, however, a mass of loose paper and undetermined claims were transformed into an organized debt of known amount, evidenced by a limited number of new types of securities.

One category of the debt was no problem: loan certificates did not have to be liquidated, and their form remained unchanged throughout the Confederation. Certificates whose value had originally been stated in terms of depreciated currency were easily reduced to specie value by the loan officers in each state under regulations which Congress enacted in 1780. Except for those issued under questionable circumstances in South Carolina and Georgia, loan certificates did not have to be formally examined; this part of the debt was already organized.[14]

Quite otherwise were the debts due to civilians, most of which had been incurred by the Quartermaster and Commissary departments. In 1782 Congress had only a vague notion of how many certificates had been issued or to what extent they had been redeemed by the states; but its policy was to merge the remaining certificates with the public debt. The states were not permitted to sink them by taxation (as they had been allowed to absorb Continental currency), and the Financier would allow the states no part in settling or evaluating the certificates held by their citizens. Under the ordinance adopted in February 1782, Morris nominated a commissioner for each state whose duty was to review all civilian claims, take in the old certificates, and issue final settlement certificates in exchange.[15]

14. On the certificates issued in South Carolina and Georgia, see Report of the Board of Treasury, Oct. 16, 1786, Papers of Cont. Cong., no. 139. Loan officers were instructed to adjust loan certificates to specie value when they were presented for interest under the indent regulations described in Chapter 12. As many of these certificates had only a small specie value, Congress in 1786 authorized loan officers to issue a "specie" certificate in lieu of certificates aggregating $100 specie or more when presented by a single holder. The new specie certificates required no liquidation; neither did the "specie loan certificates" issued in 1781, nor the certificates issued prior to Sept. 1, 1777, which were considered equal to specie under federal regulations. Certificates issued between Sept. 1, 1777 and Mar. 1, 1778 were entitled to draw interest on their face value even though their principal was subject to revaluation; consequently, they were not reduced to specie value until subscribed to the federal loan of 1790. See *Journals*, XVII, 566-69, XXIX, 869*n*, 893-94, XXX, 36-37; Nathaniel Appleton to the Board of Treasury, June 1, Oct. 20, 1785, Letterbook of Nathaniel Appleton, CCLIX, Record Group 53, Fiscal Records Section, Natl. Arch.

15. Morris to the President of Congress, Aug. 26, 1781 (enclosures), Papers of Cont. Cong., no. 137, I, 121; Morris to the President of Congress, Aug. 28, 1781, Wharton, ed., *Diplomatic Correspondence*, IV, 667-77; *Journals*, XXI, 1132, XXII, 12-14, 14*n*, 82-86.

The settlement of civilian claims was slow getting under way: appointments had to be confirmed, and there were other delays. A commissioner began working in Maryland late in 1782, and during the next year others were sent to New England, New Jersey, Delaware, Pennsylvania, and Virginia. New York and South Carolina had to wait until 1784, North Carolina until 1785. Not until 1786 was a commissioner sent to Georgia. Morris had written their instructions: "Artful Men have frequently taken advantage of the Public and . . . in many Instances public officers have taken advantage of the weak and unprotected. You will therefore always remember that it is your Duty to do Justice. In the Prosecution of this Duty you will take Care also to discover, bring to Light, and Pursue and punish Fraud and Peculation of every kind."[16]

The duties of the commissioners were not easy. They were supposed to require the submission of proper documents in proof of claims, than determine the specie value of goods or services contributed by individuals during the war, taking into account local variations in prices and the depreciation of paper money. Their task was made more difficult because many certificates presented to them had not been signed by the proper officers or did not list enough details to be evaluated. Many claimants did not even own certificates and could offer no proof but their word. Morris insisted on a thorough scrutiny of old transactions, and he held the commissioners responsible for their decisions in doubtful cases. Understandably reluctant to make judgments which might later be questioned, the commissioners worked so slowly that there were many complaints, and Congress finally relaxed the rules governing the submission of evidence. The commissioners were authorized to admit questionable claims and in doubtful cases to hold a public session wherein the claimant faced the officer with whom he had allegedly made the transaction. Even more liberal regulations were later adopted: the commissioner was allowed to take the mere oath of a claimant.[17]

16. Morris to the Commissioners for settling the Accounts of the States, Sept. 7, 1782, Morris to the President of Congress, Dec. 3, 1782, Official Letterbook D, 177-78, 435-36, Morris Correspondence, Lib. Cong.; Board of Treasury report, June 12, 1786, Papers of Cont. Cong., no. 139, 237.

17. Robert Morris to Lewis Pintard, Jan. 10, 1783, to William Barber, Mar. 18, 1784, Letterbook E, 31, Letterbook G, 59-60, Morris Correspondence, Lib. Cong.; Morris to President of Congress, Aug. 12, 1783, Papers of Cont. Cong., no. 137, 779-801; also further reports and letters, *ibid.*, III, 17-27; *Journals,* XXV, 828-35, XXVII, 540-45.

Nothing could disguise the impossibility of conducting a rigid settlement of the chaotic finances of the Revolution, at least by any methods that would not be unjust to a great many individuals or delay the settlement indefinitely. In 1786 the Board of Treasury (which succeeded Morris) lamented that "the admission of the Oath of the Claimant, in many Cases where other Testimony was defective, has undoubtedly proved a fruitful Source of augmenting the Public Expence, and of Corrupting the Virtue of the People."[18] But there was no remedy.

In the south, as we have seen, most of the certificate debt was liquidated and assumed by the states. Entering belatedly upon their duties, the commissioners found little to do. The commissioner for North Carolina was told when he arrived that most of the work was finished. In June 1785 claims settled in Virginia were only $97 and in South Carolina, $20. Commenting on this situation, the Board of Treasury observed that the expense accounts of the commissioners were greater than the value of the claims they liquidated.[19]

By the end of 1786, the settlement of civilian accounts was nearly finished, except in North Carolina and Georgia where the commissioners worked a year longer. It increased the public debt by $3,723,000—all that remained of that useful paper which had sustained the army in the darkest period of the war.

The settlement of army accounts was finished about the same time. The army's fear that its claims would not be acknowledged proved groundless. Under John Pierce and his capable deputy Joseph Howell, the settlement went forward with dispatch and a relative absence of friction. Since it was necessary to determine the amounts which the states had already paid to their lines, Pierce was assisted by agents representing the troops or appointed by the states. The local agents scrutinized muster rolls, financial records, and other documents; Pierce and Howell traveled about coordinating their efforts. When a rough calculation had been made of the total sums due the various lines, Pierce supplied the states with batches of final settlement certificates, which were passed on to officers,

18. *Ibid.*, XXX, 341-42.
19. *Ibid.*, XXIX, 584-85, XXX, 341; Letters of the Board of Treasury, July 25, Sept. 17, 1785, Aug. 21, 1786, Papers of Cont. Cong., no. 140, II, 27, 91, 259; Board of Treasury report, June 12, 1786, *ibid.*, no. 139.

soldiers, or persons who had purchased their rights. Pierce's notes embraced back pay, commutation of officers' pensions, a soldiers' bonus of $80 granted by Congress in 1778, in addition to various claims for rations, clothing, forage, and other items not received in service.[20]

Military accounts were fraught with the same uncertainties as civilian claims. In Virginia the events of war had moved so rapidly that muster rolls were not kept, and the confusion of men being drafted from one detachment to another often resulted in neither the paymasters nor the commanding officers knowing what pay the troops had received or the length of their service. Officers who might have supplied this information had frequently moved out of the state or into the backcountry. Reporting that records were deficient in all the states, Pierce proposed that he be allowed to accept an oath from any officer and, in the case of noncommissioned officers and enlisted men, a certificate from the field officer who had commanded them. Congress authorized this procedure.[21]

Like the commissioners in charge of the settlement of civilian accounts, Pierce discovered that the southern states had pre-empted his duties. Georgia had made payments to its line throughout the Revolution, and Pierce had to review all the state records before he could issue certificates for balances not already provided for. In South Carolina he never issued a single certificate directly. The state settled the accounts of its line and issued securities for balances due. This procedure was sanctioned by the federal government.[22]

20. *Journals*, XXV, 801, XXVIII, 399, XXIX, 866. There is abundant evidence of other persons' buying soldiers' rights to receive certificates in Discharges and Accounts, 1783-1785, State Papers, 1784, Md. Hall of Records. As to methods by which the accounts were settled, see Commissioner of Army Accounts, Letterbook 1784-1786, Acc. 1762, *ibid.;* Letters and Reports of John Pierce, Papers of Cont. Cong., no. 62; Walter Clark, ed., *State Records of North Carolina, 1777-1790* (Winston and Goldsboro, 1895-1905), XVIII, 381, XXI, 348, 413-14; Hamilton to the Governor of Rhode Island, Jan. 14, 1790, John Bartlett, ed., *Records of the Colony [and State] of Rhode Island* . . . (Providence, 1856-65), X, 409-10; Pierce's Register, *Seventeenth Report of the Daughters of the American Revolution*, 63 Cong., 3rd sess., Senate Doc., no. 988 (Wash., 1915), Appendix, 149-50.

21. John Pierce to the President of Congress, May 23, 1784, Papers of Cont. Cong., no. 62, 25-27; *Journals*, XXVII, 505-6, 540-45.

22. *Journals*, XXIX, 835-36; Letters of John Pierce, Oct. 14, 1785, Papers of Cont. Cong., no. 62, 87. On the absence of Pierce's certificates in South Carolina, see *Seventeenth Report of the DAR*, 152. But Treasury reports of 1790 show $233,047 in military certificates listed for South Carolina. It appears that Pierce validated the settlement which the state conducted with its line. *American State Papers, Finance*, I, 239.

North Carolina undertook a general settlement of the accounts of its line before Pierce arrived and completed it with his assistance, having already absorbed part of the debt.[23] Virginia had provided for the pay of its troops up to the beginning of 1782, but Pierce issued certificates for commutations of pensions and other items not covered by state payments. Pierce issued nearly $11,000,000 in military certificates, of which perhaps $5,000,000 represented the commutation of pensions which Congress granted the officers at the time of the Newburgh affair. Soldiers on an average got up to two or three hundred dollars in satisfaction of all their claims, while the total sums received by officers ranged from $1,500, in the case of lieutenants, to $4,400 for colonels and nearly $10,000 for generals.[24]

There remained the accounts of the dispersed host of federal officers who had handled public money during the war. The inspection of these accounts was deemed a necessary counterpart of the settlement with private creditors, for the data furnished by public servants could be measured against the claims of individuals and vice versa. All the officers had left the service with their accounts unsettled, and their claims for commissions and other remuneration could not be honored until their accounts were approved. In addition, it was supposed that many of them owed money to the government and that others were guilty of fraud and deceptions.

Congress in 1782 initiated a general settlement of the accounts of persons in charge of public funds or property during the Revolution. The settlement was as rigorous and exacting as Congress and the treasury could make it; the final outcome, some ten or fifteen years later, was a neat, finite list of balances. Everything suggests, however, that order was imposed on irreparable confusion. Even if it had been possible at a later date to calculate the inevitable complexities of time, depreciation, and local incident that had affected financial transactions, a rigorous settlement was out of the question.

23. *Journal of the House of Commons of North Carolina*, Dec. 6, 1786, Dec. 21, 1789, Dec. 15, 1790; *Laws of North Carolina*, Nov. sess., 1790, ch. 13, also Dec. sess., 1790, ch. 3; Clark, ed., *State Records of North Carolina*, XXV, 75-76.

24. Pierce issued $1,129,539 in Virginia. *American State Papers, Finance*, I, 239. Estimate of the commutation was given in 1783. *Journals*, XXIV, 286. The calculation on soldiers' and officers' claims is based on the records of the payments to the Maryland line. Commissioners of Army Accounts, Pay Account, 1784-1798, Md. Hall of Records.

Most accounts had been badly kept, and records were blank in important particulars. Purchasing committees of Congress had not kept vouchers to show that money had been applied to the purposes stated; their accounts were mysterious, leaving much to conjecture, and it was difficult to fix responsibility because accounts had remained open during the lives of successive committees. In the five executive departments, officers had frequently been drafted from the military forces; they knew little of accounting methods, failed to keep their books properly, and practiced their errors for years, uncorrected by the casual inspections of their superior officers. Morris once wrote that military officers thought keeping books and husbanding supplies rather beneath their dignity.[25]

Congress undertook the settlement of staff accounts in February 1782, directing Morris to appoint five commissioners for the Quartermaster, Commissary, Hospital, Clothier, and Marine departments. The appointees were William Denning, Jonathan Burrall, Edward Fox, Joseph Bindon, and Joseph Pennel. All were conscientious men, well qualified for their jobs. Morris reminded them: "You cannot be ignorant that the public Officers in the several Departments have been charged with Peculation, Fraud, and speculating with the public money."[26] It was their business to uncover frauds and demand satisfaction from the persons implicated.

Under Morris and his successor, the Board of Treasury, an effort was made to obtain documentary proof of all transactions. The commissioners were required to demand vouchers which would prove that money or certificates had actually been employed as stated in the accounts. This task involved the separate inspection of thousands of papers which, if they existed at all, were in many cases scattered about the country. From the standpoint of the officers whose accounts were under examination, the meticulous requirements of the commissioners were a source of needless delay and expense to themselves. Particularly inconvenienced were officers of high rank who could not clear their accounts and take their commissions until

25. See Morris to President of Congress, Apr. 20, 1782, Official Letterbook C, 198-201, Morris Correspondence, Lib. Cong.

26. Morris to the President of Congress, Feb. 18, 1782, Wharton, ed., *Diplomatic Correspondence*, V, 171-72; *Journals*, XXII, 102-4, 204, 425, XXIII, 645-46, 648, XXIV, 402; Morris to Commissioners for settling Accounts in the several Departments, Sept. 19, 1782, Official Letterbook D, 207-9, Morris Correspondence, Lib. Cong.

the papers of their subordinates were examined. A group of officers complained in 1783 that unless Congress relaxed the rules they "despaired of getting . . . [their accounts] finished during life." Their appeal was supported by a memorial from Charles Stewart, former Commissary General of Issues, who complained that documents involved in the examination of his own accounts were scattered at Albany, Fishkill, Rhode Island, Danberry, and Windham. His ex-deputies refused to pay for sending them to Philadelphia.[27]

In reply to these complaints, the commissioner, Jonathan Burrall, declared that the casual inspections made during the war were of little use in uncovering frauds. He was aware that a less rigorous procedure would be faster, but he felt it would serve no useful purpose, if Congress desired a bona fide settlement; on the other hand, he was prepared to retreat from principle, if it were Congress's wish. "Perhaps, indeed," he observed, permitting himself a touch of irony, "when we consider the very confused and incorrect management of the Purchasing Department, it will appear that no greater evil will arise from complying with the prayer of the Memorialist, than is at present to be apprehended from the vague and uncertain means of collecting the charges against them."[28]

The pedestrian tactics of the commissioners caused less delay, eventually, than the refusal of officers to submit their papers for examination. Throughout the decade many officers were still patching their records, issuing certificates, soliciting vouchers from persons with whom they had had dealings, transferring entries from one heading to another, and negotiating with their old superior officers or deputies over conflicting entries.[29] To save money and consolidate records, Congress in 1786 finally placed the settlement of accounts in the five executive departments under two commissioners, and after pleading earnestly with its former officers to submit documents, authorized the Board of Treasury in May 1788 to enter suit against those who were still delinquent.[30]

27. Thomas Jones et al. to a committee of Congress, Oct. 24, 25, 1783, Gustavus Risberg et al. to the President of Congress, Oct. 23, 1783, Charles Stewart to the President of Congress, Oct. 27, 1783, Papers of Cont. Cong., no. 137, III, 279-81, 283-85, 287-88, 271-73.

28. Burrall to Robert Morris, Nov. 4, 1783, ibid., III, 275-77.

29. See Journals, XXVIII, 61-62, 92-93, 160n; Edward Carrington to Timothy Pickering, Apr. 13, 1786, Burnett, ed., Letters, VIII, 340.

30. Robert Morris to William Denning, June 19, 1783, Official Letterbook E,

The new federal government retained the administrative staff of the Confederation Congress, and the adjustment of accounts proceeded without interruption. Although much of the spade work had been done by 1790, more than 400 accounts remained open.[31] It is impossible to say what money value they represented, for most of them were stated in terms of the fluctuating currency of the Revolution, but certainly the sums ran into millions of specie dollars. Most of the former heads of departments and their principal deputies were still charged with large amounts on the Treasury books. The most conspicuous were former Commissary General, Jeremiah Wadsworth, who had not settled for $78,000,000 currency, and ex-Quartermaster General Nathanael Greene, who had not explained the disbursement of $86,700,000 currency. But many of the deputies who served under these and other high officers had not closed accounts involving hundreds of thousands and sometimes millions of currency dollars. And there were large open accounts in other branches of the administration, particularly in the Clothier and Marine departments. Besides specific charges against individuals, there were in each department general accounts for which, apparently, nobody could be held responsible. Some $300,000 specie and $1,776,450 currency was charged to military and ordnance stores; $2,700,000 currency to Quartermaster and Commissary stores; $1,275,000 currency and $218,000 specie to branches of the Quartermaster department; $2,791,000 currency and $103,000 specie to branches of the Commissary department; $255,000 specie to the Hospital department. As events proved, these charges could not be further defined or settled on individuals.[32]

A balance stated against individuals did not necessarily imply any misbehavior on the part of officers who served during the Revolution; in most cases it merely reflected the difficulties of the settlement. On the other hand, the clearance which they eventually received was no proof of the rectitude of their conduct during the war,

370, Morris Correspondence, Lib. Cong.; *Journals*, XXIX, 905, XXX, 17-19, 34-35, 130-31, 158-59, 182n, 202-3, 239-40, XXXII, 258, XXXIV, 147-48, 159-60, 169-71.

31. See Treasury Board report, May 6, 1788, Papers of Cont. Cong., no. 138, II, 393; Benjamin Walker to Hamilton, Sept. 15, 1789, Hamilton Papers, VIII, 976-79; Lib. Cong.

32. These figures have been extracted from Late Government Balances as Struck on the Treasury Books [undated, but with notations as late as 1797], ser. 392, Record Group 53, Fiscal Records Sec., Natl. Arch.

except in a technical sense, for private advantage could be cultivated in ways that no future accounting could detect.

By the mid-1790's the settlement of domestic accounts had accomplished everything possible in reducing confusion to a semblance of order. Perhaps three hundred accounts of individuals and committees were not closed. Most were for small sums—the irreducible core of larger accounts—about which nothing more could be proved. There were a few sizable balances which might have represented real debts owed to the government,[33] but it is just as likely that they remained unsettled because expenditures could not be verified by the presentation of vouchers or other evidence which the Treasury would accept. The commissioners of the Navy Board of the Middle District, for example, were debited with $4,000,000 currency, $70,000 new emission, and $677 specie, most of which might have gone into paying salaries of naval personnel. The Board of Admiralty could not explain the disposition of $958,000 currency. The deceased Benjamin Flower, former Commissary General of Stores, was still charged with $2,000,000 currency in supplies issued by his department for which receipts had apparently never existed. Ebenezer Hazard, a paymaster in New England, could not verify the expenditure of $3,500,000 currency which had passed through his hands.

It would appear that the Treasury took a most lenient view whenever circumstances indicated that a person's inability to produce vouchers or other data arose from defective bookkeeping or the conditions of his service during the war. Though legally entitled to do so, the Treasury abstained from entering wholesale suits at law against presumed debtors of the government.[34] In the case of committees and boards of Congress, it was virtually impossible to trace individual responsibility, and there is much to suggest that the Treasury simply gave up on many accounts. This is implied by the fact that the general accounts kept in the several departments had a tendency to grow during the 1790's, and though it is impossible to be sure, one suspects that items originally charged against indi-

33. Personal Debtor Accounts, ser. 393, *ibid.* These are undated, but contain notations up to 1797 or later.

34. Report of the committee appointed to enquire into what progress has been made in the settlement of accounts of the former government, Jan. 26, 1795. Broadside, Rare Books Div., Lib. Cong.

viduals were transferred to these general accounts for which nobody could be held responsible. Early in the decade, the general accounts (exclusive of those of the Marine Department and the Admiralty) amounted to about $1,400,000 specie and $10,000,000 currency; by 1797 they had risen to about $1,700,000 specie and $23,000,000 currency.[35]

During the fifteen years in which domestic accounts were being settled, the Treasury addressed itself to the even greater task of adjusting the accounts of officers employed in foreign procurement— a process rich in sensations. Foremost were the accounts of the Secret and Commercial Committees, commonly designated *Mr. Morris's accounts* because Morris had been the pivotal figure and had conducted much of the Secret Committee's business in his own name. But there were also the accounts of foreign commissioners and agents, notably Beaumarchais, Silas Deane, William Bingham, John Ross, Oliver Pollock, Jonathan Williams, and Thomas Morris.[36]

The usual difficulties were encountered. Records were so confused and irregularly kept, especially those of the Secret and Commercial Committees, as to defy analysis. The plethora of detail was so complex that no accurate judgment could be formed about the justice of present charges or the validity of past actions. The main difficulty, as always, was the absence of vouchers: either they did not exist or they were on the other side of the Atlantic. The Treasury therefore had no documentary proof that expenditures noted in the books had been made for the purposes intended or that goods listed as shipped from Europe to the United States had been received by proper persons and applied to public use. Something could be accomplished by a comparison of different accounts, since many of them were closely related, but in the absence of documentary proof it was impossible to make a really accurate settlement. Here again, one is forced to conclude that the order to which these accounts were eventually reduced was not achieved without a great deal of presumption and interpretation on the part of the examiners.

35. Compare the previously cited documents: Late Government Balances as Struck on the Treasury Books, ser. 392, Record Group 53, Fiscal Records Sec., Natl. Arch.; and Personal Debtor Accounts, ser. 393, *ibid.*

36. Benjamin Walker to Hamilton, Sept. 15, 1789, Hamilton Papers, VIII, 976-79, Lib. Cong.

During the early years of the Revolution, Congress displayed a fairly casual attitude toward foreign accounts and was willing to accept settlements conducted by its officers abroad. In 1778 the commissioners at Paris were told to settle Beaumarchais' accounts and determine what Congress owed him; Silas Deane made these arrangements himself.[37] Franklin the same year initiated a settlement with his nephew Jonathan Williams, who served the United States at the port of Nantes. To protect himself against the insinuations of Arthur Lee, Franklin followed the mercantile custom of submitting Williams' accounts to an "impartial" board of arbiters, in this case a number of American merchants who happened to reside at Nantes. Their observations, favorable to Williams, were forwarded to Congress, though in view of Arthur Lee's intrusion into the affair, the merchants forebore rendering a final decision.[38] John Ross's accounts were also settled by arbitration; Samuel Wharton and Edward Bancroft inspected them in 1779 at Franklin's request.[39]

Congress's attitude changed after the Deane-Lee controversy brought foreign agents under heavy fire in 1778 and 1779. It became politically impossible to entrust final decisions respecting foreign accounts to any agency except the Treasury. Insofar as Congress or the Treasury had caught glimpses of accounts kept in Europe, they had found them in many cases defective and contradictory. Several of Beaumarchais' cargoes, apart from being of a quality "not only base but despicable," had arrived without invoices, and there were discrepancies between the goods declared to have been sent and those which arrived.[40] A final reason for the Treasury's desire to review foreign accounts, complete with vouchers, was that until 1789, at least, there was no substantial proof of what happened to

37. Extract from *Journals*, Apr. 13, 1778, Wharton, ed., *Diplomatic Correspondence*, II, 550.

38. Out of a lengthy correspondence on this subject, see Franklin to Arthur Lee, Mar. 13, 1779, to Joseph Wharton *et al.*, Apr. 8, 1779, *ibid.*, III, 77-78, 114-15; Jonathan Williams to Franklin and Adams, Jan. 31, 1779, Jonathan Williams to Franklin, July 22, 27, 1779, Franklin Papers, XXXVIII, 4, 44, 46, Amer. Philos. Soc.

39. Chamber of Accounts, no. 1, Phila., Jan. 5, 1781, Report of two commissioners on the accounts of John Ross, Statement of James Milligan, Auditor General's Office, Jan. 1, 1781, Arthur Lee Papers, Houghton Lib.

40. Morris to Thomas Barclay, Dec. 5, 1782, Official Letterbook D, 437-46, Morris Correspondence, Lib. Cong.; de Francey to Beaumarchais, Dec. 14, 1777, Bigelow, *Beaumarchais the Merchant*, 4-5.

most of the goods shipped from Europe to the United States on public account—the relevant documents were still abroad. In 1781 Auditor General James Milligan questioned the propriety of making any final settlement of foreign accounts until vouchers and other documents were examined at the Treasury.[41]

In 1782 Congress appointed Thomas Barclay commissioner to settle European accounts. As first envisaged, his duty was to collect documents in Europe which would be settled by the Treasury. But Financier Robert Morris argued that Barclay's judgment would have to be accepted in all doubtful cases, and that he might as well be given the authority to make a conclusive settlement on the spot. Congress was persuaded to grant Barclay this authority. The policy, however, did not last long after Morris's retirement. In settling accounts, Barclay merely transmitted general statements without accompanying documents and the Board of Treasury regarded his work as tentative and subject to review.[42]

By the end of the decade, years of work on all the Revolutionary financial records gradually revealed deficiencies in the foreign procurement accounts. In 1788 a committee of Congress observed that the Secret Committee could not account for almost $2,000,000, except by contracts with its own members, who would not submit their documents. There was no documentary evidence of what had happened to 19,700,000 livres of the 47,000,000 received from France during the war. After hearing this report, Congress directed Thomas Jefferson, Minister to France, to send the papers Barclay had accumulated to the United States for examination and comparison with other records.[43] Barclay's work was finished.

Several of the major foreign accounts had already acquired a sensational history. Among them none were more inscrutable than those of the colorful Beaumarchais, who never achieved a final settlement during his lifetime. Late in 1777 he had sent an agent,

41. Statement of James Milligan, Auditor General's Office, Jan. 1, 1781, Arthur Lee Papers, Houghton Lib.

42. At the time of his appointment Barclay was already in Europe as an American consul, and, among other duties, helping Silas Deane to arrange his papers. *Journals*, XXII, 306, 421, XXIII, 728-30, 744; Morris to Scott *et al.*, Aug. 26, 1782, Official Letterbook D, 134-40, Morris Correspondence, Lib. Cong.; Morris to Barclay, Dec. 5, Wharton, ed., *Diplomatic Correspondence*, VI, 115-19.

43. *Journals*, XXXIV, 339, 562-64. See *ibid.*, XX, 645, 681, XXIV, 234-38. Barclay had gone on a diplomatic mission to Morocco.

Théveneau de Francey, to America in an effort to collect money due him for supplies. Discrepancies were uncovered in the accounts which de Francey presented, and Congress was not certain, after hearing Arthur Lee's allegations, that the supplies had not in fact been a gift from the French Court. Trying to act fairly in the circumstances, Congress instructed the commissioners at Paris to settle Beaumarchais' accounts and also to ask the Court whether the supplies were a gift. In due time Congress was informed that the supplies were not a gift; the Court considered the United States in debt for them to Beaumarchais. The commissioners at Paris sent in Silas Deane's settlement of Beaumarchais' claims, which totaled some 5,000,000 livres.

Beaumarchais had already received 300,000 livres and 115 hogsheads of tobacco on his account with Congress, which the Treasury now stated at 4,500,000 livres, without commissions or insurance. At the suggestion of de Francey, Congress paid Beaumarchais 2,400,000 livres in bills drawn on American funds in France, payable in January 1782. He also received 432,000 livres to compensate him for the interest which would accumulate by the time the bills were due for payment. Beaumarchais immediately sold these bills at a discount to realize his money.[44]

He still claimed a balance of 3,300,000 livres, which included over a million for interest, but payment was indefinitely suspended when it was discovered that the American commissioners at Paris had given receipts to the French government for one million livres more than the United States had received. The extra million had been given to Beaumarchais by the French government and charged to the United States as a gift. Justifiably suspicious, Congress would pay Beaumarchais nothing more until the mystery was cleared up. The situation was inescapably ambiguous, as it remains to this day, and despite the repeated assertions of the Court up to 1789 that Congress owed Beaumarchais for all the supplies he had delivered, Congress would pay him nothing. Meanwhile his accounts were reviewed several times: by Deane in 1781 after his return to France; by Thomas Barclay in 1783; by Arthur Lee, acting for the Board of Treasury, who in 1787 declared that Beaumarchais owed the United

44. The bills were paid by Franklin out of French loans. *Journals,* XIV, 690-93, 746-47.

States 1,800,000 livres; and by Hamilton in 1793, who restored a balance in Beaumarchais' favor.   After 1789 the revolutionary governments of France would not support Beaumarchais' claim, which remained in dispute until 1835 when Congress paid his heirs 800,000 francs.[45]

Silas Deane had similar misfortunes, and his claims like those of Beaumarchais were not honored until after his death.   After being recalled from France, he arrived in the United States in 1778; he had not organized his financial records—indeed, he had not brought them with him.   He expected to be paid expenses and commission on presentation of a general financial statement whose main headings were corroborated by extracts from the accounts of Grand, banker to the commissioners in France.[46]   But Deane's case was complicated by his being a protagonist in the Deane-Lee imbroglio, and the stricter requirements toward which the Treasury was tending made it even more unlikely that his statement would be accepted without supporting data.   Congress sent him back to put his books in order, making it perfectly clear that he would get no commission until his papers were examined at the Treasury.   Although this treatment could be considered harsh, especially in contrast with the favor bestowed on Arthur Lee, from whom every kind of evidence was accepted in lieu of vouchers, it was probably not unjustified since Deane was known to have been deeply involved in private transactions, whereas Arthur Lee was not.

In 1781 Deane was still struggling to collect vouchers.   Apparently his accounts were not distinguished by the clarity he liked to imagine they had, because Thomas Barclay, who reviewed them in Europe, found it necessary to work on them intermittently for several years. Deane kept hoping that Congress would authorize Barclay to make

45. On the Beaumarchais claim, see de Francey to Beaumarchais, Dec. 14, 1777, Bigelow, *Beaumarchais the Merchant*, 4-5; Extract from the *Journals*, Apr. 13, 1778, Committee of Foreign Affairs to the Commissioners at Paris, May 15, 1778, Wharton, ed., *Diplomatic Correspondence*, II, 550, 582; Thomas Barclay to Franklin, Mar. 23, 1782, Bache Papers, Amer. Philos. Soc.; Accounts of Beaumarchais, June 3, 1782, Robert Morris Correspondence, Lib. Cong.; Lomenie, *Beaumarchais*, 321-35; *Journals*, XXXIV, 542-48.   An excellent account of the affair is Charles J. Stille, "Beaumarchais and 'The Lost Million,'" *Penn. Mag. of Hist. and Biog.*, 11 (1887), 1-36.

46. Deane to the President of Congress, Sept. 22, 1778, Apr. 30, 1779, Wharton, ed., *Diplomatic Correspondence*, II, 736-38, III, 148-51; Copy of Grand's General Account . . . Mar. 27, 1778, *Deane Papers*, III, 21-33.

a final settlement by arbitration, thus entitling him to his commissions. But this was a vain hope. Deane had been exposed as an
apostate to the American cause and was thereby deprived of the
open support of his friends in the United States. Barclay concluded his labors over Deane's papers in 1787, and they were trans-
ported to the United States, where the Treasury examined them in
1790.[47]

Although it seems unlikely that Deane's accounts were not without technical flaws, the major obstacle to their acceptance was the
amount of his commission. Deane charged 5 percent on the goods
he procured through Beaumarchais; together with Beaumarchais'
commission this raised the total on these goods to 15 percent, an
unreasonable figure. There were also a few objections to his expense
account and some doubt whether certain other items did not represent his private dealings. For these reasons his accounts were held
in suspension long after his death. They were finally settled in
1838, when the Treasury allowed a full commission of 5 percent on
his disbursements up to $200,000 (the amount of the Indian Contract,
which was the basis for his going to France in the first place) and
$2\frac{1}{2}$ percent on goods procured through Beaumarchais. His heirs
received $37,000.[48]

Most of the other agents who served Congress or its committees
abroad during the war had less difficulty. The settlement in Europe
of Jonathan Williams' accounts, which Franklin had arranged, was
accepted by the Treasury. Although Williams' accounts were placed
on file and not finally approved until a later date, he did not have
to wait for his commissions—in 1781 Franklin had taken care to pay

47. Congress in 1780 appointed a Mr. Joshua Johnson of Nantes to examine
Deane's accounts, but he declined. Report of a Committee on Arthur Lee's
Accounts, Jan. 15, 1781, Papers of Cont. Cong., no. 31, II, 315; Joshua Johnson
to Franklin, July 1, 1780, Franklin Papers, XIX, 1, Amer. Philos. Soc.; Deane to
Barnabas Deane, Feb. 23, 1781, *Deane Papers*, IV, 283-85; Thomas Barclay to
Congress, Dec. 21, 1781, Acc. 161, no. 248, env. 6, Foreign Affairs Sec., Natl.
Arch.; Jefferson to Jay, Jan. 2, 1786, env. 17, *ibid.;* Barclay to Franklin, Mar. 23,
1782, Bache Papers, Amer. Philos. Soc.; Deane to Wadsworth, Dec. 14, 1784,
Emmett Collection, N. Y. Pub. Lib.; Treasury Dept., Auditor's Office statement,
July 6, 1790, Deane Papers, Conn. Hist. Soc.

48. Beaumarchais once offered to pay Deane 2 percent on all the sums which
he, Beaumarchais, received from Congress if Deane were denied his claim to
5 percent. Beaumarchais to Deane, Sept. 11, 1781, *Deane Papers*, IV, 460-61;
Copy of the Accounts of Silas Deane according to the Act for settlement and
payment thereof, Deane Papers, Conn. Hist. Soc.

him the balance he claimed.[49] The settlement of John Ross's accounts in Europe by arbitration resulted in a balance of $86,000 in his favor, and although this decision was considered no more than tentative, Ross was given a credit on the books in advance of a conclusive settlement. A similar credit was granted to William Bingham. As Superintendent of Finance, Morris seized the opportunity to pay both Ross and Bingham in specie—an act which discriminated in favor of his former partners and aroused much criticism. In Bingham's case the payment proved to be somewhat premature: it was later discovered that he had charged Congress for money which he had borrowed on public account and had presumably repaid; but the Treasury had no proof that he had repaid the loan.[50] The same difficulty was encountered in settling the accounts of Oliver Pollock, a former Morris partner and Secret Committee agent at New Orleans, who charged the government for a loan he had contracted on behalf of the United States. Pollock, like Bingham, had been given a credit in advance of a final settlement, but in this case Morris was prevented by an act of Congress from giving him any money until Pollock produced evidence that he had repaid the loan.[51] In spite of these complications, however, the accounts of Ross, Bingham, and Pollock were closed by the early 1790's and never seriously challenged.

In quite a different category were the accounts of the Secret and Commercial Committees, in which were mingled the accounts of Robert and Thomas Morris. This body of papers constituted the substantive evidence in the case of Deane versus Lee, and it was presumed that a thorough examination would either indict or vindicate the central figures in the controversy. Unfortunately the accounts were so complicated and obscure, so intimately linked with

49. Deane to John Jay, Nov. 16, 1780, *Deane Papers*, IV, 252-60; Jonathan Williams' Account for clothing, 1780-1781, Acc. 161, no. 248, env. 1, Foreign Affairs Sec., Natl. Arch.

50. Report of two Commissioners on the accounts of John Ross, Chamber of Accounts, no. 1, Jan. 5, 1781, Arthur Lee Papers, Houghton Lib. On Bingham's and Ross's claims, see Report of a Committee on William Bingham's claims, Sept. 22, 1780, Report of a Committee on William Bingham's accounts, June 11 . . . 1781, Papers of Cont. Cong., no. 19, I, 349, 353; Report of a committee on the report of Mr. Pennel, Jan. 11, 1786, *ibid.*, no. 26, III, 573-76; *Journals*, XXI, 1184, XXVIII, 600, XXX, 16-17.

51. Report of a Committee, Apr. 27, 1785, Papers of Cont. Cong., no. 50, I, 1-15; Robert Morris to Duane, Oct. 11, 1782, *ibid.*, 17-19. In 1785 the Board of Treasury allowed Pollock $9,600 interest on the presumed balance in his favor.

other papers whose examination was slow and difficult, that for nearly a decade after the Revolution they defied analysis—in fact, they were never satisfactorily closed. By the mid-1790's, when the Treasury drew up what was probably its final statement, these accounts, with whatever implications of guilt or injured innocence they revealed, aroused no more than a passing interest.

The inquiry had begun early. In June 1777, the Secret Committee was ordered to turn over its papers to its successor, the Commercial Committee, whose chairman, Robert Morris, was entrusted with putting them in order. Morris took the books home with him and got leave from Congress in order to give sufficient time to the job. After nearly a year of intermittent labor, he returned the books in their original condition. Henry Laurens, his assailant in the Deane-Lee controversy, then at its height, had boasted that he could arrange them in a few days if they were given to him. He had his wish gratified but could do nothing with them. The books were then lodged with the Commercial Committee, which was instructed to hire an accountant to arrange them, but little was accomplished. In 1781 the existing members of the Commercial Committee, trying to reconstruct the previous business of the committee found the records in such disorder "as utterly to defeat all hope of their obtaining in any reasonable time, a sufficient knowledge of the state of the Department." Another committee, reporting afterwards that there was no information about military stores sent from Europe to the United States, observed: "There may be materials for such an estimate among the commercial papers, but they are represented to be in such disorder that your Committee thought it needless to make the attempt."[52]

During Morris's term as Superintendent of Finance, the accounts of the Secret and Commercial Committees were not examined any further, and just before the Financier's retirement Congress lodged them with the Comptroller of Accounts. In 1786 the Board of Treasury took them over, and Arthur Lee scrutinized them in his unremitting effort to incriminate Morris. They baffled him. Accountants were hired to put them in order, but there was little progress: In September 1789, Benjamin Walker, who was in charge of settling accounts in the five departments, advised Hamilton that

52. *Journals*, XIX, 63-64, 157, 163-64.

nothing of consequence had ever been done to the papers. At this time there was still an unexplained balance of $2,000,000 charged against the Secret Committee, to say nothing of money advanced to its successor, the Commercial Committee.

The Board of Treasury tried to extract from Morris the papers of his deceased brother Thomas, which had been given to him after his brother's death. Although they had been many years in his possession, they were apparently still so faulty that he was reluctant to submit them for examination. In 1788 a committee of Congress suggested that he be forced to surrender them in order that Congress might gain some information about the disposal of prize ships and cargoes sent into Nantes during the war. Congress so ordered, but in May 1789, it was reported that Morris was still holding up delivery of his papers, presumably including those of Thomas Morris.[53]

Morris was hunting for vouchers as late as March 1790, in an effort to prepare his accounts. It was about this time that the Treasury received the documents which Barclay had collected in Europe, and the settlement of foreign accounts gained momentum. Various charges against Morris and the Secret Committee were narrowed down, presumably on the basis of a reasonable interpretation of the evidence rather than strict accounting procedures, to a final charge of $93,312. Morris executed two bonds for this amount in 1796, secured by mortgages on his property.[54]

The details of Morris's transactions as head of the Secret Committee are hidden, but it would seem that the only circumstances which can exempt him from the charge of having embezzled public funds would be his suppression of the defalcations of his brother Thomas, who as agent at Nantes might have misappropriated cargoes

53. *Ibid.*, XXIV, 511-12, XVI, 161-62, XXX, 327, XXXII, 347, XXXIV, 562-64; State of Accounts of the Secret and Commercial Committees, May 27, 1789, Arthur Lee Papers, Houghton Lib.; Benjamin Walker to Hamilton, Sept. 15, 1789, Hamilton Papers, II, 976-79, Lib. Cong. See also *Journals*, XX, 645, 681, XXIV, 234-38.

54. Morris to John Ross, Mar. 12, 1790, Folder B, Robert Morris Papers, Div. of Public Records, Penn. Hist. and Museum Commission; Outstanding debtors, Doc. 28,793 undated, but probably 1791), Outstanding debtors, Treasury Department, Comptroller's Office, Oct. 26, 1795, Docs. 28,793 and 29,304, War Records Section, Natl. Arch.; Late Government Balances Struck on the Treasury Books (undated, but about 1789 to 1791), ser. 392, and Personal Debtors Accounts, Revolutionary and Confederation Government (undated, but about 1795 to 1798), ser. 392 and 393, Record Group 53, Fiscal Records Sec., *ibid.* See Rufus King to Robert Morris, Apr. 15, 1791, Rufus King Papers, 1788-1792, N.-Y. Hist. Soc.

sent to him on public account. To protect the reputation of his house, Robert Morris had taken responsibility for any misconduct of Thomas Morris. Yet to assume that the embezzlement was his brother's deed is gratuitous, for there is no suggestion of it anywhere; moreover, while at Nantes, Thomas Morris handled few cargoes sent by Robert Morris or the Secret Committee on public account.

Morris's execution of a bond closed off the settlement of the Secret Committee accounts: after 1796 there is no further mention of the balances against the committee or its principal members. However, the accounts of the Commercial Committee, in whose activities Morris was also involved, were not so quickly dispatched. As late as 1796 or 1797, when all the available evidence must have been at hand, there remained large sums unaccounted for. In addition to $50,000 specie for clothing shipped by Arthur Lee, there was a long open account of expenditures amounting to $607,000 specie. It is unlikely that the disposition of these sums was ever satisfactorily explained.[55]

As the first decade of the new federal government elapsed, however, an ending was finally made to the accounts of those federal agents who had once swarmed over the country and across the sea, performing their essential labor without supervision, without help, and without an accounting. A by-product of the settlement was a modest increase in the federal debt as securities were issued to officers and merchants connected with the government who had balances in their favor. The total amount was $1,160,000.[56] In the postwar years, Congress thus appropriated what remained of the Revolutionary debt.

55. Later commercial committees were charged with $20,000 in bills of exchange and $66,000 in new emission money. Personal Debtor Accounts, ser. 393, Record Group 53, Fiscal Records Sec., Natl. Arch.

56. *American State Papers, Finance,* I, 239.

Settlement of State Accounts

"The objects for which both descriptions of the debt [federal and state] were contracted, are in the main the same. Indeed, a great part of the particular debts of the states has arisen from assumptions by them on account of the Union. And it is most equitable, that there should be the same measure of retribution for all."

—Alexander Hamilton, Report
on Public Credit, 1790.

The last step in financial house cleaning was the settlement of accounts between the states and the United States—the accounts of the Confederation. Congress began the process in 1782, but it triggered so many conflicts of interest among the states that it was not completed until 1793. By then the principles which governed it were reshaped and its significance altered by the existence of the new federal government. A by-product of the settlement was the genesis of principles which justified federal assumption of state debts in 1790.

Under the Articles of Confederation the financial relations between Congress and the states and among the states themselves were based on the concept of the Union as a league of thirteen entities. The Articles provided that "all charges of War and all other expences, that shall be incurred for the common defence or general welfare, and allowed by the United States . . . shall be defrayed out of a Common Treasury." Translated into procedure, this meant that the expenses of Congress and the expenditures of the states in the general welfare were to be lumped together in one mass called the *common charges*. At a future time, when all accounts had been settled and the total amount of the common charges made known, each state would be assessed its proper share, according to the value of its land. If a state had contributed more to the war than its proper share, it would receive a credit balance; if not, a debit balance. How balances arising from the final settlement were to be discharged was not certain, but presumably the debtor states would give Congress the money to reimburse the creditor states.

The public debt lay outside this arrangement. The Nationalists established the principle that it was to be excluded from the common charges and vested solely in Congress. Consisting first of loan certificates, the public debt, as we have seen, grew by accretion as commissioners settled the claims of the Continental army and private citizens after the war. Along with the foreign debt, which was always thought to inhere in Congress, the public debt was to be kept intact and paid by the federal government out of its own revenues. This principle was not to be found in the Articles of Confederation and was never universally acknowledged, but Congress and the states acted after 1783 on the premise that the public debt was to be set apart, not included in the general settlement of accounts, nor apportioned among the states.

Further changes in principle developed as Congress addressed itself to the actual task of settling state accounts. When the Articles of Confederation were drafted, the expectation was that not all state expenses would be admissible to the common charges—only those which had been authorized by resolutions of Congress or requested by its officers. Authorized expenditures included payments on requisitions, state retirement of Continental currency and certificates at Congress's request, the expense of recruiting and equipping state lines in the Continental army and employing the militia, back pay and depreciation notes given to soldiers in compliance with Congressional resolutions, and state payments of money and certificates for delivery of supplies to federal officers. It was supposed that expenditures in the general welfare, though vast, could be exactly defined.

This notion was illusory. When the settlement of accounts got under way after the war, it proved impossible to distinguish clearly between authorized and unauthorized expenditures. In some cases, the states had spent money combating the common enemy but had failed to get Congressional authorization. Even when they had financed separate expeditions for their own purposes, who was to say that these had not contributed to the conduct of the war? On a strict accounting such outlays were not to be admitted to the common charges; in practice it was hard to exclude them.

Each state had made expenditures not authorized by Congress. Massachusetts, whose expenditures were typical of the New England states, had been exceptionally zealous in raising troops for the Continental army, and as enthusiasm waned in the later stages of the war, the towns had enlisted men by offering higher bounties than Congress prescribed. Considerable money had also been spent on naval defense and coastal fortifications. The expenditures were not authorized by Congress, but Massachusetts wanted credit for them.[1] A more debatable claim arose from the unhappy expedition which Massachusetts launched upon a British post at Penobscot, Maine. A costly venture, it left a residue of $387,000 in state debt. The general opinion outside Massachusetts was that the desire to secure possession of the area had prompted the expedition and that Massachusetts ought to bear the cost. But Massachusetts charged it against the Union.[2]

Although it did not fall within the category of unauthorized expenditures, the valuation of Continental currency was another major interest of Massachusetts. Congress had rated the old money at 40 to 1 in 1780, but this ratio soon became invalid. The money sank to 100 or 150 to 1 before it went out of circulation and thereafter had no value except as a remote speculation. Congress asked the states in 1780 to retire it by levying taxes; when they got around to acting, the money was nearly or completely worthless. During its last days, it passed at a higher value in Massachusetts than elsewhere, and consequently a great volume of currency had flowed into the state and died there. Massachusetts' taxes, which were vigorously

1. See Madison's Notes of Debates, *Journals*, XXV, 913n.

2. In Hartford the Penobscot expedition was called the "Boston scheme." John Jeffery to Jeremiah Wadsworth, Sept. 2, 1779, Wadsworth Papers, box 129, Conn. Hist. Soc. See *Journals*, XXVII, 394-95; Madison's Notes of Debates, *ibid.*, XXV, 913n; proceedings of the Massachusetts legislature, *Boston Magazine*, July 1786; Rufus King to Elbridge Gerry, Mar. 24, 1785, Nathan Dane to Jacob Wales, Jan. 31, 1786, Burnett, ed., *Letters*, VIII, 71, 294-97.

executed by a conservative government, drew into the treasury not only the state's quota of Continental money, but also a large surplus. The state therefore had a vital concern in the value Congress would place upon the old money and what credit she would be allowed for redeeming it. Massachusetts insisted on a ratio of 40 to 1, hoping thereby to obtain a large credit in the settlement of accounts or force other states to buy currency from her at this price in order to fill their own quotas. Not surprisingly, the other states protested. The issue was argued repeatedly, but never settled during the Confederation.[3]

Among the southern states, Virginia's problems were fairly typical. She also wanted the Union to assume the costs of specific ventures which had not been authorized by Congress, notably the campaigns of George Rogers Clark in the northwest. Nonresidents tended to view Clark's expeditions as a means of securing Virginia's control over the area. But Virginia had a strong bargaining position in this matter. She would not cede her claims to the Northwest unless the expense of Clark's operations was admitted to the common charges.[4]

Otherwise, her position in the general settlement was extremely precarious. As the accounting progressed during the 1780's, it became evident that a great part of her war expenses, though incurred for worthy purposes, had not been authorized by Congress. The planters of Virginia had conducted the war as a local enterprise, with little regard for the niceties of bookkeeping or the letter of Congressional requests. The state had assumed expenses that properly belonged to the federal government, blending state and federal expenses in the same accounts. One commissioner charged that this cavalier attitude was grounded in the expectation that all expenditures would be chargeable to the Union. Whatever the reason, neglect had serious consequences, particularly after the major campaigns shifted southward in 1779. With the enemy on the premises,

3. In 1784 a grand committee of Congress resolved to rate Continental money at its actual value at the time the state withdrew it. This is what was done in 1793. *Journals,* XXVII, 394-97. See numerous allusions to this question in Burnett's *Letters,* VI and VII; *Journals,* XX, 702, 750, XXI, 897, XXIII, 590-91, 831-32, XXIV, 39-42; Madison's Notes of Debates, *ibid.,* XXIII, 831-32, 854-56, 865-66.

4. Hening, ed., *Statutes of Virginia,* X, 564-66. See Monroe to Madison, May 31, 1786, Burnett, ed., *Letters,* VIII, 377.

the state government dug deeply into Virginia's resources to support the war, but, through failure to observe the rules prescribed by Congress, gained insignificant credits on the books of the federal Treasury.[5]

Virginia's predicament was shared by North Carolina and Georgia. Contrasting the pecuniary spirit of New Englanders, who always kept close accounts, with the spontaneous patriotism of Southerners, who spilled out their treasure without thought of a reckoning, a North Carolina delegate to Congress once complained: "While some of the Northern States never turned out a Serjeants guard of Militia without obtaining the sanction of Congress or of some Continental officer our State in the true Spirit of a patriot but not of an accoumptant has been expending Militia and raising State troops without taking any heed concerning the day of retribution."[6]

The day of retribution loomed large as the southern states took stock of their position in the settlement of accounts. They could not benefit greatly by the admission of one or another specific expenditure to the common charges. The southern interest could be served only by broadening the concept of the general welfare to admit claims founded in equity.

The southern states also had a vital interest in liberalizing the rules for admission of evidence in support of claims. Under regulations drawn up by Morris and later by the Board of Treasury for settling state accounts, claims for expenditures in the general welfare had to be supported at each point by documents showing how virtually every dollar had been spent. The regulations entailed much paper work which none of the state governments were capable of during the war. With the exception of South Carolina, whose accounts were in fairly good condition, there was never the slightest possibility that claims of the southern states could be supported by documents. Not only had contempt for procedural details been an

---

5. David Jameson to Madison, Aug. 15, 1781, William C. Rives Collection, Madison Papers, box 10, Lib. Cong.; Ephraim Blaine to Robert Morris, Nov. 27, 1781, Blaine Letterbook, 1780-1783, *ibid.;* Zephaniah Turner to Robert Morris, Oct. 22, 1783, Papers of Cont. Cong., no. 138, I, 453; Robert Forsyth to Col. William Davies, Aug. 4, 1781, Charles Stewart and Ephraim Blaine to Davies, Nov. 8, 1781, Davies to the Executive, Aug. 14, 1781, Jan. 19, June 17, 1782, *Cal. Va. State Papers,* II, 292-94, 587, 328-29, III, 36, 195.

6. Hugh Williamson to the Governor of North Carolina, Sept. 30, 1784, Burnett, ed., *Letters,* VII, 595.

ingrained habit, but the British invasion had spread confusion and caused the destruction of records.

Closely involved in the question of evidence was another question which grew out of state assumption of the unliquidated federal debt. The southern states had gone furthest in assuming Quartermaster and Commissary certificates and other unliquidated claims against Congress, converting them into state debts before they had been reviewed by federal commissioners. It appears that when state agents determined the value of federal certificates held by local citizens, it was likely to be on terms very favorable to the citizens. The county courts doing the work in Virginia required little in the way of evidence and freely accepted testimony in lieu of documents.[7] State securities were issued to citizens in exchange for their federal certificates, which were then lodged in the state treasury, where they formed the basis of claims for expenditures in the general welfare.

Congress had adopted a very liberal policy toward civilian creditors when the settlement was conducted by its own officers, but the Board of Treasury would not extend the same leniency to settlements by state officers. It regarded all state adjustment of individual claims made after February 20, 1782,[8] as inconclusive until reviewed by federal commissioners. This policy cast doubt on state claims for expenditures in the general welfare and meant that all their settlements would have to be re-examined, with a likely possibility that many would be invalidated.

The southern states worked to establish a more liberal rule. Led by South Carolina, which had liquidated and assumed virtually the whole federal debt held by her citizens, they demanded that the same rules which governed settlements by federal officers should be extended to those made by the states. This would ensure acceptance of state claims founded on the assumption of unliquidated federal securities.

7. See Andrew Dunscomb to the Board of Treasury, July 1, 1785, Papers of Cont. Cong., no. 139, I, 229; Abstract of Queries made by Officers of the Treasury and of Information transmitted in reply by the Commissioners (undated), Samuel Osgood Papers, N.-Y. Hist. Soc.

8. The date Congress provided for commissioners to settle individual claims. It should be noted that when states assumed public securities (issued by federal commissioners in the adjustment of claims), no re-evaluation was necessary. For the Board's policy, see *Journals*, XXIX, 536-39; Board of Treasury report, Aug. 9, 1785, Papers of Cont. Cong., no. 138, II, 381.

Another dispute, which generally aligned the south against New England, concerned the rule that each state's share of the common expenses be in proportion to the value of its land. The rule was never operative. An appraisal of land values was impracticable during the war; therefore Congress made population the standard, basing each state's quota of requisitions on the estimated number of its inhabitants, adding the proviso that the quotas were tentative and subject to retroactive adjustment whenever the value of land could be determined. Later, the use of land values raised so many difficulties that Congress proposed an amendment to the Articles of Confederation making population the rule of apportionment. The amendment was never ratified by the states, and it remained doubtful whether population or the value of land was to be the standard.[9]

It was clear that a final apportionment on either basis would be unfair. The wealth and population of the states were changing; moreover, some of the states had suffered more during the war than others. New York, in particular, always contended that the long British occupation of her main city should exempt her from part of her share of the total expenses. Her argument was similar to the plea of the southern states that the final settlement must be governed by principles of equity rather than technical requirements.[10]

The settlement of accounts thus gave rise to conflicts of interest in which no state could realize its own advantage without conceding something to the others. There was continuous bargaining throughout the Confederation. The necessity of compromise forced Congress toward expansive principles which would encompass all demands.[11]

As early as 1783, Robert Morris anticipated the final solution. He proposed a generous scheme—one of the spectacular operations by which he tried to override rather than solve problems of divergent state interests.[12] He suggested that all claims be allowed: the

9. *Journals*, XXIV, 135-37, 257-61.
10. See Morris to the President of Congress, Aug. 28, 1781, Wharton, ed., *Diplomatic Correspondence*, IV, 667-69.
11. See Hugh Williamson to the Governor of North Carolina, Sept. 30, 1784, Nathan Dane to Jacob Wales, Jan. 31, 1786, Burnett, ed., *Letters*, VII, 593-98, VIII, 294-97; Madison's Notes of Debates, *Journals*, XXV, 913n.
12. Morris to the President of Congress, Mar. 8, 1783, Morris to Gerry, Aug. 26, 1783, Wharton, ed., *Diplomatic Correspondence*, VI, 280-81, 658-61.

states should be given a blanket credit for all expenditures from the beginning of the war. There should be no attempt to apportion the total of these expenses and arrive at final balances. The states should simply be given federal securities to the full amount of their expenses. Those states which had internal debts would then be able to eliminate them by transferring federal securities to their creditors. Congress, in effect, would assume all expenses and all debts; the states as well as private individuals would be its creditors. Thus, Morris sought to evade the problems attendant on the settlement of accounts and at the same time forward his plans for political centralization.[13]

His thinking had the benefit of a year's reflection. In 1782, when Congress initiated the settlement of state accounts, there had been little perception of the difficulties. It was thought that the job could be quickly discharged by single commissioners. Congress entrusted the settlement to the commissioners appointed to adjust civilian accounts under the ordinance of February 20, 1782. The settlement, however, proved to be the work of many years. The commissioners busied themselves with the claims of individuals until 1785 or 1786, at which time they had done little or nothing on state accounts. But the states had begun to put their accounts in order, and as they realized what their problems were, they formulated their position with respect to Congressional policy.

An illuminating debate took place in connection with the funding requisition of 1783. The core of the bill was a request for a federal impost and for permanent supplementary taxes; but Congress explored other propositions to make the bill more attractive to individual states. The Massachusetts delegates took the opportunity to propose that the expense of the Penobscot expedition be made a charge against the Union. New York demanded on grounds of equity that the final apportionment should excuse the state from part of her share of the costs of the war. Virginia tried to gain the acceptance of unauthorized expenditures to the common charges. Madison proposed that all the expenditures of the states during the war be

13. See *Journals*, XXII, 14*n*, 82-86. A year earlier Morris had tried in a similar grand style to dispose of the thorny problem of the rule of apportionment by proposing that each state send a delegate to a meeting in Philadelphia which would there determine by majority vote each state's share of the total expenses of the war. Congress, however, reserved the final decision for itself.

made a charge against the Union. He was concerned mainly with getting credit for George Rogers Clark's expeditions. In return he held out the inducement that Virginia would surrender her western claims to the United States.[14]

Early drafts of the funding requisition included a range of provisions to accommodate the interests of particular states: allowances for states which had suffered extraordinary hardship during the war, admission into the common charges of all "reasonable" military expenditures, and the cession of claims to western lands. In the course of debate, however, Congress narrowed the terms. The New England and middle states were afraid that opening the common charges to unauthorized expenditures would admit a flood of extravagant claims from Virginia. The southern state's offer to cede western lands did not impress many of the delegates, who believed her incapable in any case of holding the territory. The result was the elimination of all clauses relative to the settlement of accounts, except a proposal that population be substituted for land values as the basis of apportionment. The states were also asked to cede their western claims to Congress.[15] Writing to Jefferson, Madison observed that the funding requisition, in its final form, held "no bait for Virginia." Jefferson agreed, in words forever after misunderstood by historians: "The article . . . which proposed the conversion of state into federal debts was one palatable ingredient at least in the pill we were to swallow." Jefferson, of course, was alluding not to the assumption of state debts but to the admission of Virginia's expenditures into the common charges.[16]

In 1783 Virginia was almost alone among the southern states in trying to alter the mode of settling state accounts. Her efforts

14. Madison's Notes of Debates, *ibid.*, XXIV, 114-17, 138, 162-63, XXV, 913, 913n, 919 *et seq.*; Madison to Edmund Randolph, Apr. 8, 1783, Burnett, ed., *Letters*, VII, 127.

15. *Journals*, XXIV, 170-74, 295-302, XXIV, 162-64, 172-73, 197, 255-61; Madison's Notes of Debates, *ibid.*, XXV, 946-47, 960-62; Madison to Edmund Randolph, Mar. 11, 1783, Stephen Higginson to Theophilus Parsons, Apr. 7, 1783, Burnett, ed., *Letters*, VII, 69, 122-24.

16. Madison to Jefferson, Apr. 22, 1783, *ibid.*, VII, 145-56; Jefferson to Madison, May 7, 1783, Paul Leicester Ford, ed., *The Writings of Thomas Jefferson* (N.Y., 1892-99), IV, 144. See Madison to Jefferson, May 20, 1783, Burnett, ed., *Letters*, VII, 169. This point should be clarified. Before 1789, the settlement of state accounts had nothing to do with the debt of the federal government. The final balances between the states were to be canceled by interstate payments which entailed no increase in the public debt.

to secure the admission of unauthorized expenditures were opposed by South Carolina, and even the North Carolina delegates finally voted against the proposal, possibly out of reluctance to bind their state to a deal involving cession of claims to western lands. In the next two years, however, the southern states—usually joined by Maryland—discovered their mutual interests and were voting solidly on questions relative to the settlement of accounts.

Virginia and North Carolina had generally similar problems: both had incurred heavy expenses which had not been authorized by Congress; neither had observed federal regulations; neither could produce vouchers to verify the expenditures they had made. South Carolina's interests corresponded with the other two states in one important respect: she had gone furthest of all in settling and assuming unliquidated federal securities and was vitally concerned that the settlements she had made with individual creditors should be validated and admitted to the common charges.

All the southern states cherished the notion (unjustified except in the case of South Carolina) that they had contributed more than their share to the prosecution of the war and that they would emerge from the final settlement of accounts with large balances in their favor.[17] They embraced this idea the more fervently because their citizens did not hold much of the public debt, which was concentrated in the middle states and New England. They hoped to gain a large credit in the final settlement, become creditors of the other states, and thereby equalize their financial standing in the Union.[18]

A southern bloc materialized in the debate over the requisition of 1785. South Carolina and Virginia fought hard to commit Congress to a blanket endorsement of settlements they had made with their own citizens. They also tried to get credit on current requisitions for their assumption of unliquidated federal debts and for past expenditures in the general welfare.[19] Obviously, they were

17. Among southern states, only South Carolina emerged with a large credit balance in the final settlement concluded in 1793.

18. See Monroe to Madison, May 8, 1785, Burnett, ed., *Letters*, VIII, 117.

19. Under the indent requisition of 1785 (see pp. 387-90) states got credit for paying interest on public securities; however, the south, with relatively few public securities, wanted to get credit for interest arising on unliquidated securities which they had assumed and which were in their possession. They also proposed that as settlement of state accounts progressed, balances in a state's

afraid that a final settlement would never take place, and they desired to have a system in operation which would give them an immediate return, irrespective of the final settlement, for their expenditures in behalf of the Union.

They were defeated in 1785 on a sectional vote, but the next year Congress revised the method of settling state accounts, and they found other avenues toward their objectives. Under the previous arrangement, the commissioners appointed in 1782 were to examine the accounts of the states after they had finished adjusting claims of individuals. The Board of Treasury took a stand against this procedure, complaining that the powers given to the commissioners to accept oaths and indirect evidence in lieu of documents would not be proper in examining state accounts. The commissioners might be too liberal; in any case, some would be more liberal than others, and there would be no common standard of settlement in the various states.[20] While most of the southern delegates did not share the Board's apprehension that the settlement would be too lax, it was clear that disputes would arise if the settlement in each state devolved upon a single commissioner. A centralized system based on uniform principles was indicated; Congress therefore decided to replace the commissioners with a board which would supervise the settlement in all the states.

The southern members wanted to give the new board wide discretionary powers. They backed a motion that it be given authority to admit claims for unauthorized expenditures, reporting to Congress only those which it considered most dubious. They tried to confer on the board specific authority to accept other evidence in support of claims when documents were lacking. Charles Pinckney of South Carolina revived a motion he had made the previous year which would have validated state settlement of unliquidated federal debts.

favor should be placed at interest and the amount of such interest deducted from the state's quota of requisitions. *Journals,* XXIX, 547, 579-81, 587-93, 695-96, 708-9, 739-42, 750-51, 765-71; Monroe to Madison, July 12, 1785, William Grayson to Madison, Sept. 16, 1785, James McHenry to John Hall, Sept. 28, 1785, Burnett, ed., *Letters,* VIII, 163-65, 217, 223-24.

20. *Journals,* XXVIII, 168-69, XXIX, 536-39; Board of Treasury report, Aug. 9, 1785, Papers of Cont. Cong., no. 138, II, 381; Letters of the Board of Treasury, Sept. 17, 1785, *ibid.,* no. 140, II, 91. Under a resolution of March 17, 1785, the commissioners had been ordered to discontinue the adjustment of individual claims within a year (except in Georgia and South Carolina) and start work on state accounts.

These propositions embraced the southern interest in the settlement of accounts, and the southern delegates backed them unanimously.[21]

Each of the states north of Maryland stood to benefit in some degree from a more liberal policy; their claims were not in all cases supported by documents, and they voted unanimously to allow the board to accept other kinds of evidence. But they were not willing to go much further. Although the northern and middle states had all settled and assumed unliquidated federal debts, three northern states divided on Pinckney's motion to instruct the board to validate such settlements.[22] The northern delegates were wary of opening the gates to a flood of overblown claims from the south. Generally speaking, their tactics were to hold the line against a wholesale admission of claims and at the same time try to get specific expenditures of their own states admitted to the common charges. The Massachusetts delegates, for example, had "rugged instructions" to use their "unwearied and unabated exertions" to get credit for the Penobscot expedition, extra bounties, and the state's surplus of Continental currency. In the long run, they were to find this impossible without yielding to southern demands.[23]

The ordinance of 1786 significantly relaxed the rules governing the settlement of state accounts. In acknowledgment of the fact that a strict policy was not feasible, the proposed board was instructed to take cognizance of expenditures not authorized by Congress and to accept other evidence in lieu of vouchers. These concessions were immensely valuable to the southern states, but in other respects the ordinance fell short of their desires. The board was not given the authority to approve dubious claims, and the effort to obtain blanket acceptance of state-conducted settlement of unliquidated federal debts was defeated. South Carolina and Georgia voted against the ordinance; Maryland was divided; only Virginia supported it.[24] Nevertheless, the south triumphed, for the ordinance

21. *Journals*, XXIX, 912, XXXI, 636-37, 643-44, 666-67, 741-42, 744-45, 771-79.
22. *Ibid.*, XXXI, 742-43, 771-72. But see *ibid.*, 778-79.
23. *Ibid.*, XXXI, 772-73; Rufus King to Elbridge Gerry, Mar. 24, 1785, Nathan Dane to Hon. Samuel Phillips, Jan. 20, 1786, Burnett, ed., *Letters*, VIII, 71, 71*n*, 288-89; Discussions of the Massachusetts legislature reported in the *Boston Magazine*, July 1786. Rufus King notified the Massachusetts legislature in 1786 that the southern claims would probably be allowed. He interpreted this as an advantage to Massachusetts, as their claims would also be admitted. King's letter is printed in the *Boston Magazine*, Sept., Oct., 1786.
24. North Carolina was not represented. *Journals*, XXXI, 771-72, 777-81.

relinquished technical requirements in favor of equity. Thereafter, there was really no way of refusing any claims for expenditures in the general welfare.

Within a year Congress had waived all formal requirements. The Ordinance of May 7, 1787, established a new General Board of three commissioners which had complete authority to conclude the settlement of accounts with the various states. There was no limit to its discretionary powers. The ordinance fully acknowledged the propriety of claims which were inadmissible for technical reasons and invested the Board with authority to allow them in accordance with "principles of general equity."[25]

Envisaging a quick settlement of state accounts, Congress appointed five district commissioners to collect within six months all the material which the states had to offer in support of claims. The claims were to be processed first by the commissioners themselves; if clearly authorized by resolutions of Congress and properly supported by documents, they were to be passed immediately to the credit of the state. In case of doubt, the claims and supporting documents were to be passed on to the General Board.[26]

The southern states, except South Carolina, were caught unprepared. Every state in the Union had difficulty arranging its accounts and supporting claims with documents, but the financial records of Virginia, North Carolina, and, apparently, Georgia were so fragmentary and confused as to defy organization. When the district commissioner, Mr. William Winder, arrived in Virginia, he was so appalled by the disorganization that he refused to pass any significant amount to the credit of the state, considering all claims dubious. He would not even sign a receipt for a statement of Virginia's claims, fearing that his signature might be construed as an endorsement. Instead, he insisted upon packing up all the material for presentation to the General Board.

The situation was critical for Virginia. The exhibition of her accounts in their existing disarray would probably elicit a rejection, especially in view of Winder's negative attitude. He had to be prevented from taking away the documents until there was time to

25. *Ibid.,* XXXII, 262-66.
26. *Ibid.,* XXXII, 60*n*, 141, 206-9, 223*n*, 258-66; Madison's Notes of Debates, *ibid.,* XXXIII, 729.

arrange them. In this emergency Virginia called upon Mr. William
Davies, former member of the state Board of War and a man of
experience and ability, who was put in charge of Virginia's accounts.
As he recalled, his first task was to pick a quarrel with Winder; he
did this, and the district commissioner finally departed without the
documents. Time was gained, but the status of Virginia's claims
remained precarious. The legislature called an official halt to any
further action in settling accounts while the state's delegates to
Congress applied for an extension of time.[27]

Winder also got a cold reception in North Carolina. Francis
Child, the state agent in charge of arranging accounts, was unable
to put them in any degree of order within the allotted period of
six months. Winder would not approve any of the state's claims;
nor would he affix his signature to a column of figures representing
them. Child at first refused to surrender any documents to Winder,
but the governor intervened, and Winder returned to New York with
the records.[28]

Virginia shortly experienced another setback. One of her primary
aims was to charge the expense of George Rogers Clark's campaigns
to the Union. In accepting Virginia's cession of her claims to the
Northwest, Congress had agreed to assume all reasonable expense
of the Clark expeditions. The amount was to be determined by a
board of three commissioners, one appointed by Congress, another
by the state, and a third by the other two commissioners. What
credit would be allowed depended chiefly on the attitude of the commissioners, for Clark informed the governor that vouchers could
not be found.[29]

27. Andrew Dunscomb to the Executive, May 23, 1788, William Davies to the
Executive, Feb. 25, 1794, *Cal. Va. State Papers,* IV, 444-46, VII, 44-45; William
Winder to the Board of Treasury, May 28, 1788, Board of Treasury reports, May
7, 1788, Sept. 10, 1788, Papers of Cont. Cong., no. 138, I, 309, 365, II, 77, 421.
See also *Cal. Va. State Papers,* IV, 370, 490, 557, 567-70, 662-63, and *Journals,*
XXXIV, 140n, 145-46, 203-4, 253-60, 443-44, 503-6.
28. Francis Child to Governor Johnston, July 1, 1788, Child to Johnston,
undated [Dec. 1788], Johnston to Child, Dec. 28, 1788, Clark, ed., *State Records
of North Carolina,* XXI, 480-82, 512-14; Hugh Williamson to the Governor of
North Carolina, Oct. 13, 1788, Mar. 2, 9, 1789, Burnett, ed., *Letters,* VIII, 804-5,
824-25, 825-26.
29. Hening, ed., *Statutes of Virginia,* X, 564-66; *Journals,* XXV, 560, XXVI,
112-17, XXVIII, 261; George Rogers Clark to the Governor of Virginia, Oct. 8,
1787, *Cal. Va. State Papers,* IV, 346-47.

Congress's appointee was Edward Fox, but after some time had elapsed he resigned, complaining that the salary was too low. Meanwhile, the other two commissioners, William Heth of Virginia and Colonel David Henley, went ahead under the supervision of the state governor. Alarmed by the prospect, the Board of Treasury prodded Congress to fill the vacancy created by Fox's resignation. The man appointed was John Pierce, Commissioner of Army accounts and a stickler for detail. He betrayed what Virginia's agent, William Heth, described as a narrow and parsimonious attitude. Then Pierce fell ill and could not attend the meetings of the commissioners. During his absence Heth and Henley announced an award of $500,000—considered a reasonable sum in Virginia. Congress would not formally endorse this decision, despite the Virginia legislature's threat to withhold any further payment of requisitions until the state was fully indemnified for Clark's conquest of the Northwest.[30]

By the time the new federal government began functioning, the settlement of state accounts had gained scope and momentum. Principles of equity had unfolded a boundless field for claims against the Union. The states revised estimates upward and discovered new expenditures. They appointed agents to scan old documents and scour the land for vouchers. In 1787 Congress had set a deadline of six months for the submission of claims and documents; this date was set back and a new one established, but none of the states accepted the new deadline as final. Nor was it. Two years after the inauguration of the new government, the states were still gathering material and presenting new claims. In one of its last acts, the Congress of the Confederation had appointed three commissioners to sit as the General Board and finally adjudicate state claims. The Board was retained by the new government, and the states sent agents to New York to negotiate their settlements with the Board,

---

30. *Journals*, XXVIII, 103, 258-61, 442, XXXI, 737, 741, 886n, XXXII, 165-66, 171-72, XXXIV, 134-35, 178, 180-81; Letter of the Board of Treasury, Apr. 9, 1787, Papers of Cont. Cong., no. 140, II, 411, 415; William Heth to Governor Randolph, Mar. 9, 21, Apr. 16, 1788, *Cal. Va. State Papers*, IV, 406, 414-16, 425-26; Nicholas Gilman to the President of New Hampshire, Mar. 22, 1788, Virginia delegates to William Heth, Apr. 20, 1788, Burnett, ed., *Letters*, VIII, 708-9, 723; George Lee Tuberville to Madison, Jan. 8, 1788, Madison Papers, N.Y. Pub. Lib. A statement of the account for Clark's expedition is in Theodore C. Pease, ed., *George Rogers Clark Papers, 1781-1784* (Springfield, 1924), Ill. State Hist. Lib., *Collections*, XIX.

as well as with the Treasury officials who processed the accounts.[31]
No one could forecast the Board's decisions.   In Virginia there
was serious concern about the fate of the state's claims.   The Massachusetts delegates to Congress had a vague suspicion that the appointments to the Board were "crooked" and that the Penobscot claims
would be thrown out.[32]   However, the Board's conduct was in some
degree predisposed by its commitment to principles of equity, dictated
by the Confederation Congress, and by a growing inclination, now
that the new government was formed, to reconcile differences by
granting all demands.

The settlement of accounts had already given birth to the principles which were to justify federal assumption of state debts.   Technical rules had been suspended in favor of equity, and it was virtually acknowledged that all state war expenses had been incurred
in the common cause and should be admitted as a charge against the
Union.   State debts could be considered the unabsorbed residue of
the common effort, distinguishable from federal debts only in having
been contracted by states rather than by Congress.   The creditors
of the states were in the same category as creditors of Congress and
no less deserving of payment.

Only one further idea was necessary to complete the arguments
Hamilton used in 1790 to justify federal assumption, and this idea,
too, had developed during the settlement of state accounts—equality
of sacrifice.   Nearly every state asserted that it had contributed more
than its share to the war.   For lack of an effective majority to prove
otherwise, Congress was compelled to proceed on the assumption
that the sacrifices of the states, though different, had been equal.
It therefore became an arguable question in 1790 whether states
with large debts ought not to be relieved of them by the Union,
such debts having proceeded from extra sacrifice during the war or
exceptional difficulties after the peace.   Since the states might never

31. *Journals,* XXXIV, 257-60, 262-63, 497-98, 502-3.   The members of the
General Board were William Irvine, John Taylor, and Abraham Baldwin.   Baldwin was elected to the House of Representatives in 1789 and did not serve.   The
state legislative journals for the period contain numerous references to the settlement of accounts and the activities of state agents.   See also Burnett, ed., *Letters,*
from July 1788 on, and William Davies to Governor Randolph, Dec. 1, 1790,
Cal. Va. State Papers, V, 226.

32. Samuel A. Otis to Nathan Dane, Oct. 29, 1788, Burnett, ed., *Letters,* VIII,
810-11.

be able to agree on the terms of a final settlement of accounts, it could be maintained—under the principle of equality of sacrifice—that justice would be fairly well served by making all existing debts an obligation of the Union.

With the prospect of a central government exercising paramount powers of taxation, federal assumption entered the field of practical consideration. The transfer of tax sources to Congress gave the states with large debts a further reason to demand relief. The assumption of state debts was discussed at the Constitutional Convention, and the notion of writing such a provision into the Constitution was considered. The delegates from states which were financially interested supported the idea, but they were aware that it was a divisive issue and did not press it. There was no general agreement at the Convention, and the Constitution contained nothing on this point; however the advocates of assumption chose to believe that Congress already had sufficient authority and that an express provision was unnecessary.[33]

During the interval before the inauguration of the new government, assumption was occasionally discussed in the Confederation Congress. A Massachusetts delegate predicted: "This or a Sponge . . . will be attempted at some period not far distant."[34] In December 1789, such a rumor sparked a sharp rise in the value of Massachusetts securities. About the same time, the legislature of South Carolina pointedly expressed its hopes by neglecting to provide for the interest due on the state debt in 1790.[35]

33. Jonathan Elliot, *The Debates in the Several State Conventions on the Adoption of the Federal Constitution* (Phila., 1937), 441-42, 451-52. See Rowland, *Life of George Mason*, II, 162; Max Farrand, "Compromises of the Constitution," *Amer. Hist. Rev.* 9 (1903-4), 482.

34. Samuel Alleyne Otis to the Speaker of the Massachusetts House of Representatives, Feb. 27, 1788, to Nathan Dane, Oct. 29, 1788, Burnett, ed., *Letters*, VIII, 702, 811.

35. "X" in *Massachusetts Centinel*, Mar. 20, 1790; *Annals of Congress*, II, 1371, 1415; Christopher Gore to Rufus King, June 7, July 26, Dec. 3, 1789, folios 78, 81, 94, Rufus King Papers, 1788-1792, N.-Y. Hist. Soc.

The Economics of Disunion

"The natural affects of a pure democracy are already full produced among us . . . [,] against Virtue, talents & property [,] carried on by the dregs and scum of mankind."

—Theodore Sedgwick to Nathan
Dane, July 5, 1787.

During the postwar years the approach to political centralization continued to lie in fiscal reform. As its main legacy, the Nationalist Congress of 1781-83 bequeathed to its successors a public debt and a plan of financing it that endowed the central government with the power of taxation. The financial plan (after the defeat of the impost of 1781) was the funding requisition of 1783 which, it will be recalled, included a federal duty on imports as well as additional taxes to be collected by the states but pledged to Congress. The Nationalist Congress also inaugurated a specie policy, launching a series of requisitions payable in hard money. Its successors tried to be firm in demanding specie, for after the extinction of wartime Continental currency only hard money permitted centralized receipts and disbursements.[1]

During the remainder of the Confederation period, requisitions were successful up to a point: they raised almost enough to meet the normal expense of federal administration, and, as we shall see, the states took care of the interest on the public debt. In domestic affairs the federal government was solvent, or nearly so.

1. *Journals*, XXI, 187-88. The Board of Treasury issued limited amounts of new emission money after the war. See *ibid.*, XXIV, 73-74.

Foreign debts were another matter. Congress suspended payment of interest on the debt to France after 1785 and defaulted on
installments of the principal which fell due in 1787. The default
was not irretrievable, for Congress had just begun to cash its enormous assets in western lands, which, if sold for public securities or
foreign claims, promised in time to absorb all its debts.

Congress, in short, was poor but not desperate. Nonetheless,
its plight was dangerous. In all that related to maintaining its
status in the Union or increasing its powers, it met only failure.
The funding requisition (including the request for an impost) lay
before the states until 1787 and was never operative, although it
was approved by all of them in one form or another. Meanwhile,
since Congress was unable to meet the interest on the public debt,
the states themselves began taking over payment—a process which
boded disaster to plans for political reform. It was apparent
that the Nationalists of 1783 had loaded Congress with responsibilities beyond its powers; when constitutional revision failed, the
normal tendency of the Confederation asserted itself—the nation
moved towards state-oriented public finance based on the issue and
redemption of paper. Beneath the surface, there was an implicit
rivalry between Congress and the states for appropriation of the
debt. The fate of the Union seemed to ride on the outcome. As
the states laid hands on the public debt they undermined the basis
for a constitutional enlargement of federal powers.

From the Nationalist viewpoint, the situation was the more
alarming because the states acted at the behest of the public creditors.
Once it had been gratifying to think that economic self-interest must
prompt creditors to support the federal government, but now it was
discovered that self-interest worked two ways. The demonstration
took a malignant turn when the creditors appealed to the states.

The first assault on federal control of the public debt occurred
in 1782. When Congress finally stopped payment of interest on all
loan certificates, Pennsylvania threatened to pay interest directly
to her citizens. Congress yielded to the extent of passing a special
requisition of $1,200,000 specie, under which all the states were
allowed to pay interest to holders of loan certificates, but the concession was not enough to deter Pennsylvania from executing her

own plans early the next year.[2] Employing currency finance methods, she gave the public creditors certificates of interest which were receivable in taxes. The legislature at the same time levied a tax of £225,000, payable half in interest certificates and half in hard money. Pennsylvania thus afforded creditors the security of her taxes and created in the process a kind of state paper money.[3]

Pennsylvania's action broke with Congress's debt-funding program, and, to make matters worse for Congress, other states tended to follow her example; they could thereby satisfy public creditors and indulge their taste for a paper medium. Before the end of the year, New Hampshire announced its intention of employing certificates of interest, and New Jersey had issued "revenue money" to public creditors. Stephen Higginson wrote home from Congress that Massachusetts had "the same right to take care of her subjects and they will expect it."[4]

The states had many reasons for refusing to make the sacrifice entailed in Congress's servicing the debt in specie. They were heavily engaged in reducing their own debts by levying taxes payable in defunct currencies and certificates. Virginia, for example, collected $3,250,000 in certificates and commodities from 1782 to 1785.[5] Massachusetts' taxes yielded more than $4,300,000 in specie, certificates, and old paper money from 1780 to 1786.[6] Taxes were heavy in all the states, but, as usual, they did not produce large quantities of specie; in any case there was a reluctance to surrender specie to Congress, for

2. *Journals*, XXIII, 545-47, 551-53, 564-71, 604-6. Pennsylvania's quota of the requisition was much less than the interest due her citizens, who held more than a third of the loan certificate debt. The requirement that creditors be paid in specie was also objectionable.

3. Mitchell and Flanders, eds., *Statutes of Pennsylvania*, XI, 81-91. The certificates ranged from one-quarter of a dollar to twenty dollars, thus constituting a kind of paper money. *Journals of the First Session of the House of Representatives of the Commonwealth of Pennsylvania* (Phila., 1790), 388.

4. Stephen Higginson to Theophilus Parsons, Apr. 1783, Burnett, ed., *Letters,* VII, 124. See Ferguson, "State Assumption," *Miss. Valley Hist. Rev.*, 38 (1951), 415; McCormick, *Experiment in Independence*, 176-79.

5. Total receipts from the end of the war were reported as $4,660,000, of which $1,290,000 were specie, the rest commodities and certificates. *Cal. Va. State Papers,* IV, 388; Broadside, Washington Papers, CCCXXXI, 111, Lib. Cong.; R. H. Lee to Madison, Nov. 20, 1784, Ballagh, ed., *Letters of Richard Henry Lee*, II, 299-301. See August Low, Virginia in the Critical Period, 1783-1789 (unpublished doctoral dissertation, State University of Iowa, 1941); Walter F. Dodd, "The Effect of the Adoption of the Constitution on the Finances of Virginia," *Va. Mag. of Hist. and Biog.*, 10 (1903), 369.

6. *Acts of Massachusetts, 1786-1787*, 143-50.

it always had special uses at home. The general population, moreover, did not relish the idea of paying debts in hard money. It was a common saying that Americans liked to pay their debts and get rid of them rather than set them at perpetual interest, thus mortgaging the future. The remark is interpretable only as it implies the cheap and easy methods of debt redemption employed by the states. The Congressional plan was pretty expensive for most people's tastes.

A final reason for non-compliance with federal requisitions was the knowledge that inevitably some of the states would fail to contribute their share and Congress would not have enough money to go around. Hence a willing state which sent off money had no assurance that any of it would return as interest payments to its own citizens. The state governments might legitimately inquire whether they ought not to take care of their own citizens before giving money away.

Congress soon realized that until federal taxes were established the states would rather pay their own citizens than give Congress the funds to do it. Congress also came to understand that a paper medium would have to be tolerated. Unable itself to discharge interest in specie, the federal government could not long insist that the states not pay it in certificates. Early in 1784, Congress entertained the notion of incorporating *indents,* or certificates of interest, in that part of requisitions levied to service the public debt. The Financier, who was still in office, denounced indents as a "meer shadow" and no more than another form of paper money.[7] But Congress had escaped his influence. The indent system was adopted, and, for lack of an alternative, was pursued to the end of the Confederation. The requisition of 1784 allowed the states to pay part of their quotas in indents.

Congress labored until 1787 to perfect a general system. Its goal was, first, to allow the states to service the debt under uniform regulations which would preserve federal control of it and, second, to compel the states to deliver a certain amount of specie on requisitions. The requisition of 1784 asked for $2,670,000; one-fourth of

7. See *Journals,* XXIV, 232-33, XXVI, 196-98. For Morris's attitude, see Official Letterbook G, 77-81, 97-99, 218-19, 239-40, 240-41, Morris Correspondence, Lib. Cong.

this sum was payable in indents on condition that three-fourths was paid in specie.[8] Indents were printed by the Treasury and deposited with the loan officers in each state, who turned them over to the local authority. The states were then supposed to issue indents for interest due on public securities up to the last day of 1782—and no further. When the indents had been redeemed by taxes and presented to the Treasury, along with the specie accompaniment, the state would receive credit on the current requisition. There was a deadline of a year's time to complete the process.

The scheme provided for a nation-wide payment under federal auspices. Ideally, the indents would be retired by taxation within a year and a new series issued to bring the interest another step forward. Presumably the federal government would also receive enough specie to handle its other business. Congress had the notion that indents would flow freely across state borders and be taken indiscriminately by all states for taxes. Since they were printed in small denominations, ranging from one to twenty dollars, they would provide a national circulating medium.

None of the states complied with this requisition during 1785 under the terms prescribed by Congress. Their failure owed something to the attitude of Robert Morris, who, in the last months before his resignation on November 1, 1784, would not apply himself to administering the system.[9] After his departure, several months elapsed before the Board of Treasury got under way. The delay in starting no doubt complicated matters, but the states in any case found the conditions too troublesome to observe. A year was hardly enough time to levy and collect new taxes, and many of the states made no attempt to comply with the time limitation. In some cases the states had already paid creditors through 1782 and were not deterred from issuing indents for the next year's interest—a practice which disorganized the general system. In disregard of Congress's intention, the states almost invariably refused to honor the claims of nonresidents; they would not pay out indents on any securities except

8. This amount, added to previous state payments on the $8,000,000 requisition of 1781, totaled $4,000,000, which was half the amount asked for by that requisition and all that Congress considered necessary for the year 1785. *Journals*, XXVI, 297-303, 311-13, XXX, 75.

9. See Morris to Nathaniel Appleton, July 18, Aug. 16, 1782, Official Letterbook G, 218-19, 240-41, Morris Correspondence, Lib. Cong.; *Journals*, XXVI, 196-98; Sanders, *Executive Departments*, 147.

those originally issued within their jurisdiction and presently held by their own citizens; nor would they accept out-of-state indents for taxes. Another problem arose from the unequal distribution of the debt. The southern states claimed that their citizens held so few public securities that not enough indents could be collected to fill their quotas.[10] As always, however, the great difficulty was specie: the states balked at paying large sums in hard money in order to get credit for indents.[11]

Congress's response was to tighten rather than relax the requirements. In 1785 the states were asked to contribute $3,000,000, of which two-thirds was payable in indents if a third was paid in specie.[12] This appeared to be a concession, but actually the conditions were made more exacting. Only indents covering interest due in 1783 and 1784 were acceptable, and to compel the states to redeem them promptly, Congress fixed a time limit at January 1, 1787, after which a state would have to pay any remaining balance of its indent quota in specie. An effort was made to plug loopholes. The loan officers, who were placed under the direct supervision of the Board of Treasury, could be suspended immediately for any violation of their instructions. Their instructions were to make no indents available to state authorities until the legislature had levied enough taxes to raise the specie quota of the requisition. Loan officers were also forbidden to deliver indents if the tax bill excluded indents issued by other states or those held by nonresidents or foreigners.

The same stipulations were written into the requisition of 1786, which brought interest payment to the last day of 1785 and set a deadline for compliance at July 1, 1787. To encourage the states to honor out-of-state indents, Congress rated them at a value of $1.33 for $1.00, when presented at the Treasury. All these efforts were unavailing. Congress could not control the loan officers, who handed indents over to state authorities whether or not Congress's stipulations were met. The states paid their citizens as they chose, without being coerced by the letter of federal regulations, and in 1786 the structure upon which Congress and the Board of Treasury had expended

10. The settlement of individual claims against Congress had not been completed in the southern states.
11. See *Journals*, XXXIII, 649-58.
12. The sum was three-fourths of the remaining half of the $8,000,000 requisition of October 30, 1781. *Ibid.*, XXIX, 765-71.

so much care was stricken at its foundations by the general revival
of paper money.[13]

A growing economic depression after the war had evoked the
usual demand for credit and currency expansion, rendered more
urgent because heavy debt retirements by the states had contracted
the supply of all types of paper media. By 1786 seven states had
adopted paper money—with dangerous consequences for the Congressional program. The paper money states would have to support
their currency by making it acceptable for the widest possible range
of taxes and other payments to the government: inevitably, their
specie incomes must dwindle. In recognition of this situation, Congress went so far as to allow the states to pay public creditors in
their own currencies rather than indents (since they were doing it
anyhow), but insisted on deliveries of specie before giving credit
for indents. There was little possibility, of course, that the paper
money states would pay much specie to Congress.

Treasury records for this period are obscure, contradictory, and
not illustrative of actual financial relations between Congress and
the states. A summary statement, drawn up many years later, shows
that by 1787, when two indent requisitions had run their course
and a third had been adopted, only $808,000 in indents had been
issued under the authority of the Board of Treasury. Credit for
compliance with indent requisitions was confined to the single instance of Virginia, which earned $30,000 for indents in 1786, proba-
bly as a reward for delivering $110,000 in specie.[14]

The current reports of the Board of Treasury afford a broader, if
shadowy, picture. In 1787 the Board presumed that the states had
paid the entire interest on the public debt to the end of 1785 in
indents, state certificates, or paper money, amounting in the whole
to over $6,000,000. The Board was concerned with how much of
this paper had been redeemed by taxes. According to its figures,
the total was less than $1,000,000. Putting the worst construction on
the scanty information it had, the Board supposed that at least
$4,500,000 in indents or certificates issued to pay interest was still
unredeemed and circulating as a paper medium. This figure was

13. *Ibid.*, XXI, 461-65, XXIX, 664-68.
14. Statement of the Financial Affairs of the late Confederated Government,
United States, Finance Mss., Lib. Cong.

a gross exaggeration, but it was nevertheless clear that indent requisitions had not jelled into a manageable or coordinated system of servicing the public debt, and they had failed to produce the specie income which Congress desired.[15]

Congress finally surrendered in 1787. All stipulations were waived in the requisition of that year, and the states were allowed to service the public debt in their own way. They were explicitly told that they might discharge interest in any manner they chose and still receive credit. Congress asked for $1,200,000 in specie and $1,700,000 in indents, but the two requests were separate—the states would get credit for interest payments whether or not they remitted specie. The effort to bring the interest forward from year to year in a regular fashion was abandoned; all indents issued at any time in the past were acceptable for indent balances due on all existing requisitions.[16]

INDENT ACCOUNT[17]

(in dollars)

1785

No indents authorized or Paid into Treasury

1786

Authorized emission of indents	808,473	
Paid into Treasury	29,901	
		778,572 outstanding

1787

Authorized emission of indents	955,536	
Paid into Treasury	370,257	
		1,363,851 outstanding

1788

Authorized emission of indents	451,917	
Paid into Treasury	1,041,756	
		774,012 outstanding

15. *Journals*, XXXIII, 571; undated Treasury Board report [1787], Papers of Cont. Cong., no. 139, 549.

16. *Journals*, XXXIII, 649-58.

17. Statements of the Financial Affairs of the late Confederated Government, United States, Finance Mss., Lib. Cong.; *American State Papers, Finance*, I, 27-28.

1789

| Authorized emission of indents | 19,308 |
| Paid into Treasury | 90,721 |

702,599 outstanding

Total indents paid into Treasury: 1,532,635

The new policy, which was continued in 1788, delivered the states from their predicament; they submerged Congress with indents —$370,000 in 1787 and $1,041,000 in 1788. But Congress had given over management of the public debt, yielding before the general tendency of the Confederation to revert to separate state action and currency finance methods.

More ominous than the fragmentation of debt servicing, however, was the fragmentation of the debt itself which accompanied the progressive disintegration of the indent system. By 1786 the states were advancing into Congress's last preserve: they had begun to assume public securities. As they did, the public debt disappeared into state debts.

The public creditors played a major role in the process; it was their needs which had first inspired the payment of interest in certificates, and it was their dissatisfaction with indents that caused the states to convert public securities into state securities. Although from the creditor's standpoint, indents were better than nothing, they were not much better. Their value was sustained by acceptance for the taxes levied to meet Congressional requisitions, but such taxes were a minor and sometimes neglected part of state revenue systems. There was not enough demand for indents to give them a high market value. A creditor could pay his personal taxes with them, but any surplus had to be sold in the market at a fourth to an eighth of face value. As dependents of Congress, the public creditors were isolated. In the absence of federal taxes, the more fully their securities were incorporated into the general processes of public finance and debt redemption in each state, the greater were the benefits.

In 1784 the public creditors in Pennsylvania carried an appeal to their legislature, then dominated by a radical majority that had supplanted the conservatives who held sway in the late years of the war. The creditors got the aid they wanted, but with strings attached; the legislature passed a bill early in 1785 which provided for an emission of £100,000 currency to pay interest on all public securities held by citizens of the state. An additional £50,000 was put into a land bank. Although the money was not legal tender, it was strongly supported. The major resources of the state were pledged to its redemption—a range of taxes, and by another act, the sale of unappropriated land.[18]

Congress registered a protest, and staunch Nationalists like Robert Morris and John Dickinson opposed the bill. As President of Pennsylvania, Dickinson argued that the bill would reward speculators, since a great number of securities had been bought up at a fraction of their face value, and 6 percent interest would yield speculators an actual return of 40 percent to 50 percent on their investment. He pleaded for a discrimination between original holders, who were entitled to their full reward, and mere speculators, who might be dealt with on less favorable terms. His arguments were echoed without much effect by the conservative minority in the legislature.[19]

Significantly, the usually close-knit conservative elements in Pennsylvania were divided. The "merchants and traders" of Philadelphia refused to ally themselves with the conservatives in the legislature. They were afraid of paper money, but mollified by its being moderate in amount and not legal tender. The benefits they would receive under the bill were unquestionably superior to being paid in certificates. When the monied gentlemen of Philadelphia convened in their capacity as public creditors, they urged the assembly to disregard those who would distinguish between original and secondary holders. Answering the charge that the act would sap the foundations of the Union, they replied that until Congress could pay its debts, the states must take the responsibility. There were a few complaints from unorganized citizens, who perceived the outlines

18. Mitchell and Flanders, eds., *Statutes of Pennsylvania*, XI, 454-86, 560-72. The legislation represented a deal between creditors, paper money advocates, and would-be land speculators. See Brunhouse, *Counter Revolution in Pennsylvania*, 169-72. Pennsylvania had already begun to absorb military and civilian final settlement certificates in the sale of unappropriated land.

19. *Minutes of the General Assembly of Pennsylvania*, Dec. 4, 1784, Mar. 16, 1785. See *Penn. Packet*, Feb. 7, 1785.

of a speculators' scheme, but paper money had a wide appeal, and the substantial interests behind the bill ensured its enactment.[20]

The next year Pennsylvania formally assumed public securities, calling in $5,168,000 and giving her citizens "new loan" (state) securities in their place. Before 1790 she had absorbed an additional $876,000 through land sales, bringing her holdings of public securities to about $6,000,000. During the Confederation she paid $1,134,000 interest on this assumed debt; the annual charge of $371,000 was more than her quota of indent requisitions. Pennsylvania thus fulfilled her obligation to the Union.[21]

Maryland had already acted, though on a lesser scale. When Congress stopped paying interest on loan certificates in 1782, Maryland invited her citizens to exchange their securities for state notes bearing 6 percent interest, promising to pay half the interest each year in hard money during the war and afterwards make good the arrears. The state assumed $214,712 under this act and later invested in other public securities. By 1790 her holdings amounted to $661,000.[22]

After the stoppage of interest on loan certificates, New Jersey began issuing "revenue money" to public creditors and pledged annual taxes for twenty-five years to redeem it.[23] The state did not try to conform with the indent system, considering it impossible to

20. *Penn. Packet,* Feb. 18, 24, Mar. 1, 8, 1785; Petition of the citizens of the middle counties, *ibid.,* Mar. 12, 1785; "Centinel" in *Penn. Gazette,* Feb. 2, 1785.

21. Only securities originally issued in the state and currently owned by her citizens were assumed in 1786. The next year, however, Pennsylvania issued new loan certificates in exchange for federal loan certificates which her citizens had purchased in New Jersey and Delaware. The total assumption was $6,045,126, but it must be set at a somewhat lower figure because it included loan certificates issued between Feb. 1, 1777, and Mar. 1, 1778, which were stated at face value (for purposes of drawing interest) instead of their value according to the Continental scale of depreciation. Mitchell and Flanders, eds., *Statutes of Pennsylvania,* XII, 158-64, 426-27; *Minutes of the Pennsylvania Assembly,* Nov. 12, 1787; Statement of Finances, Nov. 7, 1787, portfolio 145, no. 4, Broadside Coll., Rare Books Div., Lib. Cong.; *Journals of the First Session of the House of Representatives of Pennsylvania,* 395, 420, 422; John Nicholson to Governor Mifflin, July 2, 1791, Public Records Div., Penn. Hist. and Museum Commission.

22. The assumption was confined to loan certificates issued in Maryland and currently owned by her citizens. *Laws of Maryland made Since M, DCC, LXIII,* Nov. sess., 1782, ch. 25; *Votes and Proceedings of the Maryland House of Delegates,* Nov. 19, 1782, May 2, 1787, Nov. 12, 1790; Address of the Maryland House of Delegates to their Constituents (1787), portfolio 28, no. 24, Broadside Coll., Rare Books Div., Lib. Cong.

23. *Acts of New Jersey,* Dec. 20, 1783, ch. 21.

raise the specie which Congress required. Her citizens held a disproportionately large share of the public debt, and New Jersey felt justified in refusing to give specie to Congress while she was shouldering a considerable share of the interest on public securities.

Formally seceding from the Congressional system in 1786, New Jersey announced that her first obligation was to her own citizens. At this time, she was printing an emission of £100,000 to be put into a land bank. The public creditors were to receive payment in these bills or in revenue money, both of which were legal tender. The next year the legislature inquired into the advisability of a formal assumption of the public debt. A grand committee of the assembly proposed that public securities to the amount of £537,000 be converted into state notes. The motion lost by a close vote; the assumption was too formidable as a long-term proposition—the citizens of New Jersey held more than twice the state's supposed share of the public debt. However, New Jersey continued to pay interest on public securities, amounting to $424,000 by the end of 1790. Although stopping short of a formal assumption, the state had taken over responsibility for the public debt held within her borders.[24]

New York assumed public securities in 1786, concurrently with Pennsylvania and for similar reasons. Here, too, the assumption was fostered by a combination of creditor and paper money interests. It was rumored that leading politicians had invested heavily in securities and wanted to commit the state's revenues to their support. Under the legislative act, all federal securities were called in and state notes issued in exchange. The same act provided for an emission of £200,000 in paper money, of which £150,000 was reserved for a land bank and the remainder assigned to the payment of one-fifth of the interest due on securities to the end of 1784.[25]

The opposition to the bill in the assembly was led by William Duer, protegé of Robert Morris and a friend of Alexander Hamilton; but conservative opinion was divided, as in Pennsylvania. Although the merchants disliked paper money, they were willing to

24. McCormick, *Experiment in Independence*, 171-78, 197-204, 208-10, 211-13, Appendix II; *American State Papers, Finance*, I, 28. See "A Jersey Man," *Penn. Packet*, Feb. 15, 1790. Annual payments were said to average $86,456.

25. Monroe to Madison, Feb. 11, 1786, Madison Papers, VI, 40, Lib. Cong. New York already owned a few public securities. See *Laws of the State of New York, 1777-1801* (Albany, 1886-87), I, 678-80, 726, II, 100, 253-72.

agree to it provided that it was not made legal tender. The assembly's final act was a compromise. The currency was made legal tender only in the settlement of judgments procured by suits at law. Certain controversial features were retained: loan certificates issued in other states were excluded from the assumption, as were final settlement certificates granted to the New York line, which were being absorbed by the sale of state land.[26] As a result of the assumption and continuing receipts at the land office, New York gained possession of more than $2,300,000 in public securities, which entitled her to an annual credit of $147,500 on indent requisitions, her full quota.[27]

Prudence suggested to other states the advisability of acquiring public securities. They were still plentiful and could be purchased at a fraction of their nominal value. Lodged in state treasuries, they not only earned credits on requisitions, but constituted gilt-edged assets against the day when Congress and the states would finally settle their accounts.

Massachusetts had the will but not the ability to follow the lead of Pennsylvania and New York; her inflated state debt precluded any large ventures. She could do no more than attempt to convert part of her surplus of old Continental currency into public securities. These efforts, begun in 1786, added little to the $165,000 then in her treasury. The legislature held out to the people the hope of absorbing the state's full share of the public debt, but any possibility of this was ruled out by Shays's Rebellion and its aftermath. The government of Massachusetts did not have large holdings in 1790, and the same was true of the other New England states. New Hampshire held $33,148 and Connecticut only $8,647.[28]

26. *Journal of the Assembly of the State of New York* (printed currently), Feb. 15, 17, 18, 20, 21, 1786; *Laws of New York, 1777-1801*, II, 253-72; Petition of the New York Chamber of Commerce, *Daily Advertiser* (N.Y.), Mar. 3, 1786.

27. New York apparently made no further payment of interest to public creditors after the assumption, though she received indent credit on requisitions. *Journal of the New York Assembly*, Feb. 1, 1787, Jan. 16, 1788, Jan. 16, 1790; *American State Papers, Finance*, I, 30; *Laws of New York, 1777-1801*, II, 291-93, 301-6; *Journals*, XXXIII, 573.

28. On the effect of Shays's Rebellion, see Whitney K. Bates, State Finances of Massachusetts, 1780-1789 (unpublished master's thesis, Univ. of Wisconsin, 1948), Appendix III; *Acts of Massachusetts, 1784-1785*, 950; *ibid., 1786-1787*, 144; *A Journal of the Proceedings of the House of Representatives of the State of New Hampshire* (printed currently), Jan. 2, 1789; A Statement of the public debt of . . . Connecticut . . ., Nov. 1, 1789, Reports of the Comptroller, Conn. State Lib.

The southern states also had only minor holdings of public securities. North Carolina collected a few final settlement certificates. In 1786 a committee of the legislature recommended accepting public securities for taxes; the results seem to have been meager.[29]

Virginia did not enter the lists until 1787, when the legislature created a sinking fund, placing various revenues in the hands of the governor, who was authorized to invest in any kind of securities at his own discretion. With an inveterate local attachment, the governor employed the money to buy state military certificates, acquiring $388,000 by 1790; he purchased only $22,000 in public securities.[30]

South Carolina was occupied with her own problems. Except for loan certificates, virtually all federal debts held by her citizens had been converted into state obligations. The assumption swelled her internal debt to $4,220,000 by 1787. Damaged by war, afflicted by crop failures and declining tax revenues, South Carolina was committed beyond her resources. The state had an asset in confiscated estates, which were sold for securities, but purchasers avoided payment, and in any case the income from this source was partly anticipated by incumbrances upon the estates which the government had to discharge. Hence, no progress was made in reducing the state debt, which by 1789 had grown to $5,386,588, including a foreign debt of $496,361. The government could do little more than issue "special indents" to pay the annual interest of about $342,000. The bulk of the taxes were absorbed in the redemption of these certificates, and there was scant income for other purposes.[31] With all

29. Laws of North Carolina, Nov. sess., 1786, in Clark, ed., *State Records of North Carolina*, XXIV, 803; *Journals of the House of Commons of North Carolina*, Dec. 6, 1786.

30. Hening, ed., *Statutes of Virginia*, XII, 452-54, 781-87; *Journal of the House of Delegates of the Commonwealth of Virginia* (Richmond, 1791), Dec. 18, 1789, Nov. 8, 1790. See Arthur Lee to the Governor of Virginia, May 20, 1787, *Cal. Va. State Papers*, IV, 288-89.

31. The actual emission of indents varied from $273,000 to $535,000 annually. The South Carolina pound has been stated in terms of dollars at the rate of $4.286 to £1, which the legislature adopted in 1783. Cooper and McCord, eds., *Statutes of South Carolina*, IV, 542-43, 563-64, 627-38, 679-80, 689-99, 728-29, V, 24-36, 57-62, 129-32; Journals of the House of Representatives of South Carolina, Mar. 10, 1783, Feb. 2, 1784, Microfilm Collection of Early State Records, A. 1b, reel 20, Lib. Cong.; Report of Ways and Means Committee, Feb. 9, 1785 and undated second report, Xx, reel 1, *ibid.*; Report of the Commissioner appointed by the Intendant General of the Honorable the Board of Police (James Simpson), Dec. 19, 1780, Xx, reel 1, *ibid.*; Salley, *Entries to Indents Issued in Payment of*

that remained due to the state from sales of confiscated land, back taxes, and other sources discounted, the debt still amounted in 1789 to $4,317,000. South Carolina had no opportunity to acquire United States public securities.[32]

New England and the south were laggard, but it was an unmitigated fact that by 1786 New York, Pennsylvania, and Maryland had appropriated nearly $9,000,000—almost a third of the principal of the public debt. Other states had acquired smaller amounts and were seeking ways of getting more, while still others had made a permanent provision for the interest due to their own citizens. The distribution of the public debt, which Morris and the Nationalist Congress forestalled at the end of the war, was under way. It portended an end to major Congressional receipts and disbursements; the servicing of the debt bypassed Congress, and state revenues were committed to local purposes.

The gloomy implications of these events were dramatized by Congress's default on its foreign obligations. From the end of Morris's administration in 1784 until 1789, federal income from the states and other domestic sources did not fall greatly below domestic expenditures, and since the public debt was in the hands of the states, Congress's main problem was to meet the interest and installments of principal falling due on foreign loans.[33] This, however, could not be done. By concentrating its resources, Congress managed to save its credit in Holland, but the debt to France was sloughed off, and when Spain did not press its claims, no payment was made.[34]

Claims against South Carolina, books R-T and *passim;* Salley, *Accounts Audited Against South Carolina,* I, 3-4; William L. McDowell, The South Carolina Revolutionary Debt, 1776-1789 (unpublished master's thesis, Univ. of South Carolina, 1953), 33-34, 41, 47; Singer, *South Carolina in the Confederation,* 63, 114.

32. No evidence has been found to substantiate the claim advanced in the recent work of Forrest McDonald, *We the People: The Economic Origins of the Constitution* (Chicago, 1958), 205-6, that South Carolina's financial condition was good, nor his statement that her debt had been reduced to $2,800,000 by 1789. Neither have I been able to confirm his assertion that the state had acquired almost $2,000,000 in "federal" securities. Perhaps he has failed to distinguish between public securities and the unliquidated federal securities which the state assumed. That South Carolina had not reduced her debt would seem to be proved by the fact that her citizens subscribed $4,634,578 in state securities to the federal loan of 1790 and a residue estimated at $1,965,000 remained. *American State Papers, Finance,* I, 28, 150.

33. See table, pp. 236-37.

34. The best treatment is the unpublished doctoral dissertation by La Follette, Revolutionary Foreign Debt.

Congress defaulted entirely on the contracts made with the French government. Until November 1782 the United States was free of charges but was then obligated to start paying 5 percent interest on 10,000,000 livres. As interest fell due on other loans, the annual charge was scheduled to rise to 1,400,000 livres in 1784, and the next year to 1,640,000 livres. In 1787 the first installments of the principal were to fall due—an additional 2,500,000 livres, which brought the annual charges to 4,140,000 livres, about $766,000 in hard money.[35]

It was beyond Congress's means. The interest was paid on 10,000,000 livres (the Dutch loan guaranteed by France) until 1785, but that was the end. Congress preferred to apply its resources to keeping credit alive in Holland. France was insolvent and not a likely source of further loans; also, it was feared the Dutch would retaliate in case of default by seizure of American ships.[36]

In addition to the loan which France had guaranteed, there were two other loans in Holland: one of 5,000,000 guilders ($2,000,000) made in 1782, the other of 2,000,000 guilders ($800,000) made in 1784. In 1784 the proceeds enabled Morris to balance his accounts and meet interest due in Europe. Money continued to flow from this source for a little longer, aggregating $2,100,000 by early 1785; then the flow subsided. Congress's balance in Holland seems to have been exhausted by the end of the year, and in 1786 Treasury accounts showed no foreign receipts.[37] It is clear, how-

35. Congress became obligated to pay interest on French loans in the following sequence: (1) from November 1782, on the Dutch loan of 1781 of 5,000,000 guilders (10,000,000 livres) which France had guaranteed; (2) from 1784, according to a natural reading of the contract, on 18,000,000 livres lent through 1782; however Congress construed the contract to read that interest was not to begin until 1787; (3) from 1785, on 6,000,000 livres lent in 1783.
Congress was obligated to begin paying installments of the principal of French loans in the following sequence: (1) from 1787, on the guaranteed Dutch loan of 1781, calculated at 10,000,000 livres, in ten installments of 1,000,000 livres; (2) from 1787, on 18,000,000 livres lent through 1782, in twelve installments of 1,500,000 livres; (3) from 1797, on 6,000,000 livres lent in 1783, in six installments of 1,000,000 livres. All contracts may be found in Papers of Cont. Cong., no. 135, I and II.
36. La Follette, Revolutionary Foreign Debt, 25, 190.
37. Journals, XXVIII, 551-58. The accounts of the United States with Nicholas and Jacob Van Staphorst, the leading firm among Congress's Dutch agents, showed about $1,200,000 raised through 1785, but no balance remaining in their hands at year's end. Papers of Cont. Cong., no. 145, 215-19; Statements of Financial Affairs of the late Confederated Government, United States, Finance Mss., Lib. Cong.

RECEIPTS AND EXPENDITURES, NOV. 1, 1784 to 1789, EXCLUDING INDENTS

Nov. 1, 1784 (end of Morris's administration) to Dec. 31, 1784

RECEIPTS		EXPENDITURES	
Balance in Treasury, Nov. 1	21,986	Administrative expenses	16,245
Payments from or credits to states	54,740	Army	6,275
Other domestic incomes	2,758	Others	6,145
		Anticipations	32,379
		Balance in Treasury	18,440
	79,484		79,484

1785

RECEIPTS		EXPENDITURES	
Balance in Treasury, Jan. 1	18,440	*Domestic:*	
Domestic incomes:		Administration	85,715
Payments from or credits to states	378,866	Army	132,372
Others	26,278	Others	65,084
	405,144	Debts and anticipations	97,439
		Balance in Treasury	41,902
			422,512
Foreign incomes:		*Foreign:*	
Dutch loan, etc.	208,802	Interest on Dutch loan	209,874
	632,386		632,386

1786

RECEIPTS		EXPENDITURES	
Balance in Treasury, Jan. 1	41,902	*Domestic:*	
Domestic incomes:		Administration	117,430
Payments from or credits to states	328,872	Army	145,530
Others	9,249	Others	24,223
	338,121	Credit to South Carolina for supplies	27,730
Foreign incomes:	None	Past debts	49,681
Payments over receipts:	59,571		364,594
		Foreign:	
		Interest on Dutch loan	75,000
	439,594		439,594

RECEIPTS AND EXPENDITURES (1784-1789)

1787

Receipts			Expenditures		
Domestic incomes:			Accumulated deficit:		59,571
Payments from or credits to state	276,639		*Domestic:*		
Others	41,931	318,570	Administration	128,332	
Foreign incomes:		4,909	Army	160,406	
Payments over receipts and accumulated deficit:		105,815	Others	39,675	
			Payment of old accounts	9,318	337,731
			Foreign:		
			Interest on Dutch loan		31,992
		429,294			429,294

1788

Receipts			Expenditures		
Domestic incomes:			Accumulated deficit:		105,815
Payments from or credits to states	261,679		*Domestic:*		
Others	77,999	339,588	Administration	94,610	
Foreign incomes:		1,645	Army	196,404	
Payments over receipts and accumulated deficit:		174,189	Others	96,104	
			Payment of old accounts	10,248	397,366
			Foreign:		None
			Discrepancy in indent account:		12,241
		515,422			515,422

1789 (incomplete)

Receipts			Expenditures		
Domestic incomes:			Accumulated deficit:		174,189
Payments from or credits to states	127,837		*Domestic:*		
Others	14,432	142,269	Administration	55,741	
Foreign incomes:		None	Army	78,311	
Payments over receipts and accumulated deficit:		189,906	Others	23,339	
			Payment of old accounts	595	157,986
		332,175			332,175

ever, that a few securities were still being sold and that the money was applied to the interest falling due on existing loans. Congress raised an additional fund in 1786 by contracting with American merchants to deliver $75,000 in Holland. The merchants accepted payment at home in specie, new emission money, and Pennsylvania currency.[38] The interest was thereby sustained for another year. But it was a grim situation, for Congress was informed that a single failure would ruin its credit with Dutch investors.[39]

Eventually Congress managed to scrape through; a loan of a million guilders was opened in 1787, and although there was no rush to subscribe to it, enough money was realized from this and another loan of a million guilders in 1788 to maintain interest payments until the new government could take over the burden. Whether the United States could have kept its foreign credit alive without a reorganization of the federal system is dubious. Although the country had long-term assets, the Dutch were reported to be extremely touchy about prompt payment in hard currency. Certainly the outlook in 1786 was unpromising; already in complete default on the French loans, Congress faced the prospect within a few years of meeting installments of the principal of the Dutch loans, the first of which was scheduled for payment in 1793.[40]

Throughout the Revolution the anticipated possession of the Northwest territory had promised an easy solution of debt problems. Anxious to get the process under way and spurred by the knowledge that squatters were taking possession, Congress worked out a plan for selling the land. Under the Ordinance of 1785, surveyors from each state were to lay out an initial series of seven ranges. After a certain number of tracts had been set aside for the bounties promised the army, each state was to be allotted a quota of what remained. The quotas were to be sold at the respective loan offices in each state

38. The two contractors listed in 1786 were Constable Rucker and Co. and the firm of John McVicker and William Hill. The Constable Rucker contract, dated Dec. 7, 1785, is in Letters and Accounts, 1784-1793, Constable-Pierrepont Papers, N.Y. Pub. Lib. It provided for their payment of 232,000 livres to Ferdinand Grand, presumably on the debt to France; however, nothing was paid.

39. See John Adams to John Jay, June 16, 1787, Papers of Cont. Cong., no. 145, 225-28.

40. Willinks and Van Staphorst and Co. to John Jay, June 30, 1787, Acc. 161, no. 248, env. 4, Foreign Affairs Sec., Natl. Arch. See La Follette, Revolutionary Foreign Debt, 17-18; Charles Wilson, Anglo-Dutch Commerce and Finance in the Eighteenth Century (Cambridge, Eng., 1941), 190-91.

for public securities at a minimum price of $1.00 an acre. In effect, each state was assigned a share of the public domain for purposes of redeeming securities held by its citizens. Since depreciated public securities were accepted at face value, the land would actually sell for no more than twenty cents an acre.[41]

The Ordinance of 1785, which was criticized as abetting the decomposition of the Union, was not executed fast enough to be of much use. The surveyors were hindered by Indians and in two years had not completed seven ranges. Anxious to speed up the process, Congress threw out the original plan in 1787, abandoning pre-survey and sale at the loan offices in favor of large-scale grants. The new policy opened the way to a more rapid exploitation of the public domain, but not in time to relieve the Confederation Congress of its financial problems. Through 1788, land sales returned only $760,000 to the Treasury, an inconsiderable reduction of the public debt.[42]

Amidst all its discouragements, Congress lived in hope that the states would ratify the impost—the bright alternative to indents and other demoralizing expedients. Until 1786 there was some reason for confidence. Although few states had shown any willingness to grant the supplementary taxes requested in the funding requisition of 1783, nine of them had approved the impost in a form satisfactory to the Board of Treasury. Prospects were in some degree marred by the revival of paper money, which encouraged financial particularism, but by midyear all the states except New York had granted Congress the power to collect a specie duty on imports. It was mistakenly believed that the fate of the impost rested upon the concurrence of New York.[43]

41. Indents were not acceptable in payment under the policy of the Board of Treasury. One-seventh of the land was reserved for land bonuses promised the army. *Journals*, XXVIII, 375-81, XXXIII, 314-16.

42. Washington to David Grayson, Apr. 25, 1785, to Lafayette, July 25, 1785, Fitzpatrick, ed., *Writings of Washington*, XXVIII, 137, 208; *Journals*, XXXII, 155-57, 225-27, XXXIII, 399-401. See Madison to Edmund Pendleton, Apr. 22, 1787, Burnett, ed., *Letters*, VIII, 87; Proclamation dated July 9, 1788, Continental Congress Broadsides, Safe 4B, Mss. Div., Lib. Cong.; Undated (probably 1788) report of committee, Papers of Cont. Cong., no. 26, 701.

43. *Journals*, XXX, 7-10, 62-63, 364; Committee report, read Feb. 13, 1786, Papers of Cont. Cong., no. 26, 579; Letter of the Board of Treasury, May 31, 1786, *ibid.*, no. 140, II, 229, 232; Rufus King to Elbridge Gerry, Mar. 20, 1786, James Monroe to Jefferson, May 11, 1786, Burnett, ed., *Letters*, VIII, 335, 359.

The New York legislature was the same one which emitted paper money and assumed the public debt. Under heavy pressure it at last granted the impost, but with unacceptable conditions. The state reserved the right to control the customs officers and regulate the collection. The state's paper money was declared acceptable for the duties. Reluctantly, Congress declined these terms on the grounds that the other states would withdraw their consent to the impost. Governor Clinton was asked to summon a special session to amend the act. He refused, declaring that his right to call a special session was confined to emergencies.[44]

Before receiving Governor Clinton's reply, Congress had tried to smooth the way for the impost by remedying certain imperfections in Pennsylvania's grant. Pennsylvania was one of the few states which had endorsed both the impost and the supplementary taxes under the funding requisition of 1783; however, her agreement was conditional upon all the other states' granting both measures. Pennsylvania's taxes, including the state impost, were grouped behind her paper money and a general debt-funding program which included the payment of interest on public securities. Before surrendering her taxes and crippling her ability to sustain her own program, the state wished to ensure that Congress would have enough revenue to pay all public creditors, including her own citizens.

Congress had given up hope of obtaining supplementary taxes and was intent only on getting the impost. James Monroe and Rufus King were sent to persuade the Pennsylvania legislature to allow its grant of the impost to stand, whether or not the other states granted supplementary taxes. The delegates were not successful. The legislature cited its obligations to its citizens; Monroe reported that all factions agreed on this point, even though the ablest men fully appreciated the consequences for the federal program. Monroe said it was believed in Philadelphia that the situation must induce "a change of some kind or another."[45]

On previous occasions, Congress had reacted to extreme disappointment with strong talk. Confronted by the actions of Pennsylvania and New York, a committee declared that majority rule,

44. *Journals*, XXX, 439-44, XXXI, 513-14, 555-61.
45. *Ibid.*, XXXI, 511-13; Monroe to Madison, Sept. 12, 1786, Burnett, ed., *Letters*, VIII, 464. King was more optimistic; Rufus King to Theodore Sedgwick, Sept. 29, 1786, Sedgwick Papers, 1774-1860, box A, Mass. Hist. Soc.

not unanimity, should govern the Confederation, and if a majority of states complied with requisitions, Congress ought to have power to collect taxes in the others. It was suggested that any revenue plan (like the impost) should be legally binding on all states when ratified by eleven.[46]

The peremptory tone masked despair. Utterly depressed, the Board of Treasury declared flatly that there could be no expectation of the states' meeting their quota of requisitions. The Board prophesied it would probably be the last which Congress would make. Congress, in fact, was on the verge of accepting defeat and letting events take their course.[47]

The terms of the capitulation were obvious. The Board of Treasury proposed that the states be allowed to pay requisitions in public securities. A committee put this idea into a report, declaring that since there was now no reasonable hope of servicing the public debt either by requisitions or federal taxes, Congress should embrace the alternative: a distribution of the debt among the states. No other mode was "so reasonable or so probable of success, as that of apportioning upon the several states their quota's of the domestic debt . . . and requiring them to pay the same into the federal treasury." The report was printed. A few members said privately that even if it were not adopted, Congress would consent to the procedure if the states took it up.[48]

The idea was supremely practical; it accorded with the nature of the Union and the predilections of the states. But it signified the complete abandonment of any effort to strengthen Congress under the Articles of Confederation. Most of the states would probably have retired the bulk of the debt by cheap methods. Congress would have been left with depleted functions and little reason to claim enlarged powers. Creditors would have attached themselves to the states, and no ingredients would have remained to attract the propertied classes to the central government.

46. *Journals,* XXXI, 494-98. The printed report, dated Aug. 7, 1786, is in Continental Congress Broadsides, Mss. Div., Lib. Cong. Another major subject of the report was federal regulation of trade.

47. *Journals,* XXX, 366, XXXI, 613-19.

48. *Journals,* XXX, 63-64, 66, 366, XXXI, 521-23; John Henry to the Governor of Maryland, Aug. 30, 1786, Burnett, ed., *Letters,* VIII, 455-56; *Cal. Va. State Papers,* IV, 288-89. The printed report of Aug. 16 is in Continental Congress Broadsides, Mss. Div., Lib. Cong.

Congress's visible decline in the mid-1780's affected men of differing views and political sentiments. Many old adversaries of Robert Morris thought the Union too weak. Samuel Osgood and Arthur Lee of the Board of Treasury wrote diatribes against the states almost in the style of the Financier whom they had displaced. John Mercer, who had vowed in 1783 that he would crawl to Richmond on his bare knees to prevent adoption of the impost, now perceived such a relaxation in the "confoederal springs" that he thought there was no hope for the country unless the impost was adopted or a convention called to amend the Articles. In 1784, Richard Henry Lee, although still opposed to the impost, wondered about the advisability of an amending convention. James Monroe, who had little sympathy for the Nationalist program, sought a way to "patch" the Union together. In 1786 both he and Madison felt there was danger of the nation splitting into confederacies. Even David Howell, the wrecker of 1782, would one day become a Federalist.[49]

The stoppage of the Nationalist program of constitutional revision caused a sudden crisis. In previous years the impost had always seemed on the point of success, with all the states prepared to acquiesce in its adoption. Rhode Island and Virginia were converted by 1786, and Pennsylvania's defection that year stemmed from excess of zeal rather than lack of it. The New York assembly, though refusing again in 1787 to enact the impost on Congress's terms, nevertheless felt obliged to suggest a general amending convention. Neither the state governments nor the people were indifferent to the fate of the Union, and the leaders of the nation knew that the effort to strengthen Congress in the manner prescribed by the Articles of Confederation was hopelessly blocked. The failure of the impost coupled with the dissolution of the public debt seemed to portend an immediate and perhaps final decline of the central government.

49. John Francis Mercer to Madison, Nov. 12, 1784, Richard Henry Lee to Madison, Nov. 24, 1784, Mercer to Madison, Nov. 26, 1784, Monroe to Jefferson, June 16, 1785, Nathan Dane to Samuel Adams, Feb. 11, 1786, Monroe to the Governor of Virginia (postscript), Aug. 12, 1786, to Madison, Sept. 3, 1786, Burnett, ed., *Letters*, VII, 609-10, 615, 616, VIII, 143, 303-7, 424-25, 460-62; Madison to Monroe, Apr. 9, 1786, Madison Papers, VI, 51, Lib. Cong.; James Manning and Nathan Miller to the Governor of Rhode Island, Sept. 28, 1786, Bartlett, ed., *Records of Rhode Island*, X, 222-23; List of Antifederal Prox and Prox, "To the Freemen of the State . . ." *Providence Gazette*, Apr. 10, 17, 1790.

The disintegration of the movement for constitutional revision was the more disturbing to conservatives and propertied men because it occurred at the low point of the postwar economic depression, amid manifestations of popular discontent which increased their ever-present fear of social radicalism. Tutored in the history of proletarian uprisings in the ancient world and believing themselves to have been the chief sufferers during the late war, they were convinced that from the beginning of the Revolution the propertied classes had been exposed to mob despotism. Three years after the end of the war they were not certain that the Revolution had truly ended. The wave of paper money which by 1786 had swept over seven states and threatened to engulf the country heightened their sense of insecurity. Before the Revolution they had accepted paper money in most colonies as a normal fact of existence, but now they were likely to regard it as the habitual mode of lower-class aggression.

Rhode Island provided the conspicuous example. In 1786 the legislature adopted a land bank and issued paper money on loan, making it legal tender for private debts. Within a year the money had fallen to 4 to 1 of specie, in another year to 6 to 1, and by November 1788, 10 to 1.[50] At its first decline in the fall of 1786, the assembly compelled its acceptance at par with specie under penalties for refusal. Some merchants left the state. Disorder flared in scenes reminiscent of the opening years of the Revolution.

With remorseless consistency, the legislature began discharging the state debt by means of forced payments; all creditors except holders of certain preferred certificates known as consolidated notes were ordered to present their securities and receive a fourth of the principal in paper money. When creditors did not heed the summons, the legislature fixed a time limit after which they would forfeit their entitled payment. In the ensuing years, the legislature ordered a second, third, and fourth installment; the last payment was made in 1788, when depreciation was at least 7 to 1. Pleased with what it considered its zeal in discharging debts with minimum sacrifice to the inhabitants, the legislature then applied the method of forced payment to the redemption of consolidated notes. By the time

50. A table of depreciation compiled by a committee of the legislature, is printed in the *Providence Gazette,* Jan. 16, 1790.

Rhode Island entered the new federal union in 1790, she was practically debt-free.[51]

The procedure was not as arbitrary as it may appear. Many
creditors had probably bought their securities in the market at a
considerable discount, and perhaps there was no great injustice in
giving these people paper money worth a half or a tenth of its face
value for securities they had bought at the same rate. As the legislature further declared in justifying its conduct, Congress and all
the states had sanctioned tender laws and revalued debts during the
war.[52] But such explanations were not accepted outside Rhode
Island; public opinion did not sanction in peace the compulsory acts
to which state governments had resorted during the war.

Taken in isolation, Rhode Island's behavior might have been
viewed only as one more proof of the depravity generally attributed
to her inhabitants; but to conservative minds it exemplified trends
existing everywhere in the Union.[53] Fortunately, the evils were as
yet mainly potential. New Jersey's legal tender bills were fairly
steady, although they passed outside the state at a slowly increasing
discount. Depreciation had occurred in North Carolina and Georgia,
but in a manner thoroughly familiar to their remote inhabitants.
In New York, Pennsylvania, and South Carolina currency was not
legal tender, and it was being successfully managed despite a slight
discount in exchange for specie.

The situation could have been regarded as normal; the various
states were re-enacting their particular experience with paper money
in colonial times. But conservatives had no faith in state governments. Madison remarked of New York's currency, just being issued,
that as yet "its depreciation exists only in the foresight of those who
reason without prejudice on the subject." Paper money was a "fic-
titious" medium, unknown to natural law, injurious to trade, con-
ducive to luxury and high living, corruptive of public morality, and

51. From time to time the legislature allowed creditors to receive the installments they had forfeited by failure to take them when due. Rhode Island's
dealings in her state debt may be followed in Proceedings of the General Assembly
. . ., Bartlett, ed., *Records of Rhode Island*, X, 230, 235, 251, 266, 273, 280, 285-86,
292-94, 305-6, 312.

52. Proceedings of the General Assembly, Sept. 15, 1789, *ibid.*, X, 222-23.

53. A letter from Philadelphia printed in the *Worcester Magazine* (Massachusetts) suggested that rather than allow Rhode Island to continue to disrupt the
Union, she ought to be dropped from the Confederation or her territory divided
among adjoining states. *Worcester Magazine*, 3 (July 1787), 238.

a source of disorder in the community. "Nothing but evil," he wrote, "springs from this imaginary money." William Grayson wrote from Virginia that "the Antients were surely men of more candour than We are . . . they contended openly for an abolition of debts in so many words, while we strive as hard for the same thing under the decent & specious pretense of a circulating medium."[54]

The bias underlying such remarks is evident in the reaction of conservatives to the events in Massachusetts which came to be known as Shays's Rebellion. They denounced the so-called "rebellion" but failed to realize that it was touched off by financial policies which were as surely class legislation as any paper money bill. The background of the violence was the conservative recovery of power in 1780 and an arbitrary state program for consolidating and paying war debts. The plan was the most expensive possible under the circumstances, for the wartime currency was given preferred status. Other states sank their currency at full depreciation, the rates going as high as 1,000 to 1 of specie, and even Congress did not scruple to revalue Continental currency at 40 to 1. But Massachusetts appraised her notes not at their full depreciation, but at their value when issued.[55] A note issued in 1778, when depreciation was perhaps 4 to 1 was valued in 1781 at twenty-five cents, whereas its actual value had declined to less than two and a half cents. If Congress had followed this policy, the debt arising from Continental currency alone would have been forty or fifty million dollars, more than the actual principal of its foreign and domestic debts. The effect of Massachusetts' policy, apart from conferring unmerited gains upon individuals, was to double, at least, the state debt.[56] The debt consisted of $4,605,500 in consolidated notes, which had been issued in exchange for old paper money and certificates, besides $833,700 in notes given to the state line for pay and depreciation— a total of $5,439,200.

The interest was paid in hard money, aggregating $884,500 from July 1782 to October 1786. Taxes were very heavy, but undeterred

54. Madison to Jefferson, Aug. 12, 1786, July 18, 1787, Grayson to Madison, Mar. 12, 1786, Madison Papers, VI, 68, VII, 102, VI, 50, Lib. Cong.

55. The justification was that the currency had been issued in the form of interest-bearing treasury notes, but this fact did not alter its character as a paper medium of exchange nor retard its depreciation.

56. Bates's careful study makes this clear. Massachusetts Finances, 85-93.

by hardships inflicted on the people, the legislature proposed to redeem the principal of the army debt in three annual installments, beginning in 1784. The next year the legislature planned to attack consolidated notes, redeeming them in four annual installments. The actual yield of taxes from 1780 to the fall of 1786 was about $4,159,000, in addition to $2,480,000 raised to pay war expenses incurred before 1783. Part of these taxes were payable in miscellaneous certificates, but the common people were soon drained of these assets, which always concentrated in fewer hands, and hard money became scarce amid the growing depression. Executions against property were carried out on a large scale. It was reported in 1786 that tax collections were delinquent to the amount of $931,000.[57]

Popular unrest was evident in western Massachusetts as early as 1782, when some of the inhabitants were said to feel they had been duped by eastern patriots into supporting the rebellion against Britain.[58] The tide of protest mounted steadily. The towns sent delegates to numerous county conventions which brought up grievances, chose political candidates, wrote petitions, and, in the words of their critics, presumed to share power with the legislature. Many complaints were registered, but the main object of attack was the conservative debt-funding program.[59] Despite heavy taxes the state debt was still about $5,000,000, and the annual interest was about $290,000. Petitions to the legislature asked for a revaluation of debts; newspapers published schemes of finance which advocated a paper emission and the use of currency finance methods for redeem-

57. Address to the People by the General Court, Nov. 14, 1786, *Acts of Massachusetts, 1786-1787*, 142-64; Bates, Massachusetts Finance, 103, App. III; legislative proceedings reported in the *Boston Magazine*, Nov. 1784. See Richard B. Morris, "Insurrection in Massachusetts," Daniel Aaron, ed., *America in Crisis* (N.Y., 1952), 21-49.

58. The best study is Robert Taylor, *Western Massachusetts in the Revolution* (Providence, 1954). See also the Joseph Hawley Papers, particularly Hawley to Caleb Strong, June 24, 1782, N.Y. Pub. Lib.; Samuel A. Otis to Theodore Sedgwick, July 8, 1782, Sedgwick Papers, box A, Mass. Hist. Soc.

59. "The cause of this insurrection," Theodore Sedgwick declared to the House of Representatives in 1790, "was the oppression under which the citizens groaned, from the imposition of taxes to satisfy the public creditors." *Annals of Congress*, II, 1333; see also *ibid.*, 1381. The conservatives never had any doubt of this. See Manassah Cutler to Winthrop Sargent, Oct. 6, 1786, Winthrop Sargent Papers, Mass. Hist. Soc. Resolutions adopted by many conventions were printed in the *Worcester Magazine* and the *Boston Magazine* in 1786. See extract from the *Independent Chronicle* (Boston) in the *Worcester Magazine*, 3 (March 1787); report of proceedings of the General Court, *Boston Magazine*, Nov. and Dec. 1786.

ing the principal of the state debt. "Something of this kind must be done," observed one writer, "or the government will drive more than half of the inhabitants of many country towns into other states."[60] Finally, on August 29, 1786, an armed force of citizens under Daniel Shays attempted to intimidate the Northampton courts and prevent action against debtors. A clash with the local militia was narrowly averted. In January the insurgents were repulsed by the militia in an effort to seize the federal arsenal at Springfield.

The outbreak of violence in Massachusetts was grounded in widespread protest against the conservative formula of specie debts and heavy taxes. Only a minority of the people condoned the use of force, but there was considerable sympathy for the Shaysites. "Men who have respectable Standings and Characters and possessed of decent Shares of Property," wrote a member of Congress, "are said to countenance the general Insurgency tho' they avowedly claim less Reform (as they call it) than the others, but even they propose to reliquidate the public Debts and then pay them off in a Paper Money to be created without Funds and to make it a legal tender." Radicalism had not progressed so far in Massachusetts, but Shays's Rebellion did bring conservative debt-funding to a halt. A new legislature elected in 1787 cut direct taxes to the bone. They had averaged nearly $1,000,000 a year from 1781 to 1786; then in 1787 no direct taxes were levied. The assessment the next year was only $261,000, and it was lowered to $125,000 in 1789 and $98,500 in 1790.[61]

The state creditors received the hardest blow when they lost the excise and the impost. These taxes, which provided the most dependable hard money revenues, had hitherto been appropriated to the interest on consolidated notes. The county conventions in 1786 frequently complained that the creditors got the cream of the state's revenue. Early that year an attempt was made in the legislature to divert these incomes to the current requisition of Congress,

60. Bates, Massachusetts Finance, 118-20; "Address to the People," *Acts of Massachusetts, 1786-1787,* 142-60; proceedings of the legislature printed in *Boston Magazine,* July 1786; reprint from the *Hampshire Herald* in *Worcester Magazine,* 2 (Oct. 1786), 345-47; discussion of legislative proceedings, *ibid.,* 2 (Nov. 1786), 403; Governor Bowdoin's address and the proceedings of the General Court reported in *Boston Magazine,* Oct. 1785, Mar., Nov., Dec., 1786.

61. Charles Pettit to the President of Pennsylvania, Oct. 18, 1876, Burnett, ed., *Letters,* VIII, 487; Bates, Massachusetts Finance, 131, App. III; *Worcester Magazine,* 2 (Jan. 1787), 486-88.

part of which would otherwise have had to be raised by direct specie taxes. Some members reacted strongly, saying that the impost and excise were solemnly pledged to state creditors and were therefore irrevocable. Accused of speaking in their own interest as creditors, they shrewdly replied that their accusers were guilty of the same offense because they were not creditors. They further declared that if the state creditors lost the impost, merchants, who now held most of the securities, would find ways of evading duties.[62]

These discussions produced no immediate result, but after Shays's Rebellion the income from the impost and excise was diverted to other purposes, and the interest on the state debt was allowed to fall into arrears. Late in 1789 an "oppressed Creditor" wrote that since 1786 the conduct of successive legislatures had been a "ridiculous farce." Pretending to honor the state debt, they had shorted appropriations and applied revenue to other purposes. Another writer, complaining of legislative perfidy, said that the mere rumor that Congress would assume state debts had raised the price of state securities from 4/0 on the pound—their market value after Shays's Rebellion— to 4/7. He surmised that if Congress did assume state debts, the market price would probably be five times higher than if assumption were not carried through. "Such is the difference of trust and confidence which the creditors and others put between Representatives in Congress and Representatives in State Assemblies."[63]

These recriminations did not hide the refusal of an effective majority of the people to pay the inflated debt on the terms desired by the creditors. Before the existence of a new federal government changed conditions, the state creditors of Massachusetts faced the prospect of a revaluation of the debt or its payment by means of a paper medium. Under these circumstances they looked to the establishment of a strong central government.[64]   Even worse off

---

62. The proceedings are covered in the *Boston Magazine,* Mar., July, Nov., Dec., 1786.

63. *Massachusetts Centinel,* Nov. 11, 1789; "X," *ibid.,* Mar. 20, 1790. John Stone published in March 1790 his intention of suing the state in federal court for payment of a warrant of three years' standing. For publishing Stone's notice, the *Centinel* was accused of subverting the state government. *Ibid.,* Mar. 13, 31, 1790.

64. See Robert A. East, "The Massachusetts Conservatives in the Critical Period," Richard B. Morris, ed., *Era of the American Revolution* (N.Y., 1939), 385, 389-90; Louise B. Dunbar, *A Study of Monarchical Tendencies in the United States from 1776 to 1801* (Urbana, Ill., 1923).

were the creditors of Congress, for whom the state did little during the Confederation. As long as the program to fund and redeem the state debt was progressing, they could hope that Massachusetts would one day assume the public debt; after Shays's Rebellion they too could look only to Congress.

The rebellion undoubtedly converted the propertied classes of Massachusetts to Nationalist views. They regarded the suspension of the debt-funding program as a violation of their natural rights, and they were injured in spirit as well as in pocketbook when the leaders of the "lawless rabble" appeared in the legislature. Stephen Higginson described the tide of conservative opinion: "I never saw so great a change in the public mind, on any occasion, as has lately appeared in this State, as to the expediency of increasing the powers of Congress."[65]

Shays's Rebellion was consciously exploited by leading Nationalists in search of a common danger to unite the country.[66] Secretary of War Henry Knox, who acted as a kind of official observer for Congress, wrote that heavy taxes were only the ostensible cause of disorder; in reality the insurgents aimed at pillaging the rich and annihilating all debts by means of depreciated paper money. He said that many people in the other New England states were sympathetic —the rebellion was likely to spread. Similar rumors, including the trumped-up notion that the Shaysites were soliciting British aid, were relayed by letter and articles in the press to all parts of the country. Madison saw Shaysism emerging in Virginia. Edward Carrington advised the governor of Virginia that the rebellion in Massachusetts might bring on civil war and asked him to communicate this information to the legislature.[67] Manifestations of discontent throughout New England seemed to substantiate these fears.

65. Theodore Sedgwick to Nathan Dane, July 5, 1787, Sedgwick Papers, box 3, Mass. Hist. Soc.; Higginson to Henry Knox, Nov. 25, 1786, Knox Papers, *ibid.*

66. See Joseph Parker Warren, "The Confederation and Shays' Rebellion," *Amer. Hist. Rev.,* 11 (1905-6), 42-67.

67. Henry Knox to Washington, Oct. 23, 1786, Washington Papers, CCXXXVI, 102-3, Lib. Cong.; Madison to Washington, Nov. 8, 1786, *ibid.*, 119; William Grayson to Madison, Nov. 22, 1786, Madison to Jefferson, Sept. 6, 1787, Madison Papers, VI, 98, VIII, 3, Lib. Cong.; *Journals,* XXXI, 886-88, XXXII, 109-14; Edward Carrington to the Governor of Virginia, Dec. 8, 1786, *Cal. Va. State Papers,* IV, 195-99. The Virginia legislature received demands similar to those in Massachusetts for a revaluation of state securities. Its only response was to discontinue in 1786 the taxes hitherto levied to sink the state debt. *Journal of the Virginia House of Delegates,* Oct. 28, 1786.

Mobs besieged the legislature of New Hampshire and stopped courts
in eastern Connecticut; an "insurrection" was put down in Vermont.
Trouble was expected in New York, where the militia was readied
to intercept refugees from Massachusetts.[68] Summing up the implications, a correspondent to a Philadelphia newspaper observed that
"a federal Shays may be more successful than the Shays of Massachusetts, or a body of men may arise who form themselves into an order
of hereditary nobility . . . we are upon the very brink of a preci-
pice."[69]

Fear of social radicalism drove New England merchants and southern planters into alignment with middle state conservatives in support of the movement for the Constitution. In 1783 the Nationalists
had been a mere faction—albeit a powerful one—within the middle
states, supported elsewhere only by public creditors and individual
sympathizers, its leaders a coterie bound by ties of association and
interest to the dominant figure of Robert Morris. The Federalists
of 1787 were the Nationalists reinforced on a country-wide scale
under leaders convinced of the need for drastic action. Taking
advantage of a climate of opinion favorable to reform, they drove
the movement for constitutional revision beyond what had been
thought possible.

68. M. Cutler to Winthrop Sargent, Oct. 6, 1786, Winthrop Sargent Papers,
Mass. Hist. Soc.; *Boston Magazine*, Sept. and Oct. 1786; *Worcester Magazine*, 2
(Nov.-Mar. 1786-87), 401, 460-65, 636, 638. See Otto to Vergennes, Sept. 20, 1787,
Bancroft, *History of the Constitution*, II, 395-97.

69. "To the Freemen of the United States," quoted, *Worcester Magazine*, 3
(June 1787), 143.

Speculation in the Public Debt

*"The Ball is at our foot if we can but get the strength to kick
it . . . This Thing is of a Magnitude which you can scarcely
conceive and you cannot do a better thing than at once to
begin laying due foundations for many are now at Work."*

—Gouverneur Morris to William
Carmichael, Feb. 25, 1789.

THE PUBLIC events of the postwar years allowed ample scope
for the busy habits of speculation which American merchants acquired
during the Revolution. The mass of public securities coming on the
market after 1783 steadily gravitated into the hands of propertied
men and foreign investors. The brisk traffic in securities mounted
to a frenzy as Congress proceeded to enact Hamilton's funding program, the final vindication of all risks.

Low market prices of public securities in the years after the Revolution should not obscure the fact that securities were never dead
paper. They always had a value which rose or fell in response to acts
of Congress or the state governments. A nice profit could be turned
by dealing in low values, and men of property acquired sizable holdings, not in anticipation of a change in the structure of the Union—
though this was a long-term possibility—but for the sake of immediate,
marginal gains. There was always a ready market, and securities
became a medium of exchange, offered and accepted in the sale of
land or commodities and in discharge of debts. Most exchanges,
especially those involving large sums, appear to have been con-

ducted privately, but in Philadelphia, New York, and Boston, brokers advertised in the newspapers to attract small sellers and buyers.

The object of this speculation was a mass of securities consisting, in part, of loan certificates issued during the war and persisting through the Confederation to the amount of about $11,000,000. A larger body of securities came on the market after 1783 when the settlement of accounts with civilians and soldiers gave rise to about $17,000,000, of which final settlement certificates issued to the army (military certificates) formed approximately $11,000,000. The principal of the public debt in 1790 was about $27,400,000, and the accumulated interest was approximately $13,000,000.[1]

The "best part of the federal debt" was loan certificates, which drew the highest market price.[2] The tender regard in which they were held by Congress assured them most favorable treatment. Although freely bought and sold at a discount, they, more than any other security, were likely to remain with the original holder. They had been issued in many cases to propertied men who could afford to keep them, and Congress long made it worthwhile to do so by paying the interest. (The greater part of the loan certificate debt drew interest in bills of exchange until March 1782.) Compared with other securities, they were gilt-edged; fewer came on the market, and they were not the main object of large-scale speculation.

The speculators' best game was final settlement certificates issued to the army. It appears that nearly all the soldiers and most of the officers sold their securities soon after receiving them. Pierce's notes, as they were called, came on the market beginning in 1784 and by their volume depressed the price of all securities. They formed the bulk of the large speculative holdings.

The market price of all securities varied according to the steps which Congress or the states took to support their value. After Congress stopped all interest on loan certificates in 1782, they dropped to 20c or 25c on the dollar, which with minor fluctuations remained their basic price until 1788. This was a grade above the price of final settlement certificates issued to civilians and soldiers; they passed

1. *American State Papers, Finance,* I, 19, 239. Part of this interest had been paid by the states, but most of it was still represented by unredeemed indents or accumulated interest on securities which had never been applied for or collected.

2. Royal Flint to Jeremiah Wadsworth, Aug. 15, 1786, Wadsworth Papers, Conn. Hist. Soc.

at 10c or 15c on the dollar. Such rates prevailed generally in New England and the south, where the states did no more to support public securities than pay interest in indents. Public securities in these states were known as *balloon certificates* because they were unsupported. As late as November 1788, final settlements of this type were as low as 18c, and loan certificates of the same kind were 20c or 22c.[3]

Whenever states offered more than indents to public creditors, securities rose in value. New York began accepting final settlement certificates in the sale of unallocated lands, whereupon the price increased by a third—to 20c on the dollar.[4] New Jersey paid interest in state paper money, so far superior to indents that her final settlement certificates passed at 20c in the Philadelphia market. All public securities in Pennsylvania rose in price when the state backed them with taxes, accepted them at the land office, and finally assumed them as its own debt. Final settlement certificates which drew interest were 40c on the dollar after 1785; non-interest-bearing final settlements redeemable only at the land office were about 30c; loan certificates were over 40c.[5] The price increases which resulted from state funding, as in Pennsylvania, made profits for speculators, and Congress's decision in 1787 to sell northwestern lands in large tracts opened another field. By October 1787, the associates of the Ohio and Scioto companies had deposited $500,000 in depreciated securities at the Treasury.[6]

The role of economic motive in the formation of the Constitution is disputed by historians. For want of complete data on security holdings before 1790, it will probably never be possible to verify

3. An illuminating description of the securities market is the series of advertisements by a Philadelphia broker, explaining details to prospective customers. "Current Prices" listed by Francis White in the *Penn. Packet,* July 31, Sept. 1, 29, 1786, and the *Penn. Gazette,* Aug. 16, 23, Sept. 6, 1786. For additional price quotations, *Journals,* XXXIII, 574; Samuel Dick to Thomas Sinnickson, Mar. 18, 1784, Burnett, ed., *Letters,* VII, 473; Barnabas Deane to Silas Deane, Dec. 10, 1784, *Deane Papers,* Conn. Hist. Soc., *Collections,* 23 (1930), 207-8.

4. Richard Platt to Winthrop Sargent, May 30, 1786, Winthrop Sargent Papers, Mass. Hist. Soc.

5. See "Current Prices," cited in note 3. Pennsylvania new loan certificates, representing assumed public securities on which all past interest had been paid, sold from 33c to 38c.

6. List of securities received from the Agents to 27th Oct. 1787, by Richard Platt, Treasurer of the Ohio Company, Winthrop Sargent Papers, Mass. Hist. Soc. Indents were not accepted for western lands, so these were principal securities.

the financial stakes held by most of the leading actors in the drama. However, the general course of speculation can be described and a few clues gained about its role in politics. Everything suggests, for example, that transfers were continuous from the moment securities were issued and that most of the public debt was owned by secondary holders by the time the Constitution was drafted, certainly by the time it was ratified by nine states.

As early as December 1785, a Boston merchant informed his New York correspondent that large blocs of securities were hard to find at going prices—an increasingly frequent complaint from this time on. Loan certificates, he said, were either held by the original owners who were determined to "hazard the event of them" or were in the possession of moneyed men who would not sell cheaply; army final settlements had been gobbled up by brokers or speculators who were unwilling to sell without exacting a premium. "There are paper speculators dispersed over every part of the United States," he said. "They keep up a constant & accurate communication. The information flies from one to another in every direction like an electrical shock."[7] The truth of these observations is confirmed by a reading of contemporary mercantile correspondence. The letters of such merchants and brokers as Richard Platt, William Duer, William Constable, Andrew Craigie, Clement Biddle, and Elias Boudinot show a continuous attachment to speculation and a close scrutiny of market prices.

The most conclusive evidence of an early transfer of the public debt is the account books of the Virginia state treasury. In 1786 the state issued indents for the interest due on public securities held by her citizens. Nearly all the creditors claimed their indents, presenting securities whose total value was $1,392,000.[8] It is possible to identify the original holders of all but $15,800. Most of the securities had been issued only in the preceding year or two by federal commissioners engaged in settling accounts; yet the figures show that

7. George Flint to Constable Rucker & Co., Dec. 17, 1785, Constable Rucker & Co., Letters and Accounts, 1784-1793, Constable-Pierrepont Papers, N.Y. Pub. Lib.

8. Public securities originally issued in Virginia amounted to $1,614,000 and some had no doubt been transferred out of state, hence virtually the whole debt was presented to receive indents. *American State Papers, Finance,* I, 239.

$912,600, over 65 percent, had already passed out of the hands of the original holders.[9]

It is reasonably certain that by 1787 or 1788 the greater part of the debt not already redeemed by the states was in the possession of secondary holders of varying magnitude. It was the property of former army officers, storekeepers, lawyers and other professional men, prosperous landowners, merchants who traded in securities as an adjunct to commerce, merchants who became security brokers as their agency functions (buying or selling for others) gradually over-shadowed their other concerns. The actual organization of the new government imparted a sudden frenzy to the speculation, but at this late stage it consisted of dealings among secondary holders, augmented by a bare trickle of securities brought to market by original holders. The late exchanges merely concentrated the debt still further, drew more of it towards the commercial states, and brought in foreign purchasers.

The massive transfer of the debt is outlined in the phenomenal increase in the amount of securities recorded at the Treasury. Because states would not pay indents or interest on securities originating in other states or held by non-citizens, investors with portfolios of securities drawn from every part of the country registered them at the Treasury in order to draw indents. After Congress enacted the funding bill in 1790, persons with similar holdings often subscribed directly at the Treasury rather than submit parcels of securities to the loan offices in the various states of origin. Thus, securities recorded at the Treasury peculiarly display the holdings of interstate and foreign investors, and the great increase shows the volume of large-scale speculation. In 1782 the debt registered at the Treasury was $267,000; it rose to $939,000 in December 1785; then, as speculation mounted, it climbed to $2,680,000 by the end of 1787, $4,600,000 in March 1789 and $9,314,000 in June 1791. Meanwhile, additional millions were being subscribed at the Treasury to the loan of 1790. In October 1791, when the entire public debt stood at approximately

9. Daily Register of Interest Payments, Liquidated Debt, 1785-1787, Register of Certificates Issued for Interest Due on Loan Office Certificates and Certificates of the Liquidated Debt . . . in Virginia, 1786, vols. 1116, 1116a, 1081, Record Group 53, Fiscal Records Sec., Natl. Arch. The Pennsylvania indent books in the National Archives show similar concentrations of transferred securities, but are not complete.

$41,000,000, securities registered or subscribed at the Treasury amounted to more than $18,000,000.[10]

Although prices remained relatively low until 1789, the securities market responded immediately to every phase of the movement to strengthen the federal government. The Constitutional Convention brought a rise from less than 15c to 17c or 19c on the dollar.[11] As enough states ratified the Constitution to ensure its adoption, the price climbed to 24c or 25c, receding afterwards to about 21c, presumably as profits were taken and additional securities were offered for sale.[12] Those who had bought two years earlier had gained 40 percent on their investment, but long-range prospects justified holding on. It was certain, in view of past declarations, that the new Congress would support the debt; there remained only a question of what action would be taken and how far security values would improve. A residuum of doubt—plus an ultimate distrust of all political bodies—prevented a greater rise at this time. Nevertheless, the market tightened at existing prices, and thenceforth there was continual upward pressure, with more buyers than sellers. Declines were slight and temporary, accompanied by little selling. Large blocs of securities could usually be had only by paying a premium.

Omens remained favorable in 1789. Congress's failure to act at its first session was faintly disappointing, but its temper revealed a determination to support the debt. The choice of Alexander Hamilton as head of the Treasury and the fact that finances were put under a single executive instead of a board were recognizable aspects of a firm, conservative policy. Opposition to the new government, which some had expected, failed to materialize, and the first import duties levied by Congress returned an income deemed ample to pay interest on the debt. The country was prosperous. Trade boomed in the fall of the year as American wheat went to Europe

10. Report dated July 16, 1782, Papers of Cont. Cong., no. 137, I, 709; *Estimate of the Annual Expenditures of the Civil Department of the United States* ... (np, nd), in the library of the State Hist. Soc. of Wisc.; Statement of the Liquidated and Loan Office Debt to Dec. 31, 1787, Papers of Cont. Cong., no. 141, I, 361; *American State Papers, Finance*, I, 27, 146-50.

11. When speculation is the topic, price quotations will always refer to final settlement certificates unless otherwise specified.

12. William Constable to Jarvis, Mar. 19, 1788, Constable Letterbooks, N.Y. Pub. Lib.; Andrew Craigie to Daniel Parker, Nov. 5, 1788, Craigie Papers, box 3, Amer. Antiq. Soc., Worcester, Mass.; Constable to Jeremiah Wadsworth, Nov. 8, 1788, Wadsworth Papers, Conn. Hist. Soc.

on a scale never known before.[13]   Security prices moved upward
from 21c or 22c, where they had leveled off after the adoption of the
Constitution, to about 25c in April 1789, climbed slowly during the
summer months to 27c and 30c, then suddenly shot up from 33c in
November to 45c and 50c in December.   Within a year prices had
doubled; within three years they had nearly quadrupled.[14]

The level of 50 percent of face value was higher than the market
could sustain in mere anticipation of Congressional funding, and
without the pressure of foreign buyers, it is doubtful whether it
would have reached this figure.   Before the actual legislation was
passed, there was an inevitable doubt that the debt would be funded
at all and, beyond this, a question of what benefits would accrue to
the holders. Congress was now able to pay regular interest in hard
money—terms which were superior to anything which creditors could
have expected of the Confederation government—and it seemed likely
that they would be obliged to accept an "accommodation" of the debt
in the form of reduced interest or principal.   It was also possible
that Congress would redeem the principal of the debt, not in specie,
but only by acceptance of securities in the sale of northwestern
lands.   Further uncertainty existed about the unpaid interest which
had accumulated during the Confederation in the form of unredeemed indents or interest due on securities.   Most people doubted
that interest would be funded on equal terms with the principal;
it was possible that Congress would make no other provision than
to declare indents receivable from the states in discharge of past
requisitions.   Without violating the substance of its obligations,
Congress, in fact, had a number of alternatives, not all of which
were equally favorable to the creditors.   Under the circumstances,
50c on the dollar bespoke an optimism which many felt ought to be

13. Andrew Craigie to Daniel Parker, May 16, June 6, July 25, Sept. 1, 1789,
Craigie Papers, box 3, Amer. Antiq. Soc.; William Constable to James Jarvis,
Jan. 12, 1789, to Gouverneur Morris, July 29, Aug. 9, 1789, to John Cochrane,
Nov. 2, 1789, to Gouverneur Morris, Jan. 12, 1790, Constable Letterbooks, N.Y.
Pub. Lib.; Gouverneur Morris to William Carmichael, Apr. 27, 1789, to William
Constable, July 4, 1789, Commercial Correspondence, I, 51-53, 72-76, Gouverneur
Morris Papers, Lib. Cong.; Clement Biddle to George Joy, Sept. 9, 1789, to Richard
Smith, May 23, 1790, Clement Biddle Letterbook, Hist. Soc. of Pa.

14. Prices are extracted from numerous allusions in the Constable Letterbooks,
the Clement Biddle Letterbook, N.Y. Pub. Lib., the Craigie Papers, box 3, Amer.
Antiq. Soc. See Henry Jackson to Henry Knox, Dec. 27, 1789, Knox Papers, XXV,
78, Mass. Hist. Soc.

qualified, in the belief that a somewhat lower figure represented a more accurate calculation of risks. Others, especially the "deep" speculators of New York City, placed a higher pecuniary value on the course of events.

New York City, the national center of speculation, established prices for the entire country. Its pre-eminence was the result of a favorable location. In close touch with the activities of Congress, New York speculators received tips from legislators and federal officials. More important, the city rapidly became the clearing house for foreign investment. For reasons already indicated, nearly all foreigners who bought public securities had them converted at the United States Treasury into register's certificates which drew indents directly from the federal government. The New York merchants who handled this business became the primary agents of foreign buyers.

The city was heavily populated by speculators and securities brokers. Among firms of the first rank was William Constable and Co., a partnership formed by William Constable, Robert Morris, and, after 1787, Gouverneur Morris. Constable and Gouverneur Morris had partnerships independent of the firm and, of course, Robert Morris had numerous mercantile connections. Eventually, the Constable-Morris group became involved in the complex affairs of Daniel Parker, an American merchant resident in Europe whose New York agent was Andrew Craigie. But it is likely that neither of these firms was among the most important in the city. Although their activities do not appear so fully in the documents, Herman LeRoy and William Bayard were probably the foremost agents of Dutch capitalists investing in the American debt. Other first-rank brokers and firms, which had correspondents and sometimes roving agents in all parts of the country, were John Delafield, Watson and Greenleaf, C. and J. Shaw, Nicholas Low, Robert Gilchrist, Richard Platt, and William Duer.[15]

15. See Articles of Partnership between Herman LeRoy and William Bayard, Dec. 1, 1786, unsigned letter, dated Amsterdam, April 1791, Bayard Correspondence, 1786-1794, Bayard-Campbell-Pearsall Collection, N.Y. Pub. Lib.; Constable to Gouverneur Morris, July 25, 1789, to Robert Morris, Nov. 2, 1789, Constable Letterbooks, *ibid.*; Wilson, *Anglo-Dutch Commerce and Finance*, 191; Clement Biddle to Robert Gilchrist, Mar. 23, Dec. 24, 1789, Clement Biddle Letterbook, Hist. Soc. of Pa.; Craigie to Parker, Nov. 14, 1789, Craigie Papers, box 3, Amer. Antiq. Soc.; E. Haskell to William Duer and Richard Platt, May 25, 1788, William Duer Papers, 1785-1790, N.-Y. Hist. Soc.

The efforts of these firms and others like them to profit from the rise in security values were sadly handicapped by lack of capital. Like nearly all American merchants, their funds were usually over-extended in a variety of enterprises. Perhaps they had enough cash to buy tens of thousands in depreciated securities, but they were never in a position to take full advantage of their opportunities and strike for large segments of the debt. Those of a conservative temper —like the majority of Philadelphia merchants—were reluctant to throw their last dollar into securities. Those who were "security mad," as Constable described himself, were driven to distraction by the urge to increase the scale of their operations. Not satisfied with using their available funds to buy at low prices and hold until Congress funded the debt, they employed all their arts to expand their operating capital. They played for short-term gains as the market rose, buying and selling quickly for marginal gains. They borrowed securities, paying a fee for the use of them, with a guarantee to re-place them at a fixed time in the future; by selling the rented securi-ties and reinvesting the capital, they hoped to gain enough to be able to replace the original securities, even at higher prices, and still make a profit. Securities which they owned themselves they often preferred to use as collateral in borrowing money for larger speculations. They entered into contracts with other speculators and dealers, guaranteeing delivery of securities at stipulated prices, counting on being able to buy them at a lower figure; or, in turn, they contracted for such deliveries from others. In playing for big stakes they habitually took big risks.

American merchants had always relied on European credit, and as the market spiraled they naturally thought of involving European capital in their speculations. If foreign houses could be induced to supply the money, operations far beyond what the Americans could manage themselves were possible. The role was a promising one if the merchants could contract for delivery in Europe at prices higher than those in the United States. Theoretically, the backing of European capitalists would remove all limits to the amounts which could be purchased, and, as the debt migrated to Europe, American merchants handling the business could expect to profit at every stage of the process.

A scattering of American public securities had been held in Europe since the Revolution, but in everything but price they were a poor investment for Europeans in the immediate postwar years. This was so obvious that American merchants hardly tried to interest their European counterparts in the speculations they themselves were carrying on.[16] Foreign capitalists were properly dubious about risking money in the United States.

Their attitude began to change, apparently, with the arrival of Daniel Parker in Europe in 1785. Parker, who was a native of Watertown, Massachusetts, brought with him a bag of securities and an indubitable talent for negotiation. His primary mission was to acquire title to the assets of a bankrupt Dutch company, with whom he had been doing business, by offering public securities to the company's creditors as a guarantee of their claims. He also had some hope of employing securities as collateral in borrowing money. Parker was successful in his efforts, but his greatest accomplishment was to arouse the interest of certain Dutch houses in American public securities. A syndicate headed by Peter Stadnitski, Matthys Ooster, Karel D'Amour, and Kindreck Vollenhoven bought at least $200,000 in 1786 through Parker and his New York agent, Andrew Craigie. The same Dutch bankers no doubt had other agents, for by the beginning of 1788 their holdings had risen to at least $1,340,000.[17]

Stadnitski was the principal broker whom the Willinks and the Van Staphorsts employed to sell shares in American government loans to Dutch investors. It is possible that his early purchases of American domestic securities were part of a scheme, said to have been inspired by Parker, to wring an advantage out of Congress. The Dutch loan of 1787 had not been fully subscribed, and there was no money available to the United States to meet interest falling due in Holland on previous loans. Stadnitski offered to take up the 622,000

16. See Matthew Ridley to Major John Swan, Sept. 12, 1783, Ridley Letterbook, Ridley Papers, Mass. Hist. Soc.

17. Thomas Jefferson to Messrs. Van Staphorst, Oct. 12, 25, 1785, Acc. 161, no. 248, env. 17, Foreign Affairs Sec., Natl. Arch.; Daniel Parker to John Holker, Oct. 18, 1785, Holker Papers, XXX, 5851, Lib. Cong.; agreement between John Pierce and Andrew Craigie, Mar. 2, 1786, Copy of a Certificate respecting debt to Hollanders (Dec. 6, 1786), Notarial Copy of a Register's Certificate to . . . Ooster & Co. (May 30, 1787), Craigie Papers, box 2, Amer. Antiq. Soc.; Willinks and Staphorst to the Board of Treasury, Mar. 29, 1788, Duer Papers, II, 1784-1802, N.-Y. Hist. Soc.; Paul Demund Evans, *The Holland Land Company* (Buffalo, 1924), 3.

guilders which remained unsubscribed of the loan of 1787 on condition that 180,000 guilders of it be regarded as one year's interest on the domestic public securities held by his syndicate. Congress would thus be able to meet its obligations in Holland at the expense of conceding a year's interest in specie values on Stadnitski's securities—better treatment than any other public creditors were getting. Both Adams and Jefferson strongly opposed the scheme, and Adams managed to open another loan in Holland which saved American credit without recourse to Stadnitski's offer.[18]

As long as Jefferson remained in France, he tried to discourage the transfer of American domestic securities to foreigners. In the case of Stadnitski's offer, he felt that payment of interest on domestic public securities which foreigners had bought at a great discount would make investment in them so attractive as to obstruct the floating of further American government loans abroad. He wished, in any case, to keep the domestic debt at home. In an effort to prevent foreigners from taking it over, he suggested to the Board of Treasury that the category of the registered debt be abolished; foreigners would then be obliged to send the securities they held to the various states in which they were issued in order to receive the interest due on them. This procedure would certainly have been a deterrent to foreign investment. When Craigie in New York learned privately of Jefferson's letter, he said he would fight against such a move, possibly with the aid of his friend William Duer, who was secretary to the Board of Treasury. The policy was not adopted.[19]

The flow of foreign investment increased in 1788 as the new federal government materialized. Dutch investments were pre-eminent, but British and French capitalists soon entered the field. Disturbed conditions and the threat of war in Europe, the drift toward revolution in France, the bankruptcy of the French government, the heavy public debts of European nations—all contributed to the attractiveness of investing in the United States, whose potential resources were a broad

18. Willinks and Staphorst to the Board of Treasury, Feb. 7, 1788, Papers of Cont. Cong., no. 140, II, 497; Jefferson to the Board of Treasury, Mar. 29, 1788, Duer Papers, II, 1784-1802, N.-Y. Hist. Soc.; La Follette, Revolutionary Foreign Debt, 35-38. See Agreement, Daniel Parker and Peter Stadnitski, Mar. 22, 1788, Craigie Papers, box 2, Amer. Antiq. Soc.

19. Craigie to Daniel Parker, Aug. 19, Sept. 3, 1788, Craigie Papers, box 3, Amer. Antiq. Soc.

guarantee of the country's ability to pay. In view of the imminent formation of a government having the power to make good on Congress's reiterated declarations of intent, the current low price of American securities was very tempting.[20]

Early in 1788, before the Constitution had been approved, the Dutch firm of Peter Stadnitski and Hendrick Vollenhoven, along with Etienne L'Espinasse and Christian van Eighen, launched a considerable purchase through Parker, commissioning him to deliver $200,000 at 37½c on the dollar. The terms were favorable to Parker, who got an advance payment of $8,700 specie and the right to collect $80,000 in indents due in the United States on securities already held by the bankers. He thus acquired part of the money to make the initial purchases, and would be able to buy securities in the United States for little more than 20c on the dollar. The terms applied to the purchase of $200,000, but the contract was left open to allow him to buy an unlimited amount.[21]

The Dutch firm, which now included Nicholas Van Staphorst, Gerrit Nutges, and Johan van Franckenstein, soon expanded their order. About August 1788, they contracted with Parker for $1,000,000, later $1,200,000. The terms are not available, but the agreement followed conventional lines: Craigie in New York was to furnish proof that securities had been registered at the United States Treasury in the names of the Dutch capitalists, whereupon he would be entitled to receive payment by drawing bills of exchange on his patrons. It appears that in this contract Parker got another advance—the privilege of drawing indents due at the Treasury on $640,000 in public securities owned by the Dutch bankers.[22]

To fulfill his engagements, Parker entered into side contracts with two Americans then in Europe, Richard Smith and James Jarvis, who agreed, under penalties for failure, to deliver $250,000 and $300,000 respectively, at 25c on the dollar within a stipulated period. Each

20. See Oliver Wolcott to Oliver Wolcott, Sr., Dec. 2, 1789, George Gibbs, *Memoirs of the Administrations of Washington and John Adams* (N.Y., 1846), I, 24.

21. Agreement, Daniel Parker and Peter Stadnitski, Mar. 22, 1788, Craigie to Daniel Parker, Apr. 6, 1788, Craigie Papers, boxes 2, 3, Amer. Antiq. Soc.

22. This contract superseded an earlier one for $55,000. Agreement between Daniel Parker and Tourton & Ravel, May 22, 1788, box 2, *ibid.*; Craigie to Parker, Aug. 24, Sept. 3, Oct. 2, 1788, Craigie to Messrs. C. and R. Puller, Nov. 4, 1788, to Parker, Nov. 5, 1788, Oct. 30, 1789, box 3, *ibid.*

received a small cash advance from Parker.[23]   Meanwhile, in New
York Craigie tried to fill Parker's orders.   He had to bear the cost of
the initial purchases himself and was handicapped by lack of ready
money.   Drafts on the European capitalists were to be accompanied by
proof that the purchases had already been made.   Craigie tried to buy
on credit or at least on the basis of deferring payment until he could
draw bills, and sometimes he was able to persuade vendors of securities to accept bills payable in London at sixty or ninety days.   When
possible, he borrowed securities, contracting to return equal values
to the lender at a later date.   In addition, Craigie formed a private
partnership with Christopher Gore of Boston to purchase $100,000,
and these securities were probably applied to the fulfillment of Parker's
contracts.   By November 1788, Craigie managed to accumulate a sum
of $538,000, and by January 1789, $635,000.[24]

The orders given Daniel Parker were but one of many channels
of European investment in the public debt.   Parker's own principals
in Holland undoubtedly placed orders with other New York brokers,
particularly LeRoy and Bayard, whose large, reckless purchases in
this period were continually raising the market.   The business was so
extensive toward the end of 1788 that the firm of LeRoy and Son contemplated an application to the New York Chamber of Commerce,
requesting the Chamber to regulate commissions to be charged in
security negotiations on behalf of foreigners.[25]   Brokers in other American cities were getting direct orders from Europe.   Abroad there was
a frenzied promotion.   One American merchant wrote from Europe
in June 1789 that there were too many competitors: Some . . . are men
of broken fortune, who have nothing to lose by playing a desperate
game, others are adventurers, looking for contracts to be fulfilled at
distant periods, some have funds in their possession, and the last and

23. Agreement between Richard Smith and Daniel Parker, May 27, 1788, agreements between Daniel Parker and James Jarvis, June 18, 1788, box 2, *ibid.*
24. Among the lenders was the poet, Joel Barlow, who supplied $20,000.
Parker's subcontractors had difficulty fulfilling their agreement.   In a desperate
effort to find low-priced securities, Jarvis fell into the clutches of rival brokers
who lured him on to divulge information about Parker's affairs.   To prevent
worse consequences, Craigie finally sold Jarvis enough securities to get him out of
trouble.   Agreement between Andrew Craigie and Christopher Gore, Aug. 7, 1788,
Craigie Papers, box 2, Amer. Antiq. Soc.; Craigie to Parker, Sept. 3, Nov. 5, 1788,
Jan. 11, 24, 1789, to Moore Furman, June 7, 1790, box 3, *ibid.*
25. Craigie to Parker, Sept. 3, 1788, *ibid.*

most dangerous Class are those laying in wait to frustrate all speculations not made through a particular chain of connections."[26]

In 1789 Parker's negotiations involved Gouverneur Morris. Morris
had gone abroad early that year to restore the badly deteriorated
affairs of his friend Robert Morris, and to advance his own fortunes.
He soon became engrossed in securities speculation and in efforts to
refinance the American debt to France. Upon his arrival, he met
Parker and was at once impressed not only with the scope of Parker's
dealings, but also by Parker's fund of information about the business
on which he, Morris, had come. The two men agreed to join forces
rather than compete.[27]

Gouverneur Morris had arrived too late to secure the best advantage, and he and his partners were further handicapped by lack of
capital. As he once said in a slightly different context, he had to
"make bricks without straw." The leading partner, Robert Morris,
had large assets, but for some time he had been in perilous difficulty
because of over extending his resources: some of his bills had been
protested in Europe, and his credit had suffered as a result of his
failure to settle accounts with the federal government.[28] Another
likely associate in European dealings, William Duer, long an intimate
of Robert and Gouverneur Morris, had not, so he said, been able to
pay his creditors since the Revolution.[29] Constable himself was not
a big merchant and often found himself at wit's end trying to fill
orders sent by Gouverneur Morris.

All this did not prevent Gouverneur Morris from forming plans
on a grand scale. He and Parker talked of organizing an international
syndicate which would combine all European investors in a single company and purchase virtually the entire domestic debt of the United
States. As the first step, they hoped to organize a group of capitalists

26. E. Haskell to William Constable, June 7, 1789, William Constable Letters,
1774-1791, Constable-Pierrepont Papers, N.Y. Pub. Lib.

27. Gouverneur Morris to Robert Morris, Feb. 17, May 8, 1789, to Constable,
May 11, 1789, Commercial Correspondence, I, 12-17, 54-57, 59-60, Gouverneur
Morris Papers, Lib. Cong.

28. Gouverneur Morris to Robert Morris, Aug. 31, 1790, no. 22, *ibid.* See also
Constable to James Chalmers, Apr. 14, 1789, to Alexander Ellice, Nov. 7, 1789,
to Gouverneur Morris, Nov. 14, Dec. 9, 1789, Jan. 4, 1790, to John Inglis, Jan. 4,
1790, Constable Letterbooks, N.Y. Pub. Lib.; Robert Morris to Constable, William
Constable Letters, 1774-1791, Constable-Pierrepont Papers, *ibid.*

29. Except John Holker. William Duer to John Holker, Dec. 10, 1788, Holker
Papers, XXXII, 6288-89, Lib. Cong.

based at Antwerp and eventually force an alliance with the "Amsterdam Society," which included the Dutch houses already buying through Parker. "We flatter ourselves with the Expectation," wrote Morris, "of going nearly if not entirely for the whole." Parker's share of this operation was separate from his existing commitments; it was to be one-third; Morris and associates were to take two-thirds.[30]

The plan was much too ambitious, but its pursuit brought Gouverneur Morris to London where he gained the ear of several English capitalists, including the Barings, who had already begun to invest in American securities. Morris, in company with Parker and an English merchant, Samuel Rogers, agreed with Francis Baring, Edmund Boehm, and Thomas Hinchman to deliver $600,000 in securities before the end of the year. Craigie and Constable were to work together in New York, Craigie making the purchases, while Constable drew bills on Samuel Rogers at London. With this piece of business accomplished, Morris returned to the Continent and soon made a very favorable contract with Charles John Michael de Wolf and Francis Vanderborcht of Antwerp to deliver $65,000.[31]

The plan to combine all European investors in a single society advanced no further, but Morris was already at work on another scheme of epic proportions—the purchase of the American debt to France. He had plenty of competition. Rising American credit, the French government's need of money, and the existence of a rich securities market in Holland had suggested to many the idea of purchasing the American debt to France, selling it in Holland, and taking the gains of the promotion.

As early as 1786 a syndicate formed by the Willinks, Van Staphorsts, and Hubbard had offered France $3,703,000 for $4,400,000 of the American debt. The project failed because Congress opposed it, feeling that it was safer to risk non-payment of obligations to France than endanger American credit in Holland.[32] But as the financial position of the United States improved, the idea of refi-

30. Gouverneur Morris to Robert Morris, May 8, 1789, to Constable, May 11, 1789, Commercial Correspondence, I, 54-57, 59-60, Gouverneur Morris Papers, Lib. Cong.

31. Gouverneur Morris to Constable, Aug. 25, 1789, Feb. 26, 1790, to Charles de Wolf, Feb. 26, 1790, to Constable, Apr. 8, 10, 1790, *ibid.*, I, 87-89, II, 13, 14, 23-24.

32. La Follette, Revolutionary Foreign Debt, 55-59.

nancing its debt to France revived, and various schemes were con-
certed by Dutch, French, and even British capitalists. American
merchants were alerted by the visit of Brissot de Warville to America
in 1788. Warville came over as the agent of a Swiss banker, Stephen
Claviere, who headed a group of capitalists interested in purchasing
the debt. Warville talked with many Americans, including both the
Morrises, William Duer and, it appears, Jeremiah Wadsworth. The
Morrises and Duer agreed to accept half-interest in a promotion,
and when Gouverneur Morris arrived in Europe and discovered that
Parker, who had also talked with Warville, was already involved in
the scheme, he decided to join forces with him in this venture.[33]

Morris opened conversations with French government officials
which led to a series of formal interviews in October 1789 with
Jacques Necker, the head of French finances. Necker had already
received offers from Dutch sources and was in a position to bargain.
Although details of the negotiations are obscure, they turned upon
the amount which Morris, Parker, and Le Couteulx, a French banker
who was also a party to the scheme, would pay for the debt and
what form the payment would take. After considering other methods,
the Americans proposed purchasing and restoring to France depreciated French government securities then being offered in Amsterdam.
Necker, it seems, drove Morris to such a high offer for the whole
debt, principal and interest, that Le Couteulx backed out. This
was discouraging enough, and there were other difficulties. The
execution of the plan depended on the positive cooperation of the
United States government which, in return for being released from
the debt to France, was expected to assign an equal amount in new
federal bonds to the promoters, which they could sell in Holland.
Obviously, too, the plan required the backing of the Amsterdam
society of Dutch bankers, whom Morris had not yet consulted.[34]

33. Statement re William Duer, Dec. 21, 1788, Rufus King Papers, box 3, N.-Y.
Hist. Soc. As a side line, Morris also tried to purchase the American debts to
Spain and to the Farmers General. Gouverneur Morris to Robert Morris, Feb.
17, 1789, to Constable, May 11, 1789, to William Carmichael, July 4, Sept. 17,
1789, to Robert Morris, Oct. 6, 1789, Commercial Correspondence, I, 12-17, 59-60,
72-76, 100, 111-12, Gouverneur Morris Papers, Lib. Cong.

34. La Follette, *Revolutionary Foreign Debt*, 59-66; Davis, *Early American
Corporations*, 151-73; Gouverneur Morris to Robert Morris, May 8, 1789, to
Parker, Sept. 24, Oct. 11, 12, 1789, to Constable and Co., Oct. 27, 1789, to Wilhelm
and Jan Willink, Dec. 13, 1789, to Hamilton, Jan. 31, 1790, to Robert Morris,
Feb. 3, 1790, Commercial Correspondence, I, 54-57, 102-3, 113, 116, 121-22, 130, II,
6-7, 8, Gouverneur Morris Papers, Lib. Cong.

The Amsterdam society, including the Willinks, Staphorsts, and Hubbard, soon learned of Morris's negotiation and countered by offering Necker an alternative plan which was limited to the purchase of only 6,000,000 livres. Gouverneur Morris asked them to join in his proposal to Necker, but, except for Jacob Van Staphorst, he failed to convert them. Necker refused the plan of the Dutch bankers, but instead of joining now with Morris, they threatened, in letters to Necker and Alexander Hamilton, to oppose him if he continued. Unable to proceed without Dutch backing, Morris was checkmated; his further efforts were fruitless.[35]

The obstinacy of the Dutch bankers convinced Morris that they had ulterior motives. Writing to Hamilton, he explained that they were making large purchases of depreciated American public securities and selling shares in them to Dutch investors. The profits were so great that the bankers were determined to prevent the floating of an American government loan in Holland, which would compete with their own offerings to the Dutch public, until they had accomplished their speculations in the American domestic debt. "It is. . . essential to the success of their schemes," he wrote, "that they should be able to suspend the one loan till they have completed the other, and thus our national interests are rendered subservient to their particular negotiations."[36]

Back in the United States, foreign orders were convulsing the securities market. Purchase orders rippling out from New York caused sharp price advances all over the country. Local markets were disorganized as prices rose above what brokers were authorized

35. Gouverneur Morris to Robert Morris, Feb. 7, to Daniel Parker, Feb. 10, 1790, to William Short, Apr. 7, 1790, Commercial Correspondence, II, 8-9, 11, 22-23, Gouverneur Morris Papers, Lib. Cong.

36. The same bankers opened a small loan of $1,200,000 for the American government late in 1789 without being authorized to do so—a move which Morris interpreted as another effort to forestall his projects. Gouverneur Morris to Hamilton, Jan. 31, 1790, to Chevalier Ternant, Mar. 31, 1790, *ibid.*, II, 6-7, 21-22; La Follette, Revolutionary Foreign Debt, 60-66.

Most of the debt to France was transferred to Holland from 1790 to 1794; the United States borrowed $9,400,000 there and used it mainly to pay the debt to France. The remainder, amounting to more than $2,000,000 was sunk by a commercial operation. James Swan, an American merchant, received United States bonds for this amount, in return for which he assumed the debt, paid it by furnishing supplies to the French government. He sold the bonds in Holland. *Ibid.*, 119-25; Paul B. Trescott, Federal Finance and the American Economy, 1790-1860 (unpublished doctoral dissertation, Princeton Univ., 1954), 96-97.

by their principals to pay, and sellers retired from the market until they could learn what was behind the flurry. Agents hunted for securities in the rural areas of the south. Prices advanced 50 percent in the last two months of 1789. William Constable, who no doubt examined the books at the Register's office, wrote in November that the Dutch had "lately" taken up about four millions.[37]

At this point, however, the great speculation paused and drew breath, exhausted by its pace. It had in fact already been slowed by the difficulties inherent in international transactions. Under the usual arrangements, European investors made payment only when they had received proof that their American agents had registered securities in their names; the agent was expected to finance the initial purchase out of his own capital. American merchants were therefore placed under difficulties unless they could buy on credit or pay initially for securities with bills of exchange drawn on their European principals. Even these expedients failed as speculation mounted late in 1789—few holders of securities would sell for anything but cash. Both Constable and Craigie begged in vain for their principals in Europe to send cash, saying that they could then have as much of the public debt as they wanted. The Bank of New York, pressed to its limit by insatiable demands for money, stopped new discounts in November 1789 and called in loans falling due.[38]

Another complication arose from having to deal in bills of exchange. Ordinarily, at the same time they sent securities to their European principals, American agents drew bills of exchange against them and sold these bills for cash in American ports. As the speculation reached its climax late in 1789, bills were offered for sale in New York, Philadelphia, and Boston in such volume as to exceed demand. Occasionally, bills would come back from Europe protested, whereupon a wave of skepticism made it hard to dispose even of those which were indubitably sound. The obstacles became nearly insurmountable at the beginning of 1790 when the marketing of a

37. Constable's associate Craigie looked at the register, and it must be presumed that Constable had the same privilege, especially as his friend William Duer was secretary to the Board of Treasury and Hamilton's first assistant. See Craigie to Daniel Parker, Jan. 7, 1789, Craigie Papers, box 3, Amer. Antiq. Soc.; Constable to John Cochrane, Nov. 2, 1789, Constable Letterbooks, N.Y. Pub. Lib.

38. See Constable to Gouverneur Morris, Nov. 14, 1789, Constable to Alexander Ellice, Nov. 18, 1789, to Robert Morris, Nov. 22, 1789, Constable Letterbooks, N.Y. Pub. Lib.

fine wheat crop in Europe and the sale of public securities abroad
gave rise to such an abundance of bills on Europe that—almost for
the first time in living memory—the rate of exchange became favorable to the United States. During the first five months of the year,
British pounds were discounted from 5 percent to at least 13 percent
in exchange for currency in New York, Pennsylvania, and Virginia;
£100 sterling in drafts on London would get only the equivalent of
£87 to £95 in American ports. The unfavorable rate of exchange
increased the prices Europeans had to pay for securities already bid
up to high levels.[39]

The chief obstacles to the transfer of the American public debt
to Europe, however, were the high prices and a relative shortage of
securities. In view of the uncertainty about Congressional funding,
50c on the dollar was, as we have seen, an optimistic figure. It was
higher than securities had hitherto sold for in Europe and left no
margin of profit on existing contracts for the American agents, whose
zeal was understandably diminished. Moreover, few large blocs of
securities were offered even at this price. The situation was the
cumulative result of a seller's market which had prevailed since 1786.
Securities had been increasingly hard to find at prices most buyers
were willing to pay, and although there was always a certain turnover
at going prices and a few bargains to be had in odd places, securities
generally moved only as competition among buyers drove prices up
to new levels. Late in 1789, as everyone waited to see what Congress
would do, optimism was so pervasive that sellers had a tendency to
stand off, while the agents of European investors, whose purchases
had hitherto driven up prices, were forced out of the market by the
high rates. In the presence of all these difficulties, neither Craigie
nor Constable managed to fill their European orders.[40]

For some time they had been considering other fields of specula-

39. See Constable to Gouverneur Morris, Jan. 4, 14, 1790, to Alexander Ellice,
Jan. 14, 1790, to John Richard, Jan. 26, 1790, to Gouverneur Morris, Jan. 28,
1790, to Alexander Ellice, Feb. 17, 1790, to Gouverneur Morris, May 23, 1790,
ibid.; Gouverneur Morris to R. Claiborne, Mar. 31, 1790, to Charles de Wolf,
May 11, 1790, Commercial Correspondence, II, 20, 60, Gouverneur Morris Papers,
Lib. Cong.; Clement Biddle to Richard Smith, May 23, 1790, Clement Biddle
Letterbook, Hist. Soc. of Pa.

40. Gouverneur Morris to William Constable, Feb. 11, 1790, to William Short,
Mar. 18., 1790, Commercial Correspondence, II, 12, 18, Gouverneur Morris Papers,
Lib. Cong.

tion. Indents were one alternative. They were still cheap and plentiful because few people expected Congress to fund them on equal terms with the principal. The other possibility was state debts. The securities of states such as Massachusetts and South Carolina, and those of North Carolina, which had not yet entered the Union, could be bought at very low prices. Massachusetts' notes had been swept upward late in 1789 by rumors of federal assumption, but they were available for 30c to 33c. Virginia state securities were 20c to 30c, and in North and South Carolina, state securities were as low as 9c or 10c as late as December 1789. Whether these securities would rise depended entirely upon the action of Congress.[41]

There was no general expectation that Congress would assume state debts. There had been some talk about it in the Constitutional Convention and in the Confederation Congress, some hope of it in Massachusetts and South Carolina. The well-informed merchants of New York City were, however, very alert to the possibility. In November 1788, Craigie informed Parker that it was a "very general Opinion" that state debts would be assumed. Constable gave the same information to his principal, and in May 1789, Gouverneur Morris entered into an agreement with Daniel Parker to speculate in state securities.[42] In July, Constable, who became entranced with the idea, proposed an association of European capitalists to buy up the whole South Carolina debt. He himself tried to convert his Kentucky lands into South Carolina securities.[43]

As public securities became scarce and expensive, state debts emerged as the only remaining low values that promised sensational profits. To American brokers with European orders to fill, state securities were the solution to their problems. Much depended,

41. Henry Jackson to Henry Knox, Dec. 27, 1789, Knox Papers, XXV, 78, Mass. Hist. Soc.; Davis, *Early American Corporations*, I, 339-41; Constable to Gouverneur Morris, Dec. 1, 1789, to Robert Morris, Dec. 7, 1789 and Jan. 9, 1790, Constable Letterbooks, N.Y. Pub. Lib.; Craigie to Parker, Dec. 15, 1789, Craigie Papers, box 3, Amer. Antiq. Soc.

42. Craigie to Parker, Nov. 5, 1788, Craigie Papers, box 3, Amer. Antiq. Soc.; Constable to Gouverneur Morris, Apr. 25, 1789, Constable Letterbooks, N.Y. Pub. Lib.; Gouverneur Morris to Robert Morris, May 8, 1789, Commercial Correspondence, I, 54-57, Gouverneur Morris Papers, Lib. Cong. Robert Morris was also a partner.

43. Constable to Gouverneur Morris, July 25, 1789, to James Seagrove, Aug. 8, 1789, to Robert Hazlehurst, Aug. 27, 1789, Constable Letterbooks, N.Y. Pub. Lib.

however, on the views of the Secretary of the Treasury, whose recommendations were likely to shape Congressional policy. Hamilton's circle of friends and social companions in New York included the very speculators who could gain heavily from advance knowledge of his proposals. Craigie employed Hamilton's legal services, and Constable, who was an agreeable fellow, dined occasionally with him and counted him as a close friend. Craigie and Constable were both close associates of William Duer, assistant to the Secretary and Hamilton's intimate friend. Hamilton was scrupulous, but he could not keep from imparting information to such companions. With so much at stake, the positive details of his program were bound to leak out.[44]

On October 30, 1789, Craigie informed Daniel Parker it was his conviction, shared by Constable and Duer, that Hamilton would recommend funding indents on equal terms with the principal of the public debt and would also propose an assumption of state debts by the federal government on equal terms with public securities. In later conversations, Constable "tried" Hamilton on these subjects and was more convinced than ever, although not to the point of absolute certainty. After another dinner conversation with Hamilton, Constable also predicted that Hamilton would recommend a delay in taking up payment of interest on state securities. The interval would allow speculators to buy them while they were still relatively cheap.[45] All these predictions proved to be correct.

Constable and Craigie were by this time greatly excited about state debts. Constable wrote Gouverneur Morris that it would be impossible to fill large orders for public securities: "The only mode by which you can get hold is by buying State Paper which will undoubtedly be funded." Craigie wrote that the state debts "will undoubtedly be adopted & put on the same footing with the other Debts & it must be by means of the State Debts that all great opera-

44. Constable to Gouverneur Morris, Oct. 28, 1789, to Robert Morris, Nov. 9, 1789, to John Inglis, Jan. 4, 1790, *ibid.*; Nathan Schachner, *Alexander Hamilton* (N.Y., 1946), 238-40; Statement signed by Alexander Hamilton, Jan. 29, 1789, Craigie Papers, box 2, Amer. Antiq. Soc.; Craigie to Parker, Oct. 30, 1789, box 3, *ibid.*

45. Constable to Robert Morris, Dec. 1, 1789, to Gouverneur Morris, Dec. 1, 1789, Constable Letterbooks, N. Y. Pub. Lib. See Craigie to Parker, Nov. 14, 1789, Craigie Papers, box 3, Amer. Antiq. Soc.

tions are effected." He was as confident of this, he said, as of "any Thing that has not already happened." In November 1789, Constable began buying state securities through a correspondent, James Seagrove. A month later he raised an original order to Robert Hazlehurst & Co. of Charleston, from $20,000 to $100,000.[46] His associate, Craigie, was in Boston when rumors of assumption sparked a sudden rise in the price of Massachusetts securities; Craigie instructed his agent, Leonard Bleecker, whom he had sent to South Carolina, to buy state securities there—$200,000 if the price was right and $400,000 if credit could be obtained. By this time "numberless others" were "pushing at the same thing." South Carolina state securities rose suddenly from 10c to 20c on the dollar.[47] The stage was set for the delivery of the Secretary's report on public credit, breathlessly awaited by speculators of high and low degree.

The object of their concern was $40,000,000 in securities which the normal processes of a competitive society had by this time converted into the property of a relative few. That the debt had been transferred and that only a small minority of the population would benefit from its funding became an issue which spurred party opposition to the Federalists in the next decade and, in a later age, it served as the major premise of an economic interpretation of history. The validity of this premise, however, has never been statistically verifiable; the government did not publish security holdings at the time, and the central records of the Treasury were later nearly all destroyed by fire. Fortunately, a sufficient number of documents survived elsewhere to afford a conclusive sample of the extent of transfer and concentration. The material which is presented here was selected for analysis because it gives the original as well as the secondary holders of several million dollars in securities and therefore allows us to determine transfers on a scale never before attempted.

46. Constable to Gouverneur Morris, Dec. 1, 1789, to Seagrove, Nov. 19, 1789, to Robert Hazlehurst & Co., Dec. 15, 1789, Constable Letterbooks, N.Y. Pub. Lib.; Craigie to Samuel Rogers, Dec. 6, 1789, to Daniel Parker, Dec. 15, 1789, Craigie Papers, box 3, Amer. Antiq. Soc. Seagrove had been Constable's partner in New York City during the British occupation.

47. Henry Jackson to Henry Knox, Dec. 27, 1789, Knox Papers, XXV, 78, Mass. Hist. Soc.; Craigie to Leonard Bleecker, Dec. 19, 1789, Craigie Papers, box 3, Amer. Antiq. Soc.; Constable to Thomas Fitzsimons, Dec. 31, 1789, to Gouverneur Morris, Jan. 7, 1790, Constable Letterbooks, N.Y. Pub. Lib.

The figures for Massachusetts confirm the common belief that the debt in that state had become the property of a small number of people, that much of it had been bought up by great speculators, and that it was largely held in the eastern towns, primarily Boston.

Of $5,055,000 subscribed to the federal loan of 1790, it appears that 7 percent of all subscribers owned nearly 62 percent of the whole amount, while 42 percent of all subscribers—the thinned ranks of the original holders—had below 3 percent. Most original holdings were less than $500; by 1790 they had ceased to predominate, and

FEDERAL DEBT IN MASSACHUSETTS: CONCENTRATION[48]

	No. of Persons	Percent Of Total Persons	Combined Holdings	Percent Of Total Subscription
$1 and under 100	124	8	7,795	.1
100 and under 500	501	34	133,516	2.8
500 and under 1,000	253	17	177,672	3.8
1,000 and under 5,000	414	28	921,766	19.6
5,000 and under 10,000	81	5	561,571	11.9
10,000 and under 25,000	72	5	1,151,761	24.5
25,000 and over	35	2	1,754,273	37.3
	1480		4,708,354	
Institutional holdings			347,097	
			5,055,451	

40 percent of all subscribers held amounts exceeding $1,000. Nearly 80 percent of all securities in the state had been transferred, steadily gravitating into the hands of the well-to-do, lodging here and there in the great accumulations of brokers and large speculators.

48. Subscriptions towards a Loan to the United States . . . in the State of Massachusetts, CCLXXXI, Record Group 53, Fiscal Records Sec., Natl. Arch.; Subscription Register, Loan of 1790, Massachusetts, CCLXXXVI-VIII, *ibid.* The figures include interest. A few securities irregularly entered at the end of the registers have been disregarded, as well as $27,278 issued in trust to the French consul in Boston. All these volumes specify whether a subscriber was acting for himself or as an agent and in nearly all cases afford some identification. An element of error is unavoidable, but every effort has been made to avoid confusion of identity among subscribers.

The documents afford some identification of the subscribers. Excluding widows and heirs of undescribed status, some of whom held large amounts, 80 percent of the securities belonged to persons listed as merchants, brokers, esquires, and professional men. Sixty-one percent of all securities were owned by residents of Boston; only 9 or possibly 10 persons holding $10,000 to $25,000 and 4 persons holding more than $25,000, were nonresidents. Institutions had made fairly substantial investments: charitable associations, $45,548; towns and parishes, $30,828; Harvard College, $102,922; and the State of Massachusetts, $171,799.

Among the largest subscribers, Nathaniel Prime, Boston broker, led the list with $196,000, followed by Samuel Breck, Boston esquire, with $104,300. Then came William Philips, Boston esquire, $94,000; Jonathan Mason, Boston esquire, $89,000; William Burley, Boston broker, $93,000; Nathan Bond, Boston broker, $88,000; David Sears, Boston merchant, $72,000; John Peck, Boston broker, $65,000; and John Sprague, Dedham physician, $68,000. Repetition of family names indicates a further concentration. To the $94,000 subscribed by William Philips, one might add $49,000 subscribed by William Philips, Jr., and to the $89,000 listed for Jonathan Mason, $20,486 held by Jonathan Mason, Jr. There was no reason in 1790 to disguise ownership, so it is not likely that any subscribers were acting merely as agents without at least partial ownership of the securities they presented. And records such as these, which cover only securities entered in one state, do not show subscriptions made in other states or at the Treasury and therefore do not necessarily unveil the activities of really great speculators.

The original ownership of securities is not given in every case, and we can trace transfers only where the information is furnished—$2,112,000 in securities out of $5,055,000. Nevertheless, the extent of transfer in larger holdings can be demonstrated. Of $127,411 subscribed by Nathaniel Prime, only $79 was an original holding, and of $37,360 subscribed by Samuel Breck, not a dollar had been issued to him. David Sear's $73,046 included an original holding of $1,723; of $53,398 held by Nathan Bond, only $53 was original; of $52,159 by John Peck, $46; and of $54,995 by Jonathan Mason, $1. John Sprague, the physician, was conspicuous in that his $68,000 included

FEDERAL DEBT IN MASSACHUSETTS: TRANSFER ($2,112,775)

Subscription	Percent Transferred
$1 and under 100	30
100 and under 500	55
500 and under 1,000	60
1,000 and under 5,000	68
5,000 and under 10,000	73
10,000 and under 25,000	79
25,000 and over	91
Average over all categories	79

an original holding of $8,574. In lesser subscriptions, the rate of transfer declined. The persons in the $1,000 to $5,000 category formed a solid and substantial group of citizens which had managed to add heavily to original holdings by purchase in the market. If the subscriptions which show transfers are representative, 32 percent of their securities were original. Among subscribers in the $5,000 to $10,000 category, the indicated average is 27 percent.

Maryland had done more than Massachusetts to support the federal debt and therefore, presumably, to reduce transfers; however, the picture is much the same.[49] Complete data for the $900,000 subscribed in Maryland are available. They show that the debt was owned by 318 persons. Sixteen individuals held $455,000, above 50 percent of the whole amount, and the eight largest holders, including two partnerships and four other individuals, had $346,182, more than 38 percent. The single firm of Benjamin Stoddert and Uriah Forrest owned just over $100,000, about 11 percent of the total. Other holdings above $25,000 were those of Charles Wallace and John Muir, $56,478; John Laird, nearly $58,000; Gustavus Scott, about $50,000; James Williams, $47,550; and Edward Harris $34,094. In contrast, 48 percent of all holders, who subscribed sums of less than $500, held just $28,600—a little more than 3 percent of the debt.

49. For an extended discussion of Maryland see my article, "Speculation in the Revolutionary Debt: The Ownership of Public Securities in Maryland, 1790," *Jour. of Econ. Hist.*, 14 (1954), 35-45.

FEDERAL DEBT IN MARYLAND: CONCENTRATION[50]

Subscription	No. of Persons	Percent of Total Persons	Combined Holdings	Percent of Total Subscription
$1 and under 100	51	16	2,585	·3
100 and under 500	96	30	26,005	2.9
500 and under 1,000	48	15	33,305	3.7
1,000 and under 5,000	78	25	196,777	21.8
5,000 and under 10,000	29	9	189,283	20.9
10,000 and under 25,000	8	2.5	109,327	12.1
25,000 and over	8	2.5	346,182	38.3
	318		903,464	

The degree of transfer can be exactly stated for the entire debt.
The eight individuals subscribing sums above $25,000 had almost no
original holdings except odds and ends of old Continental currency.
Of Stoddert and Forrest's $100,257, only $124 in paper money can
possibly be considered an original holding. Wallace and Muir's
$56,478 included but $266. John Laird's $58,000, Gustavus Scott's
$50,000, and James Williams's $47,500 had all been bought in the
market. Of Edward Harris's $34,000, only $512 had been issued in
his name.

Among subscribers in the $10,000 to $25,000 category, John Weems
owned $18,666 in loan certificates issued to James Weems, which,
according to the rules by which these calculations have been made,
has been credited to him as an original holding. There was also a
Major John Davidson, whose $11,394 included $6,520 in original
holdings—he had kept the military certificates granted him at the
close of the war. But all the other large holders in this group got
their securities second-hand. The rate of transfer for the entire debt
subscribed in Maryland was 81 percent.

50. Subscriptions toward a loan to the United States . . . in the office of Thomas
Harwood, commissioner of loans in the State of Maryland, vols. 927-29, Record
Group 53, Fiscal Records Sec., Natl. Arch. The figures do not include interest.

The nature of the securities market is suggested by the fact that whereas only 63 percent of loan certificates had been transferred, the rate was 82 percent for army certificates and about 95 percent in the case of indents. The big speculators specialized in indents and army certificates.

FEDERAL DEBT IN MARYLAND: TRANSFER

Subscription	*Rate of Transfer*
$1 and under 100	33
100 and under 500	69
500 and under 1,000	71
1,000 and under 5,000	67
5,000 and under 10,000	65
10,000 and under 25,000	77
25,000 and over	97
Average over all categories	81

Pennsylvania, where we have data for $3,630,000 of the principal of the public debt, was a special case. The state had assumed public securities in 1786, giving her citizens "new loan certificates" in their stead. On the eve of Congressional funding, the procedure was reversed: the state returned public securities to her citizens and recovered the new loan certificates. We have an incomplete list of applications made by Pennsylvania citizens for a conversion of their new loan certificates into public securities.

The figures, which cover about three-fourths of the debt in Pennsylvania, reveal a degree of concentration similar to the other states. The 78 applicants who held more than $10,000 were but 9 percent of the persons covered by the data, but they held over $2,200,000—61 percent of the total amount. The 28 individuals with holdings of over $25,000 had over 40 percent. The smaller holders—277 persons who had sums of less than $500—made up a third of the applicants, but had only 1.5 percent of the total.

PUBLIC DEBT IN PENNSYLVANIA: CONCENTRATION ($3,632,162)[51]

Subscription	No. of Applicants	Percent of Applicants	Combined Holdings	Percent of all Holdings
$1 and under 100	87	10	4,523	.1
100 and under 500	190	23	50,757	1.4
500 and under 1,000	120	14	88,688	2.4
1,000 and under 5,000	277	33	694,357	19.1
5,000 and under 10,000	79	10	581,069	16.0
10,000 and under 25,000	50	6	746,189	20.6
25,000 and over	28	3	1,466,579	40.4
	831		3,632,162	

The big holders were overshadowed by a merchant-broker, Mordecai Lewis, otherwise not prominent, but who was very probably the agent and partner of William Bingham.[52] Lewis held $293,360. (The figures do not include accumulated interest.) But others had impressive sums: Matthew McConnell, $87,272; Clement Biddle, $85,688; Blair McClenachan, $74,434; Solomon Lyons, $61,251; Peter Wikoff, $57,421; Charles Pettit, $55,197; and John Olden, $55,163. A few others had sums ranging from forty to fifty thousand dollars— John M. Taylor, General Walter Stewart, and Andrew Summers, Jr.

A major fraction of the larger holdings probably represents securities owned personally by the subscriber or held jointly in partnership with others; however it is more likely than in the case of Massachusetts that the subscribers were acting as agents.[53]

The list of applications is not complete, and it is therefore possible that some of the large holders are not listed. As in Massachusetts

51. The new loan certificates exchanged were about $4,800,000. Uncatalogued petitions to exchange new loan certificates, Public Records Div., Penn. Hist. and Museum Commission.

52. An undated statement in the William Bingham Papers, Hist. Soc. of Pa., discloses that he and Lewis formed a firm under Lewis's name. The fact that Lewis was not himself a big merchant makes it very probable that the firm was operative in this period and that his purchases were made in conjunction with it.

53. Pennsylvania's assumption of federal securities in 1786 was limited to those held by residents, hence there was reason for out-of-state holders to consign securities to residents, who could then exchange them for new loan certificates.

there is an indication of further concentration of securities in family holdings. "Mrs. McClenachan" probably added her $21,400 to the $74,000 held by the well-known merchant and privateer king. Christopher Marshall, Christopher Marshall, Jr., and Charles Marshall, together owned over $50,000. Andrew and John Caldwell had $53,000.

The rate of transfer is lower than in the other states we have reviewed, but the figures cover only transfers from the time new loan certificates were being issued in 1786 until applications were begun for their conversion into federal securities. Also, Pennsylvania paid good interest on the new loan certificates, which sustained their market value and rendered them less attractive to deep speculators, presumably reducing the rate of transfer. Nonetheless, by 1790, nearly 60 percent of the securities had passed out of the hands of those who received them in 1786.

Since the list of applicants is not complete, interpretation of the figures cannot be positive, but it would appear that in Pennsylvania, as in other states, the number of public creditors of any kind had shrunk by 1790 to an inconsiderable fraction of the population. It also seems that the small holders had been decimated—only a third of the known applicants had amounts below $500. The low number of small holders and the relatively low rate of transfer in holdings up to $25,000 suggests that public securities were largely transferred and accumulated in sizable holdings by 1786, when they were exchanged for state certificates, and that many people who received the

PUBLIC DEBT IN PENNSYLVANIA: TRANSFER

Subscription	*Percent of Transfer*
$1 and under 100	47
100 and under 500	51
500 and under 1,000	42
1,000 and under 5,000	48
5,000 and under 10,000	43
10,000 and under 25,000	58
25,000 and over	73
Average over all categories	59

certificates at that time were financially able to keep them and add to them in subsequent years.

The very largest holdings consisted almost entirely of securities acquired by transfer after 1786: Mordecai Lewis's $293,000 was all transferred, as was Matthew McConnell's $87,000, Clement Biddle's $85,000, Solomon Lyon's $61,000, John Olden's $55,000, John M. Taylor's $50,000, and Andrew Summers, Jr.'s $46,000. Charles Pettit's $55,000 consisted of $6,500 in securities issued in his name and $48,500 purchased. Of the principal holdings in Pennsylvania, only those of General Walter Stewart and Blair McClenachan were original. Stewart's $48,600 included only $900 acquired by purchase. Blair McClenachan held over $66,000 issued in his name, and he had purchased an additional $8,000.

The case of Rhode Island is in most ways similar to those of other states examined here, but it presents a few arresting differences. The debt was relatively small, less than $600,000 and a small number of people owned much of it: the three largest holders had $125,000, nearly 21 percent; the top nine subscribers together had $229,000, over 38 percent. At the other end of the scale was the usual crowd of small holders, who constituted 58 percent of all subscribers, but who had only 6½ percent of the debt.

FEDERAL DEBT IN RHODE ISLAND: CONCENTRATION[54]

Subscriptions	No. of Persons	Percent of Total Persons	Combined Holdings	Percent of Total Subscription
$1 and under 100	110	26.8	4,868	.8
100 and under 500	130	31.6	34,682	5.8
500 and under 1,000	53	12.9	36,994	6.2
1,000 and under 5,000	96	23.4	206,777	34.5
5,000 and under 10,000	13	3.1	86,191	14.4
10,000 and under 25,000	6	1.5	104,090	17.4
25,000 and over	3	.7	125,339	20.9
	411		598,941	

54. Subscriptions Towards a Loan to the United States . . . in the Office of Jabez Bowen, Commissioner of Loans in the State of Rhode Island, vol. 455, Record Group 53, Fiscal Records Sec., Natl. Arch. Figures include interest.

Since the records for Rhode Island give residence and occupation in most instances, they pinpoint the geographical and social distribution of ownership. The debt was held mainly in Providence and Newport, whose citizens owned $425,122, about 71 percent of the total. With the exception of one out-of-state broker, all the nine persons holding more than $10,000 were residents of these towns. Foremost were Nicholas Brown, Providence merchant, with $63,140; Philip Allen, Providence merchant, $32,410; and Joseph Clarke, Newport esquire, $29,789. Six other subscribers held more than $10,000: Nicholas Brown, deceased, $24,815; Zachariah Allen, Providence merchant, $22,280; Jabez Bowen, Providence esquire, $19,065; Clarke and Nightingale, Providence merchants, $15,792; Welcome Arnold, Providence merchant, $11,994; and Nathan Bond, Boston merchant, $10,144.

A further breakdown of the figures shows that merchants, esquires, and professional men, whatever their place of residence, owned most of the securities. Out of $548,564, whose owners can be identified according to occupation or status, 85 percent was held by persons of this description. With few exceptions, they monopolized the larger holdings, but they also subscribed most of the securities at all levels above $500 and nearly half of those in lesser categories. This fact is important in interpreting the existence of 96 subscribers in the $1,000 to $5,000 bracket, who constituted nearly a fourth of all subscribers and held about 35 percent of the debt. Although this solid middle group included many yeomen and tradesmen, it scarcely denotes widespread participation of the common people in the ownership of securities. Owners' occupations are given for $178,000 of the $206,000 subscribed in this category; of this amount, merchants, gentlemen, and professional men subscribed over $135,000, or 75 percent.

The interesting difference in the pattern that emerges in Rhode Island is the relatively low rate of transfer. Whereas figures for Massachusetts and Maryland indicate that about 80 percent of all securities had passed from the original holders, the rate in Rhode Island was about 52 percent. There is no correlation between the rate of transfer and the size of holdings; the large as well as the small subscriber was typically one who had retained his original securities and added to them by purchase. The holdings of the nine leading subscribers, for example, illustrate the relation of original and secondary holdings: Nicholas Brown, Providence merchant, had $49,973 in original securities and $13,408 in transferred; Philip Allen held $19,865 in original purchases and $12,545 in transferred; Zachariah Allen had $16,420 in original, $5,860 in transferred; Jabez Bowen, $18,061 and $1,004; and Clarke and Nightingale, $4,741 and $11,051. The holdings of Joseph Clarke, Nicholas Brown (deceased), Welcome Arnold, and Nathan Bond were all transferred.

FEDERAL DEBT IN RHODE ISLAND: TRANSFER

Subscriptions	Percent of Transfer
$1 and under 100	27.6
100 and under 500	61.3
500 and under 1,000	64.1
1,000 and under 5,000	55.2
5,000 and under 10,000	33.8
10,000 and under 25,000	62.3
25,000 and over	44.8
Average over all categories	52.0

The relatively low rate of transfer may well imply differences in social and economic conditions as between Rhode Island and other states, or it may merely be the effect of an inactive security market. Final settlement certificates given to the army did not bulk as large in Rhode Island as in more populous states, and it was mainly these securities that fed speculation and built up the great holdings.

A final insight into the composition of the public debt is furnished by two Treasury registers. It will be recalled that the debt recorded at the Treasury was the special province of interstate speculators and foreign investors. Almost all of the documents relative to this debt have been lost, but there are two existing registers of securities which were presented at the Treasury in 1790, rather than subscribed at the loan offices in the states.[55] While the entries may not be typical, since the names of prominent foreign investors do

55. Auditor's Certificates for the Funded Debt of 1790, LXXXVII, Record Group 53, Fiscal Records Sec., Natl. Arch.; Auditor's Certificates for Treasury Credit, LXXXVIII, *ibid.*

not appear, they afford a sample of the holdings of interstate speculators. As one would expect, brokers from New York, Boston, and Philadelphia are prominent in the list.

The volumes cover subscriptions by 254 persons, amounting to $2,486,507. They do not show transfers. It is at once evident that holdings of less than $10,000 are insignificant; holdings above $10,000 form 73 percent of the total. Those above $25,000 comprise 59 percent. It is probably that large holdings were more conspicuous than even these figures suggest, for the foreign investors do not appear, and the documents are incomplete.

SUBSCRIPTIONS AT THE TREASURY: CONCENTRATION ($2,486,507)[56]

Subscription	No. of Persons	Percent of Total Persons	Combined Holdings	Percent of Total Subscription
$1 and under 100	26	10	1,072	.04
100 and under 500	32	12	7,720	.30
500 and under 1,000	26	10	20,185	.80
1,000 and under 5,000	82	32	201,217	8.10
5,000 and under 10,000	25	10	180,286	7.25
10,000 and under 25,000	41	16	605,242	24.34
25,000 and over	22	9	1,470,785	59.15
	254		2,486,507	

Many familiar names occur, headed by John Delafield, $321,642; Theodosius Fowler & Co., $202,387; Watson and Greenleaf, $125,954; and Matthew McConnell, $122,998. Except for McConnell, who was located in Philadelphia, these men were New York brokers; but Philadelphia was represented by Thomas Palmer, $82,942; Henry Kuhl, $51,344; and Edward Fox, $28,613. A Boston merchant, John Harbach, had $63,760, and Elias Boudinot of New Jersey, $36,737.

56. Volume 87 lists subscriptions formally accepted from Nov. 1790 to Jan. 12, 1791. The interest is computed and included in the table. Volume 88 is a register of subscriptions from Aug. 10 to Sept. 28, 1790, for the loan of 1790, preliminary to formal acceptance, the interest not computed. The two lists are discreet and a careful check discloses no duplications.

It is very probable that they had at least a part interest in the securities entered in their names.

The data we have for Massachusetts, Maryland, Pennsylvania, and securities entered at the Treasury constitute only a partial record, particularly of the activities of great speculators who ranged across state lines and invested in both public and state debts. The concentration of holdings doubtless exceeded what is indicated by the documents we have selected for examination. If, in an effort to obtain the largest view, we combined the data for different states and the Treasury, there is some risk of error, since, for example, a holder recorded for Pennsylvania may have entered the same securities at the Treasury. There is no reason to think that there is any such duplication in our lists, but allowing for a margin of error, it is still significant that many big holders were represented at both places. Among holders with more than $25,000 on the Pennsylvania books (without descending to lesser categories), we find Mordecai Lewis, who had at least $293,000 in the state, subscribing at least $10,500 at the Treasury; Matthew McConnell, $87,000 and $14,000; Andrew Summers, Jr., $46,000 and $13,000; Hazard and Addoms, $34,500 and $19,500; Robert Bridges, $31,000 and $18,000; Edward Fox, $30,500 and $28,600; and the Reverend Dr. Robert Blackwell, $27,000 and $64,000. Among lesser holders, it ought perhaps to be noted that Thomas Willing had $20,000 in Pennsylvania and $20,000 at the Treasury; Elias Boudinot of New Jersey, $12,700 in Pennsylvania and $36,000 at the Treasury. Robert Morris, who does not appear prominently in these particular records, had $15,800 in Pennsylvania and $12,400 subscribed in Massachusetts. Except for John Harbach, who had $20,900 in Massachusetts and $63,600 at the Treasury, the large holders in Massachusetts are not represented in the fragmentary records we have for the Treasury and other states.

The larger significance of the figures is hard to formulate precisely. What clues do they furnish as to the total number of security holders in 1790? A simple computation indicates an enormous concentration of holdings in very few hands. The $12,300,000 for which we have record—to which another million or two should probably be added in allowance for interest—was held by fewer than 3,300 individuals. A mere 100 individuals subscribed over $5,000,000, and an additional $2,600,000 was subscribed by another 170. Together, the 280 largest holders had $7,880,000—nearly two-thirds of all securities described here. Obviously, the concentration was not really this great, for many of the larger subscribers were acting as agents. How great the concentration was one cannot say. If a mere conjecture is permitted, one might estimate—by projecting the material we have over the whole public debt of $40,000,000 and making a few arbitrary assumptions—that there were probably at most no more than 15,000 to 20,000 holders of public securities in the nation. Whatever the exact count, the mass of the population certainly had no stake in the funding program of 1790. That the bulk of the debt had changed hands is attested by the high rate of transfer—79 percent in Massachusetts and 81 percent in Maryland—and by the scarcity of small holders. Of the $12,300,000 covered by our figures, holders of less than $500 numbered but 1240 persons, and they had a total of only 273,500—just 2 percent of the whole.

What the implications are for an economic interpretation of the political history of the period is an open question. The best comment which can be made is that a mere list of security holders, whoever they were, affords too narrow a context within which to discuss the establishment of the national government. Funding the public debt had always been inseparable from political reform, the means to the end, and it would be idle to attribute the work of constitutional revision, which occupied the whole decade, merely to the speculative motive. For one thing, the security holders were rather too few in number to serve as the fulcrum upon which to raise a new political structure. To assume that they fathered it, we must suppose them possessed of a degree of power and influence with which they can scarcely be credited.

The proper approach to the subject is a descriptive one. Normally, in American society of the time, a floating securities debt unredeemed by the states would soon find its way into the hands of propertied individuals. This is what happened during the Confederation, and it had no necessary reference to the prospect of constitutional revision. The speculators did not buy the debt from the people in anticipation of federal funding—the prospect was not solid enough to be the basis of investment. Indeed, such uncertainty existed that the market value of securities did not begin to rise rapidly until after the Constitution had been ratified. Only then did the buyers operate according to their estimates of what the new government was likely to do with the debt. The furious speculation that ensued was mainly in securities already transferred from the original holders, and it resulted only in a further concentration of the debt as small investors sold out to big ones. From the beginning and all the way through, security holders as a group were champions of federal powers, but it would be closer to the truth to say that the adoption of the Constitution preceded and was the cause of a speculation based on the anticipation of federal funding, rather than that the designs of speculators brought forth the Constitution and the enactment of the funding program.

PART IV

NATIONAL PUBLIC FINANCE

"Resources and Revenue Laws lay hid in Night!
'Twas said let Hamilton be, and all was right."

—Adam Stephen to Madison,
March 3, 1790.

13

Funding: The People and the Creditors

"I can consider a funding system as important, in no other respect, than as an engine of government. The only question is what that engine shall be. The influence of a clergy, nobility and armies are and ought to be put out of the question in this country; but unless some active principle of the human mind can be interested in the support of government, no civil establishment can be formed, which will not appear like useless and expensive pageants."

—Oliver Wolcott, U.S. Auditor, 1790.

THE POLITICAL and economic usages of a funded debt were well known to a generation of Americans which had beheld the role of funded debt and national bank in stabilizing the regime founded in Britain after the revolution of 1689. Scarcely had a public debt come into existence during the American Revolution than a similar role was plotted for it. Financier Robert Morris tried from 1781 to 1783, with an already sure technique and a keen sense of direction, to arrange the government's finances and fund the debt in ways calculated to strengthen Congress and foster the growth of commercial capitalism. The economics of statecraft were such a cliché of contemporary thought that newspaper articles and personal letters abounded in the very slogans which statesmen employed on weightier occasions. "A certain amount of funded debt . . . ," ran a creditors' memorial addressed to Congress in 1789, "is a national blessing. The creation of a new species of money by this means, naturally increases the circulation of cash, and extensively promotes every kind of useful undertaking in agriculture and mechanics . . . It has been well maintained that, after the revolution in England, a funding system was there encouraged as the best means of attaching the great and powerful body of stockholders to the Government . . . In short, a debt originating in the patriotism that achieved the independence, may thus be converted into a cement that shall strengthen and perpetuate the Union of America."[1]

The new scheme of government had conferred unlimited power of taxation upon Congress. Whether the political reorganization wrought in 1787 departed abruptly from the past and violated the sentiments of the people, or whether the Constitution is to be viewed as the evolutionary product of American experience and a growing sense of national identity, the transfer of the substance of power to the central government was accomplished with remarkable ease. From the first disturbances that led to the break with England, the most vital public issues had turned upon taxation, and in 1787 the states were still guarding their authority. Since Congress was admittedly weak, they were prepared to concede a duty on imports and perhaps an excise tax, but little more. The Philadelphia Convention was generally expected to propose that Congress regulate trade and to recommend appropriate taxes. The Nationalists at the Convention struck boldly for their full objective, however, and proposed to give the central government unlimited taxing power. As George Mason observed, "Whether the Constitution be good or bad, the . . . clause clearly discovers that it is a national government, and no longer a Confederation . . . The assumption of this power of laying direct taxes does, of itself entirely change the confederation of the states into one consolidated government."[2]

Nothing testifies more to the audacity of the founding fathers than their demand that the people relinquish what they had fought Britain to preserve, and there is perhaps no more convincing evidence of a growth of national feeling than that the point was carried. It would cast doubt upon the central interpretations of this study if the Antifederalists had not recognized the importance of the issue or

1. *Annals of Congress*, I, 821-25, 939.
2. *Elliot's Debates*, III, 29.

allowed it to go by default; however, they discerned in taxing power the pivotal feature of the new system. Their failure to mount a heavier assault upon it must be ascribed to the ineffectiveness that characterized all their efforts.

Fighting a rear-guard action, the Antifederalists concentrated upon the attempt to restrict Congress to indirect taxes. The New Jersey plan advanced at the Convention would have confined federal revenues to duties on imports and a stamp tax, with additional funds to be raised by requisitions on the states. In case of noncompliance with the requisition, Congress was to have the authority to "direct the collection" of taxes in a delinquent state. This scheme had its drawbacks, but it preserved a degree of local control of the purse strings, and wherever the Antifederalists had any strength they brought it forward. Every state which subjoined amendments to its ratification of the Constitution proposed that federal revenues be restricted to indirect taxes, that additional sums be raised by requisitions, and that federal collection of direct taxes be permitted only in case of default. Such an amendment was foremost among those adopted by the Antifederalist convention at Harrisburg.[3]

The challenge was turned aside by the Federalist majority in the first Congress. Although James Madison spurred the House of Representatives to consider various constitutional amendments which the states had suggested, he carefully omitted the revenue amendment from his list. Other members managed to obtain its referral to the committee appointed to consider amendments, but the committee declined to report it. Thomas Tucker of South Carolina finally offered it as a formal motion. It received scattered support, but was overwhelmingly defeated by a vote of 9 to 39. Congress did not offer the revenue amendment to the states.[4]

The high prerogative of Congress was thus sustained, but the Federalists were aware of a deep-seated aversion to direct federal taxes. Until the new government was more firmly established, they knew that taxation must be confined to duties on imports and possibly an excise on liquor. Even among Federalists there was a notion

3. *Ibid.,* I, 175-77, 323, 325, 326, 329, 335, II, 542-46. See Luther Martin's letter on the Convention, *ibid.,* I, 368-69. The states which coupled amendments with ratification were Massachusetts, South Carolina, New Hampshire, New York, and Rhode Island.

4. *Annals of Congress,* I, 431-42, 660-65, 773-77.

that direct taxes, if levied, should incorporate elements of the requisition system. From the Constitutional Convention the Connecticut delegates informed their governor: "It is probable that the principal branch of revenues will be duties on imports. What may be necessary to be raised by direct taxation is to be apportioned on the several states, according to the number of their inhabitants; and although Congress may raise the money on their own authority, if necessary, yet that authority need not be exercised, if each state will furnish its quota."[5]

The funding of the public debt consummated the Nationalist effort to achieve political centralization by fiscal reform. In drafting his proposals Hamilton's task was to adapt to current circumstances the blueprint worked out by the Nationalists in the preceding decade. Within the limits of the government's resources and the conflicting interests of the states, it was imperative that he recommend firm and decisive measures to support the public debt. Congress now had the power of taxation, and there was a peremptory expectation on the part of the creditors that past promises would be made good. An adequate provision for the debt was also deemed vital to the recovery of "public credit." The term denoted the system of high finance which Hamilton and the Federalists considered necessary to ground the Union and foster economic growth. Conservatives everywhere waited to see what Congress would do about the debt, considering this—its first major policy act—as a test of character. Congress itself felt a keen awareness that some action had to be taken which would clearly repudiate former policies and display the intention of the new regime, lest the disappointment and chagrin of those who had supported it would unhinge the Union.

The significance of Hamilton's proposals emerges only as one considers the alternatives available to him. At one extreme, he could have recommended a full compliance with the pledges made by the Confederation Congress: 6 percent interest and full payment of the principal, all in specie. At the other extreme were currency finance measures: the payment of interest in a paper medium and the redemption of principal by acceptance of securities for taxes and in purchase of western lands; or another revaluation of old securities

5. Roger Sherman and Oliver Ellsworth to Governor Huntington, Sept. 26, 1787, transmitting a printed copy of the Constitution. *Elliot's Debates*, I, 491-92.

at current market prices. There was a solid middle ground, however, because the government was in a position to force an "accommodation" upon creditors. Its ability to support the debt was so manifestly superior to that of the former government that, provided specie revenues were committed to the payment of interest, the creditors could be expected to accept a reduction of interest or principal. Hamilton, whose philosophy might otherwise have prompted him to stand squarely behind the pledges of the former government, hoped to find an accommodation because he was also proposing the assumption of state debts, and in order to make the double burden supportable, he had to find ways of reducing interest charges.

There were certain other areas in which he had a choice. He had to decide whether to incorporate the sale of western lands into the funding system; whether to fund indents (or accumulated interest) and, if so, on what terms; and what value to give old Continental currency still in private hands. A further question, which would have loomed largest of all if this had not been a Federalist Congress, was whether to distinguish between original holders and those who had bought securities in the market. One way of reducing the principal of the debt and effecting the accommodation which Hamilton desired would have been to pay secondary holders only the market price, rather than the face value, of securities purchased at a discount.

Hamilton's proposals were a skillful compromise of varying shades of conservative opinion. The rock upon which he founded his program was specie payment—of both interest and principal. Creditors were invited, if they wished, to accept other modes of payment involving western lands, but they were at liberty to demand specie. At one stroke, he repudiated the agrarian and state-oriented methods of the past and committed the new regime to high finance, which, in the minds of all Federalists, was the indispensable basis of public credit and effective government. After years of vain striving, neither Hamilton nor Congress intended to fall short of this goal.

Within the framework of specie payments, a compromise was projected. Hamilton would not seek a reduction of the debt by discriminating against holders of alienated securities. This method he dismissed as a violation of contract and subversive of public credit—understandably, since the entire loss would fall upon a segment of the population which ardently supported the new regime. Instead he proposed differential methods of funding calculated to reduce the immediate interest to something over 4 percent.

His scheme called for a new loan and the issue of federal "stock" in exchange for old securities brought in as subscriptions. The creditors were offered a variety of propositions calculated to reduce the rate of interest on the new stock below the 6 percent due on old securities. Hamilton planned to incorporate western lands in the funding operation, but not on a compulsory basis. The creditors could elect to receive two-thirds of the value of their subscription in 6 percent stock and one-third in western lands at the rate of 20c an acre. They could take the full value of their subscription in 4 percent stock and, as compensation for the reduction of interest, receive $15.80 in western lands for every $100 subscribed. If creditors were not interested in western lands, they were at liberty to receive the full value of their subscription in stock: for every $100 subscribed, $66⅔ in 6 percent stock and $26.88 in deferred 6 percent stock which would begin drawing interest only after the lapse of ten years. Finally, he proposed that $10,000,000 of the new loan be administered on different principles. If creditors would subscribe half in specie and half in securities, they might receive stock bearing an immediate interest of 5 percent.[6]

No date was set for the redemption of the stock to be issued under the new loan; the securities were redeemable only at the pleasure of the government. To protect the creditor against the possibility that general interest rates would some day fall below 4 percent, enabling the government to refinance the debt at lower figures and call in the existing stock, Hamilton proposed that the government limit its right to retire the new securities to a minute fraction of their value annually. Hoping to divest his scheme of elements of compulsion beyond the forced reduction of interest, he made allowance for creditors who refused all the alternatives. Adamant creditors could keep their old securities and receive a flat 4 percent interest, but the interest would come out of Treasury funds remaining after the subscribed debt was taken care of.

6. The report on public credit was delivered January 14, 1790, *American State Papers, Finance,* I, 15-37. It also included two proposals for granting annuities to subscribing creditors, but these were never seriously considered by Congress.

There were two or three details which occupied a minor place in the general outline of his program but were of crucial importance to the speculators who had pumped him for information. The first related to indents (or accumulated interest on old securities). It had scarcely been expected that they would be accepted in subscription to the new loan on equal terms with the principal of old securities; there was a general prejudice against paying interest on interest. For this reason, indents remained cheap and available long after securities generally had risen in the market. In what amounted to foreknowledge of the Secretary's proposals, Craigie and Constable had made every effort to invest in indents. They were not disappointed. After considering the matter in his report, Hamilton recommended that interest be funded on terms of full equality with the principal.

Certain other details of concern to speculators were involved in his proposal to assume state debts. A vital question for the big speculators, who had turned to state debts after public securities became scarce and expensive, was whether the state debts would be assumed and, if so, whether they would be funded on equal terms with public securities. A related question was whether Hamilton would advise a delay in paying interest on assumed state securities. If he called for a delay, brokers would have time to fill their European orders by cheap purchases in the market. Again, the confidence that Craigie and Constable had in the Secretary was not misplaced. Hamilton explicitly recommended the assumption of state securities on equal terms with public securities and proposed that interest payments be postponed until January 1, 1792. By implication Hamilton also advised the acceptance of old Continental money at 40 to 1. Only the speculators held any of this money, which had had almost no value in the last days of its circulation.[7]

Needless to say, the avarice of speculators was merely instrumental in Hamilton's mind to the creation of sound public policy. Within limits of Federalist imperatives and the resources at hand, his terms amounted to a reasonable formula designed to establish public credit by specie payments and at the same time afford a reduction of interest which would make it possible for Congress to take up state debts. His scheme did not confer maximum benefits on the creditors,

7. *Ibid.*, 19, 22, 25.

but it offered enough, presumably, to satisfy them and raise the value of securities.

The partisan character of his program lay mainly in his rejection of alternatives which would not have accomplished the objects of his statecraft but would have lessened inequities and satisfied the people at large. Three percent and the redemption of principal by sales of western land would have been popular and also perhaps sufficient to maintain security values at 50c on the dollar—the highest point up to this time. The reduction of interest charges which Hamilton desired could also have been accomplished by discriminating against secondary holders and accepting their securities at market value. Presumably a regular and prompt discharge of interest would then have established the credit of the new government.

Such policies were theoretically possible, and they would have corresponded to the ordinary practice of the states; but whether they were practical under the circumstances is doubtful. In view of the political revolution which had just occurred, the nature of the new government's support, the expectations of the creditors, and the power for good or ill wielded by Dutch bankers who had invested heavily in American securities, a reversion to agrarian finance might have invited disaster. Certainly it would have relinquished the main goals of Federalist policy.

Congress, except for a small minority, was thoroughly receptive to the Secretary's ideas on funding (if not on assumption). The bill, which the House finally adopted and sent to the Senate, contained his major proposals relative to accepting securities on loan virtually as he had written them. The House also concurred in the proposal to fund indents on equal terms with the principal. The only significant change was the evaluation of old paper money at 100 to 1 rather than 40 to 1. The Senate, however, deleted the provisions about western lands and stripped away all of Hamilton's alternatives except the issuance of stock. It also disapproved of funding indents or interest on equal terms with the principal, that is, at 4 percent; the Senate bill put indents at 3 percent. In subsequent negotiations the House attempted to restore 4 percent on indents, but the final act followed the Senate bill in this as well as other major details. Under the final act the subscriber of $100 in old securities was to receive $66⅔ in 6 percent stock, $33⅓ in deferred stock bearing 6 percent interest after 1800, and 3 percent stock in exchange for indents or accumulated interest on securities. Old paper money was valued at 100 to 1 and considered part of the principal of the public debt.[8]

The main attack upon the Secretary's plan was Madison's proposal to discriminate between the original and present holders of securities. It was a false issue the way Madison presented it, and his motion was very probably a tactical maneuver to accomplish other ends; yet the small opposition that existed in the House of Representatives rallied in support.

Assuming the novel role of a foe of administration, Madison argued that 6 percent interest be paid on the whole debt, but that holders of alienated securities receive only the highest market value (about 50 percent) of the securities which they subscribed to the new loan, the balance to be issued in federal stock to the original holders. The plan had a strong element of compensatory justice, which constituted its major appeal. As one writer observed: "There is something in every man's breast that bears witness to the truth of it, unless his conscience and judgment be much beclouded by large purchases and speculations."[9] Now that the nation was in a position to render justice, a proper sentiment dictated that it should pay the patriots and soldiers to whom it really was indebted for its independence, not the speculators.

Madison's motion publicly announced a rift in the aristocracy whose united efforts had produced the Constitution, and it proved to be the first move in a sustained political campaign which eventually put Jefferson into the White House. Although it ranged Madison on the side of human justice against reason of state, and thus conformed with the later creed of Jeffersonian Republicanism, a care-

---

8. *Journals of the House of Representatives of the United States* (Wash., 1826), I, 1545-46, 1586, 1619, 200-1; *Annals of Congress*, II, 1629; Oliver Wolcott to Frederick Wolcott, July 20, 1790, to Oliver Wolcott, Sr., July 27, 1790, Gibbs, *Memoirs of the Administrations of Washington and Adams*, I, 49, 50; Richard Henry Lee to William Lee, July 27, 1790, Ballagh, ed., *Letters of Richard Henry Lee*, II, 535-36; *The Public Statutes at Large of the United States of America* . . . (Boston, 1848), I, 138-44 (ch. 34, Aug. 4, 1790).

9. *Annals of Congress*, II, 1191-95; Unsigned article, *Freeman's Journal*, Feb. 10, 1790.

ful analysis suggests that his motion was dictated by political expediency rather than a concern for the common man.[10]

Madison had completely reversed his former position. The plight of the original creditors was not new, but he had never before shown any sympathy for them. In 1783 he opposed discrimination even though it was advocated by some of his colleagues from Virginia. He was silent when the issue arose at the Constitutional Convention. Two months before Hamilton delivered his report to Congress, he asked Madison for suggestions, particularly as to ways of modifying the terms upon which the debt should be funded. Madison's reply, dated November 19, 1789, contained not a word about discrimination.[11] His own explanation of the sympathy for original creditors which suddenly overcame him was that speculation attending Hamilton's report had created a new situation: previously the bulk of the old securities had lain with the original creditors, but the fury of late speculation had resulted in a wholesale transfer to secondary holders. The explanation is dubious, for the transfer of the debt had been continuous for years, and in any case the speculation produced by Hamilton's report was in state rather than public securities.

Madison's sudden turn is better explained as the opening move in a resumption of state-oriented politics. After a long career as a protagonist of central authority, he may have felt it was time he began representing the localist traditions of Virginia. A year earlier, the legislature had refused him an appointment to the United States Senate, and even to get elected to the House he had been obliged to leave his post with the old Congress and mend fences in Virginia.[12] His motion to discriminate was certain to increase his political capital in his own state, and on the level of national politics, it served notice

10. Madison's distinguished biographer, Irving Brant, attributes his action to humanitarian motives. *James Madison, Father of the Constitution, 1787-1800* (N.Y., 1950), 300.

11. Brant, *Madison, the Nationalist,* 24-25; *Elliot's Debates,* 469-75; Hamilton to Madison, Oct. 12, 1789, Madison Papers, XII, 42, Lib. Cong.; Madison to Hamilton, Nov. 19, 1789, Hamilton Papers, VIII, 999-1000, *ibid.*

12. Edward Carrington to Madison, Oct. 22, 1788, Madison to Edmund Randolph, Nov. 2, 1788, Carrington to Madison, Nov. 9, 1788, Madison to Randolph, Nov. 23, 1788, Carrington to Madison, Nov. 26, Dec. 2, 1788, Alexander White to Madison, Dec. 4, 1788, Madison to Jefferson, Dec. 8, 1788, B. Ball to Madison, Dec. 8, 1788, Hardin Barnley to Madison, Dec. 16, 1788, Madison to Eve. George, Jan. 2, 1789, to Randolph, Mar. 1, 1789, Madison Papers, X, 26, 40, 45, 55, 56, 59, 60, 62, 64, 67, 79, XI, 1, Lib. Cong.

of Virginia's independent position and raised an issue upon which to do battle. In the unlikely event that his motion was approved by Congress, the result would have been even more fortunate, for it would have blocked the assumption of state debts, which Virginia opposed. Under Madison's scheme, 6 percent interest was to be paid on the entire public debt; Congress, after adopting it, could hardly have contemplated the additional burden of state debts.

That his motion had an ulterior purpose is suggested by the fact that it was not a realistic alternative to the Secretary's plan. It had scant support in Congress; of the small minority of thirteen members of the House of Representatives who voted in favor of it, nine were Virginians.[13] One is led to doubt the force of ethical motive since it was so largely delimited by state boundaries. Outside the south, which had a sectional interest in the matter since securities had tended to flow northward into the commercial states, compensating original holders was not an idea which had widespread support. It had been talked about often enough, but Congress liquidated its debts after 1782 without taking account of transfers, and all the states had a chance to embrace the principle in their own finances; yet they had not done so, even under the aegis of popular governments.[14]

The tenor of popular complaint against the Hamiltonian formula, as found in the newspapers and private correspondence, suggests, rather, that the opposition to it was devoted, not to rewarding original creditors, but to reducing the debt and making it payable in something other than specie. Hamilton saw this point clearly. He had felt obliged to discuss the idea of discrimination in his report, only to reject it, but to him it denoted a reduction of claims to be forced upon holders of alienated securities.[15] Madison's plan

13. According to Brant, *Madison, Father of the Constitution,* 298-99. The vote was not recorded.

14. The only instance I know is that of Pennsylvania, which funded and paid interest on unalienated military certificates, but not those which had been transferred. The latter were redeemable only in purchase of land.

15. In his report to Congress, Hamilton observed that discrimination, as commonly advocated, *sometimes* implied compensating original creditors. See Richard Hildreth, *The History of the United States . . .* (N.Y., 1851), I, 165. Hildreth, an older historian who had what is probably the most accurate version in print of the issues presented by funding and assumption, says of Madison's proposal that it was "very far from meeting the views entertained on either side of it. It had been the object of those who had attempted to belittle the claims of the present holders to find an excuse in so doing for a new repudiation."

did not cater to this notion. William Maclay came over from the Senate to urge him to alter his stand and make a fight for 3 percent and the redemption of principal only by the sale of western lands. Such a provision would probably have kept the market value of securities at current levels and permitted an easy and quick extinction of the public debt. When Madison refused, without stating his reasons satisfactorily, Maclay's suspicions were aroused. "The obstinacy of this man," he growled, "has ruined the opposition."[16]

The inconsistency in Madison's behavior did not escape the baleful attention of good Federalists in Massachusetts, who were always quick to perceive the outcroppings of natural depravity. The correspondents of Theodore Sedgwick, Madison's leading opponent in the House, observed with satisfaction that the Virginian's proposal was not popular, had hardly a "single admirer" in Massachusetts. "The proposition is not calculated to meet the public smile," remarked Benjamin Lincoln. "He should have come forward, if popularity was his aim, with power in one hand and a scale [to revalue the debt] in the other[.] then the people at *large* would have got what the public creditors should lose[.] but by his mad scheme none are to be benefitted by it but a few whom the public eye have so long seen in distress that the sight is quite familiar to them." The real meaning of the support given Madison's proposal was adduced by another correspondent: "I begin to be apprehensive, that, so much is said in Congress about discrimination, reliquidation &c &c, the next step will be, to annihilate the whole debt!"[17]

Three or four members of Congress, not Madison, had the temerity to suggest a general revaluation of the debt: Samuel Livermore of New Hampshire, Thomas Scott of Pennsylvania, and, also, from the tone of their arguments, James Jackson of Georgia and Thomas Tucker of South Carolina. Thomas Scott actually moved that any provision be postponed until the debt had been "ascertained and [once more] liquidated." This undermanned attack hit the main

16. *Journal of William Maclay, United States Senator From Pennsylvania, 1789-1791* (N.Y., 1927), 194-97.

17. Lincoln to Theodore Sedgwick, Mar. 3, 1790, S. Henshaw to Sedgwick, Feb. 28, 1790, Sedgwick Papers, box A, Mass. Hist. Soc. See letters of Henry Van Schaack, Benjamin Lincoln, Thomas Dwight, and S. Henshaw to Sedgwick, Feb. 25, 26, 27, 1790, *ibid.*

issue, but did not get far. The House quickly voted it down, dismissing agrarian finance once and for all.[18]

In the debate on Madison's motion, northern and middle state delegates, with a few exceptions, opposed it on the grounds of sanctity of contract and public credit, saying, with considerable justification, that it would impair the government's credit. They also said, incorrectly, that means were not available for determining the identity of a great many original holders. Verbal support for Madison's proposal was vigorous but came almost exclusively from southern delegates, who were themselves by no means united. The advocates of discrimination damned the speculators, invoked sympathy for the original holders, and declared that the new government must be founded not on the bribery of a few, but on substantial justice to all citizens. The result was a foregone conclusion; Madison's motion was beaten 36 to 13.[19]

Outside Congress, Madison's proposal brought to focus a residual hatred of merchants, rich men, and speculators which threatened faintly to give birth to a popular movement. Scores of newspaper articles denounced the present holders. They were said to have been loyalists or at least loyalists at heart, devoid of patriotism, and given to exploiting the public distress. They were portrayed as following soldiers to betray them with false information and buy their securities at a discount. Now that the fruits of national union were to be distributed, it was cause for bitter complaint that the wicked were to be rewarded and the virtuous made hewers of wood and drawers of water. "It is wished to sacrifice the *many* to a few . . . to make noblemen and nabobs of a few New York gentlemen, at the expense of all the farmers in the United States." Benjamin Rush voiced the characteristic reply to all Federalist arguments about public credit and sanctity of contract when he wrote that a man who expected to get twenty shillings on the pound for securities bought for a tenth of that amount had a mind like a highway robber.[20]

18. Samuel Livermore made an abortive effort to commit the House to a reduction of interest. *Annals of Congress*, I, 1148-49, 1160, 1182. See also p. 1300.
19. *Ibid.*, II, 1298.
20. Correspondent to the *Penn. Gazette*, Feb. 10, 1790; Rush to Madison, Feb. 27, 1790, Madison Papers, XII, 84, Lib. Cong.

Although the wrongs done to the original holders were emphasized to make the point stronger, the purport of much of the widespread vilification of speculators was to discredit the claims of secondary holders preparatory to a downward revision of their claims.
The people disliked paying a depreciated debt raised to its nominal
value in the hands of speculators. Obscurely coupled with the idea
of justice to the original holders was the plain implication that the
debt—at least the part which had been alienated—should be redeemed
at its market value. Even Rush admitted to Madison that the "public
mind" could be quieted by a reduction of the interest to 3 percent.[21]

A few writers in the press made the point explicit. A Rhode
Island "Farmer" exhorted his countrymen to join the Union and
send forward their delegates to "diminish the value of continental
securities . . . or by a coup de main disincumber the nation of debt."[22]
In the *New Jersey Journal,* "Eumenes" struck a familiar chord, proposing that the whole debt be converted into interest-bearing notes
of small denominations, which would "pass as money" until redeemed
by taxes.[23] "Observer" in the *Gazette of the United States* thought
Congress should apportion the debt on the states and allow them to
pay it as they pleased, a mode which he described as "more familiar
& more pleasing to the people than any other possible method."[24]
"A Private Citizen" of Connecticut, whose plan was reprinted in the
Pennsylvania Gazette, brought forth the novel idea of coupling discrimination with a scheme for apportioning the debt upon individual
citizens, assessing each his share, then extinguishing the debt by levying taxes payable in securities.[25]

Given the new structure of the Union, such schemes were fantasy.
There were, however, fairly legitimate ways of reducing the debt;
Madison's proposal was taken up because it furnished an impeccable
moral position from which to damn the claims of the speculators
and initiate a revaluation or an easier method of funding. However,
the newspaper controversy scarcely influenced the debate in the House
of Representatives, whose members were overwhelmingly disposed

21. Rush to Madison, Mar. 10, 1790, Rives Coll., Madison Papers, box 12,
Lib. Cong.
22. *Providence Gazette,* May 22, 1790.
23. Reprinted in *Freeman's Journal,* Mar. 10, 1790.
24. Feb. 3, 1790.
25. Mar. 10, 1790. See "A Pennsylvanian," *ibid.,* Apr. 21, 1790.

to institute a regime of high finance, tempered by the accommodations which Hamilton had suggested. The mood of the propertied classes throughout the country was clearly explosive, especially in New England, and if Congress had not prosecuted their interests in 1790, the results would have been incalculable.

As it was, Hamilton's proposals failed to meet the expectations of some creditors. A "Connecticut Man" said he did not know one creditor who was content with 4 percent.[26] Others had their doubts that normal interest rates would fall to 4 percent within twenty years as Hamilton had predicted in justifying the reduced rate. They announced their willingness to take 6 percent and let the government redeem the principal of the debt at its pleasure.[27] Hamilton was mocked for his pretense of giving creditors a choice. Subscription to the funding plan was in fact compulsory, it was said, because those who did not participate were to get only the leavings of Treasury revenues. If Hamilton intended more than an insincere gesture, let him show it by allowing 6 percent on all securities and then permit the creditors to decide whether they wanted to subscribe.[28] His "depraved principles" were said to have given a "mortal stab" to public credit. His scheme was called unconstitutional. The query was raised how anyone could have confidence in a government which "robbed" security holders of half their property while maintaining the fiction of observing sanctity of contract.[29] One writer, styling himself "Merchant," hinted that the creditors would resist. Writing to a New York newspaper, he said that the Constitution had been adopted in order to rid the country of dishonesty and corruption, but should the same old beaten path be followed, it was still not too late to cry *"to your tents O Israel."*[30]

26. *Gazette of the United States*, Mar. 3, 1790. See "A Merchant," *Daily Advertiser* (N.Y.), Feb. 5, 1790; Gouverneur Morris to Robert Morris, July 31, 1790, to William Duer, Sept. 18, 1790, Gouverneur Morris Papers, no. 22, Lib. Cong.

27. "Remarks on the Report of the Secretary of the Treasury," *Penn. Packet,* Feb. 8, 9, 1790; "A Jersey Man," reprinted from the *Gazette of the United States* in *ibid.*, Feb, 15, 1790; "Mr. Fair Play," *Daily Advertiser* (N.Y.), Mar. 4, 1790.

28. Unsigned, reprinted from the *Daily Advertiser* (N.Y.), in *Penn. Packet,* Feb. 16, 1790; "A Citizen," *Massachusetts Centinel*, Apr. 10, 1790.

29. "Honestus," *Daily Advertiser* (N.Y.), Feb. 3, 1790; "A Merchant," *ibid.*, Feb. 5, 1790; unsigned, *Gazette of the United States*, Feb. 27, 1790; "A Connecticut Man," *ibid.*, Mar. 3, 1790; "A Farmer," *Pennsylvania Gazette*, Feb. 17, 1790; unsigned, *Freeman's Journal*, Feb. 10, 1790; "A Republican Citizen," *Maryland Journal*, Mar. 23, 1790; "A Citizen," *Massachusetts Centinel*, Apr. 10, 1790.

30. *Daily Advertiser* (N.Y.), Feb. 12, 1790.

Although some creditors may have been dissatisfied with 4 percent, especially in New England where the last ounce of flesh was always exacted, this kind of talk was mostly froth beaten up for controversial purposes. The public creditors were much more in earnest in objecting to the assumption of state debts. Except for those already speculating in state debts, the majority of public creditors would doubtless have preferred that the government commit its revenues to the public debt and let the state debts alone—at least until it could be proved that federal revenues were sufficient for both purposes. They were well aware that the reduction of interest was linked with the assumption, which they denounced as rash, adventurous, and unconstitutional. The additional load of the state debts might prove too much to handle and bring on a general default in interest payment which would impair the value of all securities. Hamilton argued that public finance was indivisible, that all debts had to be funded in a unitary system or not at all. But he did not entirely convince the public creditors, particularly those of Pennsylvania, who, unlike the Massachusetts creditors, had no major interest in assumption. Fisher Ames, one of the champions of assumption, wrote in May 1790 that the measure was sure to pass if the Pennsylvania creditors could be reconciled to it.[31] He was afraid they would send a petition to Congress requesting an immediate funding of the public debt without regard to assumption. In July, Tench Coxe informed Hamilton that assumption was gaining ground with the Philadelphia creditors, who might endorse the proposition at an early meeting. He had to report later that no such resolution had been adopted; nor had the creditors instructed a standing committee on the subject.[32]

It would be a mistake, however, to assume that Hamilton's proposals regarding the public debt seriously divided either the people or their delegates in Congress. The conception of public policy shared by most members of Congress, though generalized as serving the ultimate good of all classes, favored immediately the interests of commerce and property. The ethical considerations raised by

31. Seth Ames, ed., *Works of Fisher Ames* (Boston, 1854), I, 77-79.
32. Coxe to Hamilton, July 9, 10, 1790, Hamilton Papers, VIII, 1089, 1090, Lib. Cong.; *Penn. Packet,* July 9, 12, 1790; *Gazette of the United States,* Mar. 13, Apr. 17, 1790. Charles Pettit, a big holder of public securities, was a prominent foe of assumption.

Madison's proposal to discriminate were fairly acknowledged; yet the great majority of Congress concurred as a matter of sound judgment in rejecting any modifications of the debt beyond those Hamilton recommended. Hamilton's proposals, after all, were no more than an execution of the pledges of the Confederation Congress, and they bore a visible relationship to the strongly felt need to implement the constitutional position of the new government and establish public credit. Outside Congress, the influence of leadership was decisive in molding effective public opinion, and except in Virginia, North Carolina, and Georgia, whose local interests ranged some leaders in the opposition, the weight of authority was behind the Secretary's program. It was quite otherwise, however, with Hamilton's proposal to assume state debts. Assumption ran headlong into conflicts of state interest which split the nation's leadership, and it would surely have died in passage had it not been rescued in the hour of extremity.

Assumption: The Compromise of 1790

"To Fund—or not to fund, that is the question!
Whether 'tis better to assume the debts
By States contracted for the gen'ral weal,
And by a lib'ral scheme of finance, prove
No little, local motives guide our sages,
In Congress met, to plan a nation's fate,
And fix the credit of the States forever;
Or—by opposing—end both Credit
And the Debts together—

—*Gazette of the United States,* Apr. 14, 1790.

Hamilton, in his Report on Public Credit, proposed an assumption of state debts as an integral part of his financial plan. He reasoned that since Congress would monopolize duties on imports and probably lay excise taxes as well, the states would lose important sources of revenue, and their creditors were likely to suffer. The state creditors would be led by their interests to oppose measures to fund the public debt; their hostility to federal taxes would constitute a divisive element within the Union. Hamilton's argument was that a unified system, with all public debts paid by the federal government, was the condition for any funding at all. Morally, it was also essential that state creditors be treated on equal terms with federal creditors. The debts of the states had been contracted for the same purposes as the debt of the Union; state creditors were no less deserving than federal creditors. Hamilton therefore recommended that the United States assume, on a parity with the federal debt, all state debts which had been contracted in the general welfare. The state creditors were to subscribe their securities to the federal loan and receive new federal stock on the same terms as the public creditors. The debt of the United States would thereby be increased by an estimated $25,000,000.

The issues which Hamilton presented to the nation have seldom been satisfactorily defined by historians, whose attention has most often focused on the constitutional implications of his program.[1] Assumption is described in the context of Hamilton's grand design of effecting political centralization by fiscal devices. Possessing all the debts, Congress rather than the states would draw forth and disburse the tax revenues, and another host of creditors would owe their primary loyalty to the central government. The rise in the market value of state securities would provide additional capital for business enterprise.

The emphasis on the constitutional issue, while verifiable, is misleading unless qualified. Hamilton's goals are not in doubt, and it is true that the constitutional issue was earnestly discussed at the time. His opponents were in some degree moved by solicitude for states' rights. Nevertheless, as the debates in the House of Representatives fully disclose, the higher question was less crucial than the economic interests of the various states. Delegates from states that stood to lose from assumption were against it; those from states that hoped to gain were in favor of it; those from states whose interests were not greatly affected either way were indifferent.

A second interpretation, which stresses economic factors, appears at first glance to probe deeper. The issue is presented as a dispute between states which had large debts remaining from the Revolution and those which had already paid them. Massachusetts and South Carolina wanted to unload their heavy obligations on the Union. Heading the opposition was Virginia, which, like Maryland, North Carolina, and Georgia, had already discharged the greater part of her Revolutionary debt. What remained was less than her share of the additional taxes which would be required to support a

1. The most perceptive account in print is Hildreth's *History of the United States*, I, written over a century ago.

federal debt enlarged by the extraordinary debts of Massachusetts and South Carolina.

The flaw in this statement of the case is that in theory no state could either gain or lose from assumption, for it was to be subordinate to a final settlement of the accounts of the Union. The debts which a state sloughed off in 1790 would be charged against her in the final settlement, and if she gained at one point, she would lose at the other. It is apparent that the dispute cannot be so simply defined. The explanation lies in the financial relations that existed among the states.

Massachusetts and South Carolina, which could look forward only to a deterioration of their financial position as Congress invaded sources of taxation, were claiming immediate relief on the grounds that their debts represented expenditures in the common cause and were properly chargeable to the Union. The fact that their debts were so large proved only that they had contributed more than their share to the war. Justice required that the excess be shifted to the Union.

The defect in this reasoning was clearly apprehended by their opponents. A method already existed for adjusting inequalities in the contributions of the states to the war—the general settlement of accounts was in progress. Treasury officers were busy examining documents, and the General Board had made considerable progress in evaluating state claims for expenditures in the general welfare. A final settlement could be expected to take place within a year or two. All state expenditures, all debts, either paid or unpaid, which had been contracted for war purposes would be computed and each state assessed its share of the whole. If, as asserted, Massachusetts and South Carolina had contributed more than their share, they would be creditor states and entitled to compensation.[2]

What Massachusetts and South Carolina were in fact demanding was an assumption of their debts prior to the final settlement on the supposition that they would be creditor states. Their importunity—which their delegates to Congress carried so far as to threaten to break up the Union—sprang from a sense of the financial crisis in their states. That they would gain relief from the final settlement of accounts was not a wholly reassuring idea. The time intervening

2. See Hamilton's proposal as to how the balances were to be discharged.

before its completion could not be exactly measured. There was a doubt that it would ever take place, and after that a question whether they would receive their due. State accounts had long been a source of controversy. Congress had not been able to agree upon a rule for apportioning the common charges, and there was disagreement about what claims for expenditures in the general welfare should be allowed. The decisions of the General Board might prove unacceptable to the states. If the final settlement never matured, Massachusetts and South Carolina would be left alone with their big debts—unless assumption carried.

With the exception of Connecticut, the other states were either indifferent or hostile to assumption. The middle states were not vitally affected, and their delegates formed their opinions as individuals. The main opposition came from Maryland, Virginia, North Carolina, and Georgia, which had paid most of their debts. They had nothing to gain from assumption, and its adoption meant that until a final settlement of accounts clarified the situation, they would have to shoulder part of the liabilities of Massachusetts and South Carolina. Underlying the objection on this ground, however, was a deeper one which originated in the fear that a present assumption would actually obstruct a final settlement of accounts, or at least jeopardize the interest which they had in it.

At a disadvantage in all that related to the federal debt, the southern states had high expectations of the final settlement. There were fewer federal creditors among their citizens, and neither their people nor their governments would benefit greatly from the funding of the public debt. They hoped to get even in the final settlement; it was confidently expected that the Union would be found to owe them money for their expenditures in the general welfare. In 1790, however, they could not view the future with confidence.

The General Board, which had been set up in 1787 and continued under the new administration, had power to admit claims for expenditures not authorized by Congress and to consider other proofs when documentary evidence in support of claims was lacking. But this did not ensure the acceptance of southern claims. The confusion of their accounts had caused such delay that documents had not been presented to the General Board within the time limit fixed by Congress. At the moment, the agents of Virginia and North

Carolina were in New York, conferring with members of Congress and waiting for the right moment to ask for an extension of time.[3] It was possible that this request would be refused.

It was also possible that the General Board might feel obliged, in all conscience, to reject southern claims for lack of evidence of their validity. While the debate on assumption was going on in the House of Representatives, the Board made a preliminary report. Claims advanced by Maryland, Georgia, North Carolina, and Virginia were summarily and rather contemptuously dismissed. The members of the House, involved in a critical negotiation, quickly expunged the report from the record and rebuked the commissioners of the Board, who threw the blame upon one of their clerks.[4] Nevertheless, this preview of the final settlement did nothing to reassure the southerners.

A present assumption of state debts was likely to undermine their bargaining position. The southern delegates were afraid that the states which benefited immediately from assumption would have a positive incentive to obstruct a settlement in which the debts they had thrown upon the Union would be charged against them. Throughout the debate, the southerners returned to the idea that while assumption would satisfy some states, the others would be forced to wait and would perhaps wait in vain.[5]

Their suspicions were fed by the eagerness of Massachusetts and South Carolina for an immediate assumption. Under the Secretary's plan, the actual payment of interest on the assumed debt was not to begin until April 1792. It was distinctly possible that by then, or shortly afterwards, accounts would be settled and Massachusetts and South Carolina would receive a just recompense. Why was such a short interval so important?. Did these states really intend to carry through a settlement of accounts? The likely conclusion was that they were acting on the premise that a settlement would never take place.[6]

The substance of the matter was that one side wanted an assump-

3. *Cal. Va. State Papers*, V, 72, 105-6, 115-16, 125-26, 170-72.
4. *Ibid.*, V, 156-67, 170-72; Beverley Randolph to Madison, June 4, 1790, Madison Papers, XIII, 36, Lib. Cong.
5. *Annals of Congress*, II, 1308, 1340, 1366, 1387, 1389-92, 1394, 1490, 1493, 1509.
6. *Ibid.*, 1352, 1364, 1365, 1391-92, 1394-95.

tion of state debts before anything else, the other a settlement of accounts before anything else.

The division of states on assumption corresponded roughly with the line-up on a related issue, which, though it had constitutional implications, was also economic in its nature: Should the state debts be given a privileged status and be funded on a specie basis or should they be redeemed by currency finance methods? Left to the states, the debts would in most cases be rapidly extinguished at their depreciated value, whereas federal funding under the present regime signified high finance and specie payments. In the minds of many delegates, the resulting long-term debts and hard money taxes were suggestive of European despotism. The connection between finance and liberty was real, and it was scarcely disguised.

James Jackson of Georgia was an outspoken foe of all Hamilton's measures. Significantly, he had been one of those who had opposed paying the public debt in full. He took the floor against assumption, declaring that in most states the people were content to pay debts by the familiar methods of their ancestors. The nature of these methods was revealed in his further comment. Many states, he said, had sunk their debts by levying taxes payable in securities, and the citizens had "cheerfully submitted." His own state had paid interest on only a fraction of her debt and had steadily reduced the principal by levying taxes payable in securities. If her outstanding securities were now assumed by the federal government, they would draw interest, appreciate in value, and—added to similarly inflated securities of other states—load the Union with an enormous burden. Jackson feared for posterity. He also feared for liberty, predicting that assumption would result in a consolidated national government. For these reasons and because each state could better adjust its measures to the "convenience" of the inhabitants, he preferred state taxation.

Samuel Livermore of New Hampshire was another champion of state taxation. He objected to the enormous and unnecessary increase in the federal debt which assumption would entail. Payment ought to be left to the states; they had "their peculiar modes of raising money" and could best adapt them to the "habits and opinions" of their own citizens.[7]

7. *Ibid.*, 1379, 1378-81, 1353. Livermore also had opposed paying the public debt in full.

Andrew Moore of Virginia argued in a similar vein. He referred with approval to Virginia's certificate tax, which had sunk a large part of her debt. Her citizens, he said, had never had any idea that state certificates would be redeemed in any other way. As the certificates were not highly valued, they had been traded at a fifth of their nominal value. Moore objected to assumption because it would appreciate the remaining debts of Virginia and other states, which the nation would then have to pay in full, with interest.[8]

Hugh Williamson of North Carolina pleaded the same cause. While some states had levied taxes to pay interest on their debts, he said, North Carolina had redeemed the principal by accepting certificates for taxes. Some debts she had paid in paper money. She wished no interference with her internal arrangements; in fact, the ratifying convention had proposed a constitutional amendment to this effect—an amendment described by one member of Congress as a demand that the state be not compelled to pay twenty shillings on the pound.

It will be seen that a high regard for state prerogatives frequently went hand in hand with the desire to escape payment in full. Basically, the objection to assumption on this ground was the same as that which had crept out in the debate over funding the public debt. A minority of the House disliked a method of payment which would gratuitously raise the market value of securities and make debts hard to get rid of. The argument had one point: let the states pay their own debts and they will sink them at market value.

In considering the objections to assumption, there was also a moral issue. Southern members expressed indignation at the shameless activities of speculators who had invaded their states in advance of the news of Hamilton's report. Hugh Williamson, recently arrived from North Carolina, charged that the purpose of assumption was to make fortunes for speculators.[9] The moral issue, though it provided verbal ammunition for debate, was peripheral to the main points of dispute and made no converts for either side.

The debates in the House of Representatives were governed by the conflicting economic interests of states. The assumption clause

8. *Ibid.*, 1511, 1516, 1487-90, 1509.
9. *Iibid.*, 1487-90. He meant northern speculators. Local speculators had already absorbed the bulk of the state debt.

was incorporated in the same bill as the provision for funding the public debt. After reaching agreement on funding, the House settled down to consider assumption. At first there seemed to be a favorable majority. Of fifty-eight members, not counting the speaker, Massachusetts, Connecticut, and South Carolina mustered a bloc of sixteen to eighteen votes. Virginia and Georgia combined only thirteen, and one of these was permanently lost to the other side by the defection of Theodorick Bland. Before the arrival of the North Carolina delegates a majority consisted of thirty votes, which the advocates of assumption sought among the delegates of states whose economic interests were not materially affected. Their arguments had considerable validity: the measure could be recommended as public policy; it appealed to those who were still thinking primarily in terms of strengthening the Union; it promised to rationalize the collection of revenue, prevent conflict of interest, and extend equal treatment to all creditors. The difficulties of Massachusetts and South Carolina were real, and the appeals of their delegates had considerable effect.

The opposition, which became more coherent as debate continued, combined several shades of opinion. Some members, like Madison, would have agreed to assumption with amendments incorporating the interests of their own states. Others, though they disliked the idea and hoped for its rejection, would have reluctantly consented to it in some modified form. Still others opposed it in any form, insisting that a settlement of accounts must come first.

The extreme position was occupied by Alexander White of Virginia. Offering an amendment contrived to destroy the main proposition, he moved that assumption be restricted to sums due creditor states after the final settlement of accounts. Support for his motion came from Andrew Moore of Virginia, Samuel Livermore of New Hampshire, and Michael Jenifer Stone of Maryland.[10]

The argument on the other side was carried by Elbridge Gerry and Fisher Ames of Massachusetts and the two vocal delegates of South Carolina, William Smith and Edanus Burke. They enlarged upon the wartime sacrifices and the present distress of their states, concluding always with the idea that the debts were really those of the Union and ought to be assumed. They fiercely rejected the

10. *Ibid.*, 1342-45.

notion that a settlement of accounts should come first. "We are
told that accounts are in a train of being settled," said Fisher Ames.
"We are advised to wait the event. But, in the mean time what is
to become of the State creditors?" Echoing these sentiments, William
Smith developed the idea that assumption had been adopted with
the Constitution. When the new government was formed, he said,
the people of the states expected it to "rid them of their embarrassments." He had always believed "that when the General Government got possession of all the revenue they would provide for all
the debts of the Union."

After a short debate, White's motion was brought to vote and
defeated 32 to 18. There was some doubt as to whether it was
technically in order, since its effect was to rule out the main proposition under color of amendment. Some members who opposed
assumption may therefore have voted in the negative or withheld
their votes; however, it would appear that a majority of the House
was not at this time unconditionally opposed to assumption.[11]

The main attack came from another quarter. It was an attempt
to combine the proposition with additional clauses contrived to
safeguard the interests of the states whose welfare was jeopardized
or else to defeat assumption altogether by loading it with impractical amendments. Madison was the leader. After two weeks' discussion had disclosed where most members stood, he rose to declare
that he was not opposed to assumption in principle. He felt, however, that it should go hand in hand with a settlement of accounts
and even then could be justified only by coupling it with an arrangement which would give states which had paid their debts the fullest
credit in the final settlement.[12]

Madison had been conferring with William Davies, the agent in
charge of settling Virginia's accounts. One of their objects was to
get an extension of time for submitting materials to the General
Board. Davies had also been instructing Madison as to the "desidera-
ta" to be put into any measure relative to the settlement of accounts.
Madison was therefore prepared to bring forward a motion which
would protect Virginia's interests. He proposed that, along with
assumption, "effectual provision be made for liquidating and credit-

11. *Ibid.*, 1371, 1357, 1377.
12. *Ibid.*, 1338-40.

ing to the States, the whole of their expenditures during the war, as the same hath been or may be stated for the purpose; and, in such liquidation, the best evidence shall be received that the nature of the case will permit." His obvious purpose was to direct the General Board to accept Virginia's own version of her claims for expenditures in the general welfare. Madison further explained that he wanted an extension of the time limit which, he said, had already barred a great number of Virginia's claims. His motion was also designed to guarantee that the final settlement of accounts would actually take place by associating a provision for it with assumption.[13]

Roger Sherman of Connecticut spoke against the amendment; he, apparently, was still wary of Virginia's enormous and shadowy claims.[14] But the Massachusetts delegates were more generous. Aware of the logic of their own position, they upheld the idea that all state war expenditures were properly chargeable to the Union. They wished, however, to separate the question of assumption from any proposition about the settlement of accounts, fearing that to combine them would result in compromises, and possibly the loss of the measure which they so much desired. Their attitude, however, was not reassuring to their opponents, who interpreted it to mean that they did not intend to bring about a settlement once their debts were assumed.

Both sides finally agreed to Madison's amendment. Those who favored assumption saw it as necessary to get votes; the others supported it because it made the original proposition more equitable. The amendment was carried unanimously. The effect was to remove some of the objections to assumption and increase the chance that it would pass.[15]

But Madison was not done. Presuming, as he said, that the House had registered an intention to undertake some kind of an assumption, he brought up an amendment designed to incorporate

13. *Ibid.*, 1339-41; *Cal. Va. State Papers,* V, 115-16, 125-26, VII, 44-45. Davies found Madison "zealous" on the subject of Virginia's claims. Cf. memoranda dated Feb. 1790 for a speech on assumption, Madison Papers, XII, 84a, 84b, Lib. Cong.

14. *Annals of Congress,* II, 1341, 1376. The same was true of Benjamin Huntington of Connecticut.

15. *Ibid.,* 1384. The clause was nullified when the House rejected assumption and was not reinstated in the bill eventually adopted.

Virginia's interests in the assumption itself, in such a manner that
she would gain her ends even if the final settlement never took
place. He proposed that the assumption be broadened to include
not only existing debts, but all debts which the states had discharged
since the end of the war.   For these amounts the states were to
receive securities similar to those issued to public creditors.

Madison's proposal was somewhat less extreme than it may appear, for he very probably intended to bring forward a subsequent
motion that the states administer at least part of the taxes necessary
to support the enlarged debt. The least that can be said, however,
is that it was very risky for states' rights. It would have vastly increased the federal debt; nearly all taxes would have been collected
in the name of the federal government, and the states—as well as
individuals—made pensioners of the Union.[16] From Virginia's standpoint, however, the plan had merit in that it insured against the
possibility of a final settlement of accounts never taking place. She
would get an immediate return for debts she had paid. Only in
this way, said Madison, could assumption be made equitable. From
Virginia, Edward Carrington wrote: "Could the state be admitted
as creditors in the scheme upon their *redeemed* securities the measure
[assumption] would perhaps be satisfactory to a majority of the community. All true friends of government would unite in defending
it."[17]

The proposal was ingenious and very subtle, because if assumption passed on these terms, Virginia's interests were protected; but
on the other hand, an assumption so large was most unlikely to
pass. The Massachusetts delegates saw the point. Fisher Ames was
alarmed. He diagnosed Madison's proposal as grounded in suspicion that the final settlement would never be concluded. He wished
to make it perfectly clear that Massachusetts had no intention of

16. *Ibid.*   Madison presumably had among his papers a "Plan of American
Finance," drawn up by Gouverneur Morris, who submitted it to Jefferson while
in Paris.   Jefferson sent it on to Madison. It is virtually identical with the
scheme proposed by Madison. Gouverneur Morris gave Robert Morris a copy
of his plan but Robert Morris apparently was not impressed by it.   Another
copy is in the Washington Papers. Jefferson Papers, XLIX, 8328-32; Gouverneur
Morris to Robert Morris, July 31, 1790, Gouverneur Morris Papers, no. 22;
Washington Papers, CCXLV, 41, all in Lib. Cong.

17. My italics. Carrington to Madison, Apr. 30, 1790, Madison Papers, XIII,
16, Lib. Cong.

placing obstacles in the way. "Gentlemen have repeatedly told us," he said, "that they are not opposed to the assumption provided the liquidation and final settlement of accounts was speedily to take place." To remove all doubts on this score, he laid before the House a plan for settling accounts. The plan was so liberal that Ames' colleague, Theodore Sedgwick, was not sure he would endorse it. The states were to be credited with all expenses or debts incurred on account of the Union and "in general with all expenditures what-soever, towards general or particular defence, during the war." The plan extended the time limit for exhibiting claims and provided an automatic solution for the most vexing question relative to the final settlement: in the event Congress did not fix each state's quota of the common charges at the present session, the General Board was empowered to determine quotas.[18]

Ames was willing to give the southern states most of what they wanted and the utmost assurance that the final settlement would take place—provided they would agree to an immediate assumption. But he did not win over the southern delegates. Madison made his objection perfectly clear. "I am afraid," he said, ". . . that notwith-standing every step which may be taken, there will be unforeseen diffi-culties in the final liquidation and adjustment of the accounts; and I am persuaded if that measure should miscarry, the assumption of the State debts will work indeed an enormous injustice." Few states, he said, "will be willing to incur a load of debt for which there is not a pressing necessity, and rely upon the final settlement of accounts for redress."[19]

Madison's drastic amendment was beaten 28 to 22. The advo-cates of assumption now wished to be done with complicated amend-ments which in their view embarrassed the main proposition. They sought a decision on the clause as it stood in the Secretary's report. In some quarters, however, their support was becoming less enthusias-tic. Such members as Thomas Fitzsimons of Pennsylvania and Daniel Carroll of Maryland were apparently struck by the obstinate resistance of a strong minority. They were not so devoted to assump-tion as to be willing to risk the failure of the Secretary's whole fund-

18. *Annals of Congress,* II, 1385-86.
19. *Ibid.,* 1390, 1392.

ing program.[20] Fitzsimons, in fact, was a big public creditor, presumably more interested in the other part of the Secretary's plan, and probably not too enthusiastic in any case about sharing federal revenues with state creditors. More ominous for the fate of the measure, however, was the arrival, one by one, of three delegates from North Carolina. Hugh Williamson, the first to take his seat, ranged himself in the forefront of the opposition. His speeches were probably less effective than his vote and those of his colleagues; the House had become so evenly divided that the new arrivals swung the balance.[21]

Various attempts were now made to delete the assumption clause from the funding bill, but the effort was defeated by a vote of 29 to 27.[22] The discussion then ranged over other phases of the Secretary's report; however, the Massachusetts delegates were willing to agree to a wide ranging discussion only on the understanding that assumption would ultimately pass; otherwise they threatened to block the whole funding bill. It was obvious that the question of assumption had to be finally decided before any progress could be made.

The members were weary by this time. All that could be said on the subject had been said, and the debate lapsed into recrimination. "I confess, Sir," said Jeremiah Wadsworth at one point, "I almost begin to despair of the assumption of the State debts, and with that I shall despair of the National Government."

Finally, the vote was taken and assumption beaten, 31 to 29. Theodore Sedgwick rose and addressed the House in the name of the people of Massachusetts. In a heated speech—the kind in which he excelled—he said his state was betrayed, that the offer of justice after the settlement of accounts was little less than mockery. He was certain Congress would have to levy excise taxes to pay the public debt, and he warned that an attempt to collect them in Massachusetts would lead to violence. John Page of Virginia called him to order, but cries of "Hear him!" arose, and Sedg-

---

20. *Ibid.*, 1408. Fitzsimons warned the advocates of assumption that they should be thinking of methods of conciliation. *Ibid.*, 1398-99. Carroll began siding with the opposition. *Ibid.*, 1396, 1409, 1410, 1478. When it seemed likely that the House could not agree, both Carroll and Fitzsimons wished to drop further consideration of assumption and get on with the funding bill. Another speculator, Elias Boudinot, also abandoned assumption.

21. The North Carolina delegates arrived between March 19 and April 6. The Rhode Island delegates had not taken their seats.

22. *Annals of Congress*, II, 1480.

wick continued. When he had finished, Jackson of Georgia delivered "spirited strictures" on the tenor of his remarks.

Subsequent votes proved that the majority against assumption was solid, and the House proceeded to draw up a funding bill without it. The advocates of assumption tried to obstruct proceedings by introducing the measure as an amendment to other propositions. Members who were otherwise sympathetic wanted to get on with the funding bill; others were indignant. At last a funding bill without assumption was completed and sent to the Senate.[23]

The rejection by the House set the stage for the deal which secured the passage of assumption in return for the location of the permanent national capital on the Potomac—one of the better known incidents of backstage negotiation in American politics. From the moment Congress departed from Philadelphia in 1783, the Virginia delegates had been trying to move the capital to the Potomac. Congress, they hoped, would then be more susceptible to southern influence. Jefferson expected that a half million dollars would be laid out annually in the immediate neighborhood and that the entire Chesapeake area would feel the stimulus and experience a commercial development. Leading Virginians relished the idea of the national capital on home grounds and were apparently not too averse to making the sacrifice which it eventually required. That it would entail a sacrifice was clear—there were not enough southern votes in Congress to obtain it without support from other sections. The Virginians had been defeated in 1788 and again in 1789. When the subject was reintroduced in 1790, as the House concluded its discussion of the funding bill, Madison had little or no hope.[24]

The stage was set for negotiation when the Senate received the funding bill at the same time that a bill to establish the residence of Congress came up for consideration. The Pennsylvanians were determined to get Congress out of New York, and they wished to have at least the temporary capital for their state. Since certain mem-

23. *Ibid.*, 1513, 1525-26, 1544-46, 1588-90, 1629. See Schachner, *Hamilton*, 260. John C. Miller, *Alexander Hamilton, Portrait in Paradox* (New York, 1959), 229-54, has a spirited account of the fight over assumption.

24. James Monroe wrote up from Virginia that assumption would not be nearly so objectionable if the capital stood on the Potomac. Monroe to Jefferson, July 3, 1790, Jefferson to Dr. Gilmer, June 27, 1790, Jefferson Papers, LVI, 9544-45, 9509-10, Lib. Cong.; Monroe to Madison, July 15, 1790, Madison Papers, XIII, 58, *ibid.*

bers of their delegation felt free to throw their vote either way on the issues of assumption and the location of the capital, the Pennsylvanians had a negotiating position. They opened conversations with both New England and southern delegates, who on their own account were seeking trades. The details of what followed have never been penetrated. Madison, it appears, was afraid that the Pennsylvanians would trade votes for assumption in return for New England votes for a location at Philadelphia, in which case Virginia would be twice defeated. What spoiled this possibility, apparently, was the obstinate refusal of the New York delegates to consent to any removal from their city. They would not line up with the Pennsylvanians. Hamilton and his henchmen at length realized that no offer of the capital would consolidate enough strength among the middle states and New England delegates to assure passage of assumption. Southern votes were necessary for any trade, and the price must be the location of the permanent capital on the Potomac. Madison's apprehension of being out-maneuvered no doubt made him ready to close with the Pennsylvanians when given an opportunity. Two Virginians, Alexander White and Richard Bland Lee, were induced to change their vote, and by their action purchased the permanent capital for Virginia. The Pennsylvanians got the temporary capital for Philadelphia. The trade conferred a benefit on Virginia which she could not otherwise have won and probably staved off a complete political defeat.[25]

Jefferson in later years pretended that he was duped by Hamilton into sanctioning the trade and persuading the Virginia delegates to change their votes. It is clear, however, that Jefferson was not innocent about financial matters, as he later declared, and if uninformed on any point he had only to consult Madison, who was an expert. The fact is that Jefferson and Madison were pretty well satisfied with the bargain they made.[26]

25. James Madison, Sr., to Madison, Apr. 13, 1790, Edward Carrington to Madison, Apr. 30, 1790, Madison to Monroe, June 1, 1790, to James Madison, Sr., June 13, 1790, Note handed to Madison on Assumption, June 1, 1790, Madison Papers, XVI, 7, 16, 34, 39, 44a, Lib. Cong.; Jefferson to Randolph, June 20, 1790, to Monroe, June 20, 1790, Jefferson Papers, LV, 9455, 9459-61, *ibid.*; Memoranda concerning the residence of Congress, 1790, Notes on the Residence Bill, June 30, 1790, folios 90, 95, 105, Rufus King Papers, N.-Y. Hist. Soc. See Brant, *Madison, Father of the Constitution,* 312-15.
26. Schachner, *Hamilton,* 260-62.

Before assumption passed the House, it was further modified, and there was more bargaining. Hamilton had proposed taking over all existing state debts, which he estimated at $25,000,000; but when opposition materialized in the House, the advocates of the measure offered a compromise limiting the assumption to specific sums—in each case less than the actual debts of the various states—amounting in all to $19,300,000. This concession became inoperative when the House dropped assumption, but later, when the Senate reinstated the clause in the funding bill, the total amount to be assumed was raised to $21,500,000. New Hampshire, Connecticut, Massachusetts, and South Carolina got no extra allowances, but New York and Pennsylvania each received $200,000. Delaware's allowance was raised by $100,000. Southern opposition was mollified by conceding $500,000 more to Virginia, $800,000 to North Carolina, and $200,000 to Georgia. New Hampshire and Georgia formally complained about their small allotment. Rhode Island, coming late on the scene, was given a pittance of $200,000, to which the legislature registered a formal protest. The amount of all state debts made assumable by the final act was $21,500,000.[27]

As it emerged from the House-Senate negotiation, the final act departed from Hamilton's recommendation in placing state debts on a slightly lower footing than the federal debt. The subscriber received 6 percent stock for only four-ninths of his subscription (which, however, was computed as the total of both principal and the accumulated interest due on his old securities); an additional two-ninths in 6 percent deferred stock; and the remaining third in 3 percent stock. The slightly lower rating may have fallen below the highest expectations of speculators in state debts but was hardly enough to diminish their profits materially. It should be noted, also, that Con-

---

27. Actual debts eventually assumed under the act amounted to $18,200,000. The increased allowances were important because, if citizens of a state undersubscribed its quota, Congress paid interest to the state on the balance. The most careful discussion of the action of the Senate on the assumption clause is in Bates, Assumption of State Debts, 163-66. See *U. S. Stat. at L.*, I, 138-44 (ch. 34, Aug. 4, 1790); *Annals of Congress*, II, 1586; Bartlett, ed., *Records of Rhode Island*, X, 465-66; Amos Perry, "Rhode Island Revolutionary Debt," R.I. Hist. Soc., *Publications*, new ser., 4 (1897), 234-43; *Journals of the Proceedings of the House of Representatives of the State of New Hampshire* (Portsmouth, 1791), 51-54; Jefferson to Mr. Eppes, July 25, 1790, Jefferson Papers, LVI, 9637, Lib. Cong.; Beverley Randolph to Madison, Aug. 10, 1790, Madison Papers, XIII, 62, *ibid.*

gress adjourned without voting the taxes everybody knew would be necessary to provide for the assumed debt. Expecting difficulties on this issue and not wishing to put obstacles in his own way, Hamilton had wisely advised a delay in taking up the interest.

Action on the debt was thus completed. The remaining element of the compromise of 1790 had to do with the settlement of state accounts. The southern states were most concerned about this; they were also the states which felt their interests menaced by assumption. An act of conciliation was therefore in order.

A bill to settle state accounts was passed by the House while the final verdict on funding and assumption was still pending. Rather surprisingly, agreement was easily secured on one matter that had baffled the Confederation Congress—the rule by which the common charges of the war were to be apportioned. It was decided that each state's share of the total expense of the Revolution (excluding the public debt) should be based on population, as determined by the first census. An extension of time was allowed for the submission of claims and documents. After the final balances were struck, the states which were found to be creditors of the Union were to receive public securities like those issued to individual creditors. Nothing was said about the debtor states.[28]

The act did not quite guarantee the southern interest in the settlement of accounts. The extension of time to July 1, 1791, met their needs, but the act was not satisfactory in other respects. Although the General Board was again authorized to judge claims on the basis of equity, the Virginia delegates did not think its powers were sufficient. Virginia's commissioner, William Davies, was having trouble getting claims processed through the Treasury, and it seemed likely that many would have to be restated and probably reduced. There was also the difficulty of producing vouchers. Madison had tried to take care of this in his first amendment to the assumption proposal, under which the states were to be credited for all expenditures *as they were stated* and the best evidence received in support of claims that the nature of the case would admit. His amendment was adopted but lost when the House rejected assumption on its first trial.[29]

28. *U. S. Stat. at L.*, I, 178-79 (ch. 38, Aug. 5, 1790).
29. My italics. *Annals of Congress*, II, 1385-86; *Cal. Va. State Papers*, V, 115-16, 125-26, 141.

When the preliminary report of the General Board revealed an alarming bias against the claims of Georgia, North Carolina, Virginia, and Maryland, the southerners attempted to enlarge the Board with the appointment of two additional commissioners. The Virginians hoped that one would be from their state. The effort was at first successful. The bill for settlement of accounts, when it left the House, provided for two extra commissioners; but the Senate disagreed and the act as finally adopted retained the existing Board of only three members. Later, after assumption had passed, Madison renewed the attempt. The House quickly concurred in a bill to add two commissioners, but again the proposition was struck down in the Senate and not revived.[30]

Although the act to settle accounts was not wholly in accord with southern desires, the execution of it left them little to complain of, and it appears that southerners got everything they wanted. If one can judge by Virginia's experience after 1790, the General Board freely accepted and approved claims of every description. The commissioners permitted Davies to sit with them whenever Virginia's accounts were examined. He was surprised at their liberality; if vouchers were lacking, they accepted resolutions and other data found in state executive journals as proof that money had been spent. Davies, who interpreted the documents for them, finally came to the conclusion that lack of vouchers was a positive advantage. "I am rather inclined to hope the State will profit by the loss of the documents & vouchers," he reported to the governor, "as hitherto I have met with scarce a single payment, but what, from some of the books, I could shew its object, nor hardly one advance without evidence of its settlement: of course for want of something to be objected to, there seems a necessity of admitting the whole charge, although in many cases there would probably be exceptionable items in the account itself." In August 1791 Davies reported that not a single item had been rejected except one introduced by mistake. He wrote a few months later that the Board had adopted a mode

30. *Cal. Va. State Papers*, V, 170-72, 179-80, 183-85; *Annals of Congress*, II, 627-28, 1633, 1634, 1644-46, 1702, 1719, 1721; James Monroe to Madison, July 2, 1790, Beverley Randolph to Madison, July 12, Aug. 10, 1790, Madison Papers, X, 47, 54, 62, Lib. Cong.

of examining accounts even more summarical and superficial than that already employed.[31]

Virginia's claims multiplied in this favorable atmosphere, growing from $13,000,000 in 1790 to $26,000,000 in November 1791, and to over $28,000,000 in 1793. The increase in particular items reflected the Board's generous attitude. In 1788 William Heth had dared ask only $500,000 for the expense of securing the Northwest Territory; in 1791 William Davies demanded $1,253,877.[32] It appears that the Board entertained all sorts of claims with the utmost liberality, but prior to a final statement reduced the totals by about 10 percent and then made further reductions in specific cases. Virginia, nevertheless, emerged with a credit of $19,085,981—the largest of any state. The other southern states fared variously. It seems that Maryland was generously treated, along with South Carolina, but that the Board pared down the claims of North Carolina and, most particularly, Georgia.[33] They were probably greatly inflated. On the whole, the southern states must not have had much cause for grievance. The Board allowed $51,598,811 to the states from Maryland to Georgia—not far short of half the total of all credits for expenditures in the general welfare.

The compromise of 1790 was now complete. The major policy decisions that pressed upon the new government had involved the

31. *Cal. Va. State Papers*, V, 361, 368-69, 379-80, 415. Questioning assumption on the grounds that it invaded state sovereignty, the Governor of North Carolina nevertheless expressed satisfaction to the state assembly that as a result of it, North Carolina's public accounts would wear a "new dress." He had been told this by the state's agent in New York. Saunders, ed., *State Records of North Carolina*, XXI, 877.

32. *Cal. Va. State Papers*, V, 156-57, 393, VII, 48.

33. These details come from a manuscript in the Hamilton Papers at the Library of Congress, XX, 2701-3, attached to a copy of the Board's final report. Hamilton's compilation is the only inclusive set of figures as to the claims of the various states that has come to notice. The final report gives no particulars, merely presenting the allowances determined by the Board. According to a letter from the chief of the records section of the General Accounting Office in Washington, D. C., the commissioners of the General Board immediately destroyed their clerical statements and papers after rendering their decision. Vouchers and other documents were lost in the 1814 fire at the Treasury. Davies wrote in 1794 that the Board told him Virginia would have been a creditor to the amount of $2,000,000 if her quota of the total expenses had remained as it was during the Confederation. As a result of population changes and the inclusion of Kentucky's population, she was a debtor state to the amount of about $100,000. *Cal. Va. State Papers*, VII, 50; Report of Commissioners of the Public Debt, June 29, 1783, Record Group 53, Fiscal Records Sec., Natl. Arch.

adjustment of state interests rather than of class interests.   Even Madison's proposal to discriminate—the only challenge to the Hamil-. tonian formula for funding the public debt—was dictated by a consideration of Virginia's interests rather than a desire to appease the common people.   Agreed upon the necessity of strengthening the central government, members of Congress were in everything else the spokesmen of their states.   After they reached accord upon funding the public debt, thereby forging a suitable foundation for the new regime, the stability of the Union depended upon harmoniz-ing state interests.   Under the grand compromise by which state debts were assumed, the capital located on the Potomac, and the set-tlement of accounts brought to completion, the material interests of all the states were in some degree propitiated.   The formula was to reconcile differences by granting all demands.

Madison and Jefferson were not elated, but neither were they dissatisfied with the result.   They felt strongly that it had been necessary to make concessions in order to preserve the Union and that there were compensatory features even to the assumption.   In letters preparing leading Virginians for the news that assumption would pass, they stressed the fact that Virginia would not lose financially.   They had, of course, hoped to fund the assumed debt by state taxes, and this was their remaining objection.[34]   But the location of the capital spoke for itself.   And, as Jefferson pointed out, there were signs of an early outbreak of war in Europe.   Na-tional unity and sound credit would enable the United States to keep out of war by being powerful.   As a neutral, America would have a "gainful time of it."   He expressed relief that the great debate was over.   "This [assumption] and the funding business out of the way," he wrote, "I hope nothing else may be able to call up local principles."[35]

34. Madison to ——, July 13, 1790, to H. Rose, *et al.*, Aug. 14, 1790, Madison Papers, XIII, 59, 63, Lib. Cong.; Jefferson to Randolph, June 20, 1790, to Monroe, June 20, 1790, to Dr. Gilmer, June 27, 1790, to Dr. Eppes, July 4, 1790, to ——, July 25, 1790, to Randolph, Aug. 14, 1790, Jefferson Papers, LV, 9455, 9459-61, LVI, 9509-10, 9548-49, 9640-42, LVII, 9711, *ibid.*

35. Jefferson to ——, July 11, 1790, to Randolph, July 11, Aug. 14, 1790, Jefferson Papers, LVI, 9577-78, 9581-82, LVII, 9711, *ibid.*

The Threads Tied

"It would have been more wonderful, if no impression had been made by a depreciated debt, which from pebbles in the ocean of society, might, by a species of political diving, be made pearls in the hands of individuals."

—John Taylor, 1814

THE publication of Hamilton's report and the ensuing Congressional debate had an adverse effect on security prices. The reduction of interest, although in some degree expected, was not distinctly favorable to the creditors, some of whom may have purchased securities at as high as 50c on the dollar. Presumably Hamilton had decided upon 4 percent after much reflection, for there is reason to believe he could not have gone lower without offending important segments of the body of creditors, who were loyal supporters of the regime. Although some friends of the administration counseled 3 percent, they were moved primarily by the desire to put it within the government's power to assume state debts.[1] Many creditors, as we have seen, also had misgivings about assumption; until put to the test there was no way of knowing whether federal revenues would support both debts, or, if taxes were raised to an adequate level, whether they would be resisted.

1. Theodore Sedgwick, one of the leading champions of assumption in the House, contemplated 3 percent and invited opinion from his friends in Massachusetts. They were divided on the matter out of a concern for assumption. See letters from Thomas Dwight, Jan. 24, 1790, S. Henshaw, Jan. 27, 30, 1790, Henry Van Schaack, Feb. 25, 1790, Benjamin Lincoln, Feb. 26, 1790, Sedgwick Papers, box A, Mass. Hist. Soc. See also Oliver Wolcott, Sr., to Oliver Wolcott, Jan. 23, Feb. 8, 1790, Gibbs, *Memoirs of the Administrations of Washington and Adams,* I, 35, 38-39.

Public securities had fallen off a little just before Hamilton sent in his report. Its publication at once dropped them to the level where they had been six months earlier—36c to 38c on the dollar.[2] Madison's motion to discriminate gave a further shock to the market, but it quickly recovered when he failed to gain support in Congress. Although the rejection of discrimination by a decisive majority brought a marginal rise, securities continued to fluctuate at low values all during the debate over the funding program. Speculators could not altogether dismiss the alarming prospect that differences over assumption would prevent any action on the debt. When the House finally drew up a bill without assumption and sent it to the Senate, securities rose to about 45c.[3]

Hamilton's report had promoted the value of state securities and indents. Indents, which he had proposed to fund on equal terms with the principal of the debt, sold for 33c when principal securities were only 40c. State securities were variously affected by the proposal to assume state debts. Some, like those of Pennsylvania and Maryland, were already higher in the market than any federal securities; but South Carolina securities, which had already risen in response to rumors of assumption, remained at about 20c on the dollar pending Congressional action.[4]

While the debate was in progress, everything connected with securities speculation quivered in suspense. Speculators did not know where to turn. They plunged this way and that, took their money out of one type of security and put it into another. They rushed in and out of state debts—an exodus took place when the House rejected assumption. Every man interpreted the course of events according to his own temper. In a spirit of optimism, he could view the delay in funding as a fortuitous opportunity to pick up securities

2. Andrew Craigie to Jaret Wells, Feb. 3, 1790, Craigie Papers, box 3, Amer. Antiq. Soc.; Jno. Dougherty to Clement Biddle, Feb. 4, 1790, Clement Biddle Papers, Hist. Soc. of Pa.

3. William Constable to Benjamin Harrison, Feb. 13, 1790, to Gouverneur Morris, May 7, June 15, 1790, Constable Letterbooks, N.Y. Pub. Lib.; Clement Biddle to John Grover, Feb. 16, 1790, to Luther Martin, Feb. 16, 1790, to Capt. William Campbell, Feb. 28, 1790, to Robert Gilchrist, Apr. 16, 1790, to William Rogers, May 2, 10, 12, 27, 31, June 22, 1790, Clement Biddle Letterbook, Hist. Soc. of Pa.

4. Clement Biddle to William Rogers, Apr. 15, 1790, Clement Biddle Letterbook, Hist. Soc. of Pa.; William Constable to Gouverneur Morris, May 23, 1790, Constable Letterbooks, N.Y. Pub. Lib. State securities were cheaper than this, it appears, in South Carolina.

before they rose in value, but there was the gloomy possibility that no bill would be enacted. The situation did not afford a certain basis for judgment—all was conjecture. State debts would surely rise if they were assumed, but how far they would rise could not be known until the government started paying interest on them, and that was to be delayed a year. If assumption took place, public securities might fall, since a doubt must exist as to whether the government was capable of supporting both debts. But if state debts were not assumed, public securities could still fall, because the resentment of certain states might cripple the operation of the funding plan and impair the value of all securities.

Amidst the confusion, New York speculators had an unmistakable advantage over their rivals in other parts of the country. They were privy to the doings of Congress, and some of them, like William Constable, had inside sources of information. "Our friend [Robert Morris]," he confided to Gouverneur Morris in Europe, "promises that when the Bill comes up to the Senate He will apprise me when to strike."[5] As late as June 15, Constable was apprehensive that assumption would fail and the session break up without a funding act. Then on June 23, two or three days after the bargain had been made over the location of the capital, he wrote that it was now "understood" that state debts would be assumed. He was certain of this the next day, for he ordered a southern correspondent to buy $100,000 in North and South Carolina debts and instructed another agent to purchase to any amount.[6] All this time, Clement Biddle languished in Philadelphia, wondering whether any sort of funding bill would pass. Two weeks after Constable had ordered his buyers to strike, Biddle still thought southern state debts were a dangerous speculation, and did not believe they would be assumed. Several weeks later, after the funding bill had passed the Senate, he was still deceived.[7]

Just prior to the submission of Hamilton's report, foreign investment had slowed down because of high prices and the unfavorable rate of exchange for foreign currencies. It was checked still further

5. Constable to Gouverneur Morris, Feb. 3, 1790, Constable Letterbooks, N.Y. Pub. Lib.
6. William Constable to Gouverneur Morris, June 15, 23, 1790, to Garrett, June 24, 1790, to James Carry, June 24, 1790, *ibid.*
7. Clement Biddle to Robert Gilchrist, June 20, July 4, 21, 1790, to William Roberts, July 7, 1790 Clement Biddle Letterbook, Hist. Soc. of Pa.

by the publication of the report in Europe. Gouverneur Morris wrote from Amsterdam that Hamilton's recommendations had given so much alarm that Dutch bankers had suspended purchases. In April he wrote from London that securities brought no more than 45c on the dollar.[8] Foreign speculators apparently had the same reservations as their American counterparts about the reduction of interest, assumption of state debts, and the fiscal resources of the United States government.

By late July, however, the imminence of federal funding began to stimulate the market. In New York public securities rose to 60c and 65c by the end of the month, and state debts were 40c and 42c. Indents (which were to be funded at 3 percent) were 34c to 37c. Within the next month, public securities went up to 75c, which was so much higher than prices in Europe as to suggest buying them there and selling them in the United States. The discrepancy in prices could not have lasted long, however, since foreign investment was being resumed on a major scale. Prices advanced steadily in the United States to the end of the year, when public securities were about 80c. By February 1792, the speculative frenzy had driven them up to $1.05.[9]

Although large profits could still be made after the passage of the funding bill, there was a dearth of cheap securities promising a fabulous return on a small capital. Their appetites whetted by profits, many speculators in securities were turning to western lands. There was a general movement into land development schemes, and often the capital was supplied by the same European houses which had bought heavily in public securities.[10]

Hamiltonian funding, needless to say, vastly increased the value of the domestic debt. The principal, which was about $28,000,000, could have been purchased or retired at market value in 1786 for

8. Gouverneur Morris to William Constable, Feb. 11, 1790, to William Short, Mar. 18, 1790, to Robert Morris, Apr. 8, 1790, Commercial Correspondence, I, 12, 18, 23, Gouverneur Morris Papers, Lib. Cong.

9. New York prices were above the rest of the country. Constable to Gouverneur Morris, July 30, Aug. 4, 27, 1790, Constable Letterbooks, N.Y. Pub. Lib.; Andrew Craigie to Bossenger Foster, Aug. 4, 1790, Craigie Papers, box 3, Amer. Antiq. Soc. Davis, *Early American Corporations*, I, 340, presents a chart of security values to October 1792.

10. See the opening chapters in Evans, *The Holland Land Company*. The Constable and Craigie papers show the rapid transition from securities to land speculation.

perhaps $5,000,000. In 1790 Congress committed the nation to pay-
ing it at par and in specie, along with approximately $13,000,000
interest. In 1791 the entire debt was something less than $42,000,000,
consisting of $14,179,000 in 6 percent stock, $7,088,000 in deferred
6 percent stock, $10,500,000 in 3 percent stock, and an estimated
$7,000,000 to $10,000,000 in various categories of the debt not yet
subscribed to the new loan.[11] The market value of all these securities
rose above par after June 1791; in February 1792, 6 percent stock
was $1.20 on the dollar, deferred stock was 72c, and 3 percent stock,
70c. A person who was lucky enough to have bought a $100 security
in 1786 for about $15 and who then subscribed it to the loan of
1790 with $25 interest due on it (by no means unusual), could have
sold his holdings for $121.50 in 1792.

The funding act had included provision for an assumption of
state debts up to $21,500,000: that is, it allowed citizens to subscribe
state certificates to the loan of 1790 and receive federal stock in
exchange. The citizens of Massachusetts, Rhode Island, and South
Carolina promptly oversubscribed their state quotas by some
$1,250,000; in other states the subscription fell below the quota.
After the oversubscription was deducted, the debts assumed by the
federal government were about $17,000,000.[12] Hamilton advised that
the time limit of September 30, 1791, be extended and the assumption broadened to include all remaining state debts. Congress, however, merely set back the time limit to allow additional subscriptions in states which had not filled their quota. The amount of
state debts ultimately assumed and converted into federal securities
was $18,200,000.[13] How far the assumption raised the market value
of state securities is hard to say. Except in the case of Pennsylvania
and Maryland, whose securities were solidly funded, it certainly
multiplied their value.

It should be remembered that states, as well as individuals, were
beneficiaries of the funding legislation. Massachusetts and South
Carolina were relieved by the assumption of their debts, but the
legislation conferred a bounty on certain other states which were

11. *American State Papers, Finance*, I, 149-50.
12. Statements of Assumed Debt Subscribed at the Several Offices of the United
States, CLXXIV, Record Group 53, Fiscal Records Sec., Natl. Arch.
13. See Whitney K. Bates, The Assumption of State Debts, 1783-1793 (unpublished doctoral dissertation, Univ. of Wisconsin, 1951).

large holders of public securities. Pennsylvania, for example, had acquired about $6,000,000, upon which she drew 6 percent interest. It formed a valuable capital. She divested herself of part of it in 1789 by inviting her citizens, who had exchanged federal securities for state notes in 1786, to take back the federal securities and surrender their state notes. Within two years, nearly the whole sum then outstanding—about $4,800,000—was exchanged, greatly reducing the state debt. After assumption passed, Pennsylvania encouraged her citizens to subscribe the remaining state securities to the federal loan by offering to make good, up to 6 percent, the lower rate of interest they received on deferred and 3 percent federal stock. Her resources were by no means exhausted, for she was able to apply $89,000 in old securities to the purchase of a large tract on Lake Erie, put her finances on a cash basis, and sell securities to finance internal improvements. A treasurer's statement in 1792 showed over $800,000, mostly 3 percent stock, still in her possession.[14]

New York held $2,327,000 in public securities as a result of her previous assumption of the public debt, the acquisition of securities by taxation, and the sale of land. In 1790 she invited persons who had exchanged public securities for state notes in 1786 to return the notes for public securities. To encourage her remaining state creditors to subscribe to the federal loan, she compensated them for the reduction of interest, offering to exchange 6 percent federal stock in her possession for the deferred stock they would receive from the federal government. Although New York's holdings of public securities were thus reduced, they were still ample. The state bought 190 shares in the Bank of the United States and 100 shares in the Bank of New York.[15] In 1792, pursuing an old tradition in a new

---

14. Mitchell and Flanders, eds., *Statutes of Pennsylvania*, XIII, 263-67, XIV, 76-79, 173-76; *Journal of the 1st Session of the House of Representatives . . . of Pennsylvania*, 389; John Nicholson to Governor Mifflin, Dec. 24, 1791, State of the Continental Certificates the property of this State, undated, Extract from the Report of the Treasurer delivered to the Register General the 3rd Feby 1792, State of the different Balances on hand the first, inst., signed by Christian Febiger, Public Records Div., Penn. Hist. and Museum Commission.

15. *Journal of the House of Assembly of New York*, Jan. 16, 1790; *Laws of 1781*, III, 153-54 (13th sess., ch. 31), 214-16 (14th sess., ch. 16),*New York, 1777-256* (14th sess., ch. 49), 261 (15th sess., ch. 1). New York treated her creditors, both state and federal, less generously than Pennsylvania in compensating them for the reduction of interest.

style, she instituted a land bank, offering over half a million dollars on loan, but without recourse to an emission of paper money.[16]

The State of Maryland subscribed $930,000 to the federal loan. Like Pennsylvania, she encouraged state creditors to subscribe their securities under the assumption program, by giving them 6 percent federal stock for the 3 percent and deferred stock they received from the federal government.[17]

Other states which held federal securities also benefited in some degree from the funding act. Still others got their reward after the general settlement of accounts in 1793, when, as creditor states, they received their balances in federal stock. Massachusetts got $1,498,000, Connecticut $743,000, and South Carolina $1,450,000. South Carolina's allotment was about equal to her remaining state debt; Connecticut and Massachusetts, though not debt-free, were able to get along on moderate taxes. Through the remainder of the decade, in fact, a good many of the states were major creditors of the federal government and drew large revenues from this source. The most fortunate ones rested easily upon acquired capital, spending only their income. According to a Treasury report in 1796, New York had laid no general or direct taxes since 1788, Pennsylvania since 1789, and Maryland since 1786.[18]

The long-awaited settlement of state accounts came to an early and uneventful conclusion, when the General Board rendered its decision on June 29, 1793. The report terminated five years of steady labor by the officers of the Treasury and the Paymaster General's department, whose expert services were not interrupted by the formation of a new government. The Board's policy was distinguished by a liberality consonant with the generous sentiments befitting the reformation of the Union. Putting the total of all state expenditures in the general welfare at $114,400,000, the Board de-

16. In attempting to support the novel thesis that the Constitution did not prohibit the emission of state paper money, Forrest McDonald asserts that the loan of 1792 was on exactly the same terms as the loan of 1796, without noticing the distinction. McDonald, *We the People*, 293-96. The legislative act is in *Laws of New York, 1777-1781*, 287-300 (15th sess., ch. 25).

17. Account, 1791, with Benjamin Harwood, Trustee, Ledger A, 1783-90, f. 90, Treasurer of the Western Shore, Md. Hall of Records; *Laws of Md.*, Nov. 1790, ch. 41.

18. The sums include 4 percent interest on the balances from Dec. 31, 1789. Statements of the Funded Debt Subscribed at the Several Offices of the United States, Old Loans, Record Group 53, Fiscal Records Sec., Natl. Arch.; *American State Papers, Finance*, I, 419-41.

ducted $36,700,000—the total of all advances of the federal govern-
ment to the various states, including debts assumed in 1790. The
balance, $77,600,000, was the sum of the common charges of the
war. It was apportioned upon the various states according to their
relative population as determined by the census of 1790. Each state
was thus assessed its proper share of the common charges. Seven
states, it was found, had made expenditures (after deducting all
sums received from the United States) greater than their proper
share of the common charges. They were creditors of the Union:
New Hampshire, $75,000; Massachusetts, $1,248,000; Rhode Island,
$299,000; Connecticut, $619,000; New Jersey, $49,000; South Caro-
lina, $1,205,000; and Georgia, $20,000. Six states were debtors: New
York, $2,074,000; Pennsylvania, $76,000; Delaware, $612,000; Mary-
land, $151,000; Virginia, $100,000; and North Carolina, $500,000.[19]

After reporting their decision, the commissioners of the General
Board carefully destroyed all records which would indicate how they
had arrived at their figures.[20] The precaution was needless, for there
was no serious protest. The creditor states gladly accepted public
securities in discharge of their balances, the debtor states cheerfully
acknowledged their obligation, and that was the end of the matter.
None of the debtor states ever made any payments except New York,
who reduced her debit a little by obtaining credit for building coastal
defenses during the naval war with France.[21]

It was now possible to calculate the cost of the Revolution. Adding state expenditures and the amount of the public debt to Congressional incomes from paper money and foreign loans, we may
compute it at $158,000,000 to $168,000,000.[22] The figure is close to
contemporary estimates.

19. Report of the Commissioners of the Public Debt, June 29, 1793, LXXXIII,
Record Group 53, Fiscal Records Sec., Natl. Arch.
20. Typescript of a letter from Joseph Nourse to Peter Hagner, Mar. 4, 1833,
in the files of Records, Research, and Service Section, General Accounting Office,
Bldg. 8, Cameron Depot, Virginia.
21. See Bates, Assumption of State Debts, 230-32, which carries the narrative
as far as 1802. The debtor states were formally excused at a later date.
22. Expenditures through 1783 are calculated as follows: (1) *Paper money*—
old emission, $45,489,000; new emission, $530,000; total, $46,019,000, (2) *Foreign
aids* expended—French loans and gifts, $8,000,000; Beaumarchais' supplies and
those of the Farmers General, deducting repayment, $466,000 Spanish loan and
subsidy, $69,000; Dutch loan of 1782, $2,000,000; total, $10,535,000, (3) *Public debt*,
principal, $28,000,000, (4) *State debts assumed* in 1790, $18,200,000, (5) *State credits
in the general welfare*, $77,600,000, less $2,244,000 for included credit obtained for

An epoch was closed. The political tradition which defined individual rights against government and linked popular control of taxation with the preservation of liberty survived into the nineteenth century to become part of the doctrine of southern sectionalism; but somewhere in the course of American democracy the nation at large forgot to distinguish between the government and the people. Individual rights and local privileges were no longer regarded as standing against the authority of the government; they were to be advanced by soliciting its aid and patronage.

Americans had never scrupled to seek governmental favor, but in Revolutionary times the power of the purse signified more than competition between economic or social groups. It involved liberty. For this reason it was the primary issue in the political development of the nation. The disputes with Britain leading to independence turned on the question of taxation. Under the Articles of Confederation, the character of the Union was determined by the fact that Congress lacked power to tax, and efforts to strengthen the central government were necessarily directed towards giving Congress this power. During the war these efforts were justified by the need of repelling the foe, afterwards by Congress's obligation to discharge the public debt. The disposition of the debt became the pivotal issue in the constitutional relations between the states and the nascent central government.

A Nationalist movement arose in the last years of the war. Because it failed in its objectives, it has not received the attention it deserves. In its aims and in the social interests which it represented, it anticipated the Federalists who later secured the adoption of the Constitution and enacted Hamilton's funding program. Its leader, Robert Morris, conceived the essential elements of the Federalist synthesis of strong government and high finance, but he was unable by constitutional procedure to obtain amendment to the Articles of Confederation in the vital particular upon which all else depended— federal power of taxation. The structure he built collapsed at the end of the war; nevertheless Morris and the Nationalists laid the conditions of ultimate victory. They created a public debt which

indents redeemed, less $10,000,000 to $20,000,000 estimated interest allowed on sums expended by the states, total $55,000,000 to $65,000,000, (6) *Grand total*, $158,000,000 to $168,000,000.

inhered solely in Congress, and they added to it all claims against the federal government remaining at war's end, thus forestalling the normal process of state-oriented finance which would soon have converted all debts into state obligations. Because of the integral relation between debts, the power of taxation, and sovereignty, Congress's ownership of the debt implied a basic reorganization of the federal system and produced a tendency in that direction. In the years after the war, the task of paying the debt was the chief function of a central government which otherwise lacked compelling reasons for existence.

Liberty was involved not only in the location of the taxing power but also in the way public finance was conducted. Nearly all the states carried over from colonial times a predilection for currency finance methods. Accustomed to these modes, which suited agrarian circumstances, most people regarded specie payment as signifying permanent debts, heavy taxes—in a word, oppression. Liberty in their minds was associated with paper money. Reflecting a conservative, mercantile bias imparted by the Nationalists, Congress embraced a policy of specie payment. It could never be realized under the Articles of Confederation, and in the postwar years Congress gave ground to agrarian modes of public finance. The states serviced the public debt, employing currency finance methods and dealing solely with their own citizens. Their action signalized the decay of the Nationalist program.

Meanwhile, issues of public finance had given birth to southern sectionalism. Because of a limited commercial development, the south emerged from the Revolution with a minor share of the public debt; its inferiority in this respect was increased by the assumption of charges against Congress. In the south, to a relatively greater extent than elsewhere, the costs of the war were absorbed by the states, and the debts left over from the conflict became state rather than federal debts. Southerners therefore owned fewer public securities than citizens of other states, and their holdings were further diminished in the postwar years by constant transfers to the north. Except for South Carolina, which was concerned with getting rid of her large state debt, the south had nothing to gain financially from giving Congress the power of taxation. Eventually, when the public debt was funded in 1790, the benefits went to other sections.

A southern interest also developed in the settlement of accounts between the states. Under the Articles of Confederation, all state expenditures in the general welfare were to be deemed the common expenses of the war, and shared by all members of the Union in proportion to the value of their land. Although the southern states had made large expenditures, they had conducted the war without attention to the rules and requests of Congress. Many of their expenditures were not admissible to the common expenses, and those that were could seldom be substantiated with the documentary proof required by the federal Treasury. The southern states therefore pressed for a liberal definition of expenditures in the general welfare. Giving way, Congress at length acknowledged that virtually all state war expenditures were a charge against the Union. Before the adoption of the Constitution, it was expected that the final settlement would be implemented by an exchange of state payments— that states whose expenditures had been greater than their share of the common charges would receive compensation from states whose expenditures had been less. However, principles had been established which were to justify the assumption of state debts by the new federal government.

The pecuniary situation of Congress in the postwar years forms part of the evidence in determining just how "critical" the period was. The facts, however, do not lend themselves to categorical judgment. Clearly it was not the era of public bankruptcy and currency depreciation that historians used to depict. The states in varying degree took care of the interest on the public debt. Congress conducted its internal affairs at a slowly increasing deficit prior to 1789, but the deficit was not serious. The real problem was foreign debts. Defaulting completely on its obligations to France, Congress just managed to keep its credit alive in Holland by meeting the interest that fell due in the country. Ultimately, Congress had great assets in western lands; moreover, the demand for American products abroad would always have afforded ways of discharging foreign debts in commodities. Nevertheless, the situation would have been precarious if the Constitution had not been adopted.

The gravest crisis stemmed from the failure of constitutional revision. After 1780 there was a continuous effort to invest Congress with a duty on imports, but although twice on the verge of success, the impost amendment was defeated in 1786 under circumstances that precluded any further attempts. By that time, the states had begun to absorb the public debt upon whose existence the grant of the taxing power was predicated. Acknowledging defeat, Congress was prepared to distribute the debt among the states. It seemed that instead of a bond of union, the debt would become a source of disunion as the states justifiably committeed their resources to local programs and the functions of the central government dwindled.

The failure of consitutional revision in 1786 reflected less a division of opinion—all the states had endorsed a federal impost in principle—than the inherent difficulty of securing unanimous agreement to any proposal. It appeared that the Articles of Confederation could not by constitutional procedure be amended to give Congress the limited accretion of power which majority opinion already sanctioned. The difficulty was surmounted in the end by recourse to extra-legal procedures.

That the crisis of the Union inspired the calling of the Federal Convention indicates such a level of agreement as to suggest that there was no crisis at all; however, the movement for constitutional revision derived much of its impetus from conservative fear of social radicalism. Conservatives in New York and Pennsylvania had long regarded central government as a refuge against majority rule. The events of 1786 spread their convictions to the extremes of the nation. Paper money and Shays's Rebellion were enough to convince New England merchants and Virginia planters of the dangers of democracy. In a climate of opinion already favorable to reform, a national alliance of conservatives drove constitutional revision beyond its original goals.

The larger story of the Constitution lies outside the scope of this study. Neither the document itself nor the circumstances that led to its adoption are wholly explained by the train of events and conditions discussed here. In view of the current revision of the Beard thesis, however, the role of the public creditors deserves some consideration. Recent studies have attacked Beard's conclusions and have even raised a doubt as to whether creditors as a group supported the Constitution.[23] One's impulse is to avoid the question:

23. Robert E. Brown, *Charles Beard and the Constitution: A Critical Analysis of "An Economic Interpretation of the Constitution"* (Princeton, 1956), and McDonald, *We the People*, are the leading revisionist works.

it is often a false issue the way it is argued; it is unprovable by the methods employed to investigate it; it is not an essential point, and to emphasize it constitutes a distortion.

Beard's major thesis that the Constitution was the handiwork of the classes of American society possessing status and property cannot be ascribed to him alone. It is a theme of historical interpretation supported by the testimony of the founding fathers and sustained on the whole by historical scholarship. It does not contradict the assumption that general considerations of national welfare weighed with the men who made the Constitution, and it is not incompatible with the idea—which one of Beard's critics very aptly suggests—that state interests were instrumental in forming the attitudes of political leaders and the views of their constituents.[24] What shocked Beard's contemporaries and still provokes the most criticism was his purported demonstration that many of the founding fathers held securities and stood to profit from their work.

Beard's method of proof was to search through accounts in the federal archives and list what he discovered of the holdings of members of the Constitutional Convention. Although his declared object was merely to identify the founders as members of an economic class, the implication was that they had a profit motive. A recent critic of the Beard thesis, Forrest McDonald, has re-examined the accounts, not only for members of the Constitutional Convention, but also the ratifying conventions. He concludes that ownership of securities was sufficiently distributed between those who upheld and those who opposed the Constitution as to rule out profit motive as a general determining factor.

Although the dispute has borne fruit in stimulating new research, it will probably be inconclusive unless argued on other ground. In what relates to securities, the proof on both sides is defective. The accounts upon which the case depends relate to subscriptions to the federal loan beginning in October 1790 and continuing for several years. Few of the documents indicate whether securities were orig-

24. McDonald, *We the People,* 357. McDonald's provocative study explores an economic approach to the formation of the Union in terms of categories different from those of Beard. For an interesting critique of McDonald's work, see Jackson T. Main, "Charles A. Beard and the Constitution: A Critical Review of Forrest McDonald's *We the People," Wm. and Mary Qtly.,* 3rd ser., 17 (1960), 88-102, and "Forrest McDonald's Rebuttal," *ibid.,* 102-10.

inally issued to the subscribers or acquired by purchase—in any event, the parties to the controversy have made no effort to establish ownership of securities as early as 1787. On the basis of their findings for the 1790's, it is gratuitous to assume anything about individual holdings at the time of the Constitutional Convention.[25]

The securities held by particular persons, including former members of the Constitutional and ratifying conventions, cannot be determined with certainty even after 1790. Lacking the central Treasury records, which have been almost entirely destroyed, existing documents are so incomplete that fifty of the greatest holders in the country would not necessarily appear. A thousand big holders might escape detection.[26] Especially in the case of wealthy or professional men likely to engage in interstate speculation, it is impossible to prove that they did not own more securities than the records disclose. On the other hand, a moderate holding of securities in 1790 implies little, for whatever a man's attitude toward the Constitution, he must have been careless of his interest not to have seized the opportunity to profit in the rising market that followed its adoption. The really surprising thing is that any man prominent enough to have taken part in either the Constitutional or the ratifying conventions had not gathered at least a hatful by 1790.

The analysis of individual motive on the basis of security holdings would remain uncertain even if holdings could be exactly determined, for it would require a close knowledge of private circumstances and personal judgment that is probably irrecoverable. If, for example, a creditor was primarily interested in purchasing state lands but had not acquired the securities with which to pay for them, he would suffer a loss from the rising values which attended the formation of the new government. He would be in the same predicament if he were a member of the Ohio Company, although it would occur to him that a stronger government would foster his

25. There is material for several states which shows security holdings at various times from 1786 on—records of indent payments, and the subscriptions in Pennsylvania to the "new loan" of 1786. These have not been exploited. The material is incomplete and in most cases unrepresentative of the body of the public debt in particular states; therefore I have not used it in this study, except in the case of Virginia, where the record is full.

26. The almost complete absence of documents relating to the enormous sums subscribed or registered at the Treasury conceals many millions of the holdings most likely to be speculative.

western enterprise. If he was not concerned with land speculation, but was a citizen of Pennsylvania, Maryland, New York, or even New Jersey, and was receiving interest from the state, he could not be entirely certain in 1787 whether the new government would promote the value of his securities.

The discussion of state assumption set forth in this study may add something to the literature of the Beard controversy. That some of the states adopted public securities and paid good interest on them might be presumed to have weakened a creditor interest in a national government. Certainly the creditors in several middle states had an alternative, and a person with decided Antifederalist views might have felt free to follow his convictions. The Philadelphia merchant, Blair McClenachan, owned $74,000 in public securities, yet presided over the Harrisburg Convention. He may have regarded his state as better security than an unfledged central government; his fortune, at least, was not staked on the Constitutional Convention.[27] But McClenachan seems to have been exceptional. Even in the states that gave most to them, it would appear that the creditors hoped for an increment from the national government, particularly as successive steps were taken to establish it.[28] The proof is that in 1789 securities rose above all previous levels. In many of the states, of course, there was never any question that creditors preferred the federal government. Those in Georgia, South Carolina, North Carolina, and in New England, could expect little from their state governments—a fact quite evident by the time of the Constitutional Convention.

It seems indisputable that as a group the creditors supported the Constitution. This writer has never seen them represented in a formal statement or petition that did not endorse stronger central government. In the writings of the times they are uniformly described as adherents of the Constitution, but one should not make the mistake of imputing to them a conspiratorial role or at least of

27. McClenachan, or McClenaghan, owned his securities in 1787. Nearly all were originally issued in his name.

28. State creditors, on the other hand, could be expected to oppose the establishment of a national government which would invade state revenue sources—unless they hoped for federal assumption of state debts. McDonald, in *We the People,* lumps subscribers to the federal loan of 1790 in one category whether they subscribed state or federal securities, implying thereby that they had similar interests in 1787.

attaching any great importance to their conspiracies. Speculations were continuous throughout the Confederation. Merchants and men of property acquired securities in the normal course of business or for marginal profits, without reference to Congressional funding. The prospect of a national government promised additional returns, and as the Constitution was adopted the prospect became solid enough to warrant speculation on the basis of renewed possibilities. To eliminate entirely the role of economic motive in the political affairs of the time is as doctrinaire and as unnecessary as Beard's overstatement of it. A creditor interest certainly existed—yet it was no more than ancillary to the political development that culminated in the founding of the new government. Constitutional reform had always involved public finance. The decision to establish a national government entailed federal taxation and the payment of the debt, irrespective of the designs of creditors, who assisted the process, reaped its benefits, but did not create it. Proceeding rigidly by the axiom that related sovereignty with revenue power, the founding fathers crowned the new government with unlimited power of taxation.

By the time the public debt was funded it had become the property of a relative few. Figures covering millions in securities suggest a transfer rate of 80 percent. The degree to which the debt had concentrated into major holdings can only be inferred, since most large subscribers were brokers or acting in partnership. However the fact speaks for itself that of $12,300,000 examined in this study, 280 individuals held $7,880,000, nearly two-thirds. The increase in securities which were registered or subscribed directly at the Treasury, amounting to $18,000,000 by October 1791, suggests the magnitude of interstate and foreign speculation. As the Constitution was ratified, foreign capital poured into the domestic debt, channeled largely through New York brokers. Foreign investment drove security prices up to prohibitive levels late in 1789 and then, in some degree inspired by foreknowledge of Hamilton's proposals, spilled over into the purchase of state debts.

Funding the public debt was the economic counterpart of the adoption of the Constitution. How one regards Hamilton's specific proposals depends somewhat upon the angle from which they are viewed. Seen as the arch of the emerging Federalist system, they are partisan, partial to wealth, commercial capitalism, the north as against the south, and denotative of the extremism which begat political parties. Considered on their merits, apart from their integral relation to other measures, and as a formula for dealing with the political as well as the financial legacy of the Confederation, they appear as a reasonable compromise of varying shades of the conservative opinion which the new government represented.

The essential feature of Hamilton's program for funding the public debt was specie payment. Rejecting agrarian modes, he pledged the central government to high finance, and in this he had the overwhelming approval of Congress. In terms of the political realities of the moment, it is hard to see how he could have done otherwise. The only real challenge in Congress was Madison's motion to discriminate between original and present holders of securities, but the proposal did not offer a true alternative, had little support, and was probably no more than a political maneuver. From all that one can gather, the people at large dissented from both Madison and Hamilton—they wanted to scale down the debt, or fund and pay it at its depreciated value. They were, however, but distantly represented in a Congress determined to ground the new order in financial orthodoxy.

Popular opposition was not effective because most of the country's leaders agreed that funding on something like Hamilton's terms was necessary to complete the federal structure. It was otherwise with the assumption of state debts, which was not clearly essential to the Union, needlessly increased the federal debt, and divided the nation's leaders along lines of state interests. Assumption passed only as a result of the famous trade that gave Virginia the permanent capital. What is not generally recognized is that there was another feature of the negotiation; the compromise of 1790 also conceded southern demands in the settlement of state accounts.

Class interests were scarcely at issue in the Congressional debate over financial legislation. The views of the masses were represented in about the same degree as at the Constitutional Convention. Madison's motion kindled the popular animus against rich men and speculators, but it did not implement the popular desire to pay debts at their depreciated value. Any such idea was heresy to the overwhelming majority of Congress, whose members differed only over the separate interests of the states they represented. Assumption provoked these differences, but it reconciled Massachusetts and South Carolina to the Union, and the onus was in part removed by its incorporation into the compromise of 1790. After the first Congress had finished its work, the future adversary of the regime, Thomas Jefferson, could still declare: "It is not foreseen that anything so generative of dissensions can arise again, & therefore the friends of the government hope that, this difficulty once surmounted in the states, everything will work well."[29]

29. Jefferson to Randolph, July 11, Aug. 14, 1790, Jefferson Papers, LVI, 9581-82, LVII, 9711, Lib. Cong.

Bibliographical Essay

No full scale financial history of the Revolution and the early national period has been written in the twentieth century. The best of the older works are Charles J. Bullock, *The Finances of the United States from 1775 to 1789* (Madison, 1895) and William Graham Sumner, *The Financier and the Finances of the American Revolution* (New York, 1891). Scholarly and accurate within its range is Clarence Ver Steeg, *Robert Morris, Revolutionary Financier* (Philadelphia, 1954). Bray Hammond's *Banks and Politics in America from the Revolution to the Civil War* (Princeton, 1957) devotes four chapters to the period from 1694 to 1791.

In colonial public finance there are a few good studies of individual provinces; a bibliography may be gathered from citations in my article, "Currency Finance: An Interpretation of Colonial Monetary Practices," *William and Mary Quarterly*, 3rd ser., 10 (1953), 153-80. But apart from Curtis P. Nettels, *The Money Supply of the American Colonies Before 1720* (Madison, 1934), which is limited in its chronological span, the only general work of merit is an unpublished doctoral dissertation by Leslie Van Horn Brock, *The Currency of the American Colonies, 1700 to 1764*, University of Michigan, 1941. New approaches are exemplified in two articles by Richard A. Lester, "Currency Issues to Overcome Depressions in Pennsylvania, 1723 and 1729," and "Currency Issues to Overcome Depressions in Delaware, New Jersey, New York and Maryland, 1715-1737," *Journal of Political Economy,* 46 (1938), 324-75, and 47 (1939), 182-217.

The core of materials for this financial history, therefore, is the primary sources in manuscript and published form. Manuscript sources begin with the documents at the Library of Congress, notably the Robert Morris Papers and the unique accounts catalogued under the heading of United States, Finance. These and the massive collection of the Papers of the Continental Congress now lodged in the Foreign Affairs Section of the National Archives illuminate the policies and the activities of the federal government. Also essential are the Library of Congress collections of Madison, Jefferson, Washington, and Hamilton papers. The basic research for this study was substantially completed before Julian P. Boyd's edition of *The Papers of Thomas Jefferson* began to appear or the microfilm reproduction of The Papers of John Adams became available, but I have used both of these magnificent collections to supplement my work in the manuscript depositories and in the earlier published works of Jefferson and Adams.

Since the states were major protagonists, financial history cannot be approached solely through material relative to the central government; accordingly, much use has been made of state documents, some printed, others in manuscript or on microfilm, including statutes, legislative journals, and documentary collections. The following state archives were consulted for particular information: Pennsylvania Historical and Museum Commission, Harrisburg; Maryland Hall of Records, Annapolis; Connecticut State Library, Hartford. A selected group of representative newspapers were scanned for material relative to local affairs and reaction to federal policies.

In the eighteenth century, the distinction between public and private business was vague; hence public administration, army procurement, and mercantile activity emerge from a single body of material. The foreign scene is depicted in the magnificent Franklin Papers in the American Philosophical Society, Philadelphia; the Silas Deane Papers at the Connecticut Historical Society, Hartford; *The Deane Papers,* ed. Charles Isham, 5 volumes, New-York Historical Society, *Collections,* 19-23 (1887-91), supplemented by the published writings of Arthur and William Lee, Henry Laurens, and Franklin.

The outstanding source on domestic procurement and everything connected with the army is the Timothy Pickering Letterbooks, Revolutionary War Manuscripts, War Records Section, National Archives. The Nathanael Greene Papers at the William L. Clements Library, Ann Arbor, are also of great value. Other personal papers relating primarily to the war period are: the Ephraim Blaine Collection, the John Holker Papers, Library of Congress; the George Rogers Clark Papers, Draper Manuscripts, State Historical Society of Wisconsin (used in microfilm); the Samuel Adams and Arthur Lee Papers, Houghton Library, Harvard University; the papers of Timothy Pickering, Matthew Ridley, and Winthrop Sargent, Massachusetts Historical Society, Boston; the Jeremiah Wadsworth Papers, Connecticut Historical Society, Hartford; the Samuel Osgood Papers and the Walter Stewart Papers, New-York Historical Society, New York; the papers of James Duane, Horatio Gates, Joseph Hawley, Alexander McDougall, Robert Morris, and Abraham Yates, New York Public Library; the Chaloner and White Letterbook, Historical Society of Pennsylvania, Philadelphia; the Robert Morris Papers, Pennsylvania Historical and Museum Commission, Harrisburg; the Franklin Papers, University of Pennsylvania; [William Bingham] Territorial Papers, Florida, volume I, and Miscellaneous Papers, Foreign Affairs Section, National Archives.

Mercantile and other personal papers lead into the postwar era, the adoption of the Constitution, security speculation, and the enactment of the funding program. Of immense value are the Constable-Pierrepont Papers, including the William Constable Letterbooks, along with the Bayard-Campbell-Pearsall Collection in the New York Public Library. Of equal importance are the Andrew Craigie Papers at the American Antiquarian Society, Worcester, followed by the William Duer Papers, New-York Historical Society; the Clement Biddle Papers, Historical Society of Pennsylvania; and the Gouverneur Morris Papers, Library of Congress. These materials disclose the activities of merchants and their reaction to public events. The Theodore Sedgwick Papers, Massachusetts Historical Society, afford an intimate view of the politics of Hamiltonian funding.

Other useful collections are the Henry Knox Papers in the same library; the Rufus King Papers and the John Lamb Papers, New-York Historical Society; and the Elias Boudinot and William Bingham Papers, Historical Society of Pennsylvania.

A general source of information on public finance, particularly useful for material on holdings of the public debt in 1790, as well as the settlement of accounts with retired public officials, is the massive Old Loans Records listed as Record Group 53, Fiscal Records Section, National Archives. Statistics on the debt held in Pennsylvania were taken from the then uncatalogued Petitions To Exchange New Loan Certificates, Pennsylvania Historical and Museum Commission.

An impressive amount of source material for financial history also exists in printed form: Worthington C. Ford, ed., *Journals of the Continental Congress, 1774-1789,* 34 volumes (Washington, D. C., 1904-37) ; Francis Wharton, ed., *The Revolutionary Diplomatic Correspondence of the United States,* 6 volumes (Washington, D. C., 1889) ; Joseph Gales, comp., *The Debates and Proceedings in the Congress of the United States . . . [Annals of Congress]* (Washington, 1834); Walter Lowrie and Matthew St. Clair Clark, comps., *American State Papers, Finance,* Vol. I, 3rd ser., Documents, Legislative and Executive of the United States (Washington, 1832). Invaluable for the years before 1789 is Edmund C. Burnett, ed., *Letters of the Members of the Continental Congress,* 8 volumes (Washington, D. C., 1921-36).

Index

A

Accounts. *See* Civilian accounts; Military accounts; Staff accounts; State accounts
Adams, John, 104, 261; quoted, 75, 84; on Deane-Lee affair, 93; negotiates Dutch loan, 128-29
Adams, Samuel, opposes Nationalists, 158
Adams-Lee junto, 110; in Deane-Lee affair, 94; broken, 113
Administration, defects in, 27-28, 49, 73; merchant activities, 28, 70-105 *passim;* loan officers, 35, 53-54, 142, 225; attempted reform, 49-50, 100-1; foreign procurement, 70-94 *passim;* accounts, 73, 74, 76; interlocking agencies, 76; domestic procurement, 94-102 *passim;* investigation, of Arnold, 94-95; of Flower, 98-99; of Mifflin, 98; of Greene, 99-102; of Shippen, 99; of Wadsworth, 99-100, 101; single executives, 116, 118-20; consolidation of agencies, 131-32; contract system, 131-33; reduction of personnel, 131; centralized receipts and disbursements, 141-42; tax receivers, 142, 172. *See also* Deane-Lee affair; Staff accounts
Allen, Philip, 281, 282
Allen, Zachariah, 282
Ames, Fisher, 304, 313-14; quoted, 316-17
Armstrong, John, Jr., 162
Army pay, 134, 155, 164. *See also* Pay and depreciation certificates; State assumption of unliquidated federal debts; Final settlement certificates—military—(Pierce's) notes
Arnold, Benedict, 94-95, 99, 110
Arnold, Jonathan, 152-53, 167
Arnold, Welcome, 281, 282
Assumption. *See* State assumption of unliquidated federal debts; State assumption of public debt; Federal assumption of state debts

B

Baldwin, Abraham, 218n
Bancroft, Edward, 89n, 194
Bank of North America, 174; plan, 123; loans, 130n; functions, 135, 137-38; notes, 136, 137; established, 136-37
Bank of Pennsylvania, 56, 136n
Barclay, Thomas, settles foreign accounts, 195, 196, 197-98, 201
Baring, Francis, 265
Beal, Samuel, 81
Beard, Charles A., thesis discussed, 337-41
Beaumarchais, Caron de, 78, 88, 198; Deane-Lee affair, 92; accounts, 193, 194, 195-97. *See also* Foreign loans and subsidies
Becker, Carl, 16
Bell, Thomas, 87-88
Biddle, Clement, 254, 278, 280, 328
Bindon, Joseph, 189
Bingham, William, 278; as commissioner at St. Eustatius, 78-80; accounts, 134-35, 193, 199
Blackwell, Reverend Dr. Robert, 284
Blaine, Ephraim, 53
Bland, Theodorick, 113, 313
Bleecker, Leonard, 272

Board of Treasury (1785-1789), civilian accounts, 186; staff accounts, 189; foreign staff accounts, 195; Beaumarchais's accounts, 196-97; Robert Morris's accounts, 200, 201; state accounts, 207, 208, 213, 217; indent system, 225, 226-27; weakness of Congress, 241
Boehm, Edmund, 265
Bond, Nathan, 274, 281, 282
Boudinot, Elias, 254, 283, 284, 318n
Bowen, Ephraim, 96
Bowen, Jabez, 281, 282
Breck, Samuel, 274
Bridges, Robert, 284
Brooks, Colonel John, Newburgh affair, 159
Brown, Nicholas, Jr., 281, 282
Brown, Nicholas, Sr., 281, 282
Burke, Edanus, 313
Burley, William, 274
Burrall, Jonathan, 189; quoted, 190

C

Caldwell, Andrew, 279
Cape François, 78
Carmichael, William, 104
Carrington, Edward, 249; quoted, 316
Carroll, Daniel, 113, 166, 317, 318n
Ceronio, Stephen, 78
Chaumont, LeRoy de, 81, 83, 85, 128
Child, Francis, 216
Civilian accounts, settled by North Carolina, 182, 186; settled by South Carolina, 182-83; settled by Virginia, 182, 186; federal settlement initiated, 184, 208; difficulties, 185-86. *See also* Quartermaster and Commissary certificates; Impressments; Final settlement certificates—civilian; State accounts
Clark, George Rogers, 206, 211, 216-17
Clarke, Joseph, 281, 282
Clarke and Nightingale, 281, 282
Claviere, Stephen, 266
Clifford and Teysett, 81, 82
Clinton, Governor George, 148, 240
Collins, John, 152, 167
Connecticut, 250, 321; assumes federal debts to civilians, 181; favors assumption, 309, 313; and funding program, 332; state accounts, 333
Constable, William, 95n; securities speculation, 254, 258, 328; foreign

investment, 264, 265, 268-69; speculates in state debts, 269-70; foreknowledge of assumption, 271-72, 295
Constable Rucker and Co., 238n
Constitutional Convention, 290, 298
Continental currency, early emissions, 18-19, 25-27; initial depreciation, 27-31; total issued, 29; supported by economic controls, 32-33; table of depreciation, 32; supported by requisitions, 33-35; income from, 43, 43n; new emission, 43n, 51-52; importance, 44; further decline, 44-45; past emissions invalidated 45; stoppage of emissions, 46-47, 112; revalued, 51; new emission, fails, 64-66; terminated, 66; redemption, 67, 69; revaluation of debts, 67-69; and state accounts, 205-6, 214; as funded in 1790, 295, 296-97. *See also* Economic controls; Currency finance
Contracts. *See* Administration
Cornell, Ezekiel, 113
Cox, John, 95, 102
Coxe, Tench, 304
Craigie, Andrew, securities speculation, 254, 258; foreign investment, 260, 261, 262, 263, 265, 268-69; speculates in state debts, 269-70; foreknowledge of assumption, 271-72, 295
Creditors. *See* Public creditors
Cunningham, Gustavus, 86-87, 88
Currency act of 1751, 21-22
Currency act of 1764. *See* Restraining Act of 1764
Currency act of 1773, 22
Currency finance, historical interpretation, xiii-xiv, 3, 5, 12
    Colonial, standards of monetary value, 4, 4n; system initiated, 4-7; direct emissions, 7-8; general procedure, 8-10; British subsidy, 11, 19, 20; Massachusetts' specie system, 11, 19, 20; North Carolina, 11-12, 17, 22; South Carolina, 11-12, 15, 17, 22; Rhode Island, 11, 21; degree of success, 13-14, 18-20; Jersey, 13, 22; New York, 13, 16, 19, 20, 22; Pennsylvania, 13, 15, 16, 19, 20; Maryland, 13-14, 15, 16-17, 22; Virginia, 14, 15, 19, 20, 22; attitudes toward, 15-18, 24; in French and Indian War, 19-20; Connecticut, 20; British policy, 20-24;

Stamp Act controversy, 23-24. *See also* Land banks; Revenue power
Revolution, attitudes toward, 19, 111, 141, 144; extinction of debt, 67; federal-state relations, 140-41. *See also* Continental currency
Post-war, debt retirement, 222-23; in Pennsylvania, 222, 229, 244; in Virginia, 222; in New Jersey, 230-31, 244; in New York, 231, 244; in South Carolina, 233, 244; suggested application to public debt, 241; attitudes toward, 243, 244-45, 335; in Rhode Island, 243-44; in Georgia, 244; in North Carolina, 244; as alternative to Hamiltonian program, 292-93, 299-300, 302, 311-12; as related to assumption, 311-12. *See* Requisitions; Indent system

D
D'Amour, Karel, 260
Davidson, Major John, 276
Davies, William, 216, 314-315, 323-24
Deane, Barnabas, 96
Deane-Lee affair, 90-94, 102-4, 110; continuing effects, 175; and foreign accounts, 194
Deane, Silas, 74, 194, 196; quoted, 47n; as foreign commissioner, 81-93; recalled, 90; accounts, 172, 193, 197-98. *See also* Deane-Lee affair
Debt. *See* Public debt
Debtor-creditor conflict. *See* Currency finance
De Francey, Théveneau, 78, 196
Delafield, John, 258, 283
Delap, Samuel and J. H., 81, 82-83
Delaware, 321; state accounts, 333
Denning, William, 189
Depreciation allowance. *See* Pay and depreciation certificates; State assumption of unliquidated federal debts
De Warville, Brissot, 266
De Wolf, Charles John Michael, 265
Dickinson, John, 94, 229
Douglass, William, 18
Duer, William, 133, 159, 261, 264; opposes state assumption, 231; securities speculation, 254, 258; purchase of debt to France, 266; foreknowledge of assumption 271-72
Dutch aids. *See* Foreign loans and subsidies

E
Economic controls, federal policy, 32-33; enacted by states, 60-62; attitudes toward, 111, 115. *See also* Continental currency
Ellery, William, quoted, 49

F
Farmers-General, 266n. *See also* Foreign loans and subsidies
Federal assumption of state debts, principles established, 218-19; and the Constitutional Convention, 219; rumored, 248, 270, 272; plan divulged, 271-72; proposed, 295, 306-7; opposed by public creditors, 303-4; and state interests, 305; the constitutional issue, 307, 311-12; the economic issue, 307-8; and state accounts, 308-9, 322-24; report of General Board, 309-10; opposed by revaluationists, 311-12; debated, 312-13; and speculation, 312; White's amendment, 313-14; Madison's amendments, 314-17; defeated, 318-19; negotiation for national capital, 319-20, 325; final act, 321-22; as part of compromise, 325; benefits to states, 330-32; total, 330; program assessed, 342-43. *See also* State accounts
Federalists, program anticipated by Morris, 123-24; background of rise, 242, 336-37; gain from Shays's Rebellion, 249-50; support taxing power, 290-91; back specie payment, 293, 302-5; program assessed, 341-43
Federal taxes, denied, 31, 111-12; impost of 1781, 116-17; advocated by Nationalists, 143; additional taxes proposed, 146-52; impost defeated, 152-53, 154, 174-76; Newburgh conspiracy, 157-61; funding requisition of 1783, 164-67, 220, 221; defeated, 239-40; consequences of defeat, 242, 336-37; conferred by Constitution, 290-91; opposed by Antifederalists, 291-92. *See also* Revenue power
Fiat money. *See* Currency finance
Final settlement certificates, civilian, 145, 179, 184-86; sectional distribution, 183. *See* Civilian accounts
Final settlement certificates, military (Pierce's) notes, 145, 164, 170-71, 179-80, 186-88; sectional distribution, 183;

speculation in, 252; high rate of transfer, 277. *See also* Military accounts
Final settlement certificates, staff, 180, 202, *See also* Staff accounts
Fitzsimmons, Thomas, 166, 317-18, 318*n*
Flower, Benjamin, 98-99, 192
Foreign loans and subsidies, to 1780, 40-42, 44; French aid sought, 45-46; in 1780, 55-56; during Morris's administration, 126-30; postwar repayment, 221, 234-38, 267*n*; Dutch loan of 1787, 260-61
Fowler, Theodosius, & Co., 283
Fox, Edward, 189, 217, 283, 284
Franklin, Benjamin, 37, 45, 56, 84, 91, 194, 198-99; proposes continental land bank, 23-24; quoted, 30; Deane-Lee affair, 92-93, 94; obtains foreign loan, 126-27, 128
Franklin, William Temple, 84
Franks, Major, 94
French aids. *See* Foreign loans and subsidies
Funding (1790), *Report on Public Credit*, 292-96; alternatives, 292-93, 296; discrimination as an issue, 293-94, 297-303, 342; Congressional action, 296-97; opposed by revaluationists, 300-1; opposed by public creditors, 303-4; supported by leaders, 304-5, 342-43; increases debt, 329-30; program assessed, 341-42
Funding requisition of 1783. *See* Federal taxes

G

Gates, Horatio, 110; Newburgh affair, 162, 163
Georgia, 321; settles federal military accounts, 187; and state accounts, 207, 214-15, 323, 324, 333; opposes assumption, 307, 309, 310, 311, 313
Gerry, Elbridge, 313; quoted, 59
Gilchrist, Robert, 258
Gordon, Dr. William, 176
Gore, Christopher, 263
Gorham, Nathaniel, 166
Grayson, William, quoted, 245
Green, Captain, 88
Greene, Griffin, 96
Greene, Nathanael, 133, 158; as Quartermaster General, 95-97, 99-102; accounts, 191

H

Half-pay pensions. *See* Pensions
Hamilton, Alexander, 109, 124, 197, 200, 267; quoted, 121; tax receiver, 148, 151-52; Newburgh affair, 158, 159-60, 168; endorses federal taxes, 165-67; retires from Congress, 171; Secretary of Treasury, 218, 256, 271, 292-96, 299, 300, 301-5, 320, 322, 326-27, 330; divulges assumption, 271-72
Hancock, Thomas, quoted, 14-15
Hanson, John, 113
Harbach, John, 283, 284
Harris, Edward, 275, 276
Harrisburg Convention, 291
Harrison, Benjamin, Jr., 80
Hartford Convention, 117*n*
Hazard, Ebenezer, 192
Hazard and Addoms, 284
Hazlehurst, Robert, and Co., 272
Henley, David, 217
Heth, William, 217, 324
Hewatt, Alexander, 17
Higginson, Stephen, 249; quoted, 222; opposes Nationalists, 139, 166, 167, 171-72, 174, 175
Hinchman, Thomas, 265
Hodge, William, 86-87
Holker, John, 85, 103, 133, 173
Hornica, Fizeau, and Company, 90
Howell, David, 172, 242; opposes impost, 152-53; censured by Congress, 153-54
Howell, Joseph, 186
Hubbard, 265, 267
Hughes, Hugh, 58
Huntington, Samuel, quoted, 113

I

Implied powers, 143, 161, 164-65, 175, 240-41
Impost. *See* Federal taxes; Requisitions
Impressments, early use of, 52, 58-59; increase, 58-60; by Virginia, 60; by New York, 61; by Pennsylvania, 61-62; by Maryland, 61-62; magnitude, 62-63. *See also* Quartermaster and Commissary certificates; Economic controls
Indents, speculation in, 270, 277; as funded in 1790, 290, 293, 295, 296-97. *See also* Requisitions

Indian contract, 82
Irvine, William 218*n;* quoted, 119
Izard, Ralph, 104

J

Jackson, James, 300, 311
Jackson, Richard, 23-24
Jarvis, James, 262
Jay, John, 55, 104, 158
Jefferson, Thomas, 195, 261; on state accounts, 211; and national capital, 319-20; expresses satisfaction (1790), 325, 343
Jones, Joseph, 113

K

King Rufus, 240
Knox, Henry, 158, 249; Newburgh affair, 159, 167
Kuhl, Henry, 283

L

Laird, John, 275, 276
Land banks, initiated, 5-7; New Jersey, 6, 22, 231; Delaware, 6; New York, 6, 22, 231; Maryland, 6, 22; Pennsylvania, 6, 22, 229; Rhode Island, 6, 11, 243; Virginia, 6, 22; North Carolina, 7; South Carolina, 7; Continental bank proposal, 23-24
Langdon, John, quoted, 77
Laurens, Henry, 46, 55, 200
Laurens, John, 84, 126-27
Le Couteulx, 134*n,* 173, 266
Lee, Arthur, 194, 197, 202; Deane-Lee affair, 87, 89, 90, 92-93, 104, 196; opposes Nationalists, 139, 158, 165-66; Congressional powers, 242
Lee, Richard Bland, 320
Lee, Richard Henry, 27, 113; quoted, 75; suggests amending convention, 242
Lee, William, 90; Deane-Lee affair, 93, 104
Legal tender laws. *See* Economic controls
LeGrand, 83
LeRoy and Bayard, 258, 263
LeRoy and Son, 263
L'Espinasse, Etienne, 262
Lewis, Mordecai, 278, 280, 284
Limozin, Andrew, 81
Lincoln, Benjamin, 54; Secretary of

War, 120; Newburgh affair, 159, 167, 169; quoted, 300
Livermore, Samuel, 300, 301*n,* 311, 313
Livingston, Robert, Secretary of Foreign Affairs, 119, 171
Livingston, Walter, 133
Livingston family, 94
Loan certificates, initiated, 35; draw interest in bills of exchange, 36-39; as investment, 36-37, 39; table of loans, 38; issued for supplies, 39-40, 53-55; income from, 43, 43*n;* specie certificates of 1781, 43*n,* 55; revalued, 68-69; as public debt, 69; sectional distribution, 69*n,* 183; default in interest, 149, 151; settlement of accounts, 184; rate of transfer, 277
Loan officers. *See* Administration
Low, Nicholas, 258
Lyons, Solomon, 278, 280

M

Maclay, William, 300
McClenachan, Blair, 278, 280, 340
McClenachan, Mrs., 279
McConnell, Matthew, 278, 283, 284
McDougall, Alexander, Newburgh affair, 156
McVicker and Hill, 238*n*
Madison, James, 109, 113, 249; quoted, 46, 139, 164-65; Newburgh affair, 155, 160, 166; retires from Congress, 171; on state accounts, 210-211; on paper money, 244-45; Constitutional amendments, 291; motion for discrimination, 297, 299-300, 301-5, 325, 342; amendments to assumption bill, 313, 314-17, 322; negotiates for national capital 319-20; satisfied (1790), 325
Marine Committee, 76
Marshall, Christopher, 279; quoted, 110
Martinique, 78-79
Maryland, forbids delegates to practice trade, 103; assumes federal debts to civilians, 181, 182; settlement of state accounts, 212, 214, 323, 324, 333; assumes public debt, 230; public security holdings in, 275-77; opposes assumption, 307, 309, 310; state securities, 327; benefits from funding, 332
Mason, George, 290
Mason, Jonathan, Jr., 274
Massachusetts, 321; opposes enlargement of public debt, 176; assumes

federal debt to army, 180; settlement of State accounts, 205-6, 210, 214, 218, 333; favors assumption, 219, 307-9, 313, 315-17; post-war taxation, 222; Shays's Rebellion, 245-50; public security holdings in, 273-75; oversubscribes quota of assumed debt, 330; benefits from settlement of accounts, 332

Mease, James, 94-95

Mercer, John, 242

Mifflin, Thomas, 58, 72, 101; as Quartermaster General, 96, 97, 98

Military accounts, settlement initiated, 164, 179-80; procedure, 186-87; settled by Georgia, 187; settled by South Carolina, 187; settled by North Carolina, 188; settled by Virginia, 188. *See also* Final settlement certificates—military (Pierce's) notes; State assumption of unliquidated federal debts; State accounts

Military certificates. *See* Pay and depreciation certificates

Milligan, James, 195

Monroe, James, quoted, 240, 319*n;* advocates Congressional powers, 242

Moore, Andrew, 312, 313

Moore, Governor, 16

Morgan, Dr. John, 99

Morris, Gouverneur, 121, 329; quoted, 30; Deane-Lee affair, 102; Assistant Financier, 119; Newburgh affair, 158, 168; securities speculation, 258, 264-65; attempts to buy debt to France, 265-67; speculation in state securities, 270, 271

Morris, Robert, 27, 37, 250, 284; quoted, 8*n*, 25, 52, 74; as head of Secret Committee of Trade, 72, 75-76, 77-85, 87-89; accounts, 77-78, 103, 193, 199-202; Deane-Lee affair, 92, 93, 94, 102-4; as Superintendent of Finance, 109, 117-55 *passim*, 164, 169-70, 181, 184-5, 189, 195, 199, 207, 209-10, 210*n;* Newburgh affair, 157, 159-62, 167-68; disbandment of army, 164, 169-71; refuses compromise on federal taxation, 166-67; spurns Congressional policy, 171; investigated, 172-74; role as Nationalist leader, 174-76, 334-35; opposes indent system, 223, 224; opposes state assumption, 229; securities speculation, 258, 328; attempts to buy

debt to France, 266. *See also* Administration; Nationalists

Morris's notes, 136, 138-39, 164, 169-70, 173-74

Morris, Thomas, as foreign commissioner, 87-88; Deane-Lee affair, 90-92, 93; accounts, 193, 199, 201-2

N

Nationalists, emerge, 109, 110-11, 112-15; program, 115-17, 142-45, 146; fear results of peace, 154-55; exploit army discontent, 155; frustrated, 164-67; decline of influence, 171-72; sources of failure, 174-76; accomplishments, 334-35. *See also* Revenue power; Robert Morris; Newburgh affair; Federalists

Necker, Jacques, 266-67

Nesbitt, John Maxwell, 87-88

Newburgh affair, 155-64, 167-68

New Hampshire, 222, 250; complains of assumption, 321; benefits from settlement of accounts, 333

New Jersey, assumes federal debts to civilians, 181; assumes public debt, 222, 230-31; settlement of state accounts, 333

New Jersey plan, 291

New York, 250, 321; assumes federal debts to army, 180; assumes federal debts to civilians, 181; settlement of state accounts, 209, 210, 333; assumes public debt, 231-32; rejects impost, 239-40; suggests amending conventions, 242; negotiations for national capital, 319-20; benefits from funding, 331-32

Neufville, John de, 128

Nicholas, Robert Carter, quoted, 17-18

North Carolina, 321; assumes federal debts to civilians, 182; settles federal accounts, 186, 188; settlement of state accounts, 207, 212-16, 323, 324, 333; opposes assumption, 307, 309, 310, 312, 313

Northwest Territory. *See* Western lands

Nutges, Gerrit, 262

O

Ohio Company, 253

Olden, John, 278, 280

Ooster, Matthys, 260
Ordinance of 1785, 238-39. *See also*
Western lands
Osgood, Samuel, quoted, 139; opposes
Nationalists, 172, 176; advocates Con-
gressional powers, 242
Otis, Samuel A., 96

P

Page, John, 318
Paine, Thomas, quoted, 66, 112; Deane-
Lee affair, 102
Palmer, Thomas, 283
Paper money. *See* Currency finance
Parker, Daniel, 173; securities speculation, 258; foreign investment, 260-
65; attempts to buy debt to France,
265-67; speculates in state securities,
270
Pay and depreciation certificates, 50-51,
180-81. *See also* State assumption of
unliquidated federal debts
Peck, John, 274
Pennel, Joseph, 189
Pennsylvania, 299*n*, 321; assumes federal debt to army, 180; assumes public debt, 221-22, 228-30; rejects impost, 240-42; promotes security values, 253, 327; public securities holdings in, 277-80; negotiation for national capitol, 319-20; benefits from
funding, 331, 332; settlement of
state accounts, 333
Penobscot expedition, 205, 210, 214
Pensions, promised, 115; commutation proposed, 156-57; commutation
granted, 164; demanded by non-com-
missioned officers, 168; in settlement
of military accounts, 188
Peters, Richard, 99, 120; Newburgh affair, 158, 166
Pettit, Charles, 95-96, 102, 278, 280
Philips, William, Jr., 274
Pickering, Timothy, 67, 94, 99; quoted,
59, 97; as Quartermaster General, 97,
131-32; Newburgh affair, 163
Pierce, John, settles army accounts, 164,
170-71, 179-80, 183, 186-88; settles
Clark's accounts, 217
Pinckney, Charles, 213
Platt, Richard, 254, 258
Pliarne, Penet and Company and J.
Gruel, 91
Pollock, Oliver, 81, 193; accounts, 199

Pownall, Thomas, quoted, 14, 16; proposes continental land bank, 23-24
Price regulation. *See* Economic controls
Prime, Nathaniel, 274
Proclamation rate, 4*n*
Procurement. *See* Administration
Public creditors, favor stronger government, 114-15; advocate federal taxes,
149-52; solicit state payment, 151;
sponsor indent system, 221-22; sponsor
state assumption, 228-32; and the
Constitution, 253-54, 285-86, 337-41;
oppose features of Hamilton's program, 303-304
Public debt, as basis for Constitutional
revision, 69, 123-24, 142-45, 335; sectional distribution, 69*n*, 183, 335-36;
defined, 114, 114*n*, 179; created by
Congress, 164, 179-80, 202; post-war
growth, 180; excluded from common
charges, 204; consequences of state
assumption, 221, 234; distribution
among states contemplated, 241; and
the Constitution, 289-90. *See also*
Revenue power; Accounts; Public
creditors
Public domain. *See* Western lands

Q

Quartermaster and Commissary certificates, importance, 57; in New Jersey,
59; in New York, 59; in Pennsylvania,
60; in Virginia, 60; amount issued,
63; neglected by Congress, 63-64; defeat new emission, 64-65; redeemed
by states, 64-65, 182-83; mode of redemption, 67-68; merged with public
debt, 183, 186. *See also* Impressments; State assumption of unliquidated federal debts; Civilian accounts

R

Ramsay, David, quoted, 17, 18-19
Receipts and expenditure, factors con-
tributing to expense, 27-28; Treasury
disbursements, 28-29; federal lottery,
42; prizes, 42; specie income to 1780,
43-44; during Morris's administration,
126, 130; balance sheet of Confederation finance, 236-37; total, 333, 333*n*.
See also Continental currency; Loan
certificates; Requisitions; Foreign

loans and subsidies; Quartermaster and Commissary certificates
Reed, Joseph, quoted, 113-14
Registered debt at the Treasury. *See* Speculation
Requisitions, reasons for early failure, 30-31; in old Continental currency, 33-35, 43-44; in specific supplies, 48-49, 50, 52; act of March 18, 1780, 51-52; payments, 52-53; specie policy, 67; returns in Morris's administration, 129, 130; derogated by Nationalists, 140-41; in 1781, 141; special requisition of 1782, 151, 221; funding requisition of 1783, 166; indent system, 223-29
Restraining Act of 1764, 15, 16, 17, 18, 22
Revenue power, political significance, xiv-xvi, 111-12, 334; and the Constitution, 290; and state rights, 311-12. *See also* Federal taxes; Public debt; Currency finance
Rhode Island, defeats impost, 152-53; opposition to Nationalists, 174; accepts impost, 242; public security holdings in, 280-82; and assumption, 321, 330; settlement of state accounts, 333
Robinson, John, 14
Rogers, Samuel, 265
Ross, John, 77, 81, 86, 87, 88-89, 91, 92; accounts, 134-35, 193, 194, 199
Rush, Dr. Benjamin, 99, 301, 302
Rutledge, John, 54

S

Saint Eustatius, 78-79
Sands, Livingston and Company, 132-33
Schuyler, Philip, 119, 148, 151
Scioto Company, 253
Scott, Gustavus, 275, 276
Scott, Thomas, 300-301
Seagrove, James, 95*n*, 272
Sears, David, 274
Secret Committee of Correspondence, 76, 86
Secret Committee of Trade, functions, 77; accounts, 103-4, 172, 193, 195, 199-202
Sedgwick, Theodore, 300, 317, 326*n*; quoted, 318-19
Shaw, C. and J., 258
Shays, Daniel, 247

Shays's Rebellion, 232, 245-50
Sherman, Roger, 315
Sherwell, Robert, 95*n*
Shippen, Dr. William, director of Hospital Department, 97, 99
Smith, Richard, 262
Smith, William, 313-14
South Carolina, 321; settles and assumes federal debts, 181, 182, 186, 187, 208; state accounts, 212-15, 324, 333; favors assumption, 219, 307-309, 313; postwar difficulties, 233-34, 234*n*, 327; benefits from assumption, 330; benefits from settlement of accounts, 332
Spanish aids. *See* Foreign loans and subsidies
Speculation in public securities, during Confederation, 251-53, 253-54; affected by New Jersey's action, 253; affected by New York's action, 253; affected by Pennsylvania's action, 253; early transfer, 254-55; revealed by registered debt, 255-56, 258; reaction to new government, 256-57, 257-58; entry of foreign captal, 258-65; mercantile procedures, 259; attempted purchase of French debt, 265-67; slowed in 1789, 268-69; Hamilton's report lowers prices, 326-27, 328-29; reaction to funding debate, 327-28; post-funding, 329

   Concentration and transfer, 272; in Virginia, 254-55; in Massachusetts, 273-75; in Maryland, 275-77; in Pennsylvania, 277-80; in Rhode Island, 280-82; at the Treasury, 282-84; estimated, 284-85, 341
Speculation in state securities, prompted by foreign investment, 269-72; assumption plans divulged, 271-72
Sprague, John, 274-75
Stadnitski, Peter, 260-61, 262
Staff accounts, domestic, 180; settlement initiated, 188-89; difficulties, 189-90; final settlement, 191-93
Staff accounts, foreign, early policy, 193-95; settlement initiated, 195; Beaumarchais, 195-97; Deane, 197-98; Jonathan Williams, 198-99; Bingham, 199; Commercial Committee, 199, 200, 201, 202; Robert Morris (Secret Committee), 199-202; Thomas Morris, 199, 201-202; Oliver Pollock, 199; John Ross, 199

Stamp Act, and paper money, 23-24
State accounts, prescribed regulations, 203-4; unauthorized expenditures, 204-7, 211-12; Continental currency, 205-6; evidence, 207-8, 212; assumed federal debts, 208, 212-13; rule of apportionment, 209; Morris's formula, 209-10, 210n; funding requisition of 1783, 210-11; settlement initiated, 210; sectional cleavage, 214-16; General Board established (1787), 215; in Virginia, 215-16; in North Carolina, 216; the Clark expedition, 216-17; progress after 1789, 217-18; principle of federal assumption, 218-19, 336; in assumption debate, 308-11, 314-16, 322; General Board's policy, 323-24; involved in compromise, 325; final settlement (1793), 332-33; settlement beneficial to States, 332

State assumption of public debt, in Pennsylvania, 221-23, 228-30, 151; in Maryland, 230; in New Jersey, 231; in New York, 231-32; in Connecticut, 232; in Massachusetts, 232; in New Hampshire, 232; in North Carolina, 233; in South Carolina, 233-34; in Virginia, 233; extent, 234; political implications, 234. *See also* Indent system

State assumption of unliquidated federal debts, 50, 180-83; Connecticut, 50-51, 181; Maryland, 50-51, 181; Massachusetts, 50-51, 180; New Jersey, 50-51, 181; New York, 50-51, 181; North Carolina, 50-51, 182; South Carolina, 50-51, 182; Rhode Island, 50-51; Virginia, 50-51, 180, 182, 206-207; Pennsylvania, 180. *See also* Army pay; Pay and depreciation certificates; Quartermaster and Commissary certificates; State accounts; Civilian accounts; Military accounts

Stewart, Charles, 190
Stewart, David, 80
Stewart, Walter, 278, 280; Newburgh affair, 159
Stoddert [Benjamin] and Forrest [Uriah], 275, 276
Stone, Michael Jenifer, 313
Sullivan, John, 113
Summers, Andrew, Jr., 278, 280, 284
Swan, James, 267n

Swanick, John, 136
Swears, Cornelius, 98

T

Taxation. *See* Federal taxes; Revenue power; Requisitions; Currency finance
Taylor, John, 218n, 278, 280
Townshend Acts, and currency restriction, 16
Trumbull, Joseph, 72
Tryon, Governor, 17
Tucker, Thomas, 291, 300

V

Vanderborcht, Francis, 265
Van Eighen, Christian, 262
Van Franckenstein, Johan, 262
Van Staphorst, Jacob, 267
Van Staphorst, Nicholas, 262
Van Staphorst, Nicholas and Jacob, 235n, 260, 265, 267
Varnum, James Mitchell, 113
Vermont, 250
Virginia, 321; forbids delegates to practise trade, 103; opposes Nationalists, 174; assumes federal debt to army, 180; adjusts federal accounts, 182, 186, 188, 208; settlement of state accounts, 207-8, 210, 211-17, 314-15, 323, 324, 333; retires war debts, 222; accepts impost, 242; holdings of public securities in, 254-55; opposes assumption, 307-10, 312, 313; state accounts and assumption, 314-17
Vollenhoven, Hendrick, 262
Vollenhoven, Kindreck, 260

W

Wadsworth, Jeremiah, 54, 58; as Commissary-General, 96, 97, 99-101; accounts, 191; quoted, 318
Wadsworth and Carter, 133
Walker, Benjamin, 200-1
Wallace [Charles] and Muir [John], 275, 276
Walpole, Thomas, 83
Washington, George, 58, 59, 98, 102, 109, 119, 154-55, 158; Newburgh affair, 155, 159-60, 162-63, 167-68, 169
Watson and Greenleaf, 258, 283
Watts, John, quoted, 18
Weems, James, 276
Weems, John, 276

Western lands, as a fund to retire debts, 144, 165, 238-39, 253; Ordinance of 1785, 238-39; large-scale grants, 239; and the funding bill, 292, 293, 294, 296-97; post-funding speculation, 329
Wharton, Samuel, 194
Wharton, Thomas, 89n
White, Alexander, 313, 314, 320
Wikoff, Peter, 278
Williams, James, 275, 276

Williams, Jonathan, 91; Deane-Lee affair, 93; accounts, 193, 194, 198-99
Williamson, Hugh, 312, 318
Willing, Charles, 81
Willing, Thomas, 75, 77, 284
Willinks, 260, 265, 267
Wilson, James, 165
Winder, William, 215, 216
Wolcott, Oliver, 113